THE WORK
OF THE
INTERNATIONAL
LAW COMMISSION

SIXTH EDITION

Volume I

UNITED NATIONS
New York, 2004

UNITED NATIONS PUBLICATION

Sales No. E.04.V.6

ISBN 92-1-133576-0

TABLE OF CONTENTS

Volume I

PART III

Topics and sub-topics considered by the International Law Commission

A. TOPICS AND SUB-TOPICS ON WHICH THE COMMISSION HAS SUBMITTED FINAL REPORTS

ANNEXES

Volume II

Instruments

ANNEX

FOREWORD

The United Nations Programme of Assistance in the Teaching, Study, Dissemination and Wider Appreciation of International Law, established under General Assembly resolution 2099 (XX) of 20 December 1965, includes among its goals the dissemination, through United Nations information media, of information about international law and activities in this field. In connection with this goal, the production of a publication on the work of the International Law Commission was suggested. In accordance with this suggestion, the first edition of the present publication was prepared by the Secretariat in 1966. The second, third, fourth and fifth editions were produced by the Secretariat in 1972, 1980, 1988 and 1996, respectively, further to requests of the International Law Commission which were endorsed by the General Assembly. The present, sixth edition brings up to date the 1996 edition by incorporating therein a summary of the latest developments of the work of the Commission, as well as texts of new Commission drafts and a new codification convention.

Under Article 13, paragraph 1, of the Charter of the United Nations, the General Assembly is required to "initiate studies and make recommendations for the purpose of ... encouraging the progressive development of international law and its codification". As a means for the discharge of these responsibilities, the General Assembly, in 1947, established the International Law Commission. Between 1949, when the Commission held its first annual session, and 2003, the Commission has considered thirty-nine topics and sub-topics of international law.

The present publication is intended to provide a general introduction to the work of the International Law Commission, with sufficient references to facilitate further research. Accordingly, the publication contains, in Part I, a brief historical outline of the various attempts at the development and codification of international law up to the inception of the Commission's work and, in Part II, an account of the organization, programme and methods of work of the Commission, with particular reference to the Statute under which the Commission functions. Finally, Part III is devoted to brief descriptions of the various topics and sub-topics of international law considered by the International Law Commission. An account is also given of the actions decided upon by the General Assembly following the consideration of the topics or sub-topics by the Commission, and of the results achieved by diplomatic conferences convened by the General Assembly to consider drafts prepared by the Commission.

Annexes are appended, containing the text of the Commission's Statute, a list of present and former members of the Commission, the text of the decision of the Swiss Federal Council regarding the juridical status of the members of the Commission at the place of its permanent seat, and the full texts of final draft articles prepared by the Commission or, where appropriate, of multilateral conventions based on such draft articles, as adopted by diplomatic conferences convened under the auspices of the United Nations or the General Assembly itself.[1] The multilateral conventions contained in annex V appear in volume II.

---

[1] Final reports by the Commission to the General Assembly on a topic or sub-topic that did not contain draft articles (e.g., reservations to multilateral conventions), contained draft articles that were superceded by the Commission's later work (draft articles on arbitral procedure) or were to be regarded as suggestions (present statelessness) are not reproduced in the annexes. In addition, the Rome Statute of the International Criminal Court is not reproduced in the annexes since it was adopted on the basis of the text of the Preparatory Committee for an International Criminal Court which was a further elaboration of the Commission's draft Statute for an International Criminal Court. The latter is reproduced because of its historical significance and its relevance as part of the legislative history of the Rome Statute of the International Criminal Court.

PART I

ORIGIN AND BACKGROUND OF THE DEVELOPMENT AND CODIFICATION OF INTERNATIONAL LAW

1. Historical antecedents

The idea of developing international law through the restatement of existing rules or through the formulation of new rules is not of recent origin. In the last quarter of the eighteenth century Jeremy Bentham proposed a codification of the whole of international law, though in a utopian spirit.[2] Since his time, numerous attempts at codification have been made by private individuals, by learned societies and by Governments.

Enthusiasm for the "codification movement" — the name sometimes given to such attempts — generally stems from the belief that written international law would remove the uncertainties of customary international law by filling existing gaps in the law, as well as by giving precision to abstract general principles whose practical application is not settled.

While it is true that only concrete texts accepted by Governments can directly constitute a body of written international law, private codification efforts, that is, the research and proposals put forward by various societies, institutions and individual writers, have also had a considerable effect on the development of international law. Particularly noteworthy are the various draft codes and proposals prepared by the *Institut de Droit International*, the International Law Association (both founded in 1873) and the Harvard Research in International Law (established in 1927), which have facilitated the work of various diplomatic conferences convened to adopt general multilateral conventions of a law-making nature.[3]

Intergovernmental regulation of legal questions of general and permanent interest may be said to have originated at the Congress of

---

[2] In his *Principles of International Law* (written in the period 1786-1789), Bentham envisaged that an international code, which should be based on a detailed application of his principle of utility to the relations between nations, would not fail to provide a scheme for an everlasting peace. However, he made little effort to base his plans for such a code upon the existing law of nations.

[3] See document A/AC.10/25, "Note on the private codification of public international law".

Vienna (1814-15), where provisions relating to the regime of international rivers, the abolition of the slave trade and the rank of diplomatic agents were adopted by the signatory Powers of the Treaty of Paris of 1814. Since then, international legal rules have been developed at diplomatic conferences on many other subjects, such as the laws of war on both land and sea, the pacific settlement of international disputes, the unification of private international law, the protection of intellectual property, the regulation of postal services and telecommunications, the regulation of maritime and aerial navigation and various other social and economic questions of international concern.[4]

Although many of these conventions were isolated events dealing with particular problems and in some cases applied only to certain geographic regions, a substantial number of them resulted from a sustained effort of Governments to develop international law by means of multilateral conventions at successive international conferences.

The protection of industrial property, for instance, has been the subject of successive conferences held since 1880, and the Paris Convention on the subject, first adopted on 20 March 1883, has been progressively revised six times and amended once. Similarly, the codification of international law contained in the four Geneva Conventions of 12 August 1949 regarding the protection of war victims and in the Protocols Additional to the Geneva Conventions of 8 June 1977[5] is the direct descendant of the Geneva Red Cross Convention of 22 August 1864.

The Hague Peace Conferences of 1899 and 1907, drawing upon the work and experience of preceding conferences on the laws of war and upon the previous practice of some Governments regarding the pacific settlement of international disputes, reached agreement on several important conventions and thus greatly stimulated the movement in favour of codifying international law. The Second Peace Conference of 1907, however, feeling the lack of adequate preparation for its deliberations, proposed that some two years before the probable date of the Third Peace Conference, a preparatory committee should be established "with the tasks of collecting the various proposals to be submitted to the conference, of ascertaining what subjects are ripe for embodiment in an international regulation,

---

[4] See documents A/AC.10/5, "Historical survey of the development of international law and its codification by international conferences"; and A/AC.10/8, "Outline of the codification of international law in the inter-American system with special reference to the methods of codification".
[5] For the text of the Conventions, see United Nations, *Treaty Series,* vol. 75, p. 2. For the text of the Protocols, see ibid., vol. 1125, pp. 3 and 609.

and of preparing a programme which the Governments should decide upon in sufficient time to enable it to be carefully examined by the countries interested".[6] Arrangements for the Third Peace Conference were being made when the First World War broke out.

2. League of Nations Codification Conference

The intergovernmental effort to promote the codification and development of international law made a further important advance with the resolution of the Assembly of the League of Nations of 22 September 1924, envisaging the creation of a standing organ called the Committee of Experts for the Progressive Codification of International Law, which was to be composed so as to represent "the main forms of civilization and the principal legal systems of the world".[7] This Committee, consisting of seventeen experts, was to prepare a list of subjects "the regulation of which by international agreement" was most "desirable and realizable" and thereafter to examine the comments of Governments on this list and report on the questions which were "sufficiently ripe", as well as on the procedure to be followed in preparing for conferences for their solution. This was the first attempt on a worldwide basis to codify and develop whole fields of international law rather than simply regulating individual and specific legal problems.

After certain consultations with Governments and the League Council, the Assembly decided, in 1927, to convene a diplomatic conference to codify three topics out of the five that had been considered to be "ripe for international agreement" by the Committee of Experts, namely: (1) nationality, (2) territorial waters and (3) the responsibility of States for damage done in their territory to the person or property of foreigners.[8] The preparation of the conference was entrusted to a Preparatory Committee of five persons which was to draw up reports showing points of agreement or divergency which might serve as "bases of discussion", but not to draw up draft conventions as had been proposed by the Committee of Experts.

Delegates from forty-seven Governments participated in the Codification Conference which met at The Hague from 13 March to 12 April 1930; but the only international instruments which resulted from its work were on the topic of nationality.[9] The Conference was

---

[6] See the Final Act of the Peace Conference of 1907, in J. B. Scott, *The Hague Peace Conferences of 1899 and 1907* (1909), vol. II, pp. 289-291.
[7] League of Nations, *Official Journal, Special Supplement*, No. 21, p. 10.
[8] Ibid., No. 53, p. 9.
[9] On 12 April 1930, the Conference adopted the following instruments:

unable to adopt any conventions on the topics of territorial water or State responsibility. Although the Conference provisionally approved certain draft articles on territorial waters which later exerted influence to the extent that Governments accepted them as a statement of existing international law, it failed to adopt even a single recommendation on the subject of State responsibility.

No further experiment in codification was made by the League of Nations after 1930. But on 25 September 1931, the League Assembly adopted an important resolution on the procedure of codification, the main theme of which was the strengthening of the influence of Governments at every stage of the codification process.[10] This underlying theme was subsequently incorporated in the Statute of the International Law Commission of the United Nations, together with certain other recommendations stated in the resolution, such as the preparation of draft conventions by an expert committee, and the close collaboration of international and national scientific institutes.

3. Drafting and implementation of Article 13, paragraph 1, of the Charter of the United Nations

The Governments participating in the drafting of the Charter of the United Nations were overwhelmingly opposed to conferring on the United Nations legislative power to enact binding rules of international law. As a corollary, they also rejected proposals to confer on the General Assembly the power to impose certain general conventions on States by some form of majority vote. There was, however, strong support for conferring on the General Assembly the more limited powers of study and recommendation, which led to the adoption of the following provision in Article 13, paragraph 1:[11]

"1. The General Assembly shall initiate studies and make recommendations for the purpose of:

"a. ... encouraging the progressive development of international law and its codification."

---

1. Convention on certain questions relating to the conflict of nationality laws (League of Nations, *Treaty Series,* vol. 179, p. 89);
2. Protocol relating to military obligations in certain cases of double nationality (ibid., vol. 178, p. 227);
3. Protocol relating to a certain case of statelessness (ibid., vol. 179, p. 115);
4. Special Protocol concerning statelessness (League of Nations document C.27.M.16.1931.V).

Except for No.4, the above instruments have been in force since 1937.

[10] League of Nations, *Official Journal, Special Supplement,* No. 92, p. 9.

[11] See *Documents of the United Nations Conference on International Organization, San Francisco, 1945,* vol. III, documents 1 and 2; vol. VIII, document 1151; and vol. IX, documents 203, 416, 507, 536, 571, 792, 795 and 848.

During the second part of its first session, the General Assembly, on 11 December 1946, adopted resolution 94 (I) establishing the Committee on the Progressive Development of International Law and its Codification, sometimes known as the "Committee of Seventeen". The Committee was directed to consider the procedures to be recommended for the discharge of the General Assembly's responsibilities under Article 13, paragraph 1.

The Committee held thirty meetings from 12 May to 17 June 1947 and adopted a report recommending the establishment of an international law commission and setting forth provisions designed to serve as the basis for its statute.[12]

Several important questions of principle relating to the organization, scope, functions and methods of an international law commission were thoroughly discussed by the Committee. Some members of the Committee saw no marked distinction between the progressive development of international law and its codification. In both cases, they observed, it would be necessary to conclude international conventions before the results were binding on States. Most of the other members, however, thought that there were differences of a substantive nature between codification and progressive development, although there were divergencies in the emphasis they placed on one or the other of the two concepts.

As to the composition of an international law commission, the majority of the Committee favoured the idea that members should not be representatives of Governments but rather should serve in their individual capacities as persons of recognized competence in international law. While some members of the Committee stressed the scientific and non-political nature of the work to be performed by the proposed commission, the majority of the Committee took the view that the work of the commission should always be carried out in close cooperation with the political authorities of States and that actions in respect of the drafts prepared by the Commission should be decided upon by the General Assembly.

During the second session of the General Assembly, a large majority of the Sixth (Legal) Committee[13] favoured the setting up of an international law commission, and a draft Statute of the International Law Commission was prepared by a subcommittee of

---

[12] See *Official Records of the General Assembly, Second Session, Sixth Committee, Annex 1.*

[13] The Sixth Committee is the main committee of the General Assembly of the United Nations which is entrusted with the consideration of legal issues. See rules of procedure of the General Assembly, rule 98 (document A/520/Rev.15/Amend.2). Relevant information and documentation may be found on the official web site of the Sixth Committee. See www.un.org/law/cod/sixth.

the Sixth Committee.[14] On 21 November 1947, the General Assembly adopted resolution 174 (II), establishing the International Law Commission and approving its Statute. Since then, the Statute has been amended by six further resolutions of the General Assembly, adopted partly on the initiative of the Commission and partly on that of Governments.[15] The text of the Statute, as it now stands, is reproduced in annex I.

In accordance with the relevant provisions of the Statute (articles 3 to 10), the first elections to the International Law Commission took place on 3 November 1948, and the Commission opened the first of its annual sessions on 12 April 1949.

---

[14] See *Official Records of the General Assembly, Second Session, Sixth Committee, Annex 1g.*

[15] See General Assembly resolutions 485 (V) of 12 December 1950, 984 (X) and 985 (X) of 3 December 1955, 1103 (XI) of 18 December 1956, 1647 (XVI) of 6 November 1961 and 36/39 of 18 November 1981. The amendments relate to the expenses to be paid to the members of the Commission, the location of the Commission's meetings, the extension of the term of office of Commission members, the size of the Commission as well as the regional distribution of its membership (*see pages 16, 58, 15, 14-15 and 10-11 respectively*). In 1996, the Commission noted that its Statute, which was drafted shortly after the end of the Second World War, had never been the subject of a thorough review and revision. The Commission concluded that, on the whole, the Statute had been flexible enough to allow modifications in practice. At the same time, the Commission drew attention to some aspects of its Statute which warranted review and revision as the Commission approach its fiftieth year. The Commission recommended that consideration be given to consolidating and updating the Commission's Statute to coincide with the fiftieth anniversary of the Commission in 1999. See *Yearbook of the International Law Commission, 1996,* vol. II (Part Two), paras. 147 (a), 148 (s) and 241-243.

PART II

ORGANIZATION, PROGRAMME AND METHODS OF WORK OF THE INTERNATIONAL LAW COMMISSION

1. Object of the Commission

Article 1, paragraph 1, of the Statute of the International Law Commission provides that the "Commission shall have for its object the promotion of the progressive development of international law and its codification". Article 15 of the Statute makes a distinction "for convenience" between progressive development as meaning "the preparation of draft conventions on subjects which have not yet been regulated by international law or in regard to which the law has not yet been sufficiently developed in the practice of States" and codification as meaning "the more precise formulation and systematization of rules of international law in fields where there already has been extensive State practice, precedent and doctrine". In practice, the Commission's work on a topic usually involves some aspects of the progressive development as well as the codification of international law, with the balance between the two varying depending on the particular topic.[16]

Although the drafters of the Statute envisaged that somewhat different methods would be used in regard to progressive development, on the one hand, and codification, on the other, they thought it desirable to entrust both tasks to a single commission. Furthermore, they did not favour proposals for the setting up of separate commissions for public, for private and for penal international law. Thus article 1, paragraph 2, of the Statute states that the Commission "shall concern itself primarily with public international law, but is not precluded from entering the field of private international law". For more than fifty years, however, the Commission has worked almost exclusively in the field of public international law. In 1996, the Commission noted that in recent years it had not entered the field of private international law, except incidentally and in the course of work on subjects of public international law; moreover, it seemed unlikely that the Commission

---

[16] See *Yearbook of the International Law Commission, 1979*, vol. II (Part One), document A/CN.4/325, para. 102, and ibid., *1996*, vol. II (Part Two), paras. 156 and 157.

would be called upon to do so having regard to the work of bodies such as UNCITRAL and the Hague Conference on Private International Law.[17] In contrast, the Commission has worked extensively in the field of international criminal law, beginning with the formulation of the Nürnberg principles and the consideration of the question of international criminal jurisdiction at its first session, in 1949, and culminating in the completion of the draft Statute for an International Criminal Court at its forty-sixth session, in 1994, and the draft Code of Crimes against the Peace and Security of Mankind at its forty-eighth session, in 1996.

2. Members of the Commission

(a) Qualifications and nationality

Article 2, paragraph 1, of the Statute provides that the members of the Commission "shall be persons of recognized competence in international law". The members of the Commission are persons who possess recognized competence and qualifications in both doctrinal and practical aspects of international law.[18] The membership of the Commission often reflects a broad spectrum of expertise and practical experience within the field of international law, including international dispute settlement procedures. Members are drawn from the various segments of the international legal community, such as academia, the diplomatic corps, government ministries and international organizations.[19] Since the members are often persons working in the academic and diplomatic fields with outside

---

[17] See *Yearbook of the International Law Commission, 1996*, vol. II (Part Two), para. 155.

[18] See *Yearbook of the International Law Commission, 1974*, vol. II (Part One), document A/9610/Rev.1, para. 207.

[19] In 1976, a Member State put forward the candidature of a staff member of the Office of the High Commissioner for Refugees for election to a vacancy in the International Law Commission. The question arose as to whether the election of a staff member to the Commission would be incompatible with the staff rules and regulations that govern the activities and conduct of an international civil servant. The Legal Counsel of the United Nations indicated that the election of a staff member to the Commission would be incompatible with the staff rules and regulations of the United Nations, in particular regulation 1.2 and rule 101.6 (e) (currently 101.2 (p)). The Legal Counsel added that a similar position was taken by the Office of Legal Affairs of the United Nations in a case involving membership in the Sub-Commission on the Prevention of Discrimination and the Protection of Minorities. The question of incompatibility arose not under the provisions of the Commission's Statute but rather from the provisions of the staff regulations and rules of the United Nations and the relevant practice. The staff member withdrew his candidature. In contrast, a staff member of a specialized agency was elected to the Commission by the General Assembly in 1991 and by the Commission in 2000 to fill a casual vacancy.

professional responsibilities, the Commission is able to proceed with its work not in an ivory tower but in close touch with the realities of international life.[20] As in the case of the judges of the International Court of Justice, the members of the Commission sit in their individual capacity and not as representatives of their Governments.[21] In addition, the members of the Commission cannot be replaced by alternates or advisers.[22]

No two members of the Commission may be nationals of the same State (article 2, paragraph 2).[23] In case of dual nationality, a person is deemed to be a national of the State in which he or she ordinarily exercises civil and political rights (article 2, paragraph 3). Eligibility for election is not restricted to nationals of Member States of the United Nations, but no national of any non-member State has ever been elected to the Commission. This possibility would seem to be diminishing as the membership of the United Nations increases and becomes almost universal.[24]

(b) Election

The Committee of Seventeen, which recommended the creation of the Commission (as described in Part I), had suggested similarity between the International Court of Justice and the Commission with regard to the method of election.[25] The General Assembly, however, rejected the suggestion for a system of election jointly by the General Assembly and by the Security Council since the Court was a special case which should not serve as a precedent for the appointment of the

---

[20] See *Yearbook of the International Law Commission, 1974*, vol. II (Part One), document A/9610/Rev.1, para. 210.
[21] See *Yearbook of the International Law Commission, 1979*, vol. II (Part One), document A/CN.4/325, para. 4.
[22] See *Yearbook of the International Law Commission, 1974*, vol. II (Part One), document A/9610/Rev.1, para. 210.
[23] The Statute does not address situations in which the nationality of a member of the Commission changes after the election. In one instance, the Commission had two members who both became nationals of the United Arab Republic after the first session of the quinquennium as a result of the formation of a union between Egypt and Syria on 22 February 1958, following the election of both members by the General Assembly in 1956. One of the members resigned. In another instance, the Commission had two members who both became nationals of Germany after the fourth session of the quinquennium as a result of the accession of the German Democratic Republic to the Federal Republic of Germany with effect from 3 October 1990, following the election of both members by the General Assembly in 1986. Both members continued to serve during the last year of the quinquennium and completed the term of office for which they were elected.
[24] As of 4 December 2003, there were 191 States Members of the United Nations.
[25] See the report of the Committee on the Progressive Development of International Law and its Codification, *Official Records of the General Assembly, Second Session, Sixth Committee, Annex 1*, para. 5.

Commission and the work of codifying international law was entrusted to the General Assembly under Article 13 of the Charter of the United Nations.[26] Instead, it decided that candidates should be nominated exclusively by the Governments of States Members of the United Nations and that the election should be by the General Assembly alone (article 3). Each Member State may nominate a maximum of four candidates, of whom only two may be nationals of the nominating State (article 4).

The Secretary-General sends a letter to the Governments of Member States informing them of the upcoming election, indicating the geographical distribution of seats at the upcoming election, noting the relevant provisions of the Statute, and drawing attention to the deadline for the nomination of candidates. The names of candidates must be submitted in writing to the Secretary-General by the first of June of the election year; in exceptional circumstances a Government may substitute one candidate for another whom it has nominated not later than thirty days before the opening of the General Assembly (article 5).[27] The Secretary-General communicates the names and the curricula vitae of the candidates to Governments of States Members (article 6). The Secretary-General also submits a list of all of the candidates duly nominated to the General Assembly for the purposes of the election (article 7).

Article 8 of the Statute (echoing Article 9 of the Statute of the International Court of Justice) provides that at the election the electors shall bear in mind that the persons to be elected to the Commission should individually possess the qualifications required (that is, recognized competence in international law as stated in article 2) and that in the Commission as a whole representation of the main forms of civilization and of the principal legal systems of the world should be assured (article 8).

In 1956, the Sixth Committee of the General Assembly reached an agreement regarding the allocation of seats among the regional groups to ensure distribution between different forms of civilization and legal systems in connection with increasing the membership of the Commission from fifteen to twenty-one.[28] In 1961, different views were expressed concerning the continuation of this arrangement when the membership of the Commission was increased from twenty-one to

---

[26] See document A/C.6/193, para. 7.

[27] The General Assembly begins its regular session on the Tuesday of the third week in September. Rules of procedure of the General Assembly, rule 1, as amended in 2003. See General Assembly resolution 57/301 of 13 March 2003.

[28] See *Official Records of the General Assembly, Eleventh Session, Annexes*, agenda item 59, document A/3427, para. 13; and ibid., *Sixteenth session, Annexes*, agenda item 17, document A/4779, paras. 4 and 5.

twenty-five.[29] In 1981, the General Assembly decided to amend the Commission's Statute in order to increase the membership of the Commission from twenty-five to thirty-four and to provide for the election of a maximum number of members for each regional group.[30] Thus, article 9 of the Statute, as amended, provides that the "candidates, up to the maximum number prescribed for each regional group, who obtain the greatest number of votes and not less than a majority of the votes of the Members present and voting shall be elected".

The election is held by secret ballot, with more than one ballot being held if necessary until all members have been elected by the required majority.[31] If more than one national of the same State receives a sufficient number of votes to be elected, then the candidate who receives the largest number of votes or, if the votes are equally divided, the elder or eldest candidate shall be elected (article 9).

The Statute provides for a different election procedure to fill a vacancy that occurs during the interval between the regular elections by the General Assembly (the so-called "casual vacancies"). In such a situation, the Commission itself elects the new member to fill the vacancy for the remainder of the term having due regard to the provisions contained in articles 2 and 8 of the Statute (article 11). Vacancies in the membership of the Commission may occur for various reasons, such as death, serious illness, appointment to a new position or election to the International Court of Justice.[32] The

---

[29] See *Official Records of the General Assembly, Sixteenth Session, Annexes*, agenda item 77, document A/4939, paras. 9-12; and document A/36/371, paras. 4-6.

[30] General Assembly resolution 36/39 of 18 November 1981 provides that the members of the Commission shall be elected according to the following pattern: eight nationals from African States; seven nationals from Asian States; three nationals from Eastern European States; six nationals from Latin American States; eight nationals from Western European and other States; one national from African States or Eastern European States in rotation; and one national from Asian States or Latin American States in rotation. (The name of the regional group of Latin American States was subsequently changed to Latin American and Caribbean States. See United Nations Journals No. 88/19 of 1 February 1988, No. 88/23 of 5 February 1988 and 88/24 of 8 February 1988). The two rotational seats were allocated to a national of an African State and a national of an Asian State at the election held in 2001. See document A/56/117 and Corr.1, paras. 6-8, and General Assembly decision 56/311 of 7 November 2001.

[31] See rules 92-94 of the rules of procedure of the General Assembly (document A/520/Rev.15).

[32] In some instances, the Commission member has given written notice of resignation usually in the form of a letter addressed to the Chairman and transmitted to the Chairman through the Secretary-General of the United Nations. This has often been the case when Commission members have been elected as judges of the International Court of Justice. Commission members have also submitted letters of resignation without indicating a reason. In other instances, the Commission has taken note of the factual events resulting in a vacancy and the Chairman has declared the existence of a vacancy. Even without an express determination by the Commission of the

Secretariat includes an item concerning the filling of one or more casual vacancies as the first item on the provisional agenda of the Commission.[33] The Secretariat also issues a note announcing the existence of one or more casual vacancies and reproducing the relevant provisions of the Statute in the form of a document of the Commission for general distribution.

The Statute does not provide a nomination procedure for casual vacancies. In practice, the Secretariat may receive the submission of candidates from Governments of Member States or members of the Commission.[34] The Secretariat gives advance notice to Commission members of the candidatures received in the form of an information circular which is sent to members before the opening of the session. The Secretariat also issues a note containing the list of candidates as well as the curricula vitae of candidates in the form of a document of the Commission for general distribution, which is issued as an addendum to its previous note announcing the vacancy.[35] The

---

existence of a casual vacancy, the inclusion of such an item on the agenda adopted by the Commission may be seen as an implied determination by the Commission of the existence of a casual vacancy in the membership of the Commission at that particular session.

[33] This is the practice when a vacancy occurs before the session, as has often been the case. If a vacancy occurs during the session, the Commission may decide to include an item concerning filling a casual vacancy in the agenda for that session or defer action to the following session.

[34] At the fourth session, in 1952, the three persons elected by the Commission to fill casual vacancies were each proposed by a Commission member. The elections were held at public meetings. See *Yearbook of the International Law Commission, 1952*, vol. I, 136th meeting, paras. 5 and 10, and 183rd meeting, para. 1. At the eleventh session, in 1959, candidates were proposed by Commission members during the election to fill a casual vacancy. In a private meeting at that session, the Commission noted that article 11 of the Statute concerning casual vacancies contains no reference to article 3 requiring nominations by Governments for regular elections and therefore decided that it could consider candidatures submitted by a member of the Commission. The election to fill the casual vacancy was held at a private meeting. At the thirty-seventh session, in 1985, one candidate was proposed by a Commission member. Another individual whose name was put forward by a Commission member sent a letter to the Legal Counsel requesting that his name be withdrawn. The individual's name did not appear in the list of candidates. The election to fill casual vacancies was again held at a private meeting.

[35] The practice of issuing a Secretariat list of candidates began in 1964. Prior to 1964, information on candidatures received was circulated to members of the Commission and an informal list of candidates was prepared by the Secretariat for consideration by Commission members. (At times, the members of the Commission were also informed of candidatures by oral statements made by the Commission's Secretary.) In accordance with the decision of the Legal Counsel of the United Nations, Mr. Stavropoulos, in 1973, the Secretariat list of candidates contains the following information: names, nationalities and curricula vitae of candidates. The source of submission of the candidates is not indicated in the list. In accordance with the same decision, the Secretariat issues another document setting out the texts of communications received submitting or supporting candidatures in the form of a conference room document of the Commission restricted to Commission members. These communications are usually from Governments. In 1985, the Secretariat also

Secretariat list of candidates includes the names of candidates submitted by a Government of a Member State or by a member of the Commission.[36]

The date of election is fixed by the Commission following consultations conducted by its Chairman.[37] The Commission elects the new member to fill the vacancy by secret ballot[38] in a private meeting.[39] Since 1981, the Commission has elected members to fill

---

published the text of a communication received from a member of the Commission submitting the name of a candidate. In some instances, information concerning the source of submission of candidates has been provided orally to Governments upon request prior to the election. In 1985, the Legal Counsel, Mr. Fleischhauer, decided that the Secretariat could not follow this practice in a particular case because it was under a constraint of confidentiality due to the request of the member who had submitted the candidature not to disclose its source other than to Commission members prior to the election.

[36] There have been instances in which an individual, not a member of the Commission, has proposed himself or another person as a candidate for a casual vacancy. In 1959, a candidate was proposed by an individual who was not a member of the Commission. The Secretariat distributed informally the individual's curriculum vitae. In a private meeting of the Commission, the Secretary indicated that "The Secretariat had to have some rule to guide it in preparing a list of candidates for the Commission, otherwise the Secretariat might well be embarrassed by a bombardment of candidates from all sources. In his view it was, therefore, desirable that either a government or a member of the Commission should propose a candidate." At the same meeting, a member of the Commission proposed the individual as a candidate without committing his vote to the candidate. In 1976, the Legal Counsel received a letter from an individual requesting that his name be registered as a candidate for a vacancy and indicating that he would be proposed as a candidate by a particular member of the Commission. The individual's name was added to the Secretariat list of candidates only after it was put forward by a Government. The Secretariat document circulated to Commission members contained the letter of the Government and not the personal letter of the individual. (There is no record of his name having been put forward by any Commission member.)

[37] In practice, the Commission has held elections to fill casual vacancies arising before the opening of its session at various times. The Commission may hold an election to fill a casual vacancy arising during the session at a later time or at its next session.

[38] This practice is similar to that of the General Assembly which holds elections by secret ballot. See rule 92 of the rules of procedure of the General Assembly. In 1979, the General Assembly decided that "The practice of dispensing with the secret ballot for elections to subsidiary organs when the number of candidates corresponds to the number of seats to be filled should become standard and the same practice should apply to the election of the President and Vice-Presidents of the General Assembly, unless a delegation specifically requests a vote on a given election." See rules of procedure of the General Assembly, annex VI, para. 16. The Commission considered the question of following this practice in filling casual vacancies in 1985, 1995 and 2003. In the first instance, the Commission decided to follow the election procedure by secret ballot in a private meeting. In the second and third instances, the Commission decided to follow the acclamation procedure in a private meeting. See *Yearbook of the International Law Commission, 1995,* vol. I, 2378th meeting, paras. 7-9; and SR. 2770.

[39] Before 1954, the Commission filled casual vacancies by election in public meetings after consideration of candidates in private meetings. Since 1954, it has been the Commission's consistent practice to fill the vacancies by election (or in a few instances by acclamation) in private meetings. There are no summary records of private meetings.

vacancies following the geographical distribution provided for in resolution 36/39 of 18 November 1981. The Commission holds separate elections to fill vacancies in different regional groups.[40] Votes for candidates not belonging to the regional group for which an election is held or for more candidates than there are vacancies in the regional group are considered invalid. The candidate who receives a majority of the votes of the members who are present and voting is elected.[41] Members who abstain from voting[42] are considered as not voting.[43] When no candidate obtains the majority required as a result of the first ballot, subsequent ballots are held.[44]

The Chairman announces the result of the election in a public meeting, which is duly recorded in the summary records.[45] The Chairman notifies the newly-elected members of the election results and invites them to participate in the Commission's proceedings.

In 1955, the General Assembly invited the Commission to give its opinion concerning a proposal to provide that a vacancy should be filled by the Assembly rather than the Commission in the light of the extension of the term of office of members from three to five years.[46] The Commission decided not to recommend such a proposal since the General Assembly meets after the Commission's session and the vacancy would therefore remain unfilled for at least one session.[47]

The names of the present and former members of the Commission are listed in annex II.

(c)   Size of the Commission

The size of the membership of the Commission has been enlarged three times: from fifteen to twenty-one in 1956, under General

---

[40] In the early years, the Commission normally held a separate election for each vacancy in the alphabetical order of the name of the vacating member. In 1973, the Commission decided to vote together on two vacancies in the same regional group. The same practice was followed in 1985 with respect to three vacancies in the same regional group; a separate election was held to fill a single vacancy in a different regional group.

[41] See rule 125 of the rules of procedure of the General Assembly.

[42] A blank ballot paper constitutes an abstention.

[43] See rule 126 of the rules of procedure of the General Assembly.

[44] See rule 132 of the rules of procedure of the General Assembly.

[45] The Chairman's announcement does not mention the results of the ballot or ballots taken at the private meeting nor make reference to the persons considered. No announcement is made until all vacancies have been filled.

[46] General Assembly resolution 986 (X) of 3 December 1955. See also *Official Records of the General Assembly, Tenth Session, Annexes,* agenda item 50, document A/3028, paras. 21-26.

[47] See *Yearbook of the International Law Commission, 1956,* vol. II, document A/3159, para. 38. See also *Official Records of the General Assembly, Eleventh Session, Annexes,* agenda item 53, document A/3520, paras. 94-100.

Assembly resolution 1103 (XI) of 18 December 1956; to twenty-five in 1961, under Assembly resolution 1647 (XVI) of 6 November 1961; and to the present thirty-four in 1981, under Assembly resolution 36/39 of 18 November 1981.[48] Proposals for the enlargement were prompted by the progressive increase in the membership of the United Nations from the original fifty-one to eighty Member States in 1956, 104 Member States in 1961 and 157 Member States in 1981. A large majority of the General Assembly believed that the provision of article 8 of the Statute, requiring "in the Commission as a whole representation of the main forms of civilization and of the principal legal systems", could be better assured by increasing the size of the Commission.[49]

(d)   Terms of office and service on a part-time basis

Article 10 of the Statute originally provided that the term of office of the members of the Commission should be three years, with the possibility of re-election. However, in practice a longer term has proved beneficial to the progress of the Commission's work, and the term of office was extended to five years, first on an ad hoc and then on a permanent basis.[50]

At its twentieth session, in 1968, the Commission proposed to the General Assembly the extension of the term of office of the Commission's members from five to six or seven years. In the view of the Commission, the experience had shown that, given the time-consuming nature of the codification process, a period of six or seven years was the minimum required for the completion of a programme of work.[51] The Sixth Committee of the General Assembly has taken note of the proposal and deferred taking a decision on it to a later session.[52]

---

[48] See article 2, paragraph 1, of the Statute.
[49] See *Official Records of the General Assembly, Eleventh Session, Annexes,* agenda item 59, document A/3427; ibid., *Sixteenth Session, Annexes,* agenda item 77, document A/4939; and ibid., *Thirty-sixth Session, Plenary Meetings,* 63rd meeting, paras. 145-172, and ibid., *Annexes,* agenda item 137, document A/36/244 and Add.l.
[50] By resolution 486 (V) of 12 December 1950, the General Assembly extended the term of the Commission's members elected in 1948 to five years. In 1955, the Commission recommended a formal amendment to article 10 of its Statute, to take effect from 1 January 1957, which was accepted by the General Assembly in resolution 985 (X) of 3 December 1955. Accordingly, elections have taken place in 1948, 1953, 1956, 1961, 1966, 1971, 1976, 1981, 1986, 1991, 1996 and 2001.
[51] See *Yearbook of the International Law Commission, 1968,* vol. II, document A/7209/Rev.1, para. 98 (a).
[52] See *Official Records of the General Assembly, Twenty-fourth Session, Annexes,* agenda items 86 and 94 *(b),* document A/7746, para. 117.

By decision of the General Assembly, the Commission meets only in annual sessions, and its members, unlike judges of the International Court of Justice, do not serve on a full-time, year-round basis, although the Committee of Seventeen recommended that service be full-time.[53] Thus, the Commission is a permanent and part-time subsidiary organ of the General Assembly.[54] Members of the Commission are paid travel expenses and receive a special allowance in accordance with article 13[55] of the Commission's Statute. The Chairman, the Special Rapporteurs and the other members of the Commission have historically also been paid honorariums. [56]

---

[53] See the report of the Committee on the Progressive Development of International Law and its Codification, *Official Records of the General Assembly, Second Session, Sixth Committee, Annex 1*, para. 5 (d).

[54] See *Yearbook of the International Law Commission, 1979*, vol. II (Part One), document A/CN.4/325, para. 4.

[55] As amended by General Assembly resolution 485 (V) of 12 December 1950. The members of the Commission were paid travel expenses and received a per diem allowance under article 13 of the Statute as originally adopted. In 1950, the General Assembly noted the inadequacy of the emoluments paid to Commission members and decided to amend this provision of the Statute to provide for the payment of travel expenses and a special allowance to Commission members bearing in mind the importance of the Commission's work, the eminence of its members and the method of their election as well as considering the nature and scope of the Commission's work which requires its members to devote considerable time in attendance at its necessarily long sessions.

[56] The basic principle governing the payment of honorariums enunciated by the General Assembly in resolution 2489 (XXIII) of 21 December 1968 and reaffirmed in resolutions 3536 (XXX) of 17 December 1975 and 35/218 of 17 December 1980 was that neither a fee nor any other remuneration in addition to subsistence allowances at the standard rate would normally be paid to members of organs or subsidiary organs of the United Nations unless expressly decided upon by the General Assembly. Payment of honorariums to the members of the Commission was authorized by the General Assembly on an exceptional basis, with the rates being kept under review by the Secretary-General and occasionally revised. In 1981, the revised rates of honorariums payable to members of the Commission were as follows: Chairman — 5,000; other members — 3,000; and Special Rapporteurs who prepared reports between sessions — an additional 2,500 United States dollars. In 1998, the Secretary-General submitted a report indicating that the General Assembly might wish to consider increasing the rates of honorariums by 25 per cent, effective 1 January 1999 (document A/53/643). The General Assembly, in resolution 56/272 of 27 March 2002, decided to set at a level of one United States dollar per year the honorariums payable to the Commission. At its fifty-fourth session, in 2002, the Commission noted that resolution 56/272 was adopted after the election of its members by the General Assembly and the decision was taken without consulting the Commission; considered that the decision was not consistent in procedure or substance with either the principles of fairness on which the United Nations conducts its affairs or with the spirit of service with which members of the Commission contribute their time and approach their work; stressed that the resolution especially affected Special Rapporteurs, particularly those from developing countries, by compromising support for their research work; and decided not to collect the honorariums due to concerns about the administrative costs involved in the payment of the symbolic honorariums (see *Official Records of the General Assembly, Fifty-seventh Session, Supplement No. 10* (A/57/10), paras. 525-531). The Chairman of the Commission sent a letter to the Chairman of the Sixth Committee bringing this

In compliance with a request by the General Assembly to review the Statute and make recommendations for its revision, the International Law Commission, in 1951, recommended that the Commission should be placed on a full-time basis with a view to expediting its work.[57] When the matter was discussed in the Sixth Committee, however, most delegations believed that it was premature to make so fundamental a change in the structure of the Commission. They felt, inter alia, that a large increase in the Commission's output would impose an excessive burden on the General Assembly and Governments asked to comment on draft texts; that it would be difficult to find suitable candidates who would accept full-time appointment; and that expense was a serious consideration.[58] Accordingly, the Assembly, in resolution 600 (VI) of 31 January 1952, decided not to take any action on the matter for the time being. Suggestions for placing the Commission on a full-time basis have also been made in the debates of the Sixth Committee at various later dates, but have never been acted on by the Assembly.

(e)   Privileges and immunities

At its thirtieth session, in 1978, the Commission considered it necessary to define better the juridical status of the Commission at the place of its permanent seat in Switzerland, including the immunities, privileges and facilities to which it and its members were entitled.[59] The Commission requested the Secretary-General to study this matter and to take appropriate measures in consultation with the Swiss authorities.[60] In 1979, the Government of Switzerland decided to accord to members of the Commission for the duration of its session the same privileges and immunities to which judges of the International Court of Justice are entitled while present in Switzerland, namely, the privileges and immunities enjoyed by the heads of mission accredited to the international organizations at

---

matter to his attention (document A/C.6/57/INF/2). The Commission reiterated those views in the report on its fifty-fifth session, in 2003 (see *Official Records of the General Assembly, Fifty-eighth Session, Supplement No. 10* (A/58/10), para. 447).
[57] See *Yearbook of the International Law Commission, 1951*, vol. II, document A/1858, paras. 60-71.
[58] See *Official Records of the General Assembly, Sixth Session, Annexes*, agenda item 49, document A/2088.
[59] The members of the Commission would be entitled to the privileges and immunities of experts on mission when the Commission meets at the United Nations Headquarters in New York or in a Member State which is a party to the Convention on the Privileges and Immunities of the United Nations (article VI). United Nations, *Treaty Series*, vol. 1, pp. 15, 26.
[60] See *Yearbook of the International Law Commission, 1978*, vol. II (Part Two), para. 199.

Geneva. (See annex III.) The Commission as well as the General Assembly expressed appreciation for this decision which would facilitate the performance by its members of their functions during its sessions in Geneva.[61]

3. Structure of the Commission

(a) Officers

At the beginning of each session, the Commission elects from among its members the Chairman, the First and Second Vice-Chairmen, the Chairman of the Drafting Committee[62] and the General Rapporteur for that session.[63] The Chairman presides over the meetings of the plenary, the Bureau and the Enlarged Bureau.[64] A vice-chairman has the same powers and duties as the Chairman when designated to take the place of the Chairman.[65] The Chairman of the Drafting Committee presides over the meetings of the Drafting Committee; recommends the membership of the Drafting Committee for each topic; and introduces the report of the Drafting Committee when it is considered in plenary. The General Rapporteur is responsible for the drafting of the Commission's annual report to the General Assembly. The Commission has emphasized that the General Rapporteur should play an active part in the preparation of the report[66] (see page 46).

(b) Bureau, Enlarged Bureau and Planning Group

At each session, the Bureau, consisting of the five officers elected at that session, considers the schedule of work and other organizational matters with respect to the current session. The Enlarged Bureau, consisting of the officers elected at the current session, the former Chairmen of the Commission who are still members and the Special Rapporteurs, may also be called upon to consider issues relating to the organization, programme and methods of the Commission's work.

---

[61] See *Yearbook of the International Law Commission, 1979,* vol. II (Part Two), paras. 11-13, and General Assembly resolution 34/141 of 17 December 1979.

[62] Since 1974, the Commission has elected the Chairman of the Drafting Committee. Previously, the First Vice-Chairman of the Commission also served as Chairman of the Drafting Committee. See *Yearbook of the International Law Commission, 1979,* vol. II (Part One), document A/CN.4/325, para. 45.

[63] In accordance with the practice of the Commission, the posts of Chairman and the other four officers have been rotated among nationals of the various regional groups.

[64] The functions of the Chairman are described in greater detail in rule 106 of the rules of procedure of the General Assembly.

[65] See rule 105 of the rules of procedure of the General Assembly.

[66] See *Yearbook of the International Law Commission, 1992,* vol. II (Part Two), para. 373 *(a).*

Since the 1970s, the Commission has established a Planning Group[67] for each session and entrusted it with the task of considering the programme and methods of work of the Commission. Since 1992, the Planning Group has established a Working Group on the Long-Term Programme which is entrusted with the task of recommending topics for inclusion in the Commission's programme of work. The Working Group has been reconstituted with the same Chairman and membership during the remaining sessions of the quinquennium (*see page 29*). The Planning Group may also establish a Working Group to review and consider ways of improving the methods of work of the Commission on the basis of a request by the General Assembly or on the Commission's own initiative (*see pages 45 and 47*).

(c) Plenary

The Commission meets in plenary primarily to consider the reports of Special Rapporteurs, working groups, the Drafting Committee, the Planning Group as well as any other matters that may require consideration by the Commission as a whole. The Commission also decides in plenary to refer proposed draft articles to the Drafting Committee and to adopt provisional or final draft articles and commentaries.[68] At the end of each session, the Commission considers and adopts in plenary its annual report to the General Assembly.

The primary role of the general debate in plenary is to establish the broad approach of the Commission to a topic for the primary purpose of providing guidance to the Commission, its subsidiary organs and Special Rapporteurs on the directions to be taken.[69] This is essential to ensure that subsidiary organs, such as the Drafting Committee or a working group, are working along lines broadly acceptable to the Commission as a whole. The Commission has indicated that the Chairman of the Commission should, whenever possible, indicate the main trends of opinion revealed by the debate in plenary to facilitate the task of the Drafting Committee.[70] The Commission has also recommended that the plenary debates should

---

[67] In the early years, the Commission established the Planning Group in the Enlarged Bureau which reviewed its report. More recently, the Commission has established the Planning Group as a subsidiary body of the Commission which reports directly to it.
[68] The Commission has decided that the commentaries to draft articles should be considered in plenary as soon as possible during each session and separately from the Commission's annual report. See *Yearbook of the International Law Commission, 1994*, vol. II (Part Two), para. 399.
[69] See *Yearbook of the International Law Commission, 1996*, vol. II (Part Two), paras. 202 and 204.
[70] See *Yearbook of the International Law Commission, 1987*, vol. II (Part Two), para. 239.

be reformed to provide more structure and to allow the Chairman to make an indicative summary of conclusions at the end of the debate,[71] based if necessary on an indicative vote.[72] (*See pages 45 and 47.*)

At its forty-ninth session, in 1997, the Commission introduced the mechanism of short, thematic debates or exchanges of views in plenary on particular issues or questions raised during the consideration of a topic, the so-called "mini-debates," in order to facilitate a more focused debate on particular issues. At its fifty-fourth session, in 2002, the Commission expressed the view that the "mini-debates" were useful and constituted an important innovation in its working methods. The Commission emphasized, however, that a mini-debate should be brief, focused and not include long statements falling outside its scope.[73]

The Commission holds its plenary meetings in public[74] unless it decides otherwise, in particular when dealing with certain organizational or administrative matters.[75] The Commission's decisions on substantive and procedural matters are taken in plenary or, if such decisions are reached in a private meeting or informal consultations, announced by the Chairman in plenary.[76]

(d) Special Rapporteurs

The role of the Special Rapporteur is central to the work of the Commission.[77] Although the Statute only envisages the appointment of a Special Rapporteur in the case of progressive development (article 16 (*a*)), the practice of the Commission has been to appoint a Special Rapporteur at the early stage of the consideration of a topic, where appropriate, without regard to whether it might be classified as

---

[71] See also the discussion below of the possible role of the Special Rapporteur in this respect.
[72] See *Yearbook of the International Law Commission, 1996*, vol. II (Part Two), paras. 148 (i) and 202-211.
[73] See *Official Records of the General Assembly, Fifty-seventh Session, Supplement No. 10* (A/57/10), para. 523.
[74] See rule 60 of the rules of procedure of the General Assembly.
[75] See *Yearbook of the International Law Commission, 1979*, vol. II (Part One), document A/CN.4/325, para. 8.
[76] This is similar to the practice followed by the General Assembly. See rule 61 of the rules of procedure of the General Assembly. The summary records of the plenary meetings of the Commission are published in the Commission's *Yearbook*. In addition, the major decisions taken in plenary are summarized in the relevant chapters of the Commission's annual report to the General Assembly. See *Yearbook of the International Law Commission, 1979*, vol. II (Part One), document A/CN.4/325, para. 8.
[77] See *Yearbook of the International Law Commission, 1996*, vol. II (Part Two), paras. 185-201.

one of codification or progressive development.[78] The functions of the Special Rapporteur continue until the Commission has completed its work on the topic, provided that he or she remains a member of the Commission.[79] In the event that it becomes necessary to appoint a new Special Rapporteur, the Commission usually suspends its work on the topic for an appropriate period of time to enable the newly appointed Special Rapporteur to perform the tasks required depending on the stage of work on the topic.

Special Rapporteurs are one of the institutional features of the Commission which contribute to the efficient performance of its functions and which have served it well.[80] The Special Rapporteur performs a number of key tasks, including preparing reports on the topic, participating in the consideration of the topic in plenary, contributing to the work of the Drafting Committee on the topic, and elaborating commentaries to draft articles.

The Special Rapporteur marks out and develops the topic, explains the state of the law and makes proposals for draft articles in the

---

[78] In practice special rapporteurships tend to be distributed among members from different regions. See *Yearbook of the International Law Commission, 1996*, vol. II (Part Two), paras. 185 and 186. The Commission has appointed one of its members to serve as Special Rapporteur for each topic on its current agenda, with the exception of the appointment of two Special Rapporteurs for the topic "Question of international criminal jurisdiction," one Special Rapporteur for the topics "Formulation of the Nürnberg principles" and "Draft Code of Offences," and one Special Rapporteur for the topics "Regime of the high seas" and "Regime of territorial waters". See *Yearbook of the International Law Commission, 1949*, Report to the General Assembly, paras. 31 and 34.

[79] The Special Rapporteur for State responsibility, Roberto Ago, resigned from the Commission upon his election to the International Court of Justice in 1978. The Chairman of the Commission sent a letter to the President of the Court requesting that Judge Ago continue to be available to the Commission in his private capacity in order to assist it in finalizing the first part of its draft on State responsibility. The Court acceded to the request in order to facilitate the Commission's work on State responsibility on the understanding that Judge Ago would be available in an individual and personal capacity to assist the Commission in its consideration of the few remaining articles of a draft of which he himself had been the prime author; there was no question of his being appointed, designated or given any official title such as "expert consultant"; and priority would have to be given to his judicial duties. Mr. Ago attended the thirty-first and thirty-second sessions of the Commission, in 1979 and 1980, respectively. In 1979, he introduced to the Commission and commented on his eighth report. In 1980, he presented to the Commission the addendum to his eighth report. See *Yearbook of the International Law Commission, 1979*, vol. II (Part Two), para. 69, and ibid., *1980*, vol. II (Part Two), para. 28. The Special Rapporteur for the law of the non-navigational uses of international watercourses, Stephen M. Schwebel, after his resignation from the Commission in 1981, continued and completed his research for the third report on the topic which he had begun to prepare prior to his resignation from the Commission. See *Yearbook of the International Law Commission, 1982*, vol. II (Part Two), para. 251.

[80] See *Yearbook of the International Law Commission, 1979*, vol. II (Part One), document A/CN.4/325, para. 104.

reports on the topic.[81] The reports of Special Rapporteurs form the very basis of work for the Commission and constitute a critical component of the methods and techniques of work of the Commission established in its Statute.[82] The Commission has recommended that Special Rapporteurs specify the nature and scope of work planned for the next session to ensure that future reports meet the needs of the Commission as a whole and that reports be available to members sufficiently in advance of the session to enable study and reflection.[83] The Commission has also recommended that a consultative group be appointed by the Commission to provide input on the general direction of the report and on any particular issues the Special Rapporteur wishes to raise.[84] The Special Rapporteur usually introduces the report at the beginning of the Commission's consideration of the topic in plenary, responds to questions raised during the debate and makes concluding remarks summarizing the main issues and trends at the end of the debate.

The role of the Special Rapporteur with respect to the Drafting Committee comprises the following elements: (a) to produce clear and complete draft articles; (b) to explain the rationale behind the draft articles currently before the Drafting Committee; and (c) to reflect the view of the Drafting Committee in revised draft articles and/or commentary.[85] The Special Rapporteurs should prepare commentaries to draft articles on their respective topics which are as uniform as possible in presentation and length.[86] The Special Rapporteurs should also, as far as possible, produce draft commentaries or notes to accompany their draft articles and revise them in the light of changes made by the Drafting Committee to

---

[81] See *Yearbook of the International Law Commission, 1996,* vol. II (Part Two), para. 188. The reports of the Special Rapporteurs are reproduced in the *Yearbook* of the Commission.

[82] See *Yearbook of the International Law Commission, 1982,* vol. II (Part Two), para. 271.

[83] See *Yearbook of the International Law Commission, 1996,* vol. II (Part Two), paras. 148 *(f),* 189 and 190.

[84] The Commission further recommended that the principle of a consultative group should be recognized, without any distinction being drawn between codification and progressive development, in any revision of the Statute. See *Yearbook of the International Law Commission, 1996,* vol. II (Part Two), paras. 148 *(g)* and 191-195.

[85] See *Yearbook of the International Law Commission, 1996,* vol. II (Part Two), para. 200

[86] See *Yearbook of the International Law Commission, 1995,* vol. II (Part Two), para. 508. The main function of a commentary is to explain the text itself, with appropriate references to key decisions, doctrine and State practice to indicate the extent to which the text reflects, develops or extends the law. Generally speaking it is not the function of such commentary to reflect disagreements on the text as adopted on second reading which can be done in the Commission in plenary at the time of final adoption of the text and reflected in the Commission's report. See *Yearbook of the International Law Commission, 1996,* vol. II (Part Two), para. 198.

ensure their availability at the time of the debate of the draft articles in plenary.[87] (*See also page 47.*) The Special Rapporteur may also draft other working documents of the Commission and the Drafting Committee, as required by the Commission's progress of work on the topic.

(e) Working groups

The Commission has made use of working groups, sometimes called subcommittees, study groups or consultative groups, on particular topics. These ad hoc subsidiary bodies have been established by the Commission or by the Planning Group for different purposes and with different mandates.[88] They may be of limited membership or open-ended.[89]

The Commission has established working groups on new topics before appointing a Special Rapporteur to undertake preliminary work or to help define the scope and direction of work, including: formulation of the Nürnberg principles (1949); succession of States and Governments (1962-1963); question of treaties concluded between States and international organizations or between two or more international organizations (1970-1971); the law of the non-navigational uses of international watercourses (1974); status of the diplomatic courier and the diplomatic bag not accompanied by diplomatic courier (1977-1979); international liability for injurious consequences arising out of acts not prohibited by international law (1978 and 2002 (second part of the topic)); jurisdictional immunities of States and their property (1978); diplomatic protection (1997); and unilateral acts of States (1997).[90]

The Commission has also established working groups after appointing a Special Rapporteur[91] to consider specific issues or to determine the direction of the future work on a particular topic or sub-topic, including: arbitral procedure (1957); State responsibility (1962-1963, 1997, 1998 and 2001[92]); relations between States and international organizations (1971 (first part of the topic) and 1992

---

[87] See *Yearbook of the International Law Commission, 1996*, vol. II (Part Two), para. 148 *(h)*.

[88] See *Yearbook of the International Law Commission, 1996*, vol. II (Part Two), para. 217.

[89] The names of members of working groups of limited membership are listed in the report of the Commission on the session at which a group is established.

[90] In most cases, the chairman of such a working group has been appointed subsequently by the Commission as the Special Rapporteur for the topic.

[91] This type of group is envisaged with respect to progressive development in article 16 (*d*) and (*i*) of the Statute.

[92] The Commission established two working groups on this topic in 2001.

(second part of the topic)[93]); draft code of offences against the peace and security of mankind (1982 and 1995-1996); international liability for injurious consequences arising out of acts not prohibited by international law (1992, 1995, 1996 and 1997 (the topic as a whole), 1998 and 2000 (prevention aspect of the topic) and 2003 (liability aspect of the topic)); unilateral acts of States (1998-2000, 2001 and 2003); nationality in relation to the succession of States (1995-1996 and 1999 (first part of the topic) and 1998 (second part of the topic)); diplomatic protection (1998 and 2003); responsibility of international organizations (2002 and 2003[94]); and shared natural resources (2002).[95]

The Commission has further established working groups to handle a topic as a whole, for example, in case of urgency, including: question of the protection and inviolability of diplomatic agents and other persons entitled to special protection under international law (1972); review of the multilateral treaty-making process (1978-1979); draft code of offences against the peace and security of mankind (draft Statute for an International Criminal Court) (1990 and 1992-1994); jurisdictional immunities of States and their property (1999); and fragmentation of international law (2002-2003).[96] Whereas the Drafting Committee works on texts of articles prepared by a Special Rapporteur, a working group begins its work at an earlier stage when ideas are still developing and thus is more closely involved in the formulation of an approach and drafts.[97] Such a working group may continue its work over several sessions, with substantial continuity of membership, while the composition of the Drafting Committee changes from year to year.[98] In most cases, if the working group has undertaken careful drafting, the final product is submitted directly to the Commission in plenary, not to the Drafting Committee, to avoid duplication or even mistakes which may be made if members of the Drafting Committee have not been party to the detailed discussion which underlies a particular text. In some cases, however, the Drafting Committee may have a role in engaging in a final review of

---

[93] This working group was established by the Planning Group of the Enlarged Bureau.

[94] The Commission established two working groups on this topic in 2003.

[95] These working groups are usually chaired by the Special Rapporteur assigned to the topic.

[96] These working groups are usually of substantial size and no Special Rapporteur is appointed.

[97] For instance, the working group that elaborated the statute for an international criminal court began by focusing on some basic propositions on which agreement could be reached, before even attempting to draft any articles.

[98] See *Yearbook of the International Law Commission, 1996*, vol. II (Part Two), para. 217.

a text from the perspective of adequacy and consistency of language.[99]

Whatever its mandate, a working group is always subordinate to the Commission, the Planning Group or other Commission organ which established it. It is for the relevant organ to issue the necessary mandate, to lay down the parameters of any study, to review and, if necessary, modify proposals, and to make a decision on the product of the work.[100]

In 1996, the Commission recommended that working groups be more extensively used to resolve particular disagreements and, in appropriate cases, to expeditiously deal with whole topics; in the latter case normally acting in place of the Drafting Committee[101] (*see page 47*).

(f)   Drafting Committee

Since its first session, the Commission has made use of a Drafting Committee,[102] the composition of which has been progressively enlarged to take account of the increase in the size of the Commission. The membership of the Drafting Committee varies from session to session and, since 1992, from topic to topic at any given session, although it continues to be a single body exercising its functions under one Chairman.[103] The General Rapporteur takes part in the Drafting Committee's work and the Special Rapporteurs who have not been appointed to the Drafting Committee participate when their topics are being considered. The Drafting Committee is also constituted so as to provide equitable representation of the principal

---

[99] See *Yearbook of the International Law Commission, 1996*, vol. II (Part Two), para. 218.
[100] See *Yearbook of the International Law Commission, 1996*, vol. II (Part Two), para. 219. The final outcome of work by a working group may be an oral report of the Chairman of the working group to the Commission in plenary which is reflected in the summary records or a written report issued as a document which may be included in the Commission's report.
[101] See *Yearbook of the International Law Commission, 1996*, vol. II (Part Two), para. 148 (*k*).
[102] Committees in the nature of drafting committees were set up by the Commission to deal with specific topics or questions at its first three sessions. However, a standing Drafting Committee has been used at each session of the Commission since its fourth session, in 1952. See *Yearbook of the International Law Commission, 1979*, vol. II (Part One), document A/CN.4/325, para. 45.
[103] See *Yearbook of the International Law Commission, 1992*, vol. II (Part Two), para. 371; and ibid., *1996*, vol. II (Part Two), paras. 148 (*j*) and 214.

legal systems and the various languages[104] of the Commission within limits compatible with its drafting responsibilities.[105]

The Drafting Committee plays an important role in harmonizing the various viewpoints and working out generally acceptable solutions.[106] The Drafting Committee is entrusted not only with purely drafting points but also with points of substance which the full Commission has been unable to resolve or which seemed likely to give rise to unduly protracted discussion.[107] In practice, the Commission usually does not take a vote in the Commission at the end of its first discussion of a particular article, and leaves it to the Drafting Committee to try to draft a generally satisfactory text on the question. The Drafting Committee's proposals have very often been adopted unanimously by the Commission, sometimes without discussion. However, the Drafting Committee's texts are subject to amendments or alternative formulations submitted by members of the Commission and may be referred back to the Committee for further consideration.[108] The Commission has noted that premature referral of draft articles to the Drafting Committee, and excessive time-lags between such referral and actual consideration of draft articles in the Committee, have counter-productive effects.[109]

The report of the Chairman of the Drafting Committee to the Commission in plenary provides a detailed summary of its work on each topic, including an explanation of the draft articles that have been adopted by the Drafting Committee and are submitted for consideration and adoption by the Commission in plenary.[110] (*See also pages 45 to 47.*)

---

[104] The practice of multilingual drafting, now customary in the Commission, as opposed to mere translation from the working language of the Special Rapporteur into the other working languages, frequently brings to light unsuspected questions of substance. This has added additional responsibilities to the work of the Drafting Committee.

[105] See *Yearbook of the International Law Commission, 1987*, vol. II (Part Two), para. 238.

[106] See *Yearbook of the International Law Commission, 1987*, vol. II (Part Two), para. 237; and ibid., *1996*, vol. II (Part Two), para. 212.

[107] See *Yearbook of the International Law Commission, 1958*, vol. II, document A/3859, para. 65.

[108] See *Yearbook of the International Law Commission, 1979*, vol. II (Part One), document A/CN.4/325, para. 47.

[109] See *Yearbook of the International Law Commission, 1987*, vol. II (Part Two), paras. 235-239.

[110] There are no summary records of the meetings of the Drafting Committee which are not public meetings. However, the statement of the Chairman of the Drafting Committee is reflected in the summary records of the Commission which are published in the Commission's *Yearbook*.

4.   Programme of work

(a)   Methods for the selection of topics

Under the Statute, the Commission shall consider proposals for the progressive development of international law referred by the General Assembly (article 16) or submitted by Members of the United Nations, the principal organs of the United Nations other than the General Assembly, specialized agencies or official bodies established by intergovernmental agreements to encourage the progressive development and codification of international law (article 17). With respect to codification, the Commission is required to survey the whole field of international law with a view to selecting appropriate topics (article 18). In addition, the Commission may recommend to the General Assembly the codification of a particular topic which is considered necessary and desirable (article 18). At its first session, in 1949, the Commission decided that it had competence to proceed with its work of codification of a topic that it had recommended to the General Assembly without awaiting action by the General Assembly on such recommendation.[111] However, in practice, the Commission has generally sought endorsement by the General Assembly before engaging in the substantive consideration of a topic. The General Assembly may also request the Commission to deal with any question of codification which receives priority (article 18).

In the early years, the Commission received a number of proposals and special assignments from the General Assembly as well as proposals from the Economic and Social Council. In 1996, the Commission expressed concern that the relevant provisions of the Statute have been used infrequently in recent years and recommended that the General Assembly — and through it other bodies within the United Nations system — should be encouraged to submit to the Commission possible topics involving codification and progressive development of international law.[112]

The Commission has conducted two surveys of international law as provided for in its Statute, the first, at its first session, in 1949, on the basis of a Secretariat memorandum entitled "Survey of international law in relation to the work of codification of the International Law Commission,"[113] and the second, on the occasion of

---

[111] See *Yearbook of the International Law Commission, 1949*, Report to the General Assembly, para. 12.
[112] See *Yearbook of the International Law Commission, 1996*, vol. II (Part Two), paras. 148 (*b*) and 177.
[113] Document A/CN.4/1 (United Nations publication, Sales No. 48.V.1) reissued under the symbol A/CN.4/1/Rev.1 (United Nations publication, Sales No. 48.V.1(1)).

the Commission's twentieth session on the basis of a series of documents prepared by the Secretariat,[114] in particular a working paper entitled "Survey of International Law," prepared by the Secretary-General in response to the Commission's request.[115]

At its forty-eighth session, in 1996, the Commission analysed the scope for progressive development and codification after nearly fifty years of work by the Commission and, in order to provide a global review of the main fields of general public international law, established a general scheme of topics of international law classified under thirteen main fields of public international law, not meant to be exhaustive, that included topics already taken up by the Commission, topics under consideration by the Commission and possible future topics.[116]

Apart from the surveys, the Commission has held a periodic review of its programme of work with a view to bringing it up to date, taking into account General Assembly recommendations and the international community's current needs and discarding those topics which are no longer suitable for treatment. Such a review has sometimes taken place at the request of the General Assembly. [117]

---

[114] See *Yearbook of the International Law Commission, 1968*, vol. II, document A/7209/Rev.1, annex; and ibid., *1970*, vol. II, document A/CN.4/230.

[115] See *Yearbook of the International Law Commission, 1971*, vol. II (Part Two), document A/CN.4/245.

[116] See *Yearbook of the International Law Commission, 1996*, vol. II (Part Two), paras. 246-248 and annex II.

[117] Most recently, by its resolution 54/111 of 9 December 1999, the General Assembly encouraged the Commission to proceed with the selection of new topics for its next quinquennium corresponding to the wishes and preoccupations of States and to present possible outlines and related information for new topics to facilitate decision thereon by the Assembly. As a result of the review held at its fifty-second session, in 2000, the Commission has identified a number of topics as appropriate for inclusion in its long-term programme of work. See *Official Records of the General Assembly, Fifty-fifth Session, Supplement No. 10* (A/55/10), paras. 726-733. For earlier reviews of the Commission's programme of work, see *Yearbook of the International Law Commission, 1962*, vol. II, document A/5209, paras. 24-62; ibid., *1967*, vol. II, document A/6709/Rev.1, para. 49; ibid., *1968*, vol. II, document A/7209/Rev.1, paras. 95-101; ibid., *1969*, vol. II, document A/7610/Rev.1, para. 91; ibid., *1970*, vol. II, document A/8010/Rev.1, para. 87; ibid., *1971*, vol. II (Part One), document A/8410/Rev.1, paras. 119-128; ibid., *1972*, vol. II, document A/CN.4/254; ibid., *1973*, vol. II, document A/9010/Rev.1, paras. 134-176; ibid., *1977*, vol. II (Part Two), paras. 96-111; ibid., *1992*, vol. II (Part Two), paras. 368-370; ibid., *1995*, vol. II (Part Two), paras. 498-503; ibid., *1996*, vol. II (Part Two), paras. 244-248 and annex II; ibid., *1997*, vol. II (Part Two), para. 238; and ibid., *1998*, vol. II (Part Two), paras. 551-554.

(b) Procedure and criteria for the selection of topics

Since 1992, the selection of topics by the Commission for its future work has been carried out in accordance with the procedure under which designated members of the Commission write a short outline or explanatory summary on one of the topics included in a pre-selected list,[118] indicating: (i) the major issues raised by the topic; (ii) any applicable treaties, general principles or relevant national legislation or judicial decisions; (iii) existing doctrine; and (iv) the advantages and disadvantages of preparing a report, a study or a draft convention, if a decision is taken to proceed with the topic.[119]

The Working Group on the Long-term Programme considers the outlines or summaries on the various topics prepared by members with a view to identifying topics for possible future consideration by the Commission. The Chairman of the Working Group provides an annual oral progress report to the Planning Group at each session and submits a final written report containing a list of recommended topics accompanied by syllabuses in the last year of the quinquennium. The Planning Group considers and adopts the report which is then submitted to the Commission. The Commission considers and adopts this report in plenary and includes it in an annex to its annual report to the General Assembly. The list of topics is intended to facilitate the selection of topics by the newly-elected members of the Commission at the beginning of the next quinquennium, taking into account views expressed in the Sixth Committee. The list of topics is intended to perform a function similar to the 1949 list which guided the Commission in the selection of topics for more than fifty years.

The Commission has recommended that the work on the identification of possibles future topics continue to follow this procedure which it considers to be an improvement.[120]

In the selection of topics, the Commission has been guided by the following criteria: (i) the topic should reflect the needs of States in

---

[118] The topics may be drawn from the list of possible future topics identified by the Commission in 1996 or suggested by members of the Commission.
[119] See *Yearbook of the International Law Commission, 1992,* vol. II (Part Two), para. 369.
[120] See *Yearbook of the International Law Commission, 1996,* vol. II (Part Two), paras. 148 *(a)* and 165. For the consideration of the long-term programme of work in accordance with this procedure in subsequent years, see ibid., *1997,* vol. II (Part Two), para. 238; ibid., *1998,* vol. II (Part Two), paras. 551-554; *Official Records of the General Assembly, Fifty-fourth Session, Supplement No. 10* (A/54/10), para. 642; ibid., *Fifty-fifth Session, Supplement No. 10* (A/55/10), paras. 726-733; ibid., *Fifty-seventh Session, Supplement No. 10* (A/57/10), para. 521; and ibid., *Fifty-eighth Session, Supplement No. 10* (A/58/10), para. 439.

respect of the progressive development and codification of international law; (ii) the topic should be at a sufficiently advanced stage in terms of State practice to permit progressive development and codification; (iii) the topic should be concrete and feasible for progressive development and codification; and (iv) the Commission should not restrict itself to traditional topics, but should also consider those that reflect new developments in international law and pressing concerns of the international community as a whole.[121]

(c) Topics on the Commission's programme of work

At its first session, in 1949, the Commission reviewed, on the basis of a Secretariat memorandum entitled "Survey of international law in relation to the work of codification of the International Law Commission",[122] twenty-five topics for possible inclusion in a list of topics for study. Following its consideration of the matter, the Commission drew up a provisional list of fourteen topics selected for codification, as follows:

(a) Recognition of States and Governments;

(b) Succession of States and Governments;

(c) Jurisdictional immunities of States and their property;

(d) Jurisdiction with regard to crimes committed outside national territory;

(e) Regime of the high seas;

(f) Regime of territorial waters;[123]

(g) Nationality, including statelessness;

(h) Treatment of aliens;

(i) Right of asylum;

(j) Law of treaties;

(k) Diplomatic intercourse and immunities;

(l) Consular intercourse and immunities;

(m) State responsibility;[124] and

(n) Arbitral procedure.

---

[121] See *Yearbook of the International Law Commission, 1997,* vol. II (Part Two), para. 238; and ibid., *1998,* vol. II (Part Two), para. 553.

[122] Document A/CN.4/1 (United Nations publication, Sales No. 48.V.1) reissued under the symbol A/CN.4/1/Rev.1 (United Nations publication, Sales No. 48.V.1(1)).

[123] At its fourth session, in 1952, the Commission decided, in accordance with a suggestion of the Special Rapporteur, to use the term "territorial sea" in lieu of "territorial waters".

[124] At its fifty-third session, in 2001, the Commission decided to amend the title of the topic to "Responsibility of States for internationally wrongful acts."

The Commission agreed to the 1949 list of fourteen topics on the understanding that it was provisional and that additions or deletions might be made after further study by the Commission or in compliance with the wishes of the General Assembly. Amendments were made in the course of the Commission's consideration of certain topics. The topic of "Succession of States and Governments" was subsequently divided into three, namely succession in respect of treaties, succession in matters other than treaties,[125] and succession in respect of membership of international organizations.[126] The topics "Regime of the high seas" and "Regime of territorial waters," for the most part, were considered separately, but, at its eighth session, in 1956, the Commission grouped together systematically all the rules it had adopted under these topics in the final report on the subject "Law of the Sea".

The Commission has submitted a final report on all of the topics included in the 1949 list, except for the following:

(a)   Recognition of States and Governments;

(b)   Jurisdiction with regard to crimes committed outside national territory;

(c)   Treatment of aliens; and

(d)   Right of asylum.[127]

---

[125] The sub-topic was originally entitled "Succession of States in respect of rights and duties resulting from sources other than treaties." The Commission adopted the new title to read as above at its twentieth session, in 1968.

[126] The third sub-topic has never been the subject of substantive consideration by the Commission.

[127] The first two topics have never been the subject of substantive consideration by the Commission. The remaining two topics were the subject of partial consideration by the Commission. The topic "Treatment of aliens" was partially considered by the Commission in the course of its work on the topic "State responsibility", but this work was discontinued. It is currently being considered, to some extent, by the Commission in connection with its work on the topic "Diplomatic protection". With respect to the topic "Right of asylum," at the Commission's first session, in 1949, during the discussion of the draft Declaration on Rights and Duties of States, a proposal was submitted to include in the draft Declaration an article relating to the right of asylum. It was finally decided not to include such an article. See *Yearbook of the International Law Commission, 1949*, Report to the General Assembly, para. 23. At a later stage, the topic was specifically referred to the Commission by the General Assembly. In resolution 1400 (XIV) of 21 November 1959, the General Assembly requested the Commission, as soon as it considered it advisable, to undertake the codification of the principles and rules of international law relating to the right of asylum. The Commission took note of the General Assembly resolution and decided to defer further consideration of this question to a future session. See *Yearbook of the International Law Commission, 1960*, vol. II, document A/4425, para. 39. At its twenty-ninth session, in 1977, the Commission concluded that the topic did not appear at that time to require active consideration by the Commission in the near future. See *Yearbook of the International Law Commission, 1977*, vol. II (Part Two), para. 109.

The 1949 list of topics constituted the Commission's basic long-term programme of work for more than fifty years. The list was supplemented by the following topics:

(*a*) Draft declaration on rights and duties of States;

(*b*) Formulation of the Nürnberg principles;

(*c*) Question of international criminal jurisdiction;

(*d*) Ways and means for making the evidence of customary international law more readily available;[128]

(*e*) Draft code of offences against the peace and security of mankind;[129]

(*f*) Reservations to multilateral conventions;

(*g*) Question of defining aggression;

(*h*) Relations between States and international organizations[130] (first and second parts of the topic, the first dealing with the status, privileges and immunities of representatives of States to international organizations, and the second dealing with the status, privileges and immunities of international organizations and their personnel);

(*i*) Juridical regime of historic waters, including historic bays;[131]

(*j*) Special missions;[132]

(*k*) Question of extended participation in general multilateral treaties concluded under the auspices of the League of Nations;

(*l*) Most-favoured-nation clause;

(*m*) Question of treaties concluded between States and international organizations or between two or more international organizations;

(*n*) Question of the protection and inviolability of diplomatic agents and other persons entitled to special protection under international law;

---

[128] This topic was considered by the Commission in accordance with article 24 of its Statute.

[129] The Commission, at its thirty-ninth session, in 1987, recommended to the General Assembly that the title of the topic in English be amended to read "Draft Code of Crimes against the Peace and Security of Mankind" in order to achieve greater uniformity and equivalence between different language versions. The General Assembly agreed with this recommendation in resolution 42/151 of 7 December 1987.

[130] At its twentieth session, in 1968, the Commission decided to amend the title of the topic, without altering its meaning, by changing the word "intergovernmental" to "international."

[131] See footnote 456.

[132] The Commission initially considered this subject under the topic of ad hoc diplomacy, following the submission of the Commission's final draft on diplomatic intercourse and immunities in 1958 (*see pages 139 and 140*).

(*o*)   The law of the non-navigational uses of international watercourses;

(*p*)   Status of the diplomatic courier and the diplomatic bag not accompanied by diplomatic courier;[133]

(*q*)   Review of the multilateral treaty-making process;[134]

(*r*)   International liability for injurious consequences arising out of acts not prohibited by international law (first and second parts of the topic, the first dealing with prevention of transboundary damage from hazardous activities, and the second dealing with international liability in case of loss from transboundary harm arising out of such activities);

(*s*)   Reservations to treaties;[135]

(*t*)   Nationality in relation to the succession of States (first and second parts of the topic, the first dealing with the question of nationality of natural persons, and the second dealing with the question of nationality of legal persons);[136]

(*u*)   Diplomatic protection;

(*v*)   Unilateral acts of States;

(*w*)   Responsibility of international organizations;

(*x*)   Shared natural resources; and

(*y*)   Fragmentation of international law: difficulties arising from the diversification and expansion of international law.[137]

---

[133] This topic was preliminarily considered by the Commission under an agenda item entitled "Proposals on the elaboration of a protocol concerning the status of the diplomatic courier and the diplomatic bag not accompanied by diplomatic courier."

[134] In resolution 32/48 of 8 December 1977, the Assembly requested the Secretary-General to prepare a report on the techniques and procedures used in the elaboration of multilateral treaties. Also in that resolution, the General Assembly, bearing in mind the important contribution of the Commission to the preparation of multilateral treaties, provided for the participation of the Commission in the review in question. The Commission was invited, as were Governments, to submit its observations on the subject for inclusion in the Secretary-General's report. Pursuant to that invitation, the Commission considered the subject at its thirtieth and thirty-first sessions, in 1978 and 1979, respectively. See *Yearbook of the International Law Commission, 1979*, vol. II (Part Two), paras. 184-195. Its observations were transmitted to the Secretary-General in 1979 in the Commission's document entitled "Report of the Working Group on review of the multilateral treaty-making process." See *Yearbook of the International Law Commission, 1979*, vol. II (Part One), document A/CN.4/325.

[135] This topic was originally entitled "The law and practice relating to reservations to treaties." At its forty-seventh session, in 1995, the Commission concluded that the title of the topic should be amended to read as above.

[136] The Commission's study on the topic has proceeded under this title following the completion by the Commission of the preliminary study of the topic "State succession and its impact on the nationality of natural and legal persons" at its forty-eighth session, in 1996.

[137] The topic was originally entitled "Risks ensuing from fragmentation of

The topics listed above that were placed on the Commission's programme of work in addition to those included in the 1949 list may be divided into four categories: (1) topics that were a specific follow-up to the Commission's previous work on one of the topics included in the 1949 list; (2) topics that were not a specific follow-up to the Commission's previous work, but nonetheless relate to some extent to one of the 1949 topics; (3) topics that do not relate to any of the topics in the 1949 list; and (4) special assignments referred to the Commission by the General Assembly.

The first category comprising the topics that were referred to the Commission by the General Assembly as a specific follow-up to the consideration by the Commission of a topic included in the 1949 list includes: (*h*) relations between States and international organizations (General Assembly resolution 1289 (XIII) of 5 December 1958);[138] (*i*) juridical regime of historic waters, including historic bays (General Assembly resolution 1453 (XIV) of 7 December 1959);[139] (*j*) special missions (General Assembly resolution 1687 (XVI) of 18 December 1961);[140] (*l*) the most-favoured-nation clause (General Assembly resolution 2272 (XXII) of 1 December 1967);[141] (*m*) question of treaties concluded between States and international organizations or between two or more international organizations (General Assembly resolution 2501 (XXIV) of 12 November 1969);[142] and (*r*) international liability for injurious consequences arising out of acts not prohibited by international law (General Assembly resolution 3071 (XXVIII) of 30 November 1973).[143] The topics listed in

---

international law." At its fifty-fourth session, in 2002, the Commission decided to change the title of the topic to read as above. In addition to the last three topics listed above, the Commission identified two other topics as appropriate for inclusion in its long-programme of work, "Effect of armed conflict on treaties" and "Expulsion of aliens," at its fifty-second session, in 2000. See *Official Records of the General Assembly, Fifty-fifth Session, Supplement No. 10* (A/55/10), para. 729 and annex. The Commission noted that topics relating to corruption and humanitarian protection were worthy of further consideration at its next quinquennium. The Commission also took note of a number of useful preliminary studies on the subject of the environment, indicated that it was desirable to have a more integrated approach to feasibility studies in the field of the environment and concluded that any decision about further work in this area should be deferred until the next quinquennium. Ibid., paras. 732-733.

[138] The topic was a follow-up to the topic of diplomatic intercourse and immunities (topic *(k)* in the 1949 list above).

[139] The topic was a follow-up to the topic of the law of the sea (*see above*).

[140] The topic was also a follow-up to the topic of diplomatic intercourse and immunities.

[141] The topic was a follow-up to the topic of the law of treaties (topic *(j)* in the 1949 list above).

[142] The topic was also a follow-up to the topic of the law of treaties.

[143] The topic was a follow-up to the topic of State responsibility (topic *(m)* in the 1949 list above).

subparagraphs (*i*), (*j*) and (*m*) were referred to the Commission as a follow-up to the consideration by the General Assembly of a resolution previously adopted to that effect by a conference of plenipotentiaries.

The second category comprising the topics that were not a specific follow-up to the Commission's previous work, but nonetheless relate to one of the 1949 topics, includes: (*p*) the status of the diplomatic courier and the diplomatic bag not accompanied by diplomatic courier,[144] which relates to the topic of diplomatic intercourse and immunities; (*s*) reservations to treaties, which relates to the topic of the law of treaties;[145] (*t*) nationality in relation to the succession of States, which relates to both the topic of succession of States and Governments as well as the topic of nationality, including statelessness; and (*u*) diplomatic protection and (*w*) responsibility of international organizations both of which relate to the topic of State responsibility.[146]

The third category comprising new topics that do not relate to any of the topics in the 1949 list includes: (*o*) the law of the non-navigational uses of international watercourses; (*v*) unilateral acts of States; (*x*) shared natural resources;[147] and (*y*) fragmentation of international law.

The fourth category comprising special assignments in terms of requests by the General Assembly to the Commission to report on particular legal problems, to examine particular texts or to prepare a particular set of draft articles[148] includes: (*a*) draft declaration on rights and duties of States (General Assembly resolution 178 (II) of 21 November 1947); (*b*) formulation of the Nürnberg principles (General Assembly resolution 177 (II) of 21 November 1947); (*c*) question of international criminal jurisdiction (General Assembly

---

[144] This topic was referred to the Commission by the General Assembly for the further development and concretization of international diplomatic law (General Assembly resolutions 31/76 of 13 December 1976 and 33/139 and 33/140 of 19 December 1978).

[145] The Commission undertook work on this topic in order to address the ambiguities and gaps in the provisions concerning reservations to treaties contained, in particular, in the Vienna Convention on the Law of Treaties which was based on the Commission's earlier draft articles on the law of treaties.

[146] These topics were partially considered by the Commission in the course of its work on State responsibility. In addition, some aspects of the subject of responsibility of international organizations were examined in the course of the Commission's work on the second part of the topic "Relations between States and international organizations," dealing with the status, privileges and immunities of international organizations and their personnel.

[147] This topic relates to some extent to the Commission's previous work on the law of the non-navigational uses of international watercourses.

[148] See *Yearbook of the International Law Commission, 1979*, vol. II (Part One), document A/CN.4/325, para. 57.

resolution 260 B (III) of 9 December 1948); (*e*) draft code of offences against the peace and security of mankind (General Assembly resolution 177 (II) of 21 November 1947); (*f*) reservations to multilateral conventions (General Assembly resolution 478 (V) of 16 November 1950); (*g*) question of defining aggression (General Assembly resolution 378 (V) of 17 November 1950); (*k*) question of extended participation in general multilateral treaties concluded under the auspices of the League of Nations (General Assembly resolution 1766 (XVII) of 20 November 1962); (*n*) question of the protection and inviolability of diplomatic agents (General Assembly resolution 2780 (XXVI) of 3 December 1971); and (*q*) review of the multilateral treaty-making process (General Assembly resolution 32/48 of 8 December 1977).

Most of the topics were referred to the Commission by the General Assembly, often as a result of an earlier initiative of the Commission itself. The topics listed above in subparagraphs (*s*)-(*y*) were selected by the Commission in accordance with the new procedure for the selection of topics. With respect to these topics, the General Assembly endorsed the Commission's decisions to undertake studies on the topics of (*s*) reservations to treaties, (*t*) nationality in relation to the succession of States, (*u*) diplomatic protection and (*v*) unilateral acts of States; took note of the Commission's decision to include in its programme of work the topics of (*x*) shared natural resources and (*y*) fragmentation of international law; and requested the Commission to begin its work on the topic of (*w*) responsibility of international organizations.

The Commission has submitted a final report on all of the topics and sub-topics added to the 1949 list which are not under current consideration, except for the following: (*h*) the second part of the topic of relations between States and international organizations (status, privileges and immunities of international organizations and their personnel), (*i*) juridical regime of historic waters, including historic bays; and (*t*) the second part of the topic of nationality in relation to the succession of States (question of nationality of legal persons).[149]

The Commission is currently considering seven topics, namely: (*r*) the second part of the topic of international liability for injurious consequences arising out of acts not prohibited by international law (international liability in case of loss from transboundary harm arising out of hazardous activities); (*s*) reservations to treaties; (*u*)

---

[149] The topic (*i*) has never been the subject of substantive consideration by the Commission. The work on the other two topics (*h*) and (*t*) was discontinued by the Commission before any final report was produced.

diplomatic protection; (*v*) unilateral acts of States; (*w*) responsibility of international organizations; (*x*) shared natural resources; and (*y*) fragmentation of international law.

5.   Methods of work

(a)   *Progressive development and codification*

The drafters of the Statute conceived progressive development as a conscious effort towards the creation of new rules of international law, whether by means of the regulation of a new topic or by means of the comprehensive revision of existing rules. Accordingly, they considered that when the Commission is engaged in the progressive development of any branch of law, the consummation of the work could be achieved only by means of an international convention.[150] Thus the Statute contemplates that the Commission prepares a draft convention, and the General Assembly then decides whether steps should be taken to bring about the conclusion of an international convention. On the other hand, when the Commission's task is one of codification (namely, the more precise formulation and systematization of existing customary law), the Statute envisages two other possible conclusions to its work: (*a*) simple publication of its report; and (*b*) a resolution of the General Assembly, taking note of or adopting the report (article 23, paragraph 1). The Statute also lays down the specific steps to be taken by the Commission in the course of its work on progressive development (articles 16 and 17) and on codification (articles 18 to 23).

The Commission has indicated that the distinctions drawn in its Statute between the two processes have proved unworkable and could be eliminated in any review of the Statute.[151] Instead the Commission has proceeded with its work on the basis of a composite idea of codification and progressive development.[152] It has developed a consolidated procedure to its methods of work and applied that method in a flexible manner making adjustments that the specific features of the topic concerned or other circumstances demand.[153]

---

[150] See the report of the Committee on the Progressive Development of International Law and its Codification, *Official Records of the General Assembly, Second Session, Sixth Committee, Annex 1,* paras. 7-9. See also article 15 of the Statute of the Commission.
[151] See *Yearbook of the International Law Commission, 1996,* vol. II (Part Two), paras. 147 (a) and 156-159.
[152] See *Yearbook of the International Law Commission, 1979,* vol. II (Part One), document A/CN.4/325, para. 13.
[153] See *Yearbook of the International Law Commission, 1979,* vol. II (Part One), document A/CN.4/325, para. 16.

The Commission does not necessarily begin consideration of a topic immediately after it has been included in the programme of work. The Commission's actual consideration of a topic on its programme results, rather, from a further decision of the Commission to place a topic on its agenda. The Commission's decision to take up a topic is mainly influenced by the status of the consideration of other topics and requests by the General Assembly (e.g., special assignments or requests to give priority to certain topics or to begin work on a certain topic).[154] In some instances, the placing of a topic on the agenda has also been preceded by preliminary work undertaken by a subcommittee or working group established for this purpose (*see pages 23 and 24*).

The Commission has identified three different stages generally present in the consideration of a topic on its agenda: a first preliminary stage, devoted mainly to the organization of work and the gathering of relevant materials and precedents; a second stage, during which the Commission proceeds to a first reading of the draft articles submitted by the Special Rapporteur; and a third and final stage, devoted to a second reading of the draft articles provisionally adopted.[155]

The first stage usually comprises the following: appointment of a Special Rapporteur; formulation of a plan of work; and, where necessary or desirable, requests for data and information from Governments[156] as well as international organizations and for research projects, studies, surveys and compilations from the Secretariat.[157]

The second stage usually comprises the following: the consideration of the reports of the Special Rapporteur[158] by the Commission in plenary, and of the proposed draft articles in the plenary and in the Drafting Committee; the elaboration of draft articles with commentaries setting forth precedents, any divergences of views expressed in the Commission, and alternative solutions considered;[159] the approval of the provisional draft articles in the

---

[154] See *Yearbook of the International Law Commission, 1979*, vol. II (Part One), document A/CN.4/325, para. 22.

[155] See *Yearbook of the International Law Commission, 1979*, vol. II (Part One), document A/CN.4/325, para. 35.

[156] For example, Governments may be requested to furnish the texts of laws, decrees, judicial decisions, treaties, diplomatic correspondence and other relevant documents under article 19 of the Statute.

[157] See *Yearbook of the International Law Commission, 1979*, vol. II (Part One), document A/CN.4/325, paras. 36-43.

[158] At the Commission's request or on his initiative, the Special Rapporteur's initial presentation may be of a general and exploratory character, in the form of a working paper or preliminary report. See *Yearbook of the International Law Commission, 1979*, vol. II (Part One), document A/CN.4/325, para. 39.

[159] The content of the commentary to draft articles is addressed in article 20 of the

Drafting Committee and the draft articles with commentaries afterwards in the plenary; and the issuance of the provisional draft with commentary as a Commission document and its submission to the General Assembly, and also to Governments for their written observations.[160] As experience has shown that a shorter period failed to elicit a sufficient number of replies, Governments under the current procedure are normally given more than one year in which to study these provisional drafts and present their written observations before the Commission begins the second reading of the draft articles.[161]

The third stage usually involves the study by the Special Rapporteur of the replies received from Governments, together with any comments made in the debates of the Sixth Committee; submission of a further report to the Commission, recommending the changes in the provisional draft that seem appropriate; the consideration and approval of the revised draft in the Drafting Committee in the light of the written and oral observations from Governments; and adoption by the Commission in plenary of the final draft with commentaries[162] and a recommendation regarding further action.[163]

The task of the Commission in relation to a given topic is completed when it presents to the General Assembly a final product on that topic, which is usually accompanied by the Commission's recommendation on further action with respect to it. In some instances, the General Assembly has requested the Commission to undertake further work on a topic on which it has already submitted a final report.[164]

Statute.

[160] See *Yearbook of the International Law Commission, 1979*, vol. II (Part One), document A/CN.4/325, paras. 44-49.

[161] See *Yearbook of the International Law Commission, 1958,* vol. II, document A/3859, paras. 60 and 61.

[162] The commentaries are amended to explain the final version of the draft articles, including the solutions adopted with respect to any controversial issues, and updated to include the most recent precedents.

[163] See *Yearbook of the International Law Commission, 1979*, vol. II (Part One), document A/CN.4/325, paras. 50-56.

[164] The General Assembly may refer drafts back to the Commission for reconsideration or redrafting under article 23, paragraph 2, of the Statute. The General Assembly took such action with respect to the draft articles on arbitral procedure submitted by the Commission to the General Assembly in 1953 (General Assembly resolution 989 (X) of 14 December 1955). In addition, the General Assembly, in resolution 53/98 of 8 December 1998, invited the Commission to present any preliminary comments it might have regarding outstanding substantive issues related to the draft articles on the jurisdictional immunities of States and their property, in the light of the results of the informal consultations held pursuant to General Assembly decision 48/413 of 9 December 1993, and taking into account the developments of State practice and other factors related to this issue since the adoption of the draft articles by the Commission in 1991.

The Commission has generally considered that its drafts constitute both codification and progressive development of international law in the sense in which those concepts are defined in the Statute, and has found it impracticable to determine into which category each provision falls.[165] The Commission has usually recommended that the General Assembly take action envisaged with respect to the codification of international law under its Statute, namely: (a) to take no action, the report having already been published; (b) to take note of or adopt the report by resolution; (c) to recommend the draft to Members with a view to the conclusion of a convention; or (d) to convoke a conference to conclude a convention (article 23, paragraph 1).

As noted in Part III, the Commission recommended that the General Assembly take the following action with respect to the various draft articles in the years indicated in parentheses: (a) take no action with respect to the draft article on the contiguous zone since the report covering it had already been published (1953); (b) adopt the reports containing drafts relating to the continental shelf and fisheries (1953),[166] and the Model Rules on Arbitral Procedure (1958); (c) adopt the draft articles on nationality of natural persons in relation to the succession of States in the form of a declaration (1999); (d) recommend to Members the conclusion of a convention on arbitral procedure (1953), elimination and reduction of future statelessness (1954),[167] diplomatic intercourse and immunities (1958), special missions (1967),[168] most-favoured-nation clauses (1978), law of the non-navigational uses of international watercourses (1994),[169] and prevention of transboundary harm from hazardous activities (2001);[170] (e) convoke a conference to conclude a convention on the

---

[165] See, for instance, *Yearbook of the International Law Commission, 1951*, vol. I. pp. 123 and 132-135; ibid., *1953*, vol. II, document A/2456, para. 54; ibid., *1956*, vol. II, document A/3159, paras. 25 and 26; ibid., *1961*, vol. II, document A/4843, para. 32; ibid., *1966*, vol. II, document A/6309/Rev.1, para. 35; ibid., *1967*, vol. II, document A/6709/Rev.1 and Rev.1/Corr.l, para. 23; ibid., *1971*, vol. II (Part One), document A/8410/Rev.l, para. 50; ibid., *1974*, vol. II (Part One), document A/9610/Rev.1, para. 83; ibid., *1978*, vol. II (Part Two), para. 72; ibid., *1982*, vol. II (Part Two), para. 55 and ibid., *1996*, vol. II (Part Two), paras. 156 and 157.
[166] These drafts, later included in the all-embracing draft on the law of the sea, became the basis for two conventions adopted by the first United Nations Conference on the Law of the Sea (1958).
[167] The recommendation of the Commission was implicit in the identical provision of article 12 of the two draft conventions on the subject submitted to the General Assembly, which read: "The present Convention, having been approved by the General Assembly, shall. . . be open for signature. . . and shall be ratified."
[168] The Commission recommended to the General Assembly that appropriate measures be taken for the conclusion of a convention on special missions.
[169] The Commission recommended that a convention be elaborated by the Assembly or an international conference of plenipotentiaries.
[170] The Commission recommended that the General Assembly elaborate a

law of the sea (1956), consular intercourse and immunities (1961), law of treaties (1966), representation of States in their relations with international organizations (1971), succession of States in respect of treaties (1974), succession of States in respect of State property, archives and debts (1981), the treaties concluded between States and international organizations or between two or more international organizations (1982), status of the diplomatic courier and the diplomatic bag not accompanied by diplomatic courier and two optional protocols thereto (1989), and jurisdictional immunities of States and their property (1991); and (f) take note of the draft articles on responsibility of States for internationally wrongful acts and subsequently consider convening a conference to conclude a convention (2001).[171]

(b)   Special assignments

In performing special assignments, the question has arisen whether the Commission, should use the methods laid down in its Statute for carrying out its normal work of progressive development and codification, or whether it was free to decide on the methods to be used in such cases. The Commission has always decided that it was free to adopt special methods for special tasks.[172] The Commission often dispenses with the normal stages of its work and considers special assignments as a whole or in a working group without appointing a Special Rapporteur or holding first and second readings.[173] In such cases, the Commission reports its conclusions simply for the consideration of the General Assembly, without recommending any of the courses of action listed in article 23,

---

convention.

[171] With respect to the topic "Ways and means for making the evidence of customary international law more readily available," no recommendation by the Commission in accordance with article 23, para. 1, of the Statute was required because of the nature of the work on the topic.

[172] See, for example, the discussion at the Commission's first session concerning the procedure to be followed in its work on the draft Declaration on Rights and Duties of States, in *Yearbook of the International Law Commission, 1949*, Report to the General Assembly, para. 53. The General Assembly, in taking note of the draft Declaration and in commending it to the continuing attention of Member States and jurists of all nations (resolution 375 (IV) of 6 December 1949), appeared to accept without question the thesis stated in the Commission's report that it was within the competence of the Commission to adopt such procedure as it might deem conducive to the effectiveness of its work in respect of a special assignment even though such procedure differed from the procedures set forth in the Statute for progressive development or codification. See *Yearbook of the International Law Commission, 1949*, Report to the General Assembly, para. 53. See also *Yearbook of the International Law Commission, 1977*, vol. II (Part Two), paras. 116 and 117.

[173] See *Yearbook of the International Law Commission, 1979*, vol. II (Part One), document A/CN.4/325, paras. 57-61.

paragraph 1, of the Statute. In other cases, the Commission has used virtually the same working methods for special assignments as for progressive development and codification with the result being the submission of draft articles accompanied by commentaries, and in some instances, a recommendation for action by the General Assembly.[174]

The Commission submitted its reports with respect to the following special assignments in the years indicated in parentheses: draft declaration on rights and duties of States (1949); formulation of the Nürnberg principles (1950); question of international criminal jurisdiction (1950); question of defining aggression (1951); reservations to multilateral conventions (1951); draft code of offences against the peace and security of mankind (1951, 1954, 1994[175] and 1996); extended participation in general multilateral treaties concluded under the auspices of the League of Nations (1963); question of the protection and inviolability of diplomatic agents and other persons entitled to special protection under international law (1972); and review of the multilateral treaty-making process (1979).

The Commission's reports on the following special assignments contained draft articles with commentaries: draft declaration on rights and duties of States; formulation of the Nürnberg principles; draft code of offences against the peace and security of mankind; and question of the protection and inviolability of diplomatic agents and other persons entitled to special protection under international law. The conclusions reached by the Commission on the other special assignments did not lend themselves to the preparation of draft articles.

(c) Review of methods of work

The Commission has periodically reviewed its methods of work, at the request of the General Assembly or on its own initiative, in the light of comments and suggestions made in the Sixth Committee or in the Commission itself.[176] It has consequently introduced a number of

---

[174] With respect to the draft Statute for an International Criminal Court submitted by the Commission to the General Assembly in 1994, the Commission recommended that the General Assembly convene an international conference of plenipotentiaries to study the draft Statute and to conclude a convention on the establishment of an international criminal court (see page 100). With respect to the draft Code of Crimes against the Peace and Security of Mankind submitted by the Commission to the General Assembly in 1996, the Commission recommended that the General Assembly select the most appropriate form which would ensure the widest possible acceptance of the draft Code (see pages 94 and 95).

[175] In this year, the Commission submitted its report containing the final text of the draft Statute for an International Criminal Court (see page 100).

[176] At its twenty-ninth session, in 1977, the Commission, stated its intention to keep

changes aimed at expediting or streamlining its procedures to respond more readily to its tasks.[177]

At its tenth session, in 1958, the Commission considered various methods by which its work might be accelerated based on a working paper prepared by the Chairman of its previous session in response to observations in the Sixth Committee.[178] As a result of this review, the Commission made changes in its methods of work with respect to plenary meetings, the Drafting Committee and Government comments. The Commission concluded that it might be useful in the initial stages of preparing a draft on a difficult or complex subject to make greater use of committees or sub-committees so that less would be done in plenary. The Commission decided that in the future the Drafting Committee should be formally constituted as what it had long been in fact, namely, a committee to which could be referred not merely pure drafting points, but also points of substance which the full Commission had been unable to resolve, or which seemed likely to give rise to unduly protracted discussion. The Commission also decided to prepare its final draft at the second session following that in which the first draft had been prepared which would give more time for Governments to comment on the first drafts produced by the Commission, also for the members to consider those comments and for the Special Rapporteur to make recommendations concerning them.[179]

At its twentieth session, in 1968, the Commission reviewed its methods of work based on working papers prepared by the Secretariat.[180] As a result of this review, the Commission recommended that: the term of office of its members be extended

---

constantly under review the possibility of improving its method of work and procedures in the light of the specific features presented by the individual topics under consideration. See *Yearbook of the International Law Commission, 1977,* vol. II (Part Two), para. 120. This was reiterated at the Commission's thirty-first session, in 1979, when the Commission conducted a comprehensive review of its methods of work, while preparing its observations on the item "Review of the multilateral treaty-making process," as well as at its next session, in 1980. See *Yearbook of the International Law Commission, 1979,* vol. II (Part One), document A/CN.4/325, para. 16, and ibid., *1980,* vol. II (Part Two), para. 185, respectively.

[177] See *Yearbook of the International Law Commission, 1979,* vol. II (Part One), document A/CN.4/325, para. 16. However, in 1973, the Commission noted that "whatever improvements it may be possible to make in the methods of work of the Commission, it is clear that there is an inbuilt periodicity at work that places certain limits on the Commission's ability to respond promptly to urgent requests." See *Yearbook of the International Law Commission, 1973,* vol. II, document A/9010/Rev.1, para. 166.

[178] Document A/CN.4/L.76.

[179] See *Yearbook of the International Law Commission, 1958,* vol. II, document A/3859, paras. 59-62 and 65.

[180] See *Yearbook of the International Law Commission, 1968,* vol. II, document A/7209/Rev.1, paras. 95-102 and annex.

from five to six or seven years; an additional special allowance be made available to Special Rapporteurs to help defray expenses in connection with their work; and the staff of the Codification Division be increased so that it could provide additional assistance to the Commission and its Special Rapporteurs.[181]

At its twenty-seventh session, in 1975, the Commission established a Planning Group in the Enlarged Bureau to study the functioning of the Commission and formulate suggestions regarding its work. As an initial project, the Planning Group undertook a review of the existing workload of the Commission with a view to proposing general goals toward which the Commission might direct its efforts during its five-year term of office ending in 1981.[182] The adoption by the Commission of general goals for completion of work on the topics under consideration was received with approval in the General Assembly.[183] From 1977 on, the Commission has established a Planning Group[184] for each of its annual sessions and entrusted it with the task of considering the programme, organization and methods of work of the Commission.

At its thirtieth and thirty-first sessions, in 1978 and 1979, respectively, the Commission examined its methods of work in the context of its consideration of the topic "Review of the multilateral treaty-making process" pursuant to General Assembly resolution 32/48 of 8 December 1977.[185] The Commission established a working group to consider preliminary questions raised by the topic and to recommend to the Commission the action to be taken in response to the General Assembly's request. The Commission subsequently adopted the report of the working group[186] which contained detailed observations on the following: (1) the International Law Commission as a United Nations body; (2) the object and functions of the Commission; (3) the role of the Commission and its contribution to the treaty-making process through the preparation of draft articles; (4) the consolidated methods and techniques of work of the Commission as applied in general to the preparation of draft articles (without distinguishing between the progressive development of international

---

[181] See *Yearbook of the International Law Commission, 1968*, vol. II, document A/7209/Rev.1, para. 98.

[182] See *Yearbook of the International Law Commission, 1975*, vol. II, document A/10010/ Rev.l, paras. 139-147.

[183] See General Assembly resolution 3495 (XXX) of 15 December 1975.

[184] As mentioned previously, the Commission's current practice is to establish the Planning Group as a subsidiary body of the Commission (*see footnote 67*).

[185] See *Yearbook of the International Law Commission, 1979*, vol. II (Part Two), paras. 184-195.

[186] See *Yearbook of the International Law Commission, 1979*, vol. II (Part One), document A/CN.4/325.

law and its codification), including the functions performed by the Special Rapporteur, the Drafting Committee and the Commission during the three stages of consideration of a topic; (5) other methods and techniques employed by the Commission (for example, with respect to special assignments); (6) the relationship between the Commission and the General Assembly; and (7) the elaboration and conclusion of conventions based on draft articles prepared by the Commission following a General Assembly decision to that effect The Commission concluded, inter alia, that the techniques and procedures provided in the Statute, as they had evolved over three decades, were well adapted for the object of the Commission set forth in article 1 of the Statute, namely, the progressive development of international law and its codification. The Commission noted that it might be necessary to provide more assistance and facilities to Special Rapporteurs to enable them to perform their duties in the future and to make more use of questionnaires addressed to Governments than in the past. The Commission did not, however, recommend any major changes in its methods of work.

At its thirty-ninth session, in 1987, the Commission considered thoroughly its methods of work in all their aspects in response to General Assembly resolution 41/81 of 3 December 1986. The Planning Group established a Working Group on Methods of Work for this purpose. As a result, the Commission, while maintaining the view that tested methods should not be radically or hastily altered, agreed that some specific aspects of its procedures could usefully be reviewed. The Commission believed that the Drafting Committee, which played a key role in harmonizing the various viewpoints and working out generally acceptable solutions, should work in optimum conditions. As regards the composition of the Drafting Committee, the Commission was aware that a proper balance must be kept, notwithstanding practical constraints, between two legitimate concerns, namely that the principal legal systems and the various languages should be equitably represented in the Committee and that the size of the Committee should be kept within limits compatible with its drafting responsibilities. To facilitate the work of the Drafting Committee, the Chairman of the Commission should, whenever possible, indicate the main trends of opinion revealed by the debate in plenary. The Commission was aware that premature referral of draft articles to the Drafting Committee, and excessive time-lags between such referral and actual consideration of draft articles in the Committee, have counter-productive effects.[187]

---

[187] See *Yearbook of the International Law Commission, 1987*, vol. II (Part Two), paras. 235-239.

At its forty-fourth session, in 1992, the Commission considered thoroughly its methods of work in all their aspects as requested by the General Assembly in resolution 46/54 of 9 December 1991. On the recommendation of the Planning Group, the Commission adopted guidelines with respect to the Drafting Committee and the Commission's report. The guidelines concerning the composition and working methods of the Drafting Committee provide as follows: (a) the Drafting Committee shall continue to be a single body, under one Chairman, but may have a different membership for each topic; (b) the Drafting Committee should, as a general rule, concentrate its work on two to three topics at each session to attain greater efficiency; (c) the Chairman of the Drafting Committee, in consultation with the other officers of the Commission, shall recommend the membership for each topic; (d) membership for each topic shall be limited to no more than fourteen members and shall ensure as far as possible representation of the different working languages; (e) members who are not serving on the Drafting Committee for a given topic may attend the meetings and occasionally be authorized to speak, but should exercise restraint; (f) the Drafting Committee shall be given the necessary time for the timely completion of the tasks entrusted to it; (g) when necessary, the Drafting Committee may be given additional time for concentrated work, preferably at the beginning of a session; and (h) the Drafting Committee shall present a report to the Commission as early as possible after the conclusion of its consideration of each topic. The guidelines concerning the preparation and content of the Commission's annual report provide, inter alia, as follows: (a) the General Rapporteur should play an active part in the preparation of the report to provide the necessary coordination and consistency, bearing in mind continuing efforts to avoid an excessively long report; and (b) the report should include a summary of the work of the session as well as a list of questions on which the views of the Sixth Committee would be particularly helpful.[188]

At its forty-sixth and forty-seventh sessions, in 1994 and 1995, respectively, the Commission considered its working methods with respect to the commentaries to draft articles. The Commission reviewed the conditions under which the commentaries to draft articles are discussed and adopted. The Commission agreed that the commentaries should be taken up as soon as possible at each session in order to receive the requisite degree of attention and should be discussed separately rather than in the framework of the adoption of

---

[188] See *Yearbook of the International Law Commission, 1992*, vol. II (Part Two), paras. 371 and 373.

the annual report. The Commission noted that the content and length of the commentaries accompanying draft articles depend partly on the nature of the topic and the extent of the precedents and other relevant data. Nonetheless, the Commission encouraged its Special Rapporteurs to draft the briefest possible commentaries and pay due attention to the desirability of having the commentaries to the draft articles on the various topics as uniform as possible in presentation and length.[189]

At its forty-eighth session, in 1996, the Commission examined the procedures of its work for the purpose of further enhancing its contribution to the progressive development and codification of international law in response to General Assembly resolution 50/45 of 11 December 1995. The Planning Group established an informal working group which discussed all of the issues involved. The Commission adopted the report of the Planning Group[190] which contained the following recommendations with respect to plenary meetings, the Drafting Committee, working groups, Special Rapporteurs and the Commission's annual report: (a) the plenary debates should be reformed to provide more structure and to allow for an indicative summary of conclusions by the Chairman at the end of the debate, based if necessary on an indicative vote; (b) the Drafting Committee should continue to have a different membership for different topics; (c) working groups should be used more extensively to resolve particular disagreements and, in appropriate cases, as an expeditious way of dealing with whole topics, in the latter case normally acting in place of the Drafting Committee; (d) Special Rapporteurs should specify the nature and scope of work planned for the next session, work with a consultative group of members, produce draft commentaries or notes to accompany their draft articles, which should be revised in the light of changes made in the Drafting Committee and made available at the time of the debate in plenary, and the Special Rapporteur's reports should be available sufficiently in advance of the session; (e) the Commission should identify specific issues for comment by the Sixth Committee before the adoption of draft articles, where possible, and the Commission's report should be shorter, more thematic and should highlight and explain key issues to assist in structuring the debate on the report in the Sixth Committee.[191] The Commission also recommended that goals should

---

[189] See *Yearbook of the International Law Commission, 1995*, vol. II (Part Two), paras. 504-508.
[190] See *Yearbook of the International Law Commission, 1996*, vol. II (Part Two), paras. 142-243.
[191] For the complete list of specific recommendations, see *Yearbook of the International Law Commission, 1996*, vol. II (Part Two), para. 148.

be set at the beginning and reviewed at the end of each quinquennium, together with any preparations that should be made to facilitate adopting the plan for the next quinquennium at the beginning of its first year.[192] The General Assembly welcomed with appreciation the steps taken by the Commission in relation to its internal matters to enhance its efficiency and productivity and invited the Commission to continue taking such measures.[193]

6.   Meetings of the Commission

(a)   Rules of procedure

As a subsidiary organ of the General Assembly, the procedure of the Commission is governed by the rules of procedure of the General Assembly relating to the procedure of committees (rules 96 to 133) as well as rule 45 (duties of the Secretary-General) and rule 60 (public and private meetings) unless the Assembly or the Commission decides otherwise.[194] The Commission, at its first session, in 1949, decided that these rules of procedure should apply to the procedure of the Commission, and that the Commission should, when the need arose, adopt its own rules of procedure.[195]

(b)   Agenda

At the beginning of each session, the Commission adopts the agenda for the session. The provisional agenda is prepared by the Secretariat on the basis of the decisions of the Commission and the pertinent provisions of the Statute. The order in which items are listed in the agenda adopted does not necessarily determine their actual order of consideration by the Commission, the latter being rather a result of ad hoc decisions. The agenda of a given session is to be distinguished from the Commission's programme of work. Not every topic on the programme of work is necessarily included in the agenda of a particular session.[196] The Commission gives serious consideration to recommendations by the General Assembly to include a topic in the agenda of its next session. However, the Commission decides whether it is appropriate to follow such a recommendation, which is not

---

[192] See *Yearbook of the International Law Commission, 1996*, vol. II (Part Two), paras. 148 *(l)* and 221.
[193] See General Assembly resolution 52/156 of 15 December 1997.
[194] See Rule 161 of the rules of procedure of the General Assembly.
[195] See *Yearbook of the International Law Commission, 1949*, Report of the General Assembly, para. 5.
[196] See *Yearbook of the International Law Commission, 1979*, vol. II (Part One), document A/CN.4/325, para. 7.

reflected in the provisional agenda prepared by the Secretariat, in the light of its previous decisions concerning the plan of work for the session.

(c)   Languages

The official languages of the Commission are those of the United Nations, namely Arabic, Chinese, English, French, Russian and Spanish.[197] In the subsidiary bodies, discussion is predominantly in English and French, coinciding with the working language of the text under discussion, if applicable, but members are free to use other official languages.[198]

(d)   Decision making

The Chairman of the Commission may declare a meeting open and permit the debate to proceed when at least one quarter of the members are present. The presence, however, of a majority of the Commission's members is required for a decision to be taken. Decisions are made by a majority of the members present and voting. Members who abstain from voting are considered as not voting.[199]

In the early years of the Commission, decisions were often taken by vote. At a later stage, it became more common for the Commission to take decisions on procedural and substantive matters without a vote, by common understanding or consensus.[200] In 1996, the Commission discussed the method of voting in the plenary and subsidiary bodies and made some suggestions.[201] It was noted, that although at present the Commission and its subsidiary bodies attempted to reach consensus, it would be less burdensome and time-consuming to call for an indicative vote in certain cases, for instance, on provisional and tentative points or points of detail, with the reflection of minority views in the summary records and in the report of the Commission. "When decisions ultimately come to be taken,

---

[197] See rule 51 of the rules of procedure of the General Assembly.
[198] See *Yearbook of the International Law Commission, 1996*, vol. II (Part Two), para. 216.
[199] See *Yearbook of the International Law Commission, 1979*, vol. II (Part One), document A/CN.4/325, para. 8. See also rules 108 (Quorum), 125 (Majority required) and 126 (Meaning of the phrase "members present and voting") of the rules of procedure of the General Assembly.
[200] See *Yearbook of the International Law Commission, 1979*, vol. II (Part One), document A/CN.4/325, para. 8.
[201] See *Yearbook of the International Law Commission, 1996,* vol. II (Part Two), paras. 207-210.

again every effort should be made to reach a consensus, but if this is not possible in the time available, a vote may have to be taken."[202]

(e) Report of the Commission

At the end of each session, the Commission adopts a report to the General Assembly, covering the work of the session, on the basis of a draft prepared by the General Rapporteur with the assistance of the Special Rapporteurs concerned and the Secretariat.[203]

The report includes information concerning the organization of the session, the progress of work and the future work of the Commission on the topics given substantive consideration during the session, the texts of draft articles and commentaries adopted by the Commission during the session, any procedural recommendations of the Commission calling for a decision on the part of the General Assembly as well as other decisions and conclusions of the Commission. [204]

The structure of the report has changed from time to time.[205] At present, it is divided into the following main chapters: the first chapter deals with organizational issues; the second chapter summarizes the work of the session; the third chapter identifies specific issues on which comments of Governments would be of particular interest to the Commission; subsequent chapters are devoted to each of the different topics considered at the session; and the last chapter contains other decisions and conclusions of the Commission. The Commission may also decide to include other relevant documents, such as reports of working groups, in an annex to its report.[206]

The Commission's annual report is the means by which it keeps the General Assembly informed on a regular basis of the progress of its work on the various topics on its current programme as well as of

---

[202] See *Yearbook of the International Law Commission, 1996*, vol. II (Part Two), para. 210.

[203] See *Yearbook of the International Law Commission, 1979*, vol. II (Part One), document A/CN.4/325, para. 65.

[204] See *Yearbook of the International Law Commission, 1979*, vol. II (Part One), document A/CN.4/325, para. 66.

[205] *See page 62.*

[206] The Commission's report on its first session and as of its twenty-first session is published as *Supplement No. 10 of the Official Records of the General Assembly*. The Commission's report on its second session was published as *Supplement No. 12* and on its third to twentieth sessions as *Supplement No. 9 of the Official Records of the General Assembly*. The report is subsequently published in the *Yearbook of the International Law Commission* (volume II, except for the *1949 Yearbook* which consists of only one volume) together with a check-list of the documents issued during the session.

its achievements in the preparation of draft articles on these topics. The report is also the means by which the Commission's drafts are given the necessary publicity provided for in articles 16 and 21 of its Statute.[207]

(f) Summary records

Since its establishment, the Commission has been provided with summary records of its meetings in both provisional and final form,[208] in accordance with the consistent policy of the General Assembly.[209] At its thirty-second session, in 1980, the Commission concluded that the provision of summary records of its meetings constitutes an inescapable requirement for the procedures and methods of work of the Commission and for the process of codification of international law in general. The Commission has observed that the need for summary records in the context of its procedures and methods of work was determined by, inter alia, its functions and composition. As its task is mainly to draw up drafts providing a basis for the elaboration by States of legal codification instruments, the debates and discussions held in the Commission on proposed formulations are of paramount importance, in terms of both substance and wording, for the understanding of the rules proposed to States by the Commission. Pursuant to the Commission's Statute, members of the Commission serve in a personal capacity and do not represent Governments. Therefore, States have a legitimate interest in knowing not only the conclusions of the Commission as a whole as recorded in its reports but also those of its individual members contained in the summary records of the Commission, particularly if it is borne in mind that members of the Commission are elected by the General Assembly so as to ensure representation in the Commission of the main forms of civilization and the principal legal systems of the world. The summary records of the Commission are also a means of making its deliberations accessible to international institutions, learned societies, universities and the public in general. They play an important role, in that respect, in promoting knowledge of and interest in the process of

---

[207] See *Yearbook of the International Law Commission, 1979*, vol. II (Part One), document A/CN.4/325, para. 64.

[208] The summary records of Commission meetings are provided in provisional form to its members and are published in final form in the *Yearbook of the International Law Commission.*

[209] See General Assembly resolutions 32/151 of 19 December 1977, 34/141 of 17 December 1979, 35/163 of 15 December 1980, 36/114 of 10 December 1981, 37/111 of 16 December 1982 and all subsequent resolutions on the annual reports of the Commission to the General Assembly. See also *Yearbook of the International Law Commission, 1980*, vol. II (Part Two), para. 190.

promoting the progressive development of international law and its codification. The Commission has emphasized the importance of providing summary records of its meetings in both provisional and final form and expressed its appreciation to the General Assembly for doing so.[210]

(g)   Yearbook of the Commission

Following a request by the Commission, the General Assembly, in resolution 987 (X) of 3 December 1955, requested the Secretary-General to arrange for the printing of: (a) the principal documents (namely, studies, reports, principal draft resolutions and amendments presented to the Commission) relating to the first seven sessions, in their original languages, and the summary records of these sessions, initially in English; and (b) the principal documents and summary records relating to the subsequent sessions, in English, French and Spanish. As a result, an annual publication entitled *Yearbook of the International Law Commission* has been printed in two volumes in respect of each session (except the first session for which there is only one volume). The *Yearbook* has also been published in Russian since 1969, in Arabic since 1982 and in Chinese since 1989. Volume I of the *Yearbook* contains the summary records of the meetings of the Commission and volume II reproduces the principal documents, including the Commission's report to the General Assembly. Volume II is published in two parts, part two reproducing, since 1976, the annual report of the Commission to the General Assembly.

(h)   Limitation of documentation[211]

From time to time, the Commission has addressed the question of the applicability of United Nations regulations for the control and limitation of documentation to its own documentation.[212] The Commission noted that the length of its documentation depended upon a series of variable factors, for example: (i) as regards its annual report, the duration of the session, the topics considered, the draft articles and commentaries included and the Commission's perception

---

[210] See *Yearbook of the International Law Commission, 1980*, vol. II (Part Two), paras. 188-190.
[211] Since 1998, many documents of the Commission have been placed on the Commission's web site. See www.un.org/law/ilc/index.htm.
[212] For the Commission's discussions, see *Yearbook of the International Law Commission, 1977*, vol. II (Part Two), paras. 124-126; ibid., *1980*, vol. II (Part Two), paras. 191 and 192; ibid., *1982*, vol. II (Part Two), para. 271; and *Official Records of the General Assembly, Fifty-eighth Session, Supplement No. 10* (A/58/10), paras. 440-443.

of the need for explaining the work accomplished at that session and justifying the draft articles contained therein to the General Assembly and Member States;[213] (ii) as regards information provided by Governments and international organizations, the volume of relevant information submitted by them since it is an absolute need for the Commission to have at its disposal, in extenso and in its working languages, the replies of Governments and international organizations to its requests for information;[214] (iii) as regards the reports and working papers of the Special Rapporteurs, the scope and complexity of the topic in question, the stage of the Commission's work on the topic, the nature and number of proposals made by the Special Rapporteur, in particular draft articles with supporting data derived from, inter alia, State practice and doctrine, including analysis of relevant debates held in the General Assembly as well as comments and observations submitted by Governments;[215] and (iv) as regards research studies by the Secretariat, the nature of studies which usually reflect "treaties, judicial decisions and doctrine" as well as "the practice of States", indispensable for the Commission's study of the various topics on its programme and formulation of commentaries on the drafts it proposes to the General Assembly, according to article 20 of its Statute.[216] The Commission has repeatedly concluded that the application of regulations for the control and limitation of documentation to its own documentation would render the documents in question unfit for the purpose for which they are intended. "In the matter of legal research--and codification of international law demands legal research--limitations on the length of documents cannot be imposed."[217] This conclusion has been endorsed by the General Assembly on a number of occasions.[218]

---

[213] See *Yearbook of the International Law Commission, 1977*, vol. II (Part Two), paras. 125 and 126.

[214] The Commission indicated its understanding that regulations on the preparation of documents on the basis of Governments' replies to a questionnaire or of submissions of the agencies and programmes of the United Nations do not affect the obligation of the Secretary-General under the Statute to publish in extenso, and in the languages of the Commission, all such replies whenever the work of the Commission and its procedures and methods so require. See *Yearbook of the International Law Commission, 1980*, vol. II (Part Two), para. 191.

[215] See *Yearbook of the International Law Commission, 1982*, vol. II (Part Two), para. 271.

[216] See *Yearbook of the International Law Commission, 1980*, vol. II (Part Two), para. 192.

[217] See *Yearbook of the International Law Commission, 1977*, vol. II (Part Two), para. 123; and ibid., *1980*, vol. II (Part Two), para. 192.

[218] See General Assembly resolutions 32/151 of 19 December 1977, 34/141 of 17 December 1979, 35/163 of 15 December 1980, 36/114 of 10 December 1981, 37/111 of 16 December 1982, 38/138 of 19 December 1983 and all subsequent resolutions on the annual report of the Commission to the General Assembly.

At its fifty-fifth session, in 2003, the Commission recalled the particular characteristics of its work that make it inappropriate for page limits to be applied to its documentation.[219] In particular, the Commission noted that it was established to assist the General Assembly in the discharge of its obligation under Article 13, paragraph 1 (a), of the Charter of the United Nations. That obligation stemmed from the recognition by those involved in drafting the Charter that, if international legal rules were to be arrived at by agreement, then in many areas of international law a necessary part of the process of arriving at agreement would involve an analysis and precise statement of State practice. Accordingly, the Commission is required by its Statute to justify its proposals to the General Assembly, and ultimately to States, on the basis of evidence of existing law and the requirements of progressive development in the light of the current needs of the international community. Thus, the draft articles or other recommendations contained in the reports of the Special Rapporteurs or the Commission's report must be supported by extensive references to State practice, doctrine and precedents and be accompanied by extensive commentaries in accordance with article 20 of the Statute. The Commission noted that its documentation is also indispensable for the following reasons: (1) it constitutes a critical component in the process of consulting States and obtaining their views; (2) it assists individual States in understanding and interpreting the rules embodied in codification conventions; (3) it is part of the *travaux preparatoires* of such conventions and is frequently referred to or quoted in the diplomatic correspondence of States, in argument before the International Court of Justice and by the Court itself in its judgments; (4) it contributes to the dissemination of information about international law in accordance with the relevant United Nations programme; and (5) it forms as important a product of the Commission's work as the draft articles themselves and enables the Commission to fulfil, in accordance with its Statute, the tasks entrusted to the Commission by the General Assembly.[220]

The Commission therefore confirmed its previous conclusion that it would be entirely inappropriate to attempt in advance and in abstracto to fix the maximum length of its documentation.[221] At the

---

[219] The Commission referred to the following documentation: its annual reports, the reports of Special Rapporteurs as well as various related research projects, studies and other working documents.
[220] See *Official Records of the General Assembly, Fifty-eighth Session, Supplement No. 10* (A/58/10), paras. 440-442.
[221] See *Official Records of the General Assembly, Fifty-eighth Session, Supplement No. 10* (A/58/10), para. 443.

same time, the Commission again stressed that it and its Special Rapporteurs are fully conscious of the need to achieve economies whenever possible in the overall volume of United Nations documentation and will continue to bear such considerations in mind.[222]

(i)   Duration of the session

The Statute of the Commission does not specify the duration of its sessions. Until 1973, the Commission's sessions normally lasted ten weeks. In 1973, the General Assembly approved a twelve-week period for the Commission's twenty-sixth session, in 1974.[223] The General Assembly subsequently approved, "in the light of the importance of its existing work programme, a twelve-week period for the annual sessions of the International Law Commission, subject to review by the General Assembly whenever necessary".[224]

Since 1974, the Commission's sessions have normally lasted twelve weeks, with the exception of its thirty-eighth session, in 1986, which was reduced to ten weeks for budgetary reasons. In response to the view expressed by the Commission, the twelve-week session was restored the following year.[225] By subsequent resolutions, most recently resolution 50/45 of 11 December 1995, the Assembly expressed the view that the requirements of the work for the progressive development of international law and its codification and the magnitude and complexity of the subjects on the agenda of the Commission made it desirable that the usual duration of its sessions be maintained.

At its forty-eighth session, in 1996, the Commission considered the duration of its sessions in connection with the examination of its work procedures requested by the General Assembly in resolution 50/45. The Commission expressed the view that, in principle, it should be able to determine on a year-to-year basis the necessary length of the following session (i.e., twelve weeks or less), having regard to the state of work and any priorities laid down by the General Assembly for the completion of particular topics. The Commission favoured reverting to the previous practice of holding ten-week sessions, with the possibility of extending this to twelve

---

[222] See *Yearbook of the International Law Commission, 1982*, vol. II (Part Two), para. 271. Subsequently confirmed in *Official Records of the General Assembly, Fifty-eighth Session, Supplement No. 10* (A/58/10), para. 443.
[223] General Assembly resolution 3071 (XXVIII) of 30 November 1973.
[224] General Assembly resolution 3315 (XXIX) of 14 December 1974.
[225] See *Yearbook of the International Law Commission, 1986*, vol. II (Part Two), para. 252 and General Assembly resolution 41/81 of 3 December 1986.

weeks in particular years, as required, and especially in the last year in a quinquennium.[226] Since 1996, the Commission's forty-ninth, fifty-fourth and fifty-fifth sessions, held in 1997, 2002 and 2003, respectively, consisted of ten weeks; its fiftieth session, held in 1998, consisted of eleven weeks, and its fifty-first to fifty-third sessions, held in 1999, 2000 and 2001, respectively, consisted of twelve weeks.

(j)   Split sessions

There is no statutory provision concerning dividing the Commission's annual session into two parts. The Commission has normally held a single annual session, with the exception of the seventeenth session which was held in Geneva and Monaco in 1965 and 1966.

At its forty-fourth session, in 1992, the Commission considered the possibility of dividing its annual session into two parts in the context of the review of its programme, procedures and methods of work. The Commission considered the advantages in terms of the effectiveness of its work as well as the disadvantages in terms of administrative and financial problems. The Commission concluded that the suggestion to divide its annual session into two parts had not received enough support at that time and therefore improvements in the effectiveness of its work should continue to be sought under the current arrangements, for the time being.[227]

At its forty-eighth session, in 1996, the Commission returned to the question of holding a split session in connection with the organization and length of its sessions. Those in favour of a single session argued that a continuous session was necessary to assure the best results on priority topics, including careful consideration of proposed draft articles, while maintaining progress and direction on other topics. Those in favour of a split session argued that it would facilitate reflection and study by members, improve productivity as a result of inter-sessional preparation for the second part, encourage informal inter-sessional work, give Special Rapporteurs time to reconsider proposals, allow concentrated work by the Drafting Committee or a working group at the end of the first part or the beginning of the second part of the session, and facilitate better and more continuous attendance of members. Noting that a split session might not be significantly more expensive than a continuous session, the Commission decided to recommend that a split session be held as

---

[226] See *Yearbook of the International Law Commission, 1996,* vol. II (Part Two), paras. 148 *(m)* and 224-226.
[227] See *Yearbook of the International Law Commission, 1992,* vol. II (Part Two), para. 376.

an experiment in 1998 in order to assess the advantages and disadvantages in practice.[228]

The fiftieth session of the Commission, in 1998, was divided into two parts, with the first part of the session being held in Geneva and the second in New York. The Commission agreed to continue the practice of split sessions as of 2000, scheduling the sessions to take place in two rather evenly split parts, with a reasonable period in between.[229]

At its fifty-first session, in 1999, the Commission examined the advantages and disadvantages of holding split sessions in response to General Assembly resolution 53/102 of 8 December 1998. The Commission concluded that a split session was more efficient and effective and facilitated the uninterrupted attendance of its members based on its experience in 1998. The Commission further concluded that there were no disadvantages to a split session and that any resulting cost increase should be more than offset by increased productivity and cost-saving measures. In particular, the Commission suggested adjusting the organization of work during sessions so that one or two weeks at the end of the first part of the session and/or the beginning of the second part of the session could be devoted exclusively to the meetings which require the attendance of a limited number of the Commission's members.[230] This measure was put into effect at the fifty-third session of the Commission, in 2001, pursuant to General Assembly resolutions 54/111 of 9 December 1999 and 55/152 of 12 December 2000.[231]

The Commission reached these conclusions on the understanding that it would maintain a flexible need-based approach to the nature and duration of its sessions.[232] The Commission's fifty-second to fifty-fifth sessions, held from 2000 to 2003, consisted of two parts.

(k)   Location

The Commission has held all of its sessions in Geneva, except for its first session, which was held in New York in 1949; its sixth session, which was held at the headquarters of the United Nations

---

[228] See *Yearbook of the International Law Commission, 1996*, vol. II (Part Two), paras. 148 (n) and 227-232.
[229] See *Yearbook of the International Law Commission, 1998*, vol. II (Part Two), para. 562.
[230] See *Official Records of the General Assembly, Fifty-fourth Session, Supplement No. 10* (A/54/10), paras. 633-639.
[231] See *Official Records of the General Assembly, Fifty-sixth session, Supplement No. 10* (A/56/10), para. 260.
[232] See *Official Records of the General Assembly, Fifty-fourth Session, Supplement No. 10* (A/54/10), paras. 635 and 638.

Educational, Scientific and Cultural Organization (UNESCO) in Paris in 1954; the second part of its seventeenth session, which was held in Monaco in January 1966; and the second part of its fiftieth session, which was held in New York in 1998.

Article 12 of the Statute initially provided that the Commission would meet at the Headquarters of the United Nations, while recognizing the right of the Commission to hold meetings at other places after consultation with the Secretary-General. The Commission held its first session, in 1949, in New York. However, the Commission decided, after consulting with the Secretary-General, to hold its second to seventh sessions, from 1950 to 1955, in Geneva.[233] The Commission preferred Geneva to New York because its atmosphere and law library were more favourable for the studies of a body of legal experts and because its location simplified arrangements for its sessions by the Secretariat.[234] In 1955, the General Assembly, acting on the recommendation of the Commission,[235] amended article 12 of the Statute to provide for the Commission to meet at the European Office of the United Nations at Geneva.[236]

In introducing the practice of split sessions, the Commission has considered holding the second part of its split sessions in New York, towards the middle of the quinquennium, in order to enhance the relationship between the Commission and the General Assembly and its Sixth Committee.[237]

(l)   The International Law Seminar

Since 1965, the International Law Seminar has been a characteristic part of the Commission's sessions, and many hundreds of young professionals have been introduced to the United Nations and to the work of the Commission through the seminar. During the seminar, the

---

[233] See *Yearbook of the International Law Commission, 1949,* Report to the General Assembly, para. 40; ibid., *1950,* vol. II, document A/1316, para. 22; ibid., *1951,* vol. II, document A/1858, para. 91; ibid., *1952,* vol. II, document A/2163, para. 55; ibid., *1953,* vol. II, document A/2456, para. 173; ibid., *1954,* vol. II, document A/2693, para. 79; and ibid., *1955,* vol. II, document A/2934, para. 29. The Commission initially decided to hold its sixth session in Geneva. However, this session was held in Paris. See *Yearbook of the International Law Commission, 1954,* vol. II, document A/2693, para. 1.
[234] See *Yearbook of the International Law Commission, 1953,* vol. II, document A/2456, para. 173; and ibid., *1955,* vol. II, document A/2934, para. 26.
[235] See *Yearbook of the International Law Commission, 1955,* vol. II, document A/2934, para. 25.
[236] General Assembly resolution 984 (X) of 3 December 1955.
[237] See *Official Records of the General Assembly, Fifty-fifth Session, Supplement No. 10* (A/55/10), para. 734.

participants observe plenary meetings of the Commission, attend specially arranged lectures, and participate in small-group discussions on specific topics.

7. Relationship with Governments

Governments have an important role in every stage of the Commission's work on the progressive development of international law and its codification. Individually, they may refer a proposal or draft convention to the Commission for consideration, furnish information at the outset of the Commission's work and comment upon its drafts as the work proceeds. Collectively, they decide sometimes upon the initiation or priority of the work and always upon its outcome.

(a) Direct relationship with Governments

The Statute provides for the consideration by the Commission of proposals and draft multilateral conventions submitted directly by Members of the United Nations (article 17, paragraph 1).[238] In practice, the Commission has never received such a proposal or draft directly from a Member State but rather indirectly from the General Assembly, usually following its consideration in the Sixth Committee.

The Statute of the Commission also contains provisions designed to give Governments an opportunity to make their views known at every stage of the Commission's work. At the outset of its work, the Commission is required: (a) to circulate a questionnaire to Governments, inviting them to supply data and information relevant to items included in its plan of work for progressive development (article 16 (c)); or (b) to address to Governments a detailed request to furnish the texts of laws, decrees, judicial decisions, treaties, diplomatic correspondence and other documents relevant to the topic being studied for codification (article 19, paragraph 2). The Commission is also required to invite or request Governments to submit comments on the Commission's document containing the initial draft as well as appropriate explanations, supporting material and information supplied by Governments (article 16 (g) to (h) and article 21). Finally, the Commission is required to take into consideration such comments in preparing the final draft and explanatory report (articles 16 (i) and 22).

---

[238] The procedure to be followed in such cases is set forth in article 17, paragraph 2, of the Statute.

The Commission has noted the fundamental and basic role that materials, comments and observations submitted by Governments play in the codification methods of the Commission. The interaction between the Commission, a permanent body of legal experts serving in their personal capacity, and Governments, through a variety of means including the submission of materials and written comments and observations, is at the core of the system created by the General Assembly for the promotion, with the assistance of the Commission, of the progressive development of international law and its codification.[239]

The Commission has indicated its concern that, in practice, the data and comments submitted by Governments in relation to particular topics have in some cases tended to be limited in quantity.[240] The Commission has attempted to make the questionnaires sent to Governments more "user-friendly" by indicating clearly what is requested and why.[241] In 1958, the Commission stated in its report that it "felt little doubt that its work tended to suffer because of defects in the process of obtaining and dealing with the comments of Governments", and accordingly it decided to give Governments more time to prepare their comments.[242] The General Assembly has repeatedly noted that consulting with national organizations and individual experts concerned with international law may assist Governments in considering whether to make comments and observations on drafts submitted by the Commission and formulating their comments and observations.[243] The written comments have been supplemented by the comments made during the annual debates in the Sixth Committee on the Commission's reports to the General Assembly.[244]

---

[239] See *Yearbook of the International Law Commission, 1980,* vol. II (Part Two), para. 191. The Commission has emphasized the importance of the written comments submitted by Governments in response to the Commission's requests on particular topics as an indispensable part of the dialogue between the Commission and Governments. See *Official Records of the General Assembly, Fifty-fourth Session, Supplement No. 10* (A/54/10), para. 616.

[240] See *Yearbook of the International Law Commission, 1996,* vol. II (Part Two), para. 180; and *Official Records of the General Assembly, Fifty-fourth Session, Supplement No. 10* (A/54/10), para. 617.

[241] See *Yearbook of the International Law Commission, 1996,* vol. II (Part Two), para. 148 *(d).*

[242] See *Yearbook of the International Law Commission, 1958,* vol. II, document A/3859, paras. 60 and 61.

[243] See, for instance, General Assembly resolution 52/156 of 15 December 1997 and subsequent resolutions on the report of the International Law Commission.

[244] Until 1979, the relevant reports of the Sixth Committee to the General Assembly contained a summary of the main trends of the discussion in that Committee of the reports of the International Law Commission. For practical reasons, the summary has, since 1980, been issued as part of the Commission's documentation and entitled

After the Commission has submitted its final draft to the General Assembly on a topic, the Assembly normally requests comments of Governments on that draft. Such comments are considered by the General Assembly's Sixth Committee in connection with further consideration of the topic before the convening of the diplomatic conference or in connection with the elaboration of the convention by the General Assembly itself (e.g., special missions, prevention and punishment of crimes against diplomatic agents and other internationally protected persons, and the law of the non-navigational uses of international watercourses), or by the diplomatic conference called upon to draw up the convention on the topic concerned. Occasionally, Governments have also been invited to submit amendments to the Commission's draft articles before the opening of the diplomatic conference (e.g., consular intercourse and immunities, and law of treaties). Those amendments are subsequently referred to the conference.

(b) Relationship with the General Assembly

The General Assembly, usually on the recommendation of its Sixth Committee, has requested the Commission to study or to continue to study a number of topics, or to give priority to certain topics from among those already selected by the Commission itself; has rejected, or deferred action in respect of, certain drafts and recommendations of the Commission; has referred a draft back to the Commission for reconsideration and redrafting; has invited the Commission to present comments regarding outstanding substantive issues related to the draft articles; has decided to convoke diplomatic conferences to study and adopt draft conventions prepared by the Commission; and has decided to consider and adopt draft conventions prepared by the Commission (see page 39).[245] These collective decisions have sometimes been preceded by, or have given rise to, discussions on the appropriate role of the Assembly and its Sixth Committee in relation to the work of the Commission. These debates and a number of resolutions resulting from them have gradually formed a general pattern of working relationships between the two bodies.

"topical summaries".

[245] The General Assembly has usually taken the action recommended by the Commission with respect to its final products on the various topics and special assignments with the exception of the draft articles on arbitral procedure submitted by the Commission in 1953, most-favoured-nation clauses and status of the diplomatic courier and the diplomatic bag not accompanied by diplomatic courier. The Commission has recognized that whether a particular set of draft articles is acceptable or appropriate for adoption at a given time is essentially a matter of policy for States. See Yearbook of the International Law Commission, 1996, vol. II (Part Two), para. 182.

Although the Statute of the Commission is silent on the matter, the Commission from its first session has submitted to the General Assembly a report on the work done at each of its sessions. The well-established practice of annually considering the Commission's reports in the Sixth Committee has facilitated the development of the existing relationship between the General Assembly and the Commission. The Chairman of the Commission introduces its report in the Sixth Committee and attends the meetings during which the report is considered. The Commission also designates a Special Rapporteur to attend the Sixth Committee under the terms of paragraph 5 of General Assembly resolution 44/35 of 4 December 1989. The Chairman and the Special Rapporteur may make observations during the meetings in response to the comments of delegations and may also meet informally with delegations. Every year several members of the Commission are also designated by their States to serve on the Sixth Committee as representatives. A number of individuals who have been elected to membership in the Commission have at some time represented their States in the Sixth Committee.

The Commission has made changes with respect to the preparation and content of its report to facilitate a more structured and focused debate in the Sixth Committee. In 1992, the Commission adopted guidelines on the preparation and content of its report which provide, inter alia, as follows: (a) efforts should continue to avoid excessively long reports; (b) the report should include a chapter providing, in a summary form, a general view of the work of the session to which the report refers, including a list of questions on which the Commission would find the views of the Sixth Committee particularly helpful; (c) parts of the report indicating previous work on each topic should continue to be as brief as possible; (d) the summary of debates should be more compact, giving emphasis to trends of opinions rather than to individual views unless such an individual view was a reservation to a decision taken by the Commission; and (e) the presentation of fragmentary results that can not be properly assessed by the Sixth Committee without additional elements should be a summary, with the indication that the matter will be more fully presented in a future report.[246] The Commission has requested the Secretariat to circulate

---

[246] See *Yearbook of the International Law Commission, 1992,* vol. II (Part Two), para. 373. The Commission has extended its practice of highlighting the issues on which comment is specifically sought in a special chapter of its annual report to the General Assembly devoted to specific issues on which comments would be of particular interest to the Commission. See *Official Records of the General Assembly, Fifty-fourth Session, Supplement No. 10* (A/54/10), para. 614. This practice has been endorsed by the General Assembly which has requested the Commission to continue to pay special attention to indicating in its annual report for each topic, those specific issues, if any, on which expressions of views by Governments, either in the Sixth

the chapters of the report containing a summary of the Commission's work and the specific issues on which views from Governments would be particularly useful (Chapters II and III) as well as the text of draft articles adopted at each session shortly after the end of the session before the report is issued.[247]

The Sixth Committee has also attempted to improve its own method of consideration of the Commission's report in order to provide effective guidance for the Commission regarding its work, for example, by: (a) indicating the dates when the Commission's annual report will be considered in the Sixth Committee at the next session of the General Assembly;[248] (b) providing for the consideration of the report in late October to give delegates time to examine carefully and prepare statements on the report which is issued in September; (c) inviting the Commission, when circumstances so warrant, to request a Special Rapporteur to attend the session of the General Assembly during the discussion of the respective topic;[249] (d) encouraging the holding of informal discussions between the members of the Sixth Committee and those members of the Commission attending the session of the General Assembly;[250] and (e) structuring the debates on the report in such a manner that conditions are provided for concentrated attention to each of the main topics dealt with in the report.[251] The Sixth Committee has also made suggestions regarding the length and content of the Commission's reports to the General Assembly, including shortening the report and focusing on points

---

Committee or in written form, would be of particular interest in providing effective guidance for the Commission in its future work. See, for instance, General Assembly resolution 44/35 of 4 December 1989 and subsequent resolutions on the report of the International Law Commission.

[247] See *Yearbook of the International Law Commission, 1977,* vol. II (Part Two), para. 130 and *Official Records of the General Assembly, Fifty-eighth Session, Supplement No. 10* (A/58/10), para. 445. In 1996, the Commission recommended that the issues on which comment is specifically sought from the Sixth Committee should be identified, if possible, before the adoption of draft articles on the point and these issues should be of a more general, "strategic" character rather than issues of drafting technique. See *Yearbook of the International Law Commission, 1996,* vol. II (Part Two), paras. 148 *(c)* and 181. In 2003, the Commission further noted that Special Rapporteurs may wish to provide sufficient background and substantive elaboration to better assist Governments in developing their responses. See *Official Records of the General Assembly, Fifty-eighth Session, Supplement No. 10* (A/58/10), para. 446.

[248] This information is included in the resolution adopted by the General Assembly on the agenda item relating to the Commission's annual report.

[249] General Assembly resolution 44/35 of 4 December 1989.

[250] General Assembly resolutions 55/152 of 12 December 2000; 56/82 of 12 December 2001 and 57/21 of 19 November 2002.

[251] Some of the changes have been instituted by the Sixth Committee based on the suggestions made by the Commission. See, for instance, *Yearbook of the International Law Commission, 1977,* vol. II (Part Two), paras. 127-129; ibid., *1988,* vol. II (Part Two), paras. 581 and 582; and ibid., *1989,* vol. II (Part Two), para. 742.

requiring comments by Governments.[252] The General Assembly recommended the continuation of efforts to improve the ways in which the report of the Commission is considered in the Sixth Committee, with a view to providing effective guidance for the Commission in its work.[253]

The Sixth Committee, following its consideration of the Commission's report,[254] submits a report to the General Assembly which contains a summary of its consideration of the agenda item, including the relevant documentation, as well as one or more draft resolutions recommended for adoption by the General Assembly. The General Assembly considers and adopts a resolution on the report of the Commission, usually as recommended by the Sixth Committee without change, indicating any recommendations or instructions that it may have with respect to the Commission's work, both substantive and procedural. The General Assembly may also adopt a separate resolution or decision, again based on the recommendation of the Sixth Committee, with respect to a particular topic relating to the Commission's work when appropriate.[255]

The Sixth Committee has indicated broad policy guidelines when assigning topics to the Commission or when giving priority to some topics, and has exercised its judgement as to action in regard to the Commission's final drafts and recommendations. This policy supervision by the Sixth Committee, however, has tended to be exercised with great restraint. The fact that the Commission is a subsidiary organ of the General Assembly has not prevented wide acceptance in the Sixth Committee of the view that the Commission

---

[252] This was one of the recommendations made by the Ad Hoc Working Group of the Sixth Committee established at the forty-third session of the General Assembly, in 1988, to deal with the question of improving the ways in which the report of the Commission was considered in the Committee, with a view to providing effective guidance for the Commission in its work. The Working Group's conclusions were summarized in the oral report of its Chairman to the Sixth Committee (see document A/C.6/43/SR.40, paras. 10-18). The relevant paragraphs of the summary record of the 40th meeting of the Sixth Committee are reproduced in the topical summary of the forty-third session of the General Assembly (see document A/CN.4/L.431, annex 2).
[253] Resolutions 43/169, 44/35, 45/41, 46/54, 47/33, 48/31 and 49/51.
[254] The report of the Sixth Committee on the agenda item relating to the report of the International Law Commission, which indicates the relevant documentation, is published in the *Official Records of the General Assembly* for each session. Relevant information may also be found on the web site of the Sixth Committee. See www.un.org/law/cod/sixth.
[255] In some situations, a topic relating to the work of the Commission may be considered by the General Assembly as a separate agenda item and be the subject of a separate resolution or decision. For example, a topic on which the Commission has already submitted a final report to the General Assembly would not be covered in its subsequent annual reports to the General Assembly. Therefore, the consideration of this topic by the General Assembly would be provided for under a separate agenda item until the Assembly has concluded its consideration of the topic.

should have a substantial degree of autonomy and that it should not be subject to detailed directives from the Assembly.[256] At the same time, the Commission, at each of its sessions, takes fully into consideration the recommendations addressed to it by the General Assembly and the observations made in the Sixth Committee in connection with the Commission's work in general or its specific drafts.

The Sixth Committee, while carefully examining the Commission's reports, has never given precise instructions regarding changes in the form or contents of the Commission's provisional drafts and has refrained from modifying the final drafts submitted by the Commission before reaching the final stage of the codification process, normally the adoption of the corresponding codification convention. The eventual modification of a Commission's final draft has been left to the body entrusted with the elaboration of the convention. On three occasions, with regard to the topics "Special missions," "Question of the protection and inviolability of diplomatic agents and other persons entitled to special protection under international law" and "The law of the non-navigational uses of international watercourses", the Sixth Committee itself was entrusted with the task of elaborating the conventions with a view to their adoption by the General Assembly. In the process of elaborating the conventions, the Sixth Committee acted mutatis mutandis as a codification conference, studying in detail each of the provisions of the draft articles prepared by the International Law Commission and amending some of them. The General Assembly subsequently adopted the texts of the Convention on Special Missions and of the Optional Protocol concerning the Compulsory Settlement of Disputes relating thereto, the text of the Convention on the Prevention and Punishment of Crimes against Internationally Protected Persons, including Diplomatic Agents, as well as the text of the Convention on the Law of Non-navigational Uses of International Watercourses, as elaborated by the Sixth Committee (*see annex V, sections E, G and L, respectively*).

The General Assembly frequently invites the Commission's Special Rapporteur on a topic to attend as an expert consultant the proceedings of the body entrusted with the task of elaborating the corresponding codification convention.[257] The international conferences which have finalized the Commission's draft articles and

---

[256] See *Yearbook of the International Law Commission, 1979*, vol. II (Part One), document A/CN.4/325, para. 18.
[257] See *Yearbook of the International Law Commission, 1979*, vol. II (Part One), document A/CN.4/325, para. 93 and 98 (d).

adopted them as conventions have always paid tribute to the Commission for its efforts in codification and progressive development of international law.

Through its resolutions, the General Assembly has also contributed to establishing and improving the dialogue between the Commission and Governments. The Secretary-General forwards to the Commission and makes available to its members, as appropriate, the relevant resolutions of the General Assembly, as well as the reports and the summary records of the meetings of the Sixth Committee relating to the Commission's work. In addition, the Secretariat produces the topical summary of the Sixth Committee's consideration of the report of the Commission as part of the Commission's documentation for each session.

8.   Relationship with other bodies

Several articles of the Statute envisage the relationship which may be established between the Commission and various other bodies, both official and unofficial. The Commission may consider proposals or draft conventions submitted by principal organs of the United Nations other than the General Assembly, specialized agencies, or official bodies established by intergovernmental agreement to encourage the progressive development of international law and its codification (article 17, paragraph 1).[258] In addition, the Commission may consult with: (a) any organ of the United Nations on any subject which is within the competence of that organ (article 25, paragraph 1); (b) any international or national organizations, official or non-official (article 26, paragraph 1);[259] as well as (c) scientific institutions and individual experts (article 16 (e)).[260] Furthermore, Commission documents on subjects within the competence of organs of the United Nations are circulated to those organs which may furnish information or make suggestions (article 25, paragraph 2). The Statute also provides for the distribution of the Commission's documents to national and international organizations concerned with international law (article 26, paragraph 2).

---

[258] The article further provides for the procedure that the Commission should follow if it deems it appropriate to proceed with the study of such proposals or drafts, including circulating a questionnaire to the bodies concerned and, if desirable, making an interim report to the organ which has submitted the proposal or draft.

[259] The advisability of consultation by the Commission with intergovernmental organizations whose task is the codification of international law is specifically recognized in article 26, paragraph 4, of the Statute of the Commission.

[260] See *Official Records of the General Assembly, Fifty-fourth Session, Supplement No. 10* (A/54/10), paras. 620-627.

The Commission has received proposals from official bodies other than the General Assembly on only two occasions during the early years of its work. At its second and third sessions, in 1950 and 1951, the Commission was notified of resolutions adopted by the Economic and Social Council of the United Nations (resolutions 304 D (XI) of 17 July 1950 and 319 B III (XI) of 11 August 1950), in which the Council requested the Commission to deal with two subjects: the nationality of married women and the elimination of statelessness. The Commission dealt with these subjects in connection with the comprehensive topic of "Nationality, including statelessness", which had already been selected for codification by the Commission in 1949.

The Commission has recommended that the General Assembly — and through it other bodies within the United Nations system — be encouraged to submit to the Commission possible topics involving codification and progressive development of international law. The Commission has further recommended that it should seek to develop links with other United Nations specialized bodies with law-making responsibilities in their field and, in particular, explore the possibility of exchange of information or even joint work on selected topics.[261]

The Commission has consulted with various bodies, both official and unofficial, on particular topics, including: the Food and Agriculture Organization on the law of the sea[262] and shared natural resources;[263] the United Nations High Commissioner for Refugees on nationality including statelessness[264] and nationality in relation to the succession of States;[265] the International Committee of the Red Cross, in particular, on the draft code of crimes against the peace and security of mankind;[266] the International Association of Hydrogeologists on shared natural resources;[267] a group of experts

---

[261] See *Yearbook of the International Law Commission, 1996*, vol. II (Part Two), paras. 148 *(b)* and *(r)*, 165, 177-178 and 240.
[262] See *Yearbook of the International Law Commission, 1996*, vol. II (Part Two), para. 238 *(d)* .
[263] See *Official Records of the General Assembly, Fifty-eighth Session, Supplement No. 10* (A/58/10), paras. 373 and 453.
[264] See *Yearbook of the International Law Commission, 1952*, vol. I, SR. 155, para. 16.
[265] See *Official Records of the General Assembly, Fifty-fourth Session, Supplement No. 10* (A/54/10), para. 621.
[266] See *Official Records of the General Assembly, Fifty-fourth Session, Supplement No. 10* (A/54/10), para. 622.
[267] See *Official Records of the General Assembly, Fifty-eighth Session, Supplement No. 10* (A/58/10), paras. 373 and 453.

on the law of the sea;[268] professors at Harvard Law School[269] and various study groups[270] on State responsibility; the members of the Committee against Torture, the Committee on Economic, Social and Cultural Rights, the Human Rights Committee and the Sub-Commission on the Promotion and Protection of Human Rights on reservations to treaties;[271] the Société française de droit international on fragmentation of international law;[272] as well as the International Law Association on diplomatic protection, responsibility of international organizations and the long-term programme of work.[273]

In some instances, the Commission has invited organizations concerned to submit relevant data and materials that could assist the Commission in determining its future work on a topic as well as comments and observations on the work in progress,[274] including: relations between States and international organizations, the question of treaties concluded between two or more international organizations and reservations to treaties.[275] In 2003, the Commission, requested the Secretariat to circulate, on an annual basis, the chapter of the Commission's report on the topic of responsibility of international organizations to the United Nations, its specialized agencies as well as other international organizations for their comment.[276]

The Commission is also involved in an ongoing process of consultations, exchange of views and mutual information with scientific institutions and professors of international law, which keeps the Commission abreast of new developments and trends in scholarly research on international law. For example, members of the

---

[268] See *Yearbook of the International Law Commission, 1954*, vol. II, document A/2693, para. 63.

[269] See *Official Records of the General Assembly, Fifty-fourth Session, Supplement No. 10* (A/54/10), para. 620.

[270] Study groups established by the Government of Japan, the International Law Association and the American Society of International Law provided useful feedback to the Commission and the Special Rapporteur. See *Official Records of the General Assembly, Fifty-fourth Session, Supplement No. 10* (A/54/10), para. 621.

[271] See *Official Records of the General Assembly, Fifty-eighth Session, Supplement No. 10* (A/58/10), para. 453.

[272] See *Official Records of the General Assembly, Fifty-eighth Session, Supplement No. 10* (A/58/10), para. 454.

[273] See *Official Records of the General Assembly, Fifty-eighth Session, Supplement No. 10* (A/58/10), para. 454.

[274] The Commission has noted the fundamental and basic role that materials, comments and observations submitted by international organizations play in the codification methods of the Commission. See *Yearbook of the International Law Commission, 1980*, vol. II (Part Two), para. 191.

[275] See *Yearbook of the International Law Commission, 1971*, vol. II (Part One), document A/8410/Rev.1, para. 15; ibid., *1978*, vol. II (Part Two), paras. 148 and 150-153; and ibid., *1995*, vol. II (Part Two), para. 489.

[276] See *Official Records of the General Assembly, Fifty-eighth Session, Supplement No. 10* (A/58/10), para. 52.

Commission participated in the United Nations Colloquium on the Progressive Development and Codification of International Law[277] as well as the seminar on the work of the International Law Commission during its first fifty years, both of which were held to commemorate the fiftieth anniversary of the establishment of the Commission.[278]

Throughout the years, the Commission has maintained a close relationship with the International Court of Justice. The Commission is informed by the President of the Court of its recent activities and of the cases currently before it and the members of the Commission are given the opportunity to have an exchange views with the President.

The Commission has also established and maintained cooperative relationships with the Asian-African Legal Consultative Committee, the European Committee on Legal Cooperation and the Committee of Legal Advisers on Public International Law, the Inter-American Juridical Committee, and other regional and inter-regional organizations. The Commission is informed by representatives of these Committees of their recent activities and the members of the Commission have the opportunity to exchange views with them. For its part, the Commission is often represented by one of its members at the sessions and meetings of those bodies. The Commission has recommended that relations with other bodies, such as the regional legal bodies, should be further encouraged and developed.[279]

For a number of years, the Commission has also held consultations with the International Committee of the Red Cross on topics under consideration by the Commission as well as issues of international humanitarian law.[280]

The General Assembly has requested the Commission to continue the implementation of the relevant provisions of its Statute to further strengthen cooperation between the Commission and other bodies concerned with international law.[281]

---

[277] The proceedings of the Colloquium were published in "Making Better International Law: the International Law Commission at 50." See *Selected bibliography.*
[278] The proceedings of the seminar were published in "The International Law Commission Fifty Years After: An Evaluation." See *Selected bibliography.* See also *Official Records of the General Assembly, Fifty-fourth Session, Supplement No. 10* (A/54/10), paras. 623-625.
[279] See *Yearbook of the International Law Commission, 1996,* vol. II (Part Two), paras. 148 *(q)* and 239.
[280] See *Official Records of the General Assembly, Fifty-fourth Session, Supplement No. 10* (A/54/10), para. 622.
[281] See resolution 53/102 of 8 December 1998 and subsequent resolutions.

9.   The Secretariat

In accordance with article 14 of the Statute of the Commission, the Secretary-General of the United Nations provides the staff and facilities required by the Commission to fulfil its task. The Codification Division of the Office of Legal Affairs of the United Nations provides the Secretariat for the Commission. The Commission has recognized the essential contribution of the Codification Division. Members of the Codification Division assist the officers of the Commission by, inter alia, providing the agenda, keeping records and preparing drafts of reports to the Commission. They assist in the preparation of the commentary to draft articles, although the Commission remains of the view that this is the primary responsibility of the Special Rapporteur. In working groups, where there may be no Special Rapporteur, this assistance is invaluable. The Commission has recommended that members of the Codification Division should be encouraged to make an even greater contribution to the Commission's work.[282]

In addition to providing this substantive servicing to the Commission and its subsidiary bodies, the Codification Division undertakes considerable research to facilitate the work of the Commission.[283] At the preliminary stage of the consideration of a topic, the Codification Division may, at the Commission's request or on its own initiative, prepare substantive studies and carry out research projects to facilitate the commencement of work on the topic by the Commission and the Special Rapporteur concerned. Secretariat studies and research projects may also be requested by the Commission or the Special Rapporteur concerned at other stages in the consideration of a topic. At its thirty-second session, in 1980, the Commission noted that the studies and research projects prepared by the Codification Division are part and parcel of the consolidated method and techniques of work of the Commission and, as such, constitute an indispensable contribution to its work.[284]

The Codification Division has prepared a number of studies and surveys on general questions relating to progressive development and codification[285] as well as on particular topics on the programme of the

---

[282] See *Yearbook of the International Law Commission, 1996*, vol. II (Part Two), para. 234.
[283] See *Yearbook of the International Law Commission, 1996*, vol. II (Part Two), para. 234.
[284] See *Yearbook of the International Law Commission, 1980*, vol. II (Part Two), para. 192.
[285] For example, the Codification Division assisted the Commission in the review of its long-term programme of work by preparing surveys on international law in 1949 and 1971, as discussed above.

Commission or aspect thereof.[286] Except for those prepared in 1948 and 1949, these studies and surveys are published in volume II of the *Yearbook of the International Law Commission.*

The Codification Division has also published, primarily for the assistance of the Commission, in the *United Nations Legislative Series,* collections of laws, decrees and treaty provisions on such subjects as: the regime of the high seas; the nationality of ships; the regime of the territorial sea; diplomatic and consular privileges and immunities; the legal status, privileges and immunities of international organizations; nationality; the conclusion of treaties; the utilization of international rivers for purposes other than navigation; succession of States; the law of the sea; jurisdictional immunities of States and their property; and review of the multilateral treaty-making process. Texts of arbitral awards are also published by the Codification Division in the *Reports of International Arbitral Awards.*[287]

The Commission has recognized the increased role of the Codification Division in providing assistance to the Commission and its Special Rapporteurs, especially in the area of research and studies. The Commission has recommended that the contribution of the Codification Division to the Commission's work be maintained and reinforced.[288] The General Assembly has endorsed the Commission's recommendation for the strengthening and increased role of the Codification Division since 1977 in resolutions concerning the report of the Commission.

---

[286] See *Yearbook of the International Law Commission, 1979,* vol. II (Part One), document A/CN.4/325, para. 9.
[287] See *Selected bibliography.*
[288] See *Yearbook of the International Law Commission, 1996,* vol. II (Part Two), paras. 148 *(o)* and 233-234.

PART III

TOPICS AND SUB-TOPICS CONSIDERED BY THE INTERNATIONAL LAW COMMISSION

A. TOPICS AND SUB-TOPICS ON WHICH THE COMMISSION HAS SUBMITTED FINAL REPORTS

A brief account of the work on the topics and sub-topics on which the International Law Commission has submitted final reports to the General Assembly[289] is presented below.[290]

1. Draft Declaration on Rights and Duties of States

By resolution 178 (II) of 21 November 1947, the General Assembly instructed the International Law Commission to prepare a draft declaration on the rights and duties of States, taking as a basis of discussion the draft declaration on this subject presented by Panama[291] and certain other related documents.

At its first session, in 1949, the Commission examined article by article the Panamanian draft. It also had before it a memorandum by the Secretary-General, which reproduced inter alia comments and observations of Member States on the Panamanian draft and a detailed analysis of the United Nations discussions on the subject.[292]

At the same session, the Commission, after three readings, adopted a final draft Declaration on Rights and Duties of States in the form of fourteen articles with commentaries,[293] the text of which is reproduced in annex IV, section 1. It decided to transmit the draft to the General Assembly with its conclusion that it was for the General

---

[289] In addition, at the request of the General Assembly, the Commission submitted its final report on the topic "Review of the Multilateral Treaty-Making Process" to the Secretary-General for inclusion in his report on the subject. See footnote 134.

[290] The Commission's work on a topic or sub-topic at its various sessions is reflected in the relevant chapter of its annual report on each session which is reproduced in the corresponding *Yearbook*. The relevant documentation that was before the Commission at a particular session is also indicated in the *Yearbook*.

[291] Document A/285.

[292] Document A/CN.4/2 and Add.1 (Preparatory Study concerning a draft Declaration on the Rights and Duties of States).

[293] See *Yearbook of the International Law Commission, 1949*, Report to the General Assembly, paras. 46-52.

Assembly to decide what further course of action should be taken in relation to the draft Declaration.[294] The Commission also observed that:

> "the rights and duties set forth in the draft Declaration are formulated in general terms, without restriction or exception, as befits a declaration of basic rights and duties. The articles of the draft Declaration enunciate general principles of international law, the extent and the modalities of the application of which are to be determined by more precise rules. Article 14 of the draft Declaration is a recognition of this fact. It is, indeed, a global provision which dominates the whole draft and, in the view of the Commission, it appropriately serves as a key to other provisions of the draft Declaration in proclaiming 'the supremacy of international law'".[295]

By resolution 375 (IV) of 6 December 1949, the General Assembly commended the draft Declaration to the continuing attention of Member States and of jurists of all nations and requested Member States to furnish their comments on the draft. It also invited the suggestions of Member States on: (1) "whether any further action should be taken by the General Assembly on the draft Declaration"; and (2) "if so, the exact nature of the document to be aimed at and the future procedure to be adopted in relation to it".

As the number of States which had given their comments and suggestions was considered too small to form the basis of any definite decision regarding the draft Declaration on Rights and Duties of States, the General Assembly, in resolution 596 (VI) of 7 December 1951, decided to postpone consideration of the matter "until a sufficient number of States have transmitted their comments and suggestions, and in any case to undertake consideration as soon as a majority of the Member States have transmitted such replies".

2. Ways and means for making the evidence of customary international law more readily available

In accordance with article 24 of its Statute, the Commission, at its first session, in 1949, began consideration of ways and means for making the evidence of customary international law more readily available. At its second session, in 1950, the Commission completed consideration of this topic and submitted a report to the General

---

[294] See *Yearbook of the International Law Commission, 1949,* Report to the General Assembly, para. 53.
[295] See *Yearbook of the International Law Commission, 1949,* Report to the General Assembly, para. 52.

Assembly, containing specific ways and means suggested by the Commission.[296]

The Commission recommended that the widest possible distribution should be made of publications relating to international law issued by organs of the United Nations, particularly the *Reports* and other publications of the International Court of Justice, the United Nations *Treaty Series*, and the *Reports of International Arbitral Awards*. The Commission also recommended that the General Assembly should authorize the Secretariat to prepare the following publications:

(*a*) a Juridical Yearbook, setting forth, inter alia, significant legislative developments in various countries, current arbitral awards by ad hoc international tribunals, and significant decisions of national courts relating to problems of international law;

(*b*) a Legislative Series containing the texts of current national legislation on matters of international interest, and particularly legislation implementing multilateral international agreements;

(*c*) a collection of the constitutions of all States, with supplementary volumes to be issued from time to time for keeping it up to date;

(*d*) a list of the publications issued by Governments of all States containing the texts of treaties concluded by them, supplemented by a list of the principal collections of treaty texts published under private auspices;

(*e*) a consolidated index of the League of Nations *Treaty Series*;

(*f*) occasional index volumes of the United Nations *Treaty Series*;

(*g*) a repertoire of the practice of the United Nations with regard to questions of international law;

(*h*) additional series of the *Reports of International Arbitral Awards*, of which a first series had already been published in three volumes.

In addition, the Commission recommended that the Registry of the International Court of Justice should publish occasional digests of the Court *Reports*; that the General Assembly should call to the attention of Governments the desirability of their publishing digests of their diplomatic correspondence and other materials relating to international law; and that the General Assembly give consideration

---

[296] See *Yearbook of the International Law Commission, 1950*, vol. II, document A/1316, paras. 24-94.

to the desirability of an international convention concerning the general exchange of official publications relating to international law and relations.

Since these recommendations were made, the General Assembly has authorized the Secretary-General to issue most of the publications suggested by the Commission and certain other publications relevant to the Commission's recommendations.[297] The Governments of several Members are publishing or preparing digests of their materials relating to international law. Two conventions — the Convention concerning the Exchange of Official Publications and Government Documents between States and the Convention concerning the International Exchange of Publications — were adopted by the General Conference of UNESCO in 1958.[298]

3. Formulation of the Nürnberg principles

By General Assembly resolution 177 (II) of 21 November 1947, the Commission was directed to formulate the principles of international law recognized in the Charter of the Nürnberg Tribunal and in the judgment of the Tribunal.

At its first session, in 1949, the Commission undertook a preliminary consideration of the subject. It had before it a memorandum submitted by the Secretary-General entitled "The Charter and the Judgement of the Nürnberg Tribunal: History and Analysis."[299] In the course of this consideration, the question arose as to whether or not the Commission should ascertain to what extent the principles contained in the Charter and in the judgment constituted principles of international law. The conclusion was that since the Nürnberg principles had been unanimously affirmed by the General Assembly in resolution 95 (I) of 11 December 1946, the task entrusted to the Commission was not to express any appreciation of

---

[297] I.e., *United Nations Juridical Yearbook* (of which a provisional volume for 1962 and printed volumes for the following years have been issued); *United Nations Legislative Series* (23 volumes of which have been issued); *List of Treaty Collections* (published in 1955); *Cumulative Index* of the United Nations *Treaty Series* (of which No. 38, the latest one as of 4 December 2003, covers the *Treaty Series*, vols. 2051-2100); *Repertoire of the Practice of the Security Council* (originally published in 1954, with supplements issued subsequently); *Repertory of Practice of United Nations Organs* (originally published in 1955, with supplements issued later); and *Reports of International Arbitral Awards* (22 volumes of which have been issued). In addition, the Secretariat of the United Nations has issued *Summary of Judgements, Advisory Opinions and Orders of the International Court of Justice.*

[298] United Nations, *Treaty Series,* vol. 398, p. 9, and vol. 416, p. 51.

[299] Document A/CN.4/5.

those principles as principles of international law but merely to formulate them.

At the same session, the Commission appointed a sub-committee, which submitted a working paper containing a formulation of the Nürnberg principles. The Commission considered the working paper and retained tentatively a number of draft articles, which were referred to the sub-committee for redrafting. In considering what action should be taken with respect to the further draft submitted by the sub-committee, the Commission noted that the task of formulating the Nürnberg principles appeared to be closely connected with that of preparing a draft code of offences against the peace and security of mankind (*see Part III.A, section 7(a)*). The Commission decided to defer a final formulation of the principles until the work of preparing the draft code was further advanced. It appointed Jean Spiropoulos as Special Rapporteur for both topics and referred to him the draft prepared by the sub-committee. The Special Rapporteur was requested to submit his report on the draft to the Commission at its second session.

At its second session, in 1950, on the basis of the report presented by the Special Rapporteur,[300] the Commission adopted a final formulation of the Principles of International Law Recognized in the Charter of the Nürnberg Tribunal and in the Judgment of the Tribunal, and submitted it, with commentaries, to the General Assembly, without making any recommendation on a further action thereon.[301] The text of the formulation, which consists of seven principles, is reproduced in annex IV, section 2.

By resolution 488 (V) of 12 December 1950, the General Assembly decided to send the formulation to the Governments of Member States for comments, and requested the Commission, in preparing the draft code of offences against the peace and security of mankind, to take account of the observations made on this formulation by delegations during the fifth session of the General Assembly and of any observations which might later be received from Governments.[302]

---

[300] See *Yearbook of the International Law Commission, 1950*, vol. II, document A/CN.4/22.
[301] See *Yearbook of the International Law Commission, 1950*, vol. II, document A/1316, paras. 97-127.
[302] Observations of Member States on the Commission's formulation of the Nürnberg principles are contained in *Yearbook of the International Law Commission, 1951*, vol. II, document A/CN.4/45 and Add.1 and 2. In addition, the second report of the Special Rapporteur on a draft code of offences against the peace and security of mankind (ibid., document A/CN.4/44) contained a digest of the observations on the Commission's formulation of the Nürnberg principles made by delegations during the fifth session of the General Assembly. As requested by the General Assembly, the

4. Question of international criminal jurisdiction

The General Assembly, in resolution 260 B (III) of 9 December 1948, invited the Commission "to study the desirability and possibility of establishing an international judicial organ for the trial of persons charged with genocide or other crimes over which jurisdiction will be conferred upon that organ by international conventions", and requested the Commission, in carrying out that task, "to pay attention to the possibility of establishing a Criminal Chamber of the International Court of Justice".

The Commission considered the question of international criminal jurisdiction at its first and second sessions, in 1949 and 1950, respectively. At its first session, the Commission appointed as Special Rapporteurs to deal with this question Ricardo J. Alfaro and A. E. F. Sandström, who were requested to submit to the Commission one or more working papers on the subject. In connection with the consideration of the question, the Commission had before it the reports of the Special Rapporteurs[303] and documents prepared by the Secretariat.[304]

At its second session, in 1950, the Commission discussed the report presented by each of the Special Rapporteurs and concluded that the establishment of an international judicial organ for the trial of persons charged with genocide or other crimes was both desirable and possible. It recommended, however, against such an organ being set up as a chamber of the International Court of Justice, though it was possible to do so by amendment of the Court's Statute which, in Article 34, provides that only States may be parties in cases before the Court.[305]

After giving preliminary consideration to the Commission's report on the question of international criminal jurisdiction, the General Assembly adopted resolution 489 (V) of 12 December 1950, establishing a committee composed of the representatives of seventeen Member States for the purpose of preparing preliminary draft conventions and proposals relating to the establishment and the

---

Commission took into account the comments and observations received from Governments on the formulation of the Nürnberg principles (*see footnote 332*).

[303] For the report of Ricardo J. Alfaro, see *Yearbook of the International Law Commission, 1950,* vol. II, document A/CN.4/15, and for the report of A. E. F. Sandström, see ibid., document A/CN.4/20.

[304] Memorandum entitled "Historical survey of the question of international criminal jurisdiction" (document A/CN.4/7/Rev.1 published in United Nations publication, Sales No. 1949.V.8); and bibliography on International Criminal Law and International Criminal Court (document A/CN.4/28).

[305] See *Yearbook of the International Law Commission, 1950,* vol. II, document A/1316, paras. 128-145.

statute of an international criminal court. The committee met at Geneva in August 1951 and formulated proposals together with a draft statute for an international criminal court. Under the draft statute it was proposed that the court should have a permanent structure but should function only on the basis of cases submitted to it.

The report of the Committee,[306] containing the draft statute, was communicated to Governments for their observations. Only a few Governments commented on the draft, however, and in 1952 the Assembly, in resolution 687 (VII) of 5 December 1952, decided to set up a new committee, consisting again of representatives of seventeen Member States, which met at United Nations Headquarters in the summer of 1953. The terms of reference of the Committee were: (1) to explore the implications and consequences of establishing an international criminal court and of the various methods by which this might be done; (2) to study the relationship between such a court and the United Nations and its organs; and (3) to reexamine the draft statute. The Committee made a number of changes in the 1951 draft statute and, in respect of several articles, prepared alternative texts, one appropriate if the court were to operate separately from the United Nations and the other in case it were decided that the court should be closely linked with the United Nations. The report of the Committee[307] was placed before the Assembly at its 1954 session.

The Assembly, however, in resolution 898 (IX) of 14 December 1954, decided to postpone consideration of the question of an international criminal jurisdiction until it had taken up the report of the special committee on the question of defining aggression and had taken up again the draft code of offences against the peace and security of mankind (*see page 83*). The report of the special committee was before the General Assembly at its twelfth session, in 1957. While taking note of the report, the Assembly postponed consideration of the question of defining aggression and the draft code of offences to a later stage (*see pages 83 and 87*). A similar decision was taken by the General Assembly with respect to the question of an international criminal jurisdiction in resolution 1187 (XII) of 11 December 1957. It was felt that, since the subject was related both to the question of defining aggression and to the draft code of offences against the peace and security of mankind,

---

[306] See *Official Records of the General Assembly, Seventh Session, Supplement No. 11* (A/2136).

[307] See *Official Records of the General Assembly, Ninth Session, Supplement No. 12* (A/2645).

consideration should be deferred until such time as the Assembly again took up the two related items.

The matter was subsequently brought to the attention of Member States in 1968 by the Secretary-General[308] in connection with placing the item on the report of the Special Committee on the Question of Defining Aggression on the agenda of the General Assembly. The Assembly's General Committee decided, however, that it would not be desirable at that stage, prior to the completion of the Assembly's consideration of the question of defining aggression, for the items "International criminal jurisdiction" and "Draft Code of Offences against the Peace and Security of Mankind" to be included in the agenda and that those items should be taken up only at a later session when further progress had been made in arriving at a generally agreed definition of aggression.[309] The General Assembly adopted its agenda as proposed by the General Committee.

The same question was again brought to the attention of Member States by the Secretary-General in a memorandum addressed to the General Committee in 1974,[310] when a draft definition of aggression was submitted to the General Assembly (*see page 84*). In allocating the item on the question of defining aggression to the Sixth Committee, the Assembly commented that it had decided to take note of the Secretary-General's observations and to consider whether it should take up again the question of a draft code of offences against the peace and security of mankind and the question of an international criminal jurisdiction.[311]

The question of international criminal jurisdiction was raised again in the context of the Commission's work on a draft code of offences against the peace and security of mankind (*see Part III. A, section 7*).

5.   Reservations to multilateral conventions

The question of reservations to multilateral conventions arose out of difficulties encountered by the Secretary-General in his capacity as depositary of the Convention on the Prevention and Punishment of the Crime of Genocide, which had been adopted by the General

---

[308] See *Official Records of the General Assembly, Twenty-third Session, Annexes*, vol. I, agenda item 8, document A/BUR/171/Rev.1, para. 4.
[309] See *Official Records of the General Assembly, Twenty-third Session, Annexes*, vol. I, agenda item 8, document A/7250, para. 10.
[310] See *Official Records of the General Assembly, Twenty-ninth Session, Annexes*, agenda item 8, document A/BUR/182, para. 26.
[311] See *Official Records of the General Assembly, Twenty-ninth Session, Annexes*, agenda item 86, document A/9890, para. 2.

Assembly on 9 December 1948.[312] The Secretary-General, as depositary of multilateral conventions, had substantially followed the practice of the League of Nations. Under this practice, in the absence of stipulations in a convention regarding the procedure to be followed in the making and accepting of reservations, the Secretary-General accepted in definitive deposit an instrument of ratification or accession offered with a reservation only after it had been ascertained that there was no objection on the part of any of the other States directly concerned. This practice, however, was contested by some Member States and, in 1950, the Secretary-General asked the General Assembly for directions on the procedure he should follow.[313] The General Assembly, by resolution 478 (V) of 16 November 1950, requested an advisory opinion from the International Court of Justice on reservations to the Genocide Convention. The Assembly also invited the Commission, in the course of its work on the codification of the law of treaties, to study the question of reservations to multilateral conventions in general, both from the point of view of codification and from that of the progressive development of international law, and to report to the Assembly at its sixth session, in 1951.

In pursuance of this resolution, the Commission, in the course of its third session, in 1951, gave priority to a study of the question of reservations to multilateral conventions.[314] It had before it a "Report on Reservations to Multilateral Conventions,"[315] submitted by the Special Rapporteur on the topic of the law of treaties, as well as two memoranda, submitted by two other members of the Commission.[316] In its report to the Assembly, the Commission stated that the criterion of compatibility of a reservation with the object and purpose of a convention — applied by the International Court of Justice in its advisory opinion on reservations to the Genocide Convention[317] — would not be suitable for application to multilateral conventions in

---

[312] United Nations, *Treaty Series*, vol. 78, p. 277.

[313] See *Official Records of the General Assembly, Fifth Session, Annexes*, agenda item 56, document A/1372.

[314] At this session, the Commission recalled its preliminary discussion of the question at its second session, in 1950, on the basis of the report of the Special Rapporteur on the topic of the law of treaties (document A/CN.4/23).

[315] See *Yearbook of the International Law Commission, 1951*, vol. II, document A/CN.4/41.

[316] See *Yearbook of the International Law Commission, 1951*, vol. II, documents A/CN.4/L.9 and A/CN.4/L.14.

[317] The Court declared that a State which has made and maintained a reservation which has been objected to by one or more of the parties to the Convention but not by others, can be regarded as a party to the Convention if the reservation is compatible with the object and purpose of the Convention; otherwise that State cannot be regarded as a party. International Court of Justice, *Reports of Judgments, Advisory Opinions and Orders, 1951*, p. 29.

general; while no single rule uniformly applied could be wholly satisfactory, a rule suitable for application in the majority of cases could be found in the practice theretofore followed by the Secretary-General, with some modifications.[318]

The General Assembly, in resolution 598 (VI) of 12 January 1952, endorsed the Commission's recommendation that clauses on reservations should be inserted in future conventions; stated that the Court's advisory opinion should be followed in regard to the Genocide Convention; and asked the Secretary-General, in respect of future United Nations conventions, to act as depositary for documents containing reservations or objections thereto without passing on the legal effect of such documents. The documents were to be communicated to all States concerned, to which it would be left to draw the legal consequences. In 1959, the General Assembly, in resolution 1452 (XIV) of 7 December 1959, asked the Secretary-General to follow the same practice with respect to United Nations conventions concluded before, as well as after, the Assembly's resolution of 1952.

The Commission returned again to the subject in the course of its preparation of draft articles on the law of treaties (*see Part III.A, section 14*) and the question of treaties concluded between States and international organizations or between two or more international organizations (*see Part III.A, section 20*). Articles 19 to 23 of the 1969 Vienna Convention on the Law of Treaties[319] and of the 1986 Vienna Convention on the Law of Treaties between States and International Organizations or between International Organizations[320] deal with reservations to treaties. The Commission also took up the subject in the context of its work on the topic of reservations to treaties (*see Part III.B, section 1*).

6. Question of defining aggression

The General Assembly, in resolution 378 (V) of 17 November 1950, decided to refer to the Commission a proposal made by the Union of Soviet Socialist Republics in connection with the agenda item "Duties of States in the event of the outbreak of hostilities" and all the records of the First (Political and Security) Committee of the Assembly dealing with the question, so that the Commission might take them into consideration and formulate its conclusions as soon as possible.

---

[318] See *Yearbook of the International Law Commission, 1951*, vol. II, document A/1858, paras. 12-34.
[319] See annex V, section F.
[320] See annex V, section K.

The Soviet proposal provided that the General Assembly, "considering it necessary ... to define the concept of aggression as accurately as possible," declares, inter alia, that "in an international conflict that State shall be declared the attacker which first commits" one of the acts enumerated in the proposal.[321]

At its third session, in 1951, the Commission considered the question whether it should enumerate aggressive acts or try to draft a definition of aggression in general terms.[322] The sense of the Commission was that it was undesirable to define aggression by a detailed enumeration of aggressive acts, since no enumeration could be exhaustive. It also considered it inadvisable unduly to limit the freedom of judgement of the competent organs of the United Nations by a rigid and necessarily incomplete list of acts constituting aggression. It was therefore decided that the only practical course was to aim at a general and abstract definition. But the Commission's efforts to draw up a general definition were not successful.

During the same session, however, the matter was reconsidered in connection with the preparation of the draft Code of Offences against the Peace and Security of Mankind (*see Part III.A, section 7 (a)*). The Commission then decided to include among the offences defined in the draft Code any act of aggression and any threat of aggression.[323]

At its sixth session, the General Assembly examined the question of defining aggression and concluded, in resolution 599 (VI) of 31 January 1952, that it was both "possible and desirable, with a view to ensuring international peace and security and to developing international criminal law, to define aggression by reference to the elements which constitute it". At the Assembly's request, the Secretary-General submitted a detailed report to the Assembly at its seventh session covering all aspects of the question.[324]

On 20 December 1952, the Assembly, in resolution 688 (VII), established a fifteen-member special committee which was requested to submit to the Assembly's ninth session, in 1954, "draft definitions

---

[321] See *Official Records of the General Assembly, Fifth Session, Annexes*, agenda item 72, document A/C.1/608.

[322] The Commission considered the question on the basis of chapter II of the second report of the Special Rapporteur for the draft code of offences against the peace and security of mankind entitled "The Possibility and Desirability of a Definition of Aggression" (see *Yearbook of the International Law Commission, 1951*, vol. II, document A/CN.4/44) as well as memoranda and proposals presented by other members of the Commission (see ibid., documents A/CN.4/L. 6-8, 10-12 and 19).

[323] See *Yearbook of the International Law Commission, 1951*, vol. II, document A/1858, para. 53.

[324] See *Official Records of the General Assembly, Seventh Session, Annexes*, agenda item 54, document A/2211.

of aggression or draft statements of the notion of aggression". The special committee met at United Nations Headquarters from 24 August to 21 September 1953. Several different texts aimed at defining aggression were presented. The committee, however, decided unanimously not to put the texts to a vote but to transmit them to the General Assembly and to Member States for comments.[325] Comments were received from eleven Member States.

By resolution 895 (IX) of 4 December 1954, the General Assembly established another special committee, consisting of nineteen members, and requested it to report to the eleventh session of the General Assembly, in 1956. The nineteen-member committee met at United Nations Headquarters from 8 October to 9 November 1956. It did not adopt a definition but decided to transmit its report to the Assembly, summarizing the views expressed on the various aspects of the matter, together with the draft definitions previously submitted to it.[326]

At its twelfth session, in 1957, the General Assembly, in resolution 1181 (XII) of 29 November 1957, took note of the special committee's report. By the same resolution, the Assembly decided to invite the views of twenty-two States admitted to the United Nations since 14 December 1955, and to renew the request for comments of other Member States. It also decided to refer the replies of Governments to a new committee, composed of the Member States which had served on the General Committee of the Assembly at its most recent regular session, and entrusted the committee with the procedural task of studying the replies "for the purpose of determining when it shall be appropriate for the General Assembly to consider again the question of defining aggression".

The committee, which met at the United Nations Headquarters from 14 to 24 April 1959, decided that the fourteen replies received did not indicate any change of attitude and agreed to postpone further consideration of the question until April 1962, unless an absolute majority of its members favoured an earlier meeting in the light of new developments. The committee met again at United Nations Headquarters in 1962, 1965 and 1967, but on each occasion found itself unable to determine any particular time as appropriate for the Assembly to resume consideration of the question of defining aggression. The activities of this committee came to an end in 1967,

---

[325] See *Official Records of the General Assembly, Ninth Session, Supplement No. 11* (A/2638).
[326] See *Official Records of the General Assembly, Twelfth Session, Supplement No. 16* (A/3574).

when the General Assembly decided to undertake again substantive consideration of the question of the definition of aggression.[327]

Recognizing "that there is a widespread conviction of the need to expedite the definition of aggression", the General Assembly, by resolution 2330 (XXII) of 18 December 1967, established a Special Committee on the Question of Defining Aggression, composed of thirty-five Member States, "to consider all aspects of the question so that an adequate definition of aggression may be prepared". The Special Committee held seven sessions, one every year from 1968 to 1974. At its 1974 session, the Special Committee adopted by consensus a draft definition of aggression and recommended it to the General Assembly for adoption.[328] On 14 December 1974, the Assembly adopted by consensus the Definition of Aggression as recommended by the Special Committee. The Assembly also called the attention of the Security Council to the Definition and recommended that the Security Council should, as appropriate, take account of that Definition as guidance in determining, in accordance with the Charter, the existence of an act of aggression.[329]

7. Draft Code of Offences against the Peace and Security of Mankind[330]

(a) Draft Code of Offences (1954)

The task of preparing a draft code of offences against the peace and security of mankind was entrusted to the Commission in 1947, by General Assembly resolution 177 (II) of 21 November 1947, the same resolution that requested it to formulate the Nürnberg principles (see page 75).

The Commission began its consideration of the draft code of offences at its first session, in 1949, when the Commission appointed Jean Spiropoulos as Special Rapporteur for the subject. It proceeded with its work at its third, fifth and sixth sessions, in 1951, 1953 and 1954, respectively. In connection with its work on the draft code of offences, the Commission had before it the reports of the Special

---

[327] For the reports of the committee, see documents A/AC.91/2, 3 and 5.
[328] See *Official Records of the General Assembly, Twenty-ninth Session, Supplement No. 19* (A/9619).
[329] The text of the Definition of Aggression is contained in General Assembly resolution 3314 (XXIX), annex. See also *Official Records of the General Assembly, Twenty-ninth Session, Annexes*, agenda item 86, document A/9890.
[330] At its thirty-ninth session, in 1987, the Commission recommended to the General Assembly that it amend the title of the topic in English so that it would read "Draft Code of Crimes against the Peace and Security of Mankind." The General Assembly agreed with this recommendation in resolution 42/151 of 7 December 1987.

Rapporteur,[331] information received from Governments[332] as well as documents prepared by the Secretariat.[333]

At its third session, in 1951, the Commission completed a draft Code of Offences against the Peace and Security of Mankind and submitted it to the General Assembly, together with commentaries thereto.[334]

In the course of the preparation of the text, the Commission considered that it was not necessary to indicate the exact extent to which the various Nürnberg principles had been incorporated in the draft Code. As to the scope of the draft Code, the Commission decided to limit the Code to offences containing a political element and endangering or disturbing the maintenance of international peace and security. It therefore omitted such matters as piracy, traffic in dangerous drugs, traffic in women and children, slavery, counterfeiting of currency, and damage to submarine cables. The Commission also decided that it would deal only with the criminal responsibility of individuals and that no provisions should be included with respect to crimes by abstract entities.[335] (The Nürnberg Tribunal had stated in its judgment that: "Crimes against international law are committed by men, not by abstract entities, and only by punishing individuals who commit such crimes can the provisions of international law be enforced."[336]) Thus, offences enumerated in the draft Code were characterized as "crimes under international law, for which the responsible individuals shall be punishable".[337]

The Commission refrained from providing for institutional arrangements for implementing the Code; it thought that, pending the

---

[331] See *Yearbook of the International Law Commission, 1950*, vol. II, document A/CN.4/25; ibid., *1951*, vol. II, document A/CN.4/44; and ibid., *1954*, vol. II, document A/CN.4/85.

[332] See *Yearbook of the International Law Commission, 1950*, vol. II, document A/CN.4/19 and Add.1 and 2; *Official Records of the General Assembly, Seventh Session, Annexes*, agenda item 54, document A/2162 and Add.1 as well as document A/2162/Add.2. The Commission also examined the comments and observations received from Governments on the formulation of the Nürnberg principles (see *Yearbook of the International Law Commission, 1951*, vol. II, document A/CN.4/45 and Add.1 and 2).

[333] See *Yearbook of the International Law Commission, 1950*, vol. II, document A/CN.4/39 as well as document A/CN.4/72.

[334] See *Yearbook of the International Law Commission, 1951*, vol. II, document A/1858, paras. 57 and 59.

[335] See *Yearbook of the International Law Commission, 1951*, vol. II, document A/1858, para. 52 (a, b and c).

[336] Trial of the Major War Criminals before the International Military Tribunal, Nürnberg, 14 November 1945-1 October 1946, published at Nürnberg, Germany, 1947, p. 223.

[337] See *Yearbook of the International Law Commission, 1951*, vol. II, document A/1858, para. 59, article 1.

establishment of an international criminal court, the Code might be applied by national courts.[338] As the Commission deemed it impracticable to prescribe a definite penalty for each offence, it was left to the competent tribunal to determine the penalty for any offence under the Code, taking into account the gravity of the particular offence.[339]

At its sixth session, in 1951, the General Assembly postponed consideration of the draft Code until its next session, in view of the fact that the draft had only recently been communicated to Governments for comments. At the Assembly's seventh session, in 1952, the item was omitted from the final agenda on the understanding that the matter would continue to be considered by the International Law Commission.

The Commission accordingly took up the matter again at its fifth session, in 1953, and requested the Special Rapporteur, Jean Spiropoulos, to prepare a new report for submission at the sixth session.

At its sixth session, in 1954, the Commission considered the report of the Special Rapporteur[340] which discussed the observations received from Governments and proposed certain changes in the text previously adopted by the Commission. The Commission decided to modify its previous text in certain respects and added a new offence to the list of crimes, namely, the intervention by the authorities of a State in the internal or external affairs of another State by means of coercive measures. It also decided to omit the condition that inhuman acts against a civil population were crimes only when committed in connection with other offences defined in the draft Code. The rule regarding crimes committed under order by a superior was reworded to say that the perpetrator of such a crime would be responsible if, under the circumstances at the time, it was possible for him not to comply with the order. In addition, the Commission decided to omit the provision dealing with the punishment of the offences defined in the draft Code, as the Commission considered that the question of penalties could more conveniently be dealt with at a later stage, after it had been decided how the Code was to become operative.[341]

---

[338] See *Yearbook of the International Law Commission, 1951*, vol. II, document A/1858, para. 52 (d).
[339] See *Yearbook of the International Law Commission, 1951*, vol. II, document A/1858, para. 59, article 5 and its commentary.
[340] See *Yearbook of the International Law Commission, 1954*, vol. II, document A/CN.4/85.
[341] See *Yearbook of the International Law Commission, 1954*, vol. II, document A/2693, paras. 50 and 51.

At the same session, the Commission adopted the revised draft Code of Offences against the Peace and Security of Mankind, with commentaries.[342] The text of the draft Code as revised in 1954 is reproduced in annex IV, section 3 (a).

The General Assembly, in resolution 897 (IX) of 4 December 1954, considering that the draft Code raised problems closely related to that of the definition of aggression, decided to postpone further consideration of the draft Code until the new special committee on the question of defining aggression had submitted its *report (see page 83)*. The report of the special committee was before the General Assembly at its twelfth session, in 1957. At that session, the General Assembly took note of the report and decided to postpone consideration of the question of aggression to a later stage *(see page 83)*. In view of that decision and the consideration that the draft Code raised problems related to the question of defining aggression, the General Assembly, in resolution 1186 (XII) of 11 December 1957, deferred consideration of the draft Code until such time as it took up again the question of defining aggression. In the same resolution, the General Assembly requested the Secretary-General to transmit the text of the draft Code to Member States for comment, and to submit their replies to the General Assembly at such time as the item might be placed on its provisional agenda.

As mentioned earlier *(see page 79)*, the item was brought to the attention of the General Assembly in 1968 and again in 1974. The Assembly decided at its twenty-third session, in 1968, not to take up the item. At its twenty-ninth session, in 1974, it decided to consider whether it should take up again the question of a draft code of offences against the peace and security of mankind.

The Commission, in its report on the work of its twenty-ninth session, in 1977, referred to the advisability of the General Assembly giving consideration to the draft Code, including the possibility of its review by the Commission if the Assembly so wished.[343]

The Assembly, at its thirty-second session, in 1977, acting on the request of seven Member States, decided to include in its agenda the item entitled "Draft Code of Offences against the Peace and Security of Mankind", and to allocate it to the Sixth Committee. However, because of lack of time, the Assembly agreed to defer consideration of the item until its thirty-third session.[344] At that session, the General

---

[342] See *Yearbook of the International Law Commission, 1954*, vol. II, document A/2693, paras. 49 and 54.

[343] See *Yearbook of the International Law Commission, 1977*, vol. II (Part Two), para. 111.

[344] See *Official Records of the General Assembly, Thirty-second Session, Annexes*, agenda item 131, document A/32/470.

Assembly adopted resolution 33/97 of 16 December 1978, by which, inter alia, it requested the Secretary-General to invite Member States and relevant international intergovernmental organizations to submit their comments and observations on the draft Code, including comments on the procedure to be adopted, and to prepare a report to be submitted to the Assembly at its thirty-fifth session, in 1980.

The comments received further to General Assembly resolution 33/97 were circulated at the thirty-fifth session of the General Assembly, in 1980.[345] At the same session, the General Assembly, in resolution 35/49 of 4 December 1980, requested the Secretary-General to reiterate his invitation to Member States and relevant international intergovernmental organizations to submit or update their comments and observations and in particular to inform him of their views on the procedure to be followed in the future consideration of the item, including the suggestion to have the item referred to the International Law Commission.

(b)   Draft Code of Crimes (1996)

The General Assembly, by resolution 36/106 of 10 December 1981, invited the International Law Commission to resume its work with a view to elaborating the draft Code of Offences against the Peace and Security of Mankind and to examine it with the required priority in order to review it, taking duly into account the results achieved by the process of the progressive development of international law.

Accordingly, at its thirty-fourth session, in 1982, the Commission included the item "Draft Code of Offences against the Peace and Security of Mankind" in its agenda and appointed Doudou Thiam as Special Rapporteur for the subject.

The Commission proceeded with its work on the draft code from its thirty-fifth session, in 1983, to its forty-third session, in 1991, and at its forty-sixth and forty-seventh sessions, in 1994 and 1995, respectively. In connection with its further consideration of the draft code, the Commission had before it the reports of the Special Rapporteur,[346] comments and observations received from

---

[345] Document A/35/210 and Add.1 and 2 and Add.2/Corr.1.

[346] See *Yearbook of the International Law Commission, 1983,* vol. II (Part One), document A/CN.4/364; ibid., *1984,* vol. II (Part One), document A/CN.4/377; ibid., *1985,* vol. II (Part One), document A/CN.4/387; ibid., *1986,* vol. II (Part One), document A/CN.4/398; ibid., *1987,* vol. II (Part One), document A/CN.4/404; ibid., *1988,* vol. II (Part One), document A/CN.4/411; ibid., *1989,* vol. II (Part One), document A/CN.4/419 and Add.l; ibid., *1990,* vol. II (Part One), document A/CN.4/430 and Add.l; ibid., *1991,* vol. II (Part One), document A/CN.4/435 and Add.l; ibid., *1992,* vol. II (Part One), document A/CN.4/442; ibid., *1993,* vol. II (Part One), document A/CN.4/449 (the tenth and eleventh reports of the Special

Governments and international organizations[347] as well as documents prepared by the Secretariat.[348]

At its thirty-fourth session, in 1982, the Commission established a Working Group chaired by the Special Rapporteur that held a preliminary exchange of views on the requests addressed to the Commission by the General Assembly in its resolution 36/106. On the recommendation of the Working Group, the Commission indicated its intention to proceed during its thirty-fifth session to a general debate in plenary on the basis of a first report to be submitted by the Special Rapporteur. The Commission further indicated that it would submit to the General Assembly, at its thirty-eighth session, the conclusions of that debate.

The General Assembly, in resolution 37/102 of 16 December 1982, requested the Commission, in conformity with resolution 36/106 of 10 December 1981, to submit to the General Assembly at its thirty-eighth session a preliminary report, inter alia, on the scope and the structure of the draft code.

At its thirty-fifth session, in 1983, the Commission proceeded to a general debate on the basis of the first report of the Special Rapporteur,[349] which focused on three questions: (1) the scope of the draft; (2) the methodology to be followed; and (3) the implementation of the code. On the question of methodology, the Commission considered it advisable to include an introduction recalling the general principles of criminal law, such as the non-retroactivity of criminal law and the theories of aggravating or mitigating circumstances, complicity, preparation and justified acts.[350] On the other two questions, the views of the Commission were as follows:

"(a) The International Law Commission is of the opinion that the draft code should cover only the most serious international offences. These offences will be determined by reference to a

---

Rapporteur published in the *1992* and *1993 Yearbooks,* respectively, were devoted entirely to the question of the possible establishment of an international criminal jurisdiction); and ibid., *1994,* vol. II (Part One), document A/CN.4/460; as well as document A/CN.4/466.

[347] See *Yearbook of the International Law Commission, 1982,* vol. II (Part One), document A/CN.4/358 and Add.1-4; ibid., *1983,* vol. II (Part One), document A/CN.4/369 and Add.1 and 2; ibid., *1985,* vol. II (Part One), document A/CN.4/392 and Add.1 and 2; ibid., *1987,* vol. II (Part One), document A/CN.4/407 and Add.1 and 2; ibid., *1990,* vol. II (Part One), document A/CN.4/429 and Add.1-4; and ibid., *1993,* vol. II (Part One), document A/CN.4/448 and Add.1.

[348] Documents A/CN.4/365 and A/CN.4/368 and Add.1.

[349] See *Yearbook of the International Law Commission, 1983,* vol. II (Part One), document A/CN.4/364.

[350] See *Yearbook of the International Law Commission, 1983,* vol. II (Part Two), para. 67.

general criterion and also to the relevant conventions and declarations pertaining to the subject;

"(b) With regard to the subjects of law to which international criminal responsibility can be attributed, the Commission would like to have the views of the General Assembly on this point, because of the political nature of the problem;

"(c) With regard to the implementation of the code:

(i) Since some members consider that a code unaccompanied by penalties and by a competent criminal jurisdiction would be ineffective, the Commission requests the General Assembly to indicate whether the Commission's mandate extends to the preparation of the statute of a competent international criminal jurisdiction for individuals;

(ii) Moreover, in view of the prevailing opinion within the Commission, which endorses the principle of criminal responsibility in the case of States, the General Assembly should indicate whether such jurisdiction should also be competent with respect to States."[351]

The General Assembly, in resolution 38/132 of 19 December 1983, invited the Commission to continue its work on the elaboration of the draft code of offences against the peace and security of mankind by elaborating, as a first step, an introduction and a list of the offences in conformity with its report on the work of its thirty-fifth session.

At its thirty-sixth session, in 1984, the Commission proceeded to a general debate on the draft code on the basis of the second report[352] of the Special Rapporteur, which dealt with two questions, namely the offences covered by the 1954 draft and the offences classified since 1954. In its own report to the General Assembly on the work of that session, the Commission expressed its intention to limit the scope *ratione personae* of the draft code to the criminal responsibility of individuals, without prejudice to subsequent consideration of the possible application to States of the notion of international criminal responsibility, and to begin by drawing up a provisional list of offences while bearing in mind the drafting of an introduction summarizing the general principles of international criminal law relating to offences against the peace and security of mankind. The offences which were mentioned for possible inclusion in the code included, in addition to the offences covered in the 1954 draft,

---

[351] See *Yearbook of the International Law Commission, 1983*, vol. II (Part Two), para. 69.

[352] See *Yearbook of the International Law Commission, 1984*, vol. II (Part One), document A/CN.4/377.

colonialism, apartheid, serious damage to the human environment, economic aggression, the use of atomic weapons and mercenarism.[353]

At its thirty-ninth session, the General Assembly, in resolution 39/80 of 13 December 1984, requested the Commission to continue its work on the elaboration of the draft code of offences against the peace and security of mankind by elaborating an introduction as well as a list of the offences, taking into account the progress made at the thirty-sixth session of the Commission, as well as the views expressed during the thirty-ninth session of the General Assembly.

The Commission began the first reading of the draft code at its thirty-seventh session, in 1985. At its thirty-eighth session, in 1986, the Commission discussed again the problem of the implementation of the code and announced its intention to examine carefully any guidance that might be furnished on various possible options (system of territoriality, system of personality, universal system and system of international criminal jurisdiction).

At its thirty-ninth session, in 1987, the Commission recommended to the General Assembly that it amend the title of the topic in English so that it would read "Draft Code of Crimes against the Peace and Security of Mankind",[354] a recommendation which the General Assembly endorsed in its resolution 42/151 of 7 December 1987.

At its forty-third session, in 1991, the Commission adopted on first reading the draft Code of Crimes against the Peace and Security of Mankind, which included the following crimes: aggression; threat of aggression; intervention; colonial domination and other forms of alien domination; genocide; apartheid; systematic or mass violations of human rights; exceptionally serious war crimes; recruitment, use, financing and training of mercenaries; international terrorism; illicit traffic in narcotic drugs; and wilful and severe damage to the environment. The Commission decided to defer the questions of applicable penalties and the crimes which could involve an attempt until the second reading of the draft. The Commission noted that the draft Code constituted the first part of the Commission's work on the topic and that the Commission would continue its work on the question of an international criminal jurisdiction (*see sub-section (c) below*). In accordance with articles 16 and 21 of its Statute, the Commission decided to transmit the draft Code, through the

---

[353] See *Yearbook of the International Law Commission, 1984*, vol. II (Part Two), para. 65.
[354] See *Yearbook of the International Law Commission, 1987*, vol. II (Part Two), para. 65.

Secretary-General, to Governments for their comments and observations.[355]

The General Assembly, in resolution 46/54 of 9 December 1991, expressed its appreciation to the Commission for the completion of the provisional draft articles on the draft Code of Crimes against the Peace and Security of Mankind and urged Governments to present in writing their comments and observations on the draft, as requested by the Commission. The request to Governments for their comments and observations on the draft was reiterated by the General Assembly in resolution 47/33 of 25 November 1992. The General Assembly, in resolution 48/31 of 9 December 1993, requested the Commission to resume at its forty-sixth session the consideration of the draft Code.

At its forty-sixth session, in 1994, the Commission began the second reading of the draft code, which was completed at its next session, in 1995. The second reading was held on the basis of the twelfth and thirteenth reports of the Special Rapporteur[356] and in the light of the comments and observations received from Governments.[357] The twelfth report, considered by the Commission at its forty-sixth session, in 1994, focused only on the general part of the draft dealing with the definition of crimes against the peace and security of mankind, characterization and general principles. The Special Rapporteur also indicated his intention to limit the list of crimes to be considered during the second reading to offences whose characterization as crimes against the peace and security of mankind was hard to challenge. At that session, after considering the report, the Commission decided to refer the draft articles dealt with therein to the Drafting Committee, it being understood that the work on the draft code and on the draft statute for an international criminal court should be coordinated by the Special Rapporteur on the draft code and by the Chairman and members of the Drafting Committee and of the Working Group on a draft statute for an international criminal court (*see sub-section (c) below*).

At its forty-seventh session, in 1995, the Commission considered the thirteenth report of the Special Rapporteur. The Special Rapporteur had omitted from his report 6 of the 12 crimes included on first reading, namely: the threat of aggression; intervention; colonial domination and other forms of alien domination; apartheid; the recruitment, use, financing and training of mercenaries; and wilful

---

[355] See *Yearbook of the International Law Commission, 1991*, vol. II (Part Two), paras. 170-175.
[356] See *Yearbook of the International Law Commission, 1994*, vol. II (Part One), document A/CN.4/460; as well as document A/CN.4/466.
[357] See *Yearbook of the International Law Commission, 1993*, vol. II (Part One), document A/CN.4/448 and Add.1.

and severe damage to the environment, in response to the strong opposition, criticisms or reservations of certain Governments with respect to those crimes. Accordingly, the report focused on the remaining crimes contained in the draft code adopted on first reading, namely: aggression, genocide, systematic or mass violations of human rights, exceptionally serious war crimes, international terrorism and illicit traffic in narcotic drugs.[358] The Commission decided to refer to the Drafting Committee articles dealing with aggression, genocide, systematic or mass violations of human rights and exceptionally serious war crimes, on the understanding that the Drafting Committee, in formulating those articles, would bear in mind and at its discretion deal with all or part of the draft articles adopted on first reading concerning intervention; colonial domination and other forms of alien domination; apartheid; recruitment, use, financing and training of mercenaries; and international terrorism. The Commission also decided to continue consultations as regards articles dealing with illicit traffic in narcotic drugs, and wilful and severe damage to the environment. With respect to the latter, the Commission decided to establish a Working Group that would meet at the beginning of the forty-eighth session to examine the possibility of covering in the draft code the issue of wilful and severe damage to the environment.[359]

At the forty-eighth session of the Commission, in 1996, the Working Group examined this issue and proposed to the Commission that this crime be considered as a war crime, a crime against humanity or a separate crime against the peace and security of mankind. The Commission decided by a vote to refer to the Drafting Committee only the text prepared by the Working Group for inclusion of wilful and severe damage to the environment as a war crime.[360]

At the same session, the Commission adopted the final text of the draft Code of Crimes against the Peace and Security of Mankind, with commentaries,[361] consisting of 20 articles divided into two parts: Part One, General Provisions (articles 1-15) and Part Two, Crimes against the Peace and Security of Mankind (articles 16-20). Part One contains provisions relating to the scope and application of the Code (article 1), individual responsibility (article 2), punishment (article 3),

---

[358] See *Yearbook of the International Law Commission, 1995*, vol. II (Part Two), paras. 38 and 39.
[359] See *Yearbook of the International Law Commission, 1995*, vol. II (Part Two), para. 140.
[360] See *Yearbook of the International Law Commission, 1996*, vol. II (Part Two), paras. 43 and 44.
[361] See *Yearbook of the International Law Commission, 1996*, vol. II (Part Two), paras. 45 and 50.

responsibility of States (article 4), order of a Government or a superior (article 5), responsibility of the superior (article 6), official position and responsibility (article 7), establishment of jurisdiction (article 8), obligation to extradite or prosecute (article 9), extradition of alleged offenders (article 10), judicial guarantees (article 11), *non bis in idem* (article 12), non-retroactivity (article 13), defences (article 14), and extenuating circumstances (article 15). Part Two includes the following crimes: aggression (article 16), genocide (article 17), crimes against humanity (article 18), crimes against United Nations and associated personnel (article 19), and war crimes (article 20). The text of the draft Code as adopted in 1996 is reproduced in annex IV, section 3 (b).

The Commission adopted the draft Code with the following understanding:

> "with a view to reaching consensus, the Commission has considerably reduced the scope of the Code. On first reading in 1991, the draft Code comprised a list of 12 categories of crimes. Some members have expressed their regrets at the reduced scope of coverage of the Code. The Commission acted in response to the interest of adoption of the Code and of obtaining support by Governments. It is understood that the inclusion of certain crimes in the Code does not affect the status of other crimes under international law, and that the adoption of the Code does not in any way preclude the further development of this important area of law."[362]

As agreed to upon the adoption of the draft code on first reading, in 1991, the Commission returned to the questions of penalties and attempt during the second reading. With regard to penalties, the Commission decided to include a general provision indicating that the punishment of an individual for a crime against the peace and security of mankind must be commensurate with the character and gravity of the crime (article 3) rather than to provide specific penalties for each crime. With regard to attempt, the Commission decided to address individual criminal responsibility for attempt with respect to all of the crimes except aggression (article 2, paragraph 3(g)).

The Commission considered various forms which the draft Code of Crimes against the Peace and Security of Mankind could take, including an international convention adopted by a plenipotentiary conference or the General Assembly, incorporation of the Code in the statute of an international criminal court, or adoption of the Code as a

---

[362] See *Yearbook of the International Law Commission, 1996*, vol. II (Part Two), para. 46.

declaration by the General Assembly. The Commission recommended that the General Assembly select the most appropriate form which would ensure the widest possible acceptance of the draft Code.[363]

The General Assembly, in resolution 51/160 of 16 December 1996, expressed its appreciation to the Commission for the completion of the draft Code; drew the attention of the States participating in the Preparatory Committee on the Establishment of an International Criminal Court to the relevance of the draft Code to their work (*see page 101*); and requested the Secretary-General to invite Governments to submit, before the end of the fifty-third session of the General Assembly, their written comments and observations on action which might be taken in relation to the draft Code.

(c)   Draft Statute for an International Criminal Court

At its thirty-fifth session, in 1983, the Commission had before it the first report of the Special Rapporteur for the draft code which focused, inter alia, on the implementation of the code.[364] Following a general debate on the basis of this report, the Commission requested the General Assembly to indicate whether the Commission's mandate with respect to the draft code extended to the preparation of the statute of a competent international criminal jurisdiction for individuals since some members considered that a code unaccompanied by penalties and by a competent criminal jurisdiction would be ineffective.[365]

At its thirty-eighth session, in 1986, the Commission had before it the fourth report of the Special Rapporteur which addressed, inter alia, the implementation of the code.[366] After considering this report, the Commission indicated that it would examine carefully any guidance that might be furnished on the various options for the implementation of the code set out in its report and reminded the General Assembly of the conclusion concerning the ineffectiveness of a code unaccompanied by penalties and a competent jurisdiction contained in the report on the work of its thirty-fifth session, in 1983.[367]

---

[363] See *Yearbook of the International Law Commission, 1996*, vol. II (Part Two), paras. 47 and 48.
[364] See *Yearbook of the International Law Commission, 1983*, vol. II (Part One), document A/CN.4/364.
[365] See *Yearbook of the International Law Commission, 1983*, vol. II (Part Two), para. 69(c)(i).
[366] See *Yearbook of the International Law Commission, 1986*, vol. II (Part One), document A/CN.4/398.
[367] See *Yearbook of the International Law Commission, 1986*, vol. II (Part Two), para. 185.

From 1986 to 1989, the General Assembly requested the Secretary-General to seek the views of Members States regarding the Commission's conclusions concerning the implementation of the draft code.[368]

At its thirty-ninth session, in 1987, the Commission had before it the fifth report of the Special Rapporteur[369] which included draft article 4 on the *aut dedere aut punire* principle which was intended to fill the existing gap with regard to jurisdiction. The Commission considered issues relating to an international criminal court in the context of its discussion of draft article 4. The Commission referred the draft article to the Drafting Committee which was unable to formulate a text for article 4 due to lack of time.

At its fortieth session, in 1988, the Commission provisionally adopted draft article 4 (Obligation to try or extradite) which relied on national courts to enforce the code without ruling out the consideration of an international criminal court at a later stage.[370]

In 1989, the General Assembly considered a new agenda item entitled "International criminal responsibility of individuals and entities engaged in illicit trafficking in narcotic drugs across national frontiers and other transnational criminal activities: establishment of an international criminal court with jurisdiction over such crimes".[371] In resolution 44/39 of 4 December 1989, the Assembly requested the Commission, when considering at its forty-second session the draft code of crimes against the peace and security of mankind, to address the question of establishing an international criminal court or other international criminal trial mechanism with jurisdiction over persons alleged to have committed crimes which may be covered under such a code, including persons engaged in illicit trafficking in narcotic drugs across national frontiers, and to devote particular attention to that question in its report on that session.

At its forty-second session, in 1990, the Commission had before it the eighth report of the Special Rapporteur on the draft code, part three of which dealt with the statute of an international criminal court.[372] The Commission considered extensively the question of the

---

[368] See General Assembly resolutions 41/75 of 3 December 1986, 42/151 of 7 December 1987, 43/164 of 9 December 1988 and 44/32 of 4 December 1989.
[369] See *Yearbook of the International Law Commission, 1987*, vol. II (Part One), document A/CN.4/404.
[370] See *Yearbook of the International Law Commission, 1988*, vol. II (Part Two), paras. 213 and 280 (commentary to article 4).
[371] See *Official Records of the General Assembly, Forty-fourth Session, Annexes*, vol. II, agenda item 152, document A/44/195.
[372] See *Yearbook of the International Law Commission, 1990*, vol. II (Part One), document A/CN.4/430 and Add.1.

possible establishment of an international criminal jurisdiction for two main reasons: first, the question concerning the draft code's implementation and, in particular, the possible creation of an international criminal jurisdiction to enforce its provisions had always been foremost in the Commission's concerns regarding the topic, and, second, the specific request addressed to the Commission by the General Assembly in resolution 44/39 of 4 December 1989. After considering the report, the Commission decided to establish a Working Group to prepare a response by the Commission to the request by the Assembly.[373]

By its resolutions 45/41 of 28 November 1990 and 46/54 of 9 December 1991, the General Assembly invited the Commission, within the framework of the draft code, to consider further and analyse the issues raised in the report concerning the question of an international criminal jurisdiction.

From 1991 to 1993, the Special Rapporteur for the draft code submitted three reports which addressed issues relating to the question of an international criminal jurisdiction.[374]

At its forty-fourth session, in 1992, the Commission decided to set up a Working Group to consider further and analyse the main issues relating to the question of an international criminal jurisdiction. The Working Group, at the same session, drew up a report to the Commission, which contained, inter alia, a set of specific recommendations on a number of issues related to the possible establishment of an international criminal jurisdiction.[375] The structure suggested in the Working Group's report consisted, in essence, of an international criminal court established by a statute in the form of a multilateral treaty agreed to by States parties. The proposed court would, in the first phase of its operations, at least, exercise jurisdiction only over private persons, as distinct from States. Its jurisdiction should be limited to crimes of an international character defined in specified international treaties in force, including the crimes defined in the draft code of crimes against the peace and security of mankind upon its adoption and entry into force, but not limited thereto. A State should be able to become a party to the statute of the court without thereby becoming a party to the code. The court would be a facility for States parties to its statute (and also, on

---

[373] For the report of the Working Group, see document A/CN.4/L.454.
[374] See *Yearbook of the International Law Commission, 1991,* vol. II (Part One), document A/CN.4/435 and Add.1; ibid., *1992,* vol. II (Part One), document A/CN.4/442; and ibid., *1993,* vol. II (Part One), document A/CN.4/449.
[375] Document A/CN.4/L.471, reproduced in *Yearbook of the International Law Commission, 1992,* vol. II (Part Two), annex. See also *Yearbook of the International Law Commission, 1992,* vol. II (Part Two), para. 99.

defined terms, other States) which could be called into operation when and as soon as required and which, in the first phase of its operation, at least, should not have compulsory jurisdiction and would not be a standing full-time body. Furthermore, whatever the precise structure of the court or other mechanisms, it must guarantee due process, independence and impartiality in its procedures.[376]

The Commission noted, at the same session, that a structure along the lines suggested in the Working Group's report could be a workable system but that further work on the issue required a renewed mandate from the General Assembly to draft a statute, and that it was now for the General Assembly to decide whether the Commission should undertake the project for an international criminal jurisdiction, and on what basis.[377]

The General Assembly, in resolution 47/33 of 25 November 1992, took note with appreciation of the chapter of the report of the Commission on the work of its forty-fourth session, entitled "Draft Code of Crimes against the Peace and Security of Mankind", which was devoted to the question of the possible establishment of an international criminal jurisdiction; invited States to submit to the Secretary-General, if possible before the forty-fifth session of the Commission, written comments on the report of the Working Group on the question of an international criminal jurisdiction; and requested the Commission to continue its work on the question by undertaking the project for the elaboration of a draft statute for an international criminal court as a matter of priority as from its next session, beginning with an examination of the issues identified in the report of the Working Group and in the debate in the Sixth Committee with a view to drafting a statute on the basis of the report of the Working Group, taking into account the views expressed during the debate in the Sixth Committee as well as any written comments received from States, and to submit a progress report to the Assembly at its forty-eighth session.

At its forty-fifth session, in 1993, the Commission decided to reconvene the Working Group it had established at the previous session to continue its work, as requested by the General Assembly in resolution 47/33 as referred to above.[378] The Working Group prepared

---

[376] See *Yearbook of the International Law Commission, 1992,* vol. II (Part Two), para. 11 and annex, para. 4.
[377] See *Yearbook of the International Law Commission, 1992,* vol. II (Part Two), paras. 11 and 104.
[378] The Commission had before it comments of Governments on the report of the Working Group established at the previous session submitted pursuant to General Assembly resolution 47/33 (see *Yearbook of the International Law Commission, 1993,* vol. II (Part One), document A/CN.4/452 and Add.1-3.)

a preliminary draft statute for an international criminal court and commentaries thereto.[379] Though the Commission was not able to examine the draft articles in detail at the forty-fifth session and to proceed with their adoption, it felt that, in principle, the proposed draft articles provided a basis for examination by the General Assembly at its forty-eighth session. The Commission therefore decided to annex the report of the Working Group containing the draft statute to its report to the General Assembly. The Commission stated that it would welcome comments by the General Assembly and Member States on the specific questions referred to in the commentaries to the various articles, as well as on the draft articles as a whole. It furthermore decided that the draft articles should be transmitted, through the Secretary-General, to Governments for their comments.[380]

The General Assembly, in resolution 48/31 of 9 December 1993, took note with appreciation of chapter II of the report of the Commission on the work of its forty-fifth session, entitled "Draft Code of Crimes against the Peace and Security of Mankind", which was devoted to the question of a draft statute for an international criminal court; invited States to submit to the Secretary-General, as requested by the Commission, written comments on the draft articles proposed by the Working Group on a draft statute for an international criminal court; and requested the Commission to continue its work as a matter of priority on the question with a view to elaborating a draft statute, if possible at its forty-sixth session, in 1994, taking into account the views expressed during the debate in the Sixth Committee as well as any written comments received from States.

At its forty-sixth session, in 1994, the Commission decided to reestablish the Working Group on a draft statute for an international criminal court. The Working Group re-examined the preliminary draft statute for an international criminal court annexed to the Commission's report at the preceding session,[381] and prepared the draft statute,[382] taking into account, inter alia, the comments by Governments on the report of the Working Group submitted to the Commission at its previous session,[383] and the views expressed during

---

[379] For the revised report of the Working Group, see document A/CN.4/L.490 and Add.1 reproduced in *Yearbook of the International Law Commission, 1993,* vol. II (Part Two), annex.
[380] See *Yearbook of the International Law Commission, 1993,* vol. II (Part Two), paras. 99 and 100.
[381] See *Yearbook of the International Law Commission, 1993,* vol. II (Part Two), annex.
[382] For the final revised report of the Working Group, see document A/CN.4/L.491/Rev.2 and Add.1-3.
[383] See *Yearbook of the International Law Commission, 1994,* vol. II (Part One),

the debate in the Sixth Committee of the General Assembly at its forty-eighth session on the report of the International Law Commission on the work of its forty-fifth session.[384]

The draft statute consisted of 60 articles which were divided into eight main parts: Part One on Establishment of the Court; Part Two on Composition and Administration of the Court; Part Three on Jurisdiction of the Court; Part Four on Investigation and Prosecution; Part Five on the Trial; Part Six on Appeal and Review; Part Seven on International Cooperation and Judicial Assistance; and Part Eight on Enforcement. In drafting the statute, the Working Group did not purport to adjust itself to any specific criminal legal system but, rather, to amalgamate into a coherent whole the most appropriate elements for the goals envisaged, having regard to existing treaties, earlier proposals for an international court or tribunals and relevant provisions in national criminal justice systems within the different legal traditions. Careful note was also taken of the various provisions regulating the International Tribunal for the Prosecution of Persons Responsible for Serious Violations of International Humanitarian Law Committed in the Territory of the Former Yugoslavia since 1991. It was also noted that the Working Group conceived the statute for an international criminal court as an attachment to a future international convention on the matter and drafted the statute's provisions accordingly.[385]

The Commission adopted the draft Statute for an International Criminal Court, together with its commentaries,[386] prepared by the Working Group, and decided, in accordance with article 23 of its Statute, to recommend to the General Assembly that it convene an international conference of plenipotentiaries to study the draft statute and to conclude a convention on the establishment of an international criminal court.[387] The text of the draft statute is reproduced in annex IV, section 9.[388]

The General Assembly, in resolution 49/53 of 9 December 1994, welcomed the report of the Commission on the work of its forty-sixth session, including the recommendations contained therein, and

---

document A/CN.4/458 and Add.1-8.
[384] Document A/CN.4/457, section B.
[385] See *Yearbook of the International Law Commission, 1994*, vol. II (Part Two), paras. 84-86.
[386] See *Yearbook of the International Law Commission, 1994*, vol. II (Part Two), paras. 88 and 91.
[387] See *Yearbook of the International Law Commission, 1994*, vol. II (Part Two), para. 90.
[388] The draft statute adopted by the Commission is reproduced because of its historical significance and its relevance as part of the legislative history of the Rome Statute of the International Criminal Court.

decided to establish an ad hoc committee open to all States Members of the United Nations or members of specialized agencies to review the major substantive and administrative issues arising out of the draft statute prepared by the Commission and, in the light of that review, to consider arrangements for the convening of an international conference of plenipotentiaries. It also decided that the Ad Hoc Committee should submit its report to the General Assembly at the beginning of its fiftieth session in 1995. By the same resolution, the General Assembly invited States to submit to the Secretary-General written comments on the draft statute and requested the Secretary-General to invite such comments from relevant international organs. It further requested the Secretary-General to submit to the Ad Hoc Committee a preliminary report with provisional estimates of the staffing, structure and costs of the establishment and operation of an international criminal court. The General Assembly decided to include in the provisional agenda of its fiftieth session an item entitled "Establishment of an international criminal court", in order to study the report of the Ad Hoc Committee and the written comments submitted by States and to decide on the convening of the proposed international conference of plenipotentiaries, including its timing and duration.

The Ad Hoc Committee on the Establishment of an International Criminal Court met from 3 to 13 April and from 14 to 25 August 1995, during which time the Committee reviewed the issues arising out of the draft statute prepared by the Commission and considered arrangements for the convening of an international conference.[389]

The General Assembly, in resolution 50/46 of 11 December 1995, decided to establish a preparatory committee to discuss further the major substantive and administrative issues arising out of the draft statute prepared by the Commission and, taking into account the different views expressed during the meetings, to draft texts with a view to preparing a widely acceptable consolidated text of a convention for an international criminal court as a next step towards consideration by a conference of plenipotentiaries.

The Preparatory Committee on the Establishment of an International Criminal Court met from 25 March to 12 April and from 12 to 30 August 1996, during which time the Committee discussed further the issues arising out of the draft statute and began preparing a widely acceptable consolidated text of a convention for an international criminal court.[390]

---

[389] See *Official Records of the General Assembly, Fiftieth session, Supplement No. 22* (A/50/22).
[390] See *Official Records of the General Assembly, Fifty-first session, Supplement No.*

The General Assembly, in resolution 51/207 of 17 December 1996, decided to hold a diplomatic conference of plenipotentiaries in 1998 with a view to finalizing and adopting a convention on the establishment of an international criminal court. The Assembly also decided that the Preparatory Committee would meet in 1997 and 1998 in order to complete the drafting of the text for submission to the Conference.

The Preparatory Committee met from 11 to 21 February, from 4 to 15 August and from 1 to 12 December 1997, during which time the Committee continued to prepare a widely acceptable consolidated text of a convention for an international criminal court.[391]

The General Assembly, in resolution 52/160 of 15 December 1997, decided to hold the United Nations Diplomatic Conference of Plenipotentiaries on the Establishment of an International Criminal Court, open to all States Members of the United Nations or members of specialized agencies or of the International Atomic Energy Agency, at Rome from 15 June to 17 July 1998. In the same resolution, the General Assembly requested the Secretary-General to invite to the Conference the following organizations to participate as observers: organizations and other entities that had received a standing invitation from the Assembly pursuant to its relevant resolutions to participate as observers in its sessions and work, as well as interested regional intergovernmental organizations and other interested international bodies, including the International Tribunal for the Prosecution of Persons Responsible for Serious Violations of International Humanitarian Law Committed in the Territory of the Former Yugoslavia since 1991 and the International Criminal Tribunal for the Prosecution of Persons Responsible for Genocide and Other Serious Violations of International Humanitarian Law Committed in the Territory of Rwanda and Rwandan Citizens Responsible for Genocide and Other Such Violations Committed in the Territory of Neighbouring States, between 1 January 1994 and 31 December 1994. In addition, the Secretary-General was requested to invite to the Conference to participate in accordance with the resolution and the rules of procedure to be adopted by the Conference non-governmental organizations accredited by the Preparatory Committee with due regard to the provisions of part VII of Economic and Social Council resolution 1996/31 of 25 July 1996, and in particular to the relevance of their activities to the work of the Conference. The Assembly further requested the Preparatory

---

22 (A/51/22), vols. I and II.
[391] Documents A/AC.249/1997/L.5, A/AC.249/1997/L.8/Rev.1 and A/AC.249/1997/L.9/Rev.1.

Committee to continue its work in accordance with General Assembly resolution 51/207 and, at the end of its sessions, to transmit to the Conference the text of a draft convention on the establishment of an international criminal court prepared in accordance with its mandate.

The Preparatory Committee met from 16 March to 3 April 1998, during which time the Committee completed the preparation of the draft Statute of an International Criminal Court, which was transmitted to the Conference.[392]

The Conference met in Rome from 15 June to 17 July 1998.[393] It was attended by 160 States as well as by the observers of the Palestine Liberation Organization, sixteen intergovernmental organizations and other entities, five specialized agencies and related organizations, and nine United Nations programmes and bodies. Furthermore, representatives of 135 non-governmental organizations participated in the work of the Conference in accordance with General Assembly resolution 52/160 of 15 December 1997.

The Conference had before it the draft Statute which was assigned to the Committee of the Whole for its consideration. The Conference entrusted the Drafting Committee, without reopening substantive discussion on any matter, with coordinating and refining the drafting of all texts referred to it without altering their substance, formulating drafts and giving advice on drafting as requested by the Conference or by the Committee of the Whole and reporting to the Conference or to the Committee of the Whole as appropriate.

On 17 July 1998, the Conference adopted the Rome Statute of the International Criminal Court[394] which consists of a preamble and 128 articles contained in thirteen parts: Part 1. Establishment of the Court; Part 2. Jurisdiction, Admissibility and Applicable Law; Part 3. General Principles of Criminal Law; Part 4. Composition and Administration of the Court; Part 5. Investigation and Prosecution; Part. 6. The Trial; Part 7. Penalties; Part 8. Appeal and Revision; Part 9. International Cooperation and Judicial Assistance; Part 10.

---

[392] See *Official Records of the United Nations Diplomatic Conference of Plenipotentiaries on the Establishment of an International Criminal Court, Rome, 15 June-17 July 1998*, vol. III, Reports and other documents (United Nations publication, Sales No. 02.I.5), document A/CONF.183/2/Add.1.

[393] For the Final Act of the Conference, see *Official Records of the United Nations Diplomatic Conference of Plenipotentiaries on the Establishment of an International Criminal Court, Rome, 15 June-17 July 1998*, vol. I, Final documents (United Nations publication, Sales No. 02.I.5), document A/CONF.183/10.

[394] See *Official Records of the United Nations Diplomatic Conference of Plenipotentiaries on the Establishment of an International Criminal Court, Rome, 15 June-17 July 1998*, vol. I, Final documents (United Nations publication, Sales No. 02.I.5), document A/CONF.183/9.

Enforcement; Part 11. Assembly of States Parties; Part 12. Financing; and Part 13. Final Clauses.

The Statute, which is subject to ratification, acceptance or approval, was opened for signature on 17 July 1998, in accordance with its provisions, until 17 October 1998 at the Ministry of Foreign Affairs of Italy and, subsequently, until 31 December 2000, at United Nations Headquarters in New York. It remains open for accession by all States. The Rome Statute entered into force on 1 July 2002. As of 19 November 2003, ninety-two States had ratified the Rome Statute.[395]

The Final Act of the Conference,[396] of which six resolutions adopted by the Conference form an integral part, was signed on 17 July 1998. In one of the resolutions, resolution E, the Conference recommended that a review conference pursuant to article 123 of the Rome Statute consider the crimes of terrorism and drug crimes with a view to arriving at an acceptable definition and their inclusion in the list of crimes within the jurisdiction of the Court. By another resolution, resolution F, the Conference established the Preparatory Commission for the International Criminal Court consisting of representatives of States-signatories of the Final Act and other States which had been invited to participate in the Conference. The Preparatory Commission was entrusted with the preparation of a number of proposals for the practical arrangements for the establishment and coming into operation of the Court, including the draft texts of the rules of procedure and evidence and of the elements of crimes, as well as proposals for a provision on aggression *(see subsection (d) below)*.

In successive resolutions adopted from 1998 to 2001, the General Assembly requested the Secretary-General to convene and reconvene the Preparatory Commission to carry out its mandate set forth in Resolution F and, in that connection, to discuss ways to enhance the effectiveness and acceptance of the Court. The General Assembly also requested the Secretary-General to invite, as observers to the Preparatory Commission, representatives of organizations and other entities that have received a standing invitation from the General Assembly, pursuant to its relevant resolutions,[397] to participate in the

---

[395] The Rome Statute of the International Criminal Court is not reproduced in the annexes of this publication since it was adopted on the basis of the text of the Preparatory Committee which further elaborated the Commission's draft statute for an international criminal court.

[396] See *Official Records of the United Nations Diplomatic Conference of Plenipotentiaries on the Establishment of an International Criminal Court, Rome, 15 June-17 July 1998*, vol. I, Final documents (United Nations publication, Sales No. 02.I.5), document A/CONF.183/10.

[397] Resolutions 253 (III), 477 (V), 2011 (XX), 3208 (XXIX), 3237 (XXIX), 3369

capacity of observers in its sessions and work, and also to invite as observers to the Preparatory Commission representatives of interested regional intergovernmental organizations and other interested international bodies, including the International Tribunal for the Prosecution of Persons Responsible for Serious Violations of International Humanitarian Law Committed in the Territory of the Former Yugoslavia since 1991 and the International Criminal Tribunal for the Prosecution of Persons Responsible for Genocide and Other Serious Violations of International Humanitarian Law Committed in the Territory of Rwanda and Rwandan Citizens Responsible for Genocide and Other Such Violations Committed in the Territory of Neighbouring States, between 1 January 1994 and 31 December 1994. The General Assembly further noted that non-governmental organizations could participate in the work of the Preparatory Commission in accordance with the rules of procedure of the Commission.[398]

From 1999 to 2002, the Preparatory Commission held ten sessions during which it prepared a number of proposals relating to the establishment and operation of the Court, including the draft Rules of Procedure and Evidence and the draft Elements of Crimes, which were transmitted to the Assembly of States Parties to the Rome Statute of the International Criminal Court.[399]

The General Assembly, in resolution 56/85 of 12 December 2001, requested the Secretary-General to make the preparations

---

(XXX), 31/3, 33/18, 35/2, 35/3, 36/4, 42/10, 43/6, 44/6, 45/6, 46/8, 47/4, 48/2, 48/3, 48/4, 48/5, 48/237, 48/265, 49/1, 49/2, 50/2, 51/1, 51/6, 51/204, 52/6, 53/5, 53/6, 53/216, 54/5, 54/10, 54/195, 55/160 and 55/161.

[398] See General Assembly resolutions 53/105 of 8 December 1998, 54/105 of 9 December 1999, 55/155 of 12 December 2000 and 56/85 of 12 December 2001.

[399] See Proceedings of the Preparatory Commission at its first, second and third sessions (16-26 February, 26 July-13 August and 29 November-17 December 1999) (document PCNICC/1999/L.5/Rev.1 and Add.1 and 2); Proceedings of the Preparatory Commission at its fourth session (13-31 March 2000) (document PCNICC/2000/L.1/Rev.1 and Add.1 and Add.2); Proceedings of the Preparatory Commission at its fifth session (12-30 June 2000) (document PCNICC/2000/L.3/Rev.1); Proceedings of the Preparatory Commission at its sixth session (27 November-8 December 2000) (document PCNICC/2000/L.4/Rev.1 and Add.1-3); Proceedings of the Preparatory Commission at its seventh session (26 February-9 March 2001) (document PCNICC/2001/L.1/ Rev.1 and Add.1-3); Proceedings of the Preparatory Commission at its eighth session (24 September-5 October 2001) (document PCNICC/ 2001/L.3/Rev.1 and Add.1); Proceedings of the Preparatory Commission at its ninth session (8-19 April 2002) (document PCNICC/2002/L.1/Rev.1 and Add.1 and 2); and Proceedings of the Preparatory Commission at its tenth session (1-12 July 2002) (document PCNICC/2002/L.4/Rev.1); as well as Report of the Preparatory Commission for the International Criminal Court (contained in documents PCNICC/2000/1 and Add.1 and 2; PCNICC/2001/1 and Add.1-4; PCNICC/2002/1 and Add.1 and 2; and PCNICC/2002/2 and Add.1-3). See also a Guide to the Report of the Preparatory Commission prepared by the Secretariat (document PCNICC/2002/3 and Corr.1).

necessary to convene, in accordance with article 112, paragraph 1, of the Rome Statute,[400] the Assembly of States Parties upon the entry into force of the Rome Statute. The General Assembly noted that the United Nations and the Secretary-General may participate, without the right to vote, in the work of the Assembly of States Parties. The General Assembly requested the Secretary-General to invite, as observers to the meeting of the Assembly of States Parties, representatives of intergovernmental organizations and other entities that have received a standing invitation from the General Assembly, pursuant to its relevant resolutions,[401] to participate in the capacity of observers in its sessions and work, and also to invite as observers to the Assembly representatives of interested regional intergovernmental organizations and other international bodies invited to the Rome Conference or accredited to the Preparatory Commission for the International Criminal Court. The General Assembly also noted that non-governmental organizations invited to the Rome Conference, registered to the Preparatory Commission for the International Criminal Court or having consultative status with the Economic and Social Council of the United Nations whose activities are relevant to the activities of the Court may participate in the work of the Assembly of States Parties in accordance with agreed rules.

At its first session, in 2002, the Assembly of States Parties considered the report of the Preparatory Commission and adopted a number of instruments based on the drafts prepared by the Preparatory Commission, including the Rules of Procedure and Evidence and the Elements of Crimes.[402]

(d) Crime of aggression

Article 5 of the Rome Statute of the International Criminal Court provides that the Court shall exercise jurisdiction over the crime of aggression once a provision has been adopted defining the crime and setting out the conditions for the exercise of jurisdiction with respect to this crime. Such a provision must be consistent with the Charter of the United Nations.[403]

---

[400] As mentioned above, the Rome Statute entered into force on 1 July 2002.

[401] Resolutions 253 (III), 477 (V), 2011 (XX), 3208 (XXIX), 3237 (XXIX), 3369 (XXX), 31/3, 33/18, 35/2, 35/3, 36/4, 42/10, 43/6, 44/6, 45/6, 46/8, 47/4, 48/2, 48/3, 48/4, 48/5, 48/237, 48/265, 49/1, 49/2, 50/2, 51/1, 51/6, 51/204, 52/6, 53/5, 53/6, 53/216, 54/5, 54/10, 54/195, 55/160 and 55/161.

[402] See *Official Records of the Assembly of States Parties to the Rome Statute of the International Criminal Court, First Session, New York, 3-10 September 2002* (ICC-ASP/1/3, United Nations publication, Sales No. 03.V.2), paras. 16-23.

[403] See *Official Records of the United Nations Diplomatic Conference of Plenipotentiaries on the Establishment of an International Criminal Court, Rome, 15*

The Rome Conference, which adopted the Statute, also adopted resolution F on the establishment of the Preparatory Commission for the International Criminal Court, which was annexed to the Final Act of the Conference (*see page 104*).[404] The Preparatory Commission was entrusted with the preparation of proposals for a provision on aggression, including the definition and the elements of the crime of aggression as well as the conditions under which the International Criminal Court will exercise its jurisdiction with regard to this crime. The proposals are to be submitted to the Assembly of States Parties of the Court at a review conference, with a view to arriving at an acceptable provision on the crime of aggression for inclusion in the Statute. The provisions relating to the crime of aggression will enter into force for the States Parties in accordance with the relevant provisions of the Statute.[405]

The Preparatory Commission considered the crime of aggression at its second to tenth sessions held from 1999 to 2002.[406] At its second session, in 1999, the Preparatory Commission agreed to establish the Working Group on the Crime of Aggression at its next session.[407] At its tenth session, the Preparatory Commission agreed to include in its report to the Assembly of States Parties the discussion paper[408] on the

June-17 July 1998, vol. I, Final documents (United Nations publication, Sales No. 02.I.5), document A/CONF.183/9, article 5.

[404] See *Official Records of the United Nations Diplomatic Conference of Plenipotentiaries on the Establishment of an International Criminal Court, Rome, 15 June-17 July 1998*, vol. I, Final documents (United Nations publication, Sales No. 02.I.5), document A/CONF.183/10, Annex I, F.

[405] Rome Statute, articles 121 and 123.

[406] See Proceedings of the Preparatory Commission at its first, second and third sessions (16-26 February, 26 July-13 August and 29 November-17 December 1999) (document PCNICC/1999/L.5/Rev.1, paras. 12, 15, 16 and 20); Proceedings of the Preparatory Commission at its fourth session (13-31 March 2000) (document PCNICC/2000/L.1/Rev.1, paras. 9 and 11); Proceedings of the Preparatory Commission at its fifth session (12-30 June 2000) (document PCNICC/2000/L.3/Rev.1, paras. 9 and 12); Proceedings of the Preparatory Commission at its sixth session (27 November-8 December 2000) (document PCNICC/2000/L.4/Rev.1, paras. 10 and 11); Proceedings of the Preparatory Commission at its seventh session (26 February-9 March 2001) (document PCNICC/2001/L.1/Rev.1, paras. 9, 11 and 14); Proceedings of the Preparatory Commission at its eighth session (24 September-5 October 2001) (document PCNICC/2001/L.3/Rev.1, paras. 10, 11 and 14); Proceedings of the Preparatory Commission at its ninth session (8-19 April 2002) (document PCNICC/2002/L.1/Rev.1, para. 14); Proceedings of the Preparatory Commission at its tenth session (1-12 July 2002) (document PCNICC/2002/L.4/Rev.1, paras. 9, 10 and 16); and Report of the Preparatory Commission for the International Criminal Court (document PCNICC/2002/2, paras. 8 and 9 as well as document PCNICC/2002/2/Add.2).

[407] See Proceedings of the Preparatory Commission at its first, second and third sessions (16-26 February, 26 July-13 August and 29 November-17 December 1999) (document PCNICC/1999/L.5/Rev.1), para. 16.

[408] Document PCNICC/2002/WGCA/RT.1/Rev.2.

definition and elements of the crime of aggression prepared by the Coordinator of the Working Group, together with a list of all proposals and related documents on the crime of aggression issued by the Preparatory Commission as well as the historical review of developments relating to aggression[409] prepared by the Secretariat for transmission to the Assembly of States Parties.[410]

The General Assembly, in resolutions 55/155 of 12 December 2000 and 56/85 of 12 December 2001, noted the importance of the growing participation in the work of the Working Group on the Crime of Aggression.

At its first session, in September 2002, the Assembly of States Parties adopted a resolution on the continuity of work in respect of the crime of aggression, by which it took the following decisions: (1) a special working group on the crime of aggression shall be established, open on an equal footing to all States Members of the United Nations or members of specialized agencies or of the International Atomic Energy Agency, for the purpose of elaborating the proposals for a provision on aggression in accordance with the Rome Statute (article 5, paragraph 2) and Resolution F (paragraph 7); (2) the special working group shall submit such proposals to the Assembly for consideration at a Review Conference; and (3) the special working group shall meet during the regular sessions of the Assembly or at any other time that the Assembly deems appropriate and feasible.[411] The Assembly subsequently decided that the Special Working Group on the Crime of Aggression should meet during annual sessions of the Assembly, while leaving open the possibility of informal inter-sessional meetings depending upon the availability of funding for such a meeting by any Government wishing to do so.[412]

At its second session, in 2003, the Assembly of States Parties took note of the oral report of the Chairman of the Special Working Group on the Crime of Aggression and decided, as recommended by the Chairman, to annex to its report the discussion paper on the definition and elements of the crime of aggression prepared by the

---

[409] Document PCNICC/2002/WGCA/L.1 and Add.1 reproduced in "Historical Review of Developments relating to Agression" (United Nations publication, Sales No. E.03.V.10).

[410] See Report of the Preparatory Commission for the International Criminal Court (document PCNICC/2002/2, para. 9, as well as document PCNICC/2002/2/Add.2).

[411] Resolution ICC-ASP/1/Res.1 of 9 September 2002. See *Official Records of the Assembly of States Parties to the Rome Statute of the International Criminal Court, First Session, New York, 3-10 September 2002* (ICC-ASP/1/3, United Nations publication, Sales No. 03.V.2), p. 328.

[412] See *Official Records of the Assembly of States Parties to the Rome Statute of the International Criminal Court, First Session (First and Second Resumptions), New York, 3-7 February and 21-23 April 2003* (ICC-ASP/1/3/Add.1, United Nations publication, Sales No. 03.V.8), paras. 37 and 38.

Coordinator of the Working Group on the Crime of Aggression during the Preparatory Commission.[413]

8.   Nationality, including statelessness

At its first session, in 1949, the Commission selected nationality including statelessness as a topic for codification without, however, including it in the list of topics to which it gave priority.

During its second session, in 1950, the Commission was notified of resolution 304 D (XI) of the Economic and Social Council on the nationality of married women, adopted on 17 July 1950, in which the Council proposed that the Commission undertake the drafting of a convention, embodying the principles recommended by the Commission on the Status of Women. After considering the resolution, the Commission deemed it appropriate to entertain the proposal of the Council in connection with its work on the topic of nationality, including statelessness.

At its third session, in 1951, the Commission was notified of another resolution of the Economic and Social Council, resolution 319 B III (XI) of 11 August 1950, urging the Commission to prepare at the earliest possible date a draft international convention or conventions for the elimination of statelessness. The Commission noted that this matter could be considered within the framework of the topic of nationality, including statelessness. At the same session, the Commission decided to initiate work on this topic.

The Commission considered the topic from its third session, in 1951, to its sixth session, in 1954. It appointed Manley O. Hudson and Roberto Córdova as the successive Special Rapporteurs for the topic at its third and fourth sessions, in 1951 and 1952, respectively. At the latter session, the Commission also invited Dr. Ivan S. Kerno to serve as an individual expert of the Commission on the question of elimination or reduction of statelessness. In connection with its work on this topic, the Commission had before it the reports of the Special

---

[413] See *Official Records of the Assembly of States Parties to the Rome Statute of the International Criminal Court, Second Session, New York, 8-12 September 2003* (ICC-ASP/2/10, United Nations publication, Sales No. 03.V.13), para. 44.

Rapporteurs,[414] comments by Governments,[415] documents prepared by the Secretariat[416] as well as memoranda prepared by the expert.[417]

(a) Nationality of married persons

At its fourth session, in 1952, the Special Rapporteur submitted to the Commission, as a part of his report on nationality, including statelessness, a draft of a convention on nationality of married persons.[418] The draft followed very closely the terms proposed by the Commission on the Status of Women and approved by the Economic and Social Council. The Commission, however, decided that the question of the nationality of married women could not suitably be considered by it separately but only in the context, and as an integral part, of the whole subject of nationality. The Commission therefore did not take further action with respect to the draft.[419]

The problem of the nationality of married women continued to be under consideration by other organs of the United Nations. In 1955, the General Assembly took note of the preamble and the first three substantive articles of the draft Convention on the Nationality of Married Women, which had been drafted by the Commission on the Status of Women. After the final clauses of the draft Convention were prepared by the Third (Social) Committee, the Assembly, by resolution 1040 (XI) of 29 January 1957, adopted the Convention, which came into force on 11 August 1958.[420]

(b) Future statelessness

At its fourth session, in 1952, the Commission also had before it, as a part of the report submitted by the Special Rapporteur, Mr. Hudson, a

---

[414] For the report of Manley O. Hudson, see *Yearbook of the International Law Commission, 1952,* vol. II, document A/CN.4/50; and for the reports of Roberto Córdova, see ibid., *1953,* vol. II, documents A/CN.4/64 and A/CN.4/75; and ibid., *1954,* vol. II, documents A/CN.4/81 and A/CN.4/83.

[415] Document A/CN.4/82 and Add.1-8 reproduced in *Yearbook of the International Law Commission, 1954,* vol. II, document A/2693, annex.

[416] See *Yearbook of the International Law Commission, 1950,* vol. II, document A/CN.4/33; ibid., *1951,* vol. II, document A/CN.4/47; and ibid., *1954,* vol. II, documents A/CN.4/81 and A/CN.4/84; as well as document A/CN.4/56 and Add.1. In addition, the Secretariat published a volume in the *United Nations Legislative Series* entitled *"Laws Concerning Nationality"* (ST/LEG/SER.B/4, United Nations publication, Sales No. 1954.V.1) and supplement thereto (ST/LEG/SER.B/9, United Nations publication, Sales No. 59.V.3).

[417] Documents A/CN.4/66 and A/CN.4/67.

[418] See *Yearbook of the International Law Commission, 1952,* vol. II, document A/CN.4/50, annex II.

[419] See *Yearbook of the International Law Commission, 1952,* vol. II, document A/2163, para. 30.

[420] United Nations, *Treaty Series,* vol. 309, p. 65.

working paper dealing with statelessness.[421] The Commission then requested the Special Rapporteur to prepare, for consideration at its fifth session, a draft convention on the elimination of statelessness and one or more draft conventions on the reduction of future statelessness.

At its fifth session, in 1953, on the basis of a report containing draft articles submitted by the new Special Rapporteur, Mr. Córdova,[422] the Commission adopted on first reading two draft conventions, one on the elimination of future statelessness and another on the reduction of future statelessness, which were then transmitted to Governments for comment.

At its sixth session, in 1954, the Commission discussed the observations made by Governments on the two draft conventions and redrafted some of the articles in the light of their comments. At the same session, the Commission adopted the final drafts of both conventions.[423] In submitting these final drafts to the General Assembly, the Commission said:

"The most common observation made by Governments was that some provisions of their legislation conflicted with certain articles of the draft conventions. Since statelessness is, however, attributable precisely to the presence of those provisions in municipal law, the Commission took the view that this was not a decisive objection for, if Governments adopted the principle of the elimination, or at least the reduction, of statelessness in the future, they should be prepared to introduce the necessary amendments in their legislation."[424]

The draft conventions, each consisting of eighteen articles, aimed, on the one hand, at facilitating the acquisition of the nationality of a country by birth within its borders and, on the other hand, at avoiding the loss of a nationality except when another nationality was acquired. The convention on the elimination of future statelessness (the draft of which is reproduced in annex IV, section 4), would impose stricter obligations on the contracting parties than the one which had the more modest aim of merely reducing statelessness. The Commission stated in its report that it would be for the General

---

[421] See *Yearbook of the International Law Commission, 1952*, vol. II, document A/CN.4/50, annex III.
[422] See *Yearbook of the International Law Commission, 1953*, vol. II, document A/CN.4/64.
[423] See *Yearbook of the International Law Commission, 1954*, vol. II, document A/2693, para. 25.
[424] See *Yearbook of the International Law Commission, 1954*, vol. II, document A/2693, para. 12.

Assembly to consider to which of the draft conventions preference should be given.[425]

At the Assembly's 1954 session, the majority of representatives in the Sixth Committee expressed the opinion that the time was not ripe for immediate consideration of the substance of the draft conventions and that the positions of Member States with respect to the draft conventions had not yet been sufficiently ascertained. The Sixth Committee, however, approved a draft resolution under which the General Assembly would express "its desire that an international conference of plenipotentiaries be convened to conclude a convention for the reduction or elimination of future statelessness as soon as at least twenty States have communicated to the Secretary-General their willingness to cooperate in such a conference". This resolution was subsequently adopted by the General Assembly on 4 December 1954 as resolution 896 (IX).

The United Nations Conference on the Elimination or Reduction of Future Statelessness[426] met at Geneva from 24 March to 18 April 1959, with representatives of thirty-five States participating. The Conference decided to use as the basis for its discussion the draft convention on the reduction of future statelessness — one of the two drafts prepared by the International Law Commission — and adopted provisions aimed at reducing statelessness at birth.

It did not, however, reach agreement as to how to limit the freedom of States to deprive citizens of their nationality in cases where such deprivation would render them stateless. Consequently, the Conference recommended to the competent organs of the United Nations that it be reconvened at the earliest possible time in order to complete its work.

The second part of the Conference, in which representatives of thirty States participated, met in New York from 15 to 28 August 1961. The Conference adopted the Convention on the Reduction of Statelessness,[427] which was opened for signature from 30 August 1961 to 31 May 1962. Signatures are subject to ratification. The Convention is open for accession by any non-signatory State entitled to become a party. The Convention, which is reproduced in annex V, section B, entered into force on 13 December 1975. By 3 October 2003, twenty-seven States were parties to the Convention.

---

[425] See *Yearbook of the International Law Commission, 1954*, vol. II, document A/2693, para. 14.

[426] For the Final Act of the Conference, see document A/CONF.9/14.

[427] United Nations, *Treaty Series*, vol. 989, p. 175.

(c)   Present statelessness

At its fifth session, in 1953, the Special Rapporteur, Mr. Córdova, prepared an interim report and drafts of conventions bearing on the problem of the elimination or reduction of existing statelessness.[428] The Commission requested the Special Rapporteur to devote further study to the matter and prepare a report for the Commission's sixth session, in 1954.

At its sixth session, in 1954, the Commission had before it the report of the Special Rapporteur,[429] containing four draft instruments dealing with elimination or reduction of present statelessness. In the course of the Commission's consideration of the report, the Special Rapporteur withdrew three of the proposed drafts. The Commission accepted as the basis of its discussion the fourth draft instrument proposed by the Special Rapporteur, the Alternative Convention on the Reduction of Present Statelessness.

The Commission considered that it was not feasible to suggest measures for the total and immediate elimination of present statlessness and that present statelessness could only be reduced if stateless persons acquired a nationality which would normally be that of the country of residence. Since, however, the acquisition of nationality is in all countries governed by certain statutory conditions, including residence qualifications, the Commission considered that for the purpose of improving the condition of statelessness it would be desirable that stateless persons should be given the special status of "protected person" in their country of residence prior to the acquisition of nationality. Stateless persons possessing this status would have all civil rights, and would also be entitled to the diplomatic protection of the Government of the country of residence; the protecting State might impose on them the same obligations as it imposed on nationals.[430]

At the same session, the Commission formulated its proposals accordingly and adopted them in the form of seven articles with commentaries.[431] They were submitted to the General Assembly as part of its final report on nationality, including statelessness. In submitting the proposals, the Commission said: "In view of the great difficulties of a non-legal nature which beset the problem of present

---

[428] See *Yearbook of the International Law Commission, 1953*, vol. II, document A/CN.4/75.

[429] See *Yearbook of the International Law Commission, 1954*, vol. II, document A/CN.4/81.

[430] See *Yearbook of the International Law Commission, 1954*, vol. II, document A/2693, paras. 29 and 31.

[431] See *Yearbook of the International Law Commission, 1954*, vol. II, document A/2693, paras. 26-37.

statelessness, the Commission considered that the proposals adopted, though worded in the form of articles, should merely be regarded as suggestions which Governments may wish to take into account when attempting a solution of this urgent problem."[432]

(d) Multiple nationality

At its sixth session, in 1954, the Commission held a general discussion on the subject of multiple nationality and had before it a report of the Special Rapporteur, Mr. Córdova,[433] and a memorandum by the Secretariat[434] on this subject. Several members expressed the opinion that the Commission should content itself with the work it had done so far in the field of nationality, and the Commission thereupon decided to "defer any further consideration of multiple nationality and other questions relating to nationality".[435]

The Commission returned to the question of nationality in the context of its work on the topic of nationality in relation to the succession of States (*see Part III.A, section 24*).

9. Law of the sea

(a) Regime of the high seas

At its first session, in 1949, the Commission selected the regime of the high seas as a topic for codification to which it gave priority and appointed J. P. A. François as Special Rapporteur for it.

The Commission considered this topic at its second, third, fifth, seventh and eighth sessions, in 1950, 1951, 1953, 1955 and 1956, respectively. In connection with its work on the topic, the Commission had before it the reports of the Special Rapporteur,[436]

---

[432] See *Yearbook of the International Law Commission, 1954*, vol. II, document A/2693, para. 36. The draft articles to be regarded as suggestions are not reproduced in the annexes of this publication.
[433] See *Yearbook of the International Law Commission, 1954*, vol. II, document A/CN.4/83.
[434] See *Yearbook of the International Law Commission, 1954*, vol. II, document A/CN.4/84.
[435] See *Yearbook of the International Law Commission, 1954*, vol. II, document A/2693, para. 39.
[436] See *Yearbook of the International Law Commission, 1950*, vol. II, document A/CN.4/17; ibid., *1951*, vol. II, document A/CN.4/42; ibid., *1952*, vol. II, document A/CN.4/51; ibid., *1953*, vol. II, documents A/CN.4/60 and A/CN.4/69; ibid., *1954*, vol. II, document A/CN.4/79; and ibid., *1956*, vol. II, documents A/CN.4/97 and A/CN.4/103.

information provided by Governments and international organizations[437] as well as documents prepared by the Secretariat.[438]

At its second session, in 1950, the Commission surveyed the various questions falling within the scope of the general topic of the regime of the high seas, e.g., nationality of ships, safety of life at sea, slave trade, submarine telegraph cables, resources of the high seas, right of pursuit, right of approach, contiguous zones, sedentary fisheries and the continental shelf.

At its third session, in 1951, the Commission, on the basis of the second report of the Special Rapporteur,[439] provisionally adopted draft articles on the following subjects: the continental shelf; resources of the sea; sedentary fisheries; and contiguous zone.

At its fifth session, in 1953, the Commission, after examining these provisional draft articles once again in the light of comments of Governments, prepared final drafts on the following three questions: continental shelf; fisheries; and contiguous zone. The Commission recommended that the Assembly adopt by resolution the part of the report covering the draft articles on the continental shelf.[440] In respect of the draft articles on fisheries, the Commission recommended that the General Assembly should approve the articles by resolution and enter into consultation with the Food and Agriculture Organization of the United Nations with a view to the preparation of a convention or conventions on the subject in conformity with the general principles embodied in the articles.[441] As the Commission had not yet adopted draft articles on the territorial sea, it recommended that the General

---

[437] See *Yearbook of the International Law Commission, 1950*, vol. II, document A/CN.4/19; ibid., *1953*, vol. II, document A/CN.4/70; ibid., *1954*, vol. II, document A/CN.4/86; and ibid., *1956*, vol. II, documents A/CN.4/97/Add.1 and Add.3, A/CN.4/99 and Add.1 to 9 and A/CN.4/100; as well as document A/CN.4/55 and Add.1, Add.1/Rev.1 and Add.2-6 incorporated in *Yearbook of the International Law Commission, 1953*, vol. II, document A/2456, annex II.

[438] See *Yearbook of the International Law Commission, 1950*, vol. II, documents A/CN.4/30 and A/CN.4/32; and document A/CN.4/38. In addition, the Secretariat published volumes in the *United Nations Legislative Series* entitled *"Laws and Regulations on the Regime of the High Seas"* (volume I of which covers laws and regulations relating to continental shelf, contiguous zones and supervision of foreign vessels on the high seas (ST/LEG/SER.B/1, United Nations publications, Sales No. 1951.V.2) and volume II covers laws relating to jurisdiction over crimes committed abroad or on the high seas (ST/LEG/SER.B/2, United Nations publications, Sales No. 1952.V.1)) and *"Laws Concerning the Nationality of Ships"* (ST/LEG/SER.B/5 and Add.1, United Nations publication, Sales No. 1956.V.1) as well as a supplement to those volumes (ST/LEG/SER.B/8, United Nations publication, Sales No. 59.V.2).

[439] See *Yearbook of the International Law Commission, 1951*, vol. II, document A/CN.4/42.

[440] See *Yearbook of the International Law Commission, 1953*, vol. II, document A/2456, paras. 62 and 91.

[441] See *Yearbook of the International Law Commission, 1953*, vol. II, document A/2456, paras. 94 and 102.

Assembly take no action with regard to the draft article on the contiguous zone, since the report covering the article was already published.[442]

The General Assembly, by resolution 798 (VIII) of 7 December 1953, decided to defer action until all the problems relating to the regime of the high seas and the regime of territorial waters had been studied by the Commission and reported upon by it to the Assembly. The question of the continental shelf was again brought before the Assembly at its ninth session, in 1954, by ten Member States, which asked the Assembly to avoid undue delay in giving substantive consideration to the question. By resolution 899 (IX) of 14 December 1954, the Assembly again deferred action and requested the Commission to submit its final report on the regime of the high seas, the regime of territorial waters and all related problems in time for their consideration by the Assembly at its eleventh session, in 1956.

At its seventh session, in 1955, the Commission considered certain subjects concerning the high seas which had not been dealt with in its 1953 report and adopted, on the basis of the Special Rapporteur's sixth report,[443] a provisional draft on the regime of the high seas, which was submitted to Governments for comments. The Commission also communicated the draft articles relating to the conservation of the living resources of the sea, which comprised a part of the provisionally adopted draft on the regime of the high seas, and the relevant chapter of its report to the organizations represented by observers at the International Technical Conference on the Conservation of the Living Resources of the Sea, which was convened by the Secretary-General in pursuance of General Assembly resolution 900 (IX) of 14 December 1954 and was held at Rome from 18 April to 10 May 1955. In preparing the articles dealing with the conservation of the living resources of the sea, the Commission took account of the report of that Conference.[444] At its eighth session, in 1956, the Commission examined replies from Governments and from the International Commission for the Northwest Atlantic Fisheries and drew up a final report on the subjects relating to the high seas, which was incorporated by the Commission in its consolidated draft on the law of the sea (*see subsection (c) below*).

---

[442] See *Yearbook of the International Law Commission, 1953*, vol. II, document A/2456, paras. 105 and 114.
[443] See *Yearbook of the International Law Commission, 1954*, vol. II, document A/CN.4/79.
[444] *Report of the International Technical Conference on the Conservation of the Living Resources of the Sea, 18 April-10 May 1955, Rome* (United Nations publication, Sales No. 1955.II.B.2).

(b)   Regime of the territorial sea[445]

At its first session, in 1949, the Commission selected the regime of the territorial waters as a topic for codification without, however, including it in the list of topics to which it gave priority. At its third session, in 1951, in pursuance of a recommendation contained in General Assembly resolution 374 (IV) of 6 December 1949, the Commission decided to initiate work on the regime of the territorial waters and appointed Mr. François as Special Rapporteur for that topic as well.

The Commission considered this topic at its fourth and from its sixth to eighth sessions, in 1952 and from 1954 to 1956, respectively. In connection with its work on this topic, the Commission had before it the reports of the Special Rapporteur[446] and information provided by Governments.[447]

At its fourth session, in 1952, the Special Rapporteur submitted a report[448] dealing in particular with the question of baselines and bays. With regard to the delimitation of the territorial sea of two adjacent States, the Commission, at that session, decided to ask Governments for information concerning their practice and for any observations they might consider useful. The Commission also decided that the Special Rapporteur should be free to consult with experts with a view to elucidating certain technical aspects of the problem. The group of experts met at The Hague in April 1953 under the chairmanship of the Special Rapporteur.[449] In his third report on the regime of the territorial sea,[450] which was submitted to the Commission in 1954, the

---

[445] At its fourth session, in 1952, the Commission decided, in accordance with a suggestion of the Special Rapporteur, to use the term "territorial sea" in lieu of "territorial waters". See *Yearbook of the International Law Commission, 1952*, vol. II, document A/2163, para. 37. The General Assembly, in its relevant resolutions, continued using the term "territorial waters" in the title of the topic.

[446] See *Yearbook of the International Law Commission, 1952*, vol. II, document A/CN.4/53; ibid., *1953*, vol. II, document A/CN.4/61 and Add.1; ibid., *1954*, vol. II, document A/CN.4/77; and ibid., *1956*, vol. II, document A/CN.4/97; as well as amendments proposed by the Special Rapporteur to the provisional articles concerning the regime of the territorial sea in document A/CN.4/93 (ibid., *1955*, vol. II).

[447] See *Yearbook of the International Law Commission, 1953*, vol. II, document A/CN.4/71 and Add.1 and 2; and ibid., *1956*, vol. II, documents A/CN.4/97/Add.2 and A/CN.4/99 and Add.1-9; as well as document A/CN.4/90 and Add.1-6 incorporated in *Yearbook of the International Law Commission, 1955*, vol. II, document A/2934, annex.

[448] See *Yearbook of the International Law Commission, 1952*, vol. II, document A/CN.4/53.

[449] For the report of the experts, see the annex to the addendum to the second report of the Special Rapporteur. See *Yearbook of the International Law Commission, 1953*, vol. II, document A/CN.4/61/Add.1.

[450] See *Yearbook of the International Law Commission, 1954*, vol. II, document A/CN.4/77.

Special Rapporteur incorporated changes suggested by the experts and also took into account the comments received from Governments on the delimitation of the territorial sea between two adjacent States.

At its sixth and seventh sessions, in 1954 and 1955, the Commission adopted provisional articles concerning the regime of the territorial sea, with commentaries, and invited Governments to furnish their observations on the articles.

At its eighth session, in 1956, the Commission drew up its final report on the territorial sea, incorporating a number of changes deriving from the replies from Governments, which was incorporated by the Commission in its consolidated draft on the law of the sea.[451]

(c)   Consolidated draft on the law of the sea

At the Commission's eighth session, in 1956, all the draft provisions adopted by the Commission concerning the law of the sea were recast so as to constitute a single coordinated and systematic body of rules. At the same session, the Commission adopted a final draft on the law of the sea, containing seventy-three articles and commentaries thereto.[452] The Commission noted that, in order to give effect to the project as a whole, it would be necessary to have recourse to conventional means. Accordingly, in submitting the final draft to the General Assembly in 1956, it recommended that the General Assembly should summon an international conference of plenipotentiaries.[453]

In accordance with the recommendation of the Commission, the General Assembly, by resolution 1105 (XI) of 21 February 1957, decided to convene an international conference of plenipotentiaries "to examine the law of the sea, taking account not only of the legal but also of the technical, biological, economic and political aspects of the problem, and to embody the results of its work in one or more international conventions or such other instruments as the conference may deem appropriate".

The United Nations Conference on the Law of the Sea met at Geneva from 24 February to 27 April 1958. Of the eighty-six States represented there, seventy-nine were Members of the United Nations

---

[451] For the use of the Commission in its work on the subject of the territorial sea, the Secretariat published a volume in the *United Nations Legislative Series* entitled *"Laws and Regulations on the Regime of the Territorial Sea"* (ST/LEG/SER.B/6, United Nations publication, Sales No. 1957.V.2).

[452] See *Yearbook of the International Law Commission, 1956*, vol. II, document A/3159, para. 33.

[453] See *Yearbook of the International Law Commission, 1956*, vol. II, document A/3159, paras. 27 and 28.

and seven were members of specialized agencies though not of the United Nations.

The final report of the Commission on the law of the sea had been referred to the Conference by the General Assembly as the basis for its consideration of the various problems involved in the development and codification of the law of the sea. In addition to this, the Conference had before it more than thirty preparatory documents, prepared by the United Nations Secretariat, by certain specialized agencies and by a number of independent experts invited by the Secretary-General to submit studies on various specialized topics. One question which had not been covered in the report of the Commission, namely, the question of free access to the sea of land-locked countries, was dealt with in a memorandum submitted to the Conference by a preliminary conference of land-locked States which met at Geneva from 10 to 14 February 1958 prior to the convening of the United Nations Conference.[454]

In view of the wide scope of the work before it, the Conference established five main committees: First Committee (territorial sea and contiguous zone); Second Committee (high seas: general regime); Third Committee (high seas: fishing and conservation of living resources); Fourth Committee (continental shelf); and Fifth Committee (question of free access to the sea of land-locked countries). Each committee submitted to the plenary meeting of the Conference a report summarizing the results of its work and appending draft articles as approved. The Conference agreed to embody these draft articles, some in amended form, in the following four separate conventions: the Convention on the Territorial Sea and the Contiguous Zone; the Convention on the High Seas; the Convention on Fishing and Conservation of the Living Resources of the High Seas; and the Convention on the Continental Shelf. The work of the Fifth Committee did not result in a separate convention, but its recommendations were included in article 14 of the Convention on the Territorial Sea and the Contiguous Zone and in articles 2, 3 and 4 of the Convention on the High Seas.[455]

---

[454] See *Official Records of the United Nations Conference on the Law of the Sea, Geneva, 24 February-27 April 1958,* vol. VII, Fifth Committee (Question of Free Access to the Sea of Land-Locked Countries) (United Nations publication, Sales No. 58.V.4, vol. VII), Annexes, document A/CONF.13/C.5/L.1.

[455] In pursuance of a resolution adopted by the First United Nations Conference on Trade and Development at Geneva in June 1964, the General Assembly, on 10 February 1965, decided to convene an international conference of plenipotentiaries to consider the question of transit trade of land-locked countries and to embody the results of its work in a convention and such other instruments as it might deem appropriate. The United Nations Conference on Transit Trade of Land-locked Countries, at which the Governments of fifty-eight States were represented, met in

In addition to the four Conventions, the Conference adopted an Optional Protocol of Signature concerning the Compulsory Settlement of Disputes, which provides for the compulsory jurisdiction of the International Court of Justice, or, if the parties so prefer, for submission of the dispute to arbitration or conciliation. The texts of the Conventions and Protocol are reproduced in annex V, section A. The Conference also adopted nine resolutions on various subjects, including the matter of convening a second United Nations Conference on the Law of the Sea.[456]

The Final Act of the Conference was signed on 29 April 1958. All the Conventions remained open for signature until 31 October 1958, by all States Members of the United Nations or of any of the specialized agencies and by any other States invited by the General Assembly to become a party; since that date they have been open to accession by all such States. The Optional Protocol was open to all States becoming parties to any of the Conventions. The Conventions were subject to ratification. The Optional Protocol was subject to ratification, where necessary, according to the constitutional requirements of the signatory States. Each of the Conventions was to come into force on the thirtieth day following the date of deposit of the twenty-second instrument of ratification or accession with the Secretary-General of the United Nations.

New York from 7 June to 8 July 1965. The Conference adopted the Convention on Transit Trade of Land-locked States and two resolutions. United Nations, *Treaty Series*, vol. 597, p. 3.

[456] United Nations, *Treaty Series*, vol. 450, p. 58. Resolution VII on Regime of Historic Waters was adopted as a follow-up to the adoption by the Conference of paragraph 6 of article 7 of the Convention on the Territorial Sea and Contiguous Zone, under which the regime established by the Convention for bays "shall not apply to so-called 'historic' bays". Further to this resolution, the General Assembly, by resolution 1453 (XIV) of 7 December 1959, requested the Commission:

". . . as soon as it considers it advisable, to undertake the study of the question of the juridical regime of historic waters, including historic bays, and to make such recommendations regarding the matter as the Commission deems appropriate."

The Commission requested the Secretariat to undertake a preliminary study of the topic and decided at its fourteenth session, in 1962, to include the topic in its programme of work, but without setting any date for the start of its consideration or appointing a Special Rapporteur. The Secretariat study is reproduced in the *Yearbook of the International Law Commission, 1962*, vol. II, document A/CN.4/143. At its nineteenth session, in 1967, the Commission considered whether to proceed with the study of this topic. The Commission's report summarized the views expressed as follows:

"Most members doubted whether the time had yet come to proceed actively with either of these topics. Both were of considerable scope and raised some political problems, and to undertake either of them at the present time might seriously delay the completion of work on the important topics already under study." (See *Yearbook of the International Law Commission, 1967*, vol. II, document A/6709/Rev.1, para. 45.)

The Convention on the High Seas[457] and the Optional Protocol of Signature concerning the Compulsory Settlement of Disputes[458] came into force on 30 September 1962. The Convention on the Continental Shelf[459] came into force on 10 June 1964; the Convention on the Territorial Sea and the Contiguous Zone[460] on 10 September 1964; and the Convention on Fishing and Conservation of the Living Resources of the High Seas[461] on 20 March 1966. By 3 October 2003, fifty-one States were parties to the Convention on the Territorial Sea and the Contiguous Zone, sixty-two States were parties to the Convention on the High Seas, thirty-seven States were parties to the Convention on Fishing and Conservation of the Living Resources of the High Seas, fifty-seven States were parties to the Convention on the Continental Shelf and thirty-seven States were parties to the Optional Protocol of Signature concerning the Compulsory Settlement of Disputes.

On 10 December 1958, the General Assembly, by resolution 1307 (XIII), asked the Secretary-General to convene a second United Nations Conference on the Law of the Sea to consider further the questions of the breadth of the territorial sea and fishery limits, questions which had been left unsettled by the first Conference on the Law of the Sea. Eighty-eight States were represented at the second Conference, which was held in Geneva from 17 March to 26 April 1960. The Conference failed to adopt any substantive proposal on the two questions before it. It did, however, approve a resolution expressing the need for technical assistance in making adjustments to their coastal and distant-waters fishing in the light of developments in international law and practice.[462]

At its twenty-fifth session, the General Assembly, by resolution 2750 C (XXV) of 17 December 1970, decided, inter alia, to convene in 1973 a conference on the law of the sea which would deal with the establishment of an equitable international regime — including an international machinery — for the seabed and the ocean floor and the subsoil thereof beyond the limits of national jurisdiction. The conference would also deal with issues concerning the regimes of the high seas, the continental shelf, the territorial sea (including the question of its breadth and the question of international straits and

---

[457] United Nations, *Treaty Series*, vol. 450, p. 82.
[458] United Nations, *Treaty Series*, vol. 450, p. 169.
[459] United Nations, *Treaty Series*, vol. 499, p. 311.
[460] United Nations, *Treaty Series*, vol. 516, p. 205.
[461] United Nations, *Treaty Series*, vol. 559, p. 285.
[462] See *Official Records of the Second United Nations Conference on the Law of the Sea, Geneva, 17 March-26 April 1960* (United Nations publication, Sales No. 60.V.6), Annexes, document A/CONF.19/L.15, annex.

contiguous zone), fishing and conservation of the living resources of the high seas (including the question of preferential rights of coastal States), the preservation of the marine environment (including, inter alia, the prevention of pollution) and scientific research. The Assembly, by the same resolution, instructed the Committee on the Peaceful Uses of the Sea-Bed and the Ocean Floor beyond the Limits of National Jurisdiction provided for in General Assembly resolution 2467A (XXIII) of 21 December 1968, enlarged to eighty-six members, to act as a preparatory body for the 1973 conference and to prepare draft treaty articles embodying the international regime — including an international machinery — for the area and resources of the seabed and ocean floor, and the subsoil thereof, beyond the limits of national jurisdiction, and a comprehensive list of subjects and issues relating to the law of the sea and draft articles on such subjects and issues.[463]

The Conference held eleven sessions, from 1973 to 1982. On 10 December 1982, it adopted the United Nations Convention on the Law of the Sea,[464] which includes 320 articles and nine annexes. It also adopted a Final Act to which are annexed, inter alia, resolutions and a statement of understanding. The Convention remained open for signature until 9 December 1984 at the Ministry of Foreign Affairs of Jamaica and also, from 1 July 1983 until 9 December 1984, at United Nations Headquarters in New York. It entered into force on 16 November 1994, twelve months after the date of deposit of the sixtieth instrument. As of 3 October 2003, one hundred forty-three States had deposited instruments of ratification. It may be noted that a number of articles of the 1982 Convention are based on those of the 1958 Conventions. In accordance with paragraph 1 of article 311 of the 1982 Convention, that Convention shall prevail, as between States Parties, over the Geneva Conventions on the Law of the Sea of 29 April 1958.

---

[463] In 1970, the Secretariat published a volume in the *United Nations Legislative Series* entitled *"National Legislation and Treaties Relating to the Territorial Sea, the Contiguous Zone, the Continental Shelf, the High Seas and to Fishing and Conservation of the Living Resources of the Sea"*(ST/LEG/SER.B/15, United Nations publication, Sales No. 70.V.9) followed by three volumes entitled *"National Legislation and Treaties Relating to the Law of the Sea"* (ST/LEG/SER.B/16, United Nations publication, Sales No. 74.V.2; ST/LEG/SER.B/18, United Nations publication, Sales No. 76.V.2; and ST/LEG/SER.B/19, United Nations publication, Sales No. 80.V.3) in 1974, 1976 and 1980, with the main purpose being to provide as complete and up-to-date information as possible for the participants in the Third United Nations Conference on the Law of the Sea.
[464] United Nations, *Treaty Series,* vol. 1833, p. 3.

10. Arbitral procedure

At its first session, in 1949, the Commission selected arbitral procedure as one of the topics for codification to which it gave priority and appointed Georges Scelle as Special Rapporteur. The Commission considered this topic at its second, fourth, fifth, ninth and tenth sessions, in 1950, 1952, 1953, 1957 and 1958, respectively. In connection with its work on this topic, the Commission had before it the reports of the Special Rapporteur,[465] information provided by Governments[466] as well as documents prepared by the Secretariat.[467]

At its fourth session, in 1952, the Commission, adopted on first reading a draft on arbitral procedure and communicated it to Governments for comment. At its fifth session, in 1953, the Commission adopted the revised draft on arbitral procedure, which was at that time intended as a final draft.[468] In its report on the fifth session to the General Assembly, the Commission expressed the view that this final draft, as adopted, called for action on the part of the Assembly of the kind contemplated in article 23, paragraph 1 (c), of the Statute of the Commission, namely, that the draft should be recommended to Member States with a view to the conclusion of a convention; the Commission recommended accordingly.[469]

The Commission emphasized that the draft had a dual aspect, representing both a codification of existing law on international arbitration and a formulation of what the Commission considered to be desirable developments in the field. Thus the Commission had taken as a basis the traditional features of arbitral procedure in the settlement of international disputes, such as those relating to the undertaking to arbitrate, the constitution and powers of an arbitral tribunal, the general rules of evidence and procedure, and the award of arbitrators. At the same time, the Commission had also provided certain procedural safeguards for securing the effectiveness, in

---

[465] See *Yearbook of the International Law Commission, 1950,* vol. II, document A/CN.4/18; ibid., *1951,* vol. II, document A/CN.4/46; ibid., *1952,* vol. II, document A/CN.4/57; ibid., *1957,* vol. II, document A/CN.4/109; and ibid., *1958,* vol. II, document A/CN.4/113.

[466] See *Yearbook of the International Law Commission, 1950,* vol. II, document A/CN.4/19; as well as document A/CN.4/68 and Add.1 and 2 incorporated in *Yearbook of the International Law Commission, 1953,* vol. II, document A/2456, annex I.

[467] See *Yearbook of the International Law Commission, 1950,* vol. II, document A/CN.4/35; as well as documents A/CN.4/29, A/CN.4/36 and A/CN.4/92 (United Nations publication, Sales No. 1955.V.1).

[468] See *Yearbook of the International Law Commission, 1953,* vol. II, document A/2456, para. 57.

[469] See *Yearbook of the International Law Commission, 1953,* vol. II, document A/2456, para. 55.

accordance with the original common intention of the parties, of the undertaking to arbitrate. For example, in order to prevent one of the parties from avoiding arbitration by claiming that the dispute in question was not covered by the undertaking to arbitrate, the draft provided for a binding decision by the International Court of Justice as to the arbitrability of the dispute. Similarly, in order to avoid the frustration that might be caused by one party withdrawing its arbitrator, the draft provided for the immutability of the tribunal once it had been formed, except in specified cases. The draft also included provisions for the drawing up of the compromis — an agreement concerning the undertaking to arbitrate and the arrangements for arbitration proceedings, e.g., nomination of arbitrators, the date and place for the proceedings — by the arbitral tribunal in cases where the parties had failed to reach agreement on the subject.[470]

The draft was considered by the General Assembly at its eighth and tenth sessions, in 1953 and 1955, where it was subjected to considerable criticism, particularly in view of the Commission's recommendation for the conclusion of a convention on the subject. The Assembly, in resolution 989 (X) of 14 December 1955, noting that a number of suggestions for improvements on the draft had been put forward in the comments submitted by Governments and in the observations made in the Sixth Committee at the eighth and tenth sessions of the General Assembly, invited the Commission to consider the comments of Governments and the discussions in the Sixth Committee in so far as they may contribute further to the value of the draft on arbitral procedure, and to report to the General Assembly at its thirteenth session.

At its ninth session, in 1957, the Commission appointed a committee to consider the matter in the light of the General Assembly resolution. In accordance with the conclusion of the committee, the Commission considered the ultimate object to be attained in reviewing the draft on arbitral procedure, in particular, whether this object should be a convention or simply a set of model rules which States might use, either wholly or in part, in the drawing up of provisions for inclusion in international treaties and special arbitration agreements. The Commission decided in favour of the second alternative. In doing so, the Commission recognized that the draft, as it stood, went beyond what the majority of Governments would be prepared to accept in advance as a general multilateral convention on arbitration. The Commission, however, was of the opinion that the recasting of the draft with a view to attracting the

---

[470] See *Yearbook of the International Law Commission, 1953*, vol. II, document A/2456, paras. 15-52.

signature and ratification of a majority of Governments would mean a complete revision, involving in all probability an alteration in the whole concept on which the draft was based. In these circumstances, the Commission took the view that it would be preferable to leave the substance of the draft intact and present it to the General Assembly as a set of draft articles which States could use as models in concluding bilateral or multilateral arbitral agreements or in submitting particular disputes to ad hoc arbitration.

At its tenth session, in 1958, the Commission adopted, on the basis of a report by the Special Rapporteur,[471] a set of "Model Rules on Arbitral Procedure" followed by a general commentary.[472] In submitting the final set to the General Assembly, the Commission recommended that the Assembly by resolution adopt the report.[473] The text of the Model Rules on Arbitral Procedure is reproduced in annex IV, section 5.

With reference to the scope and purpose of the Model Rules, which were intended to apply to arbitrations between States, the Commission observed:

"... now that the draft is no longer presented in the form of a potential general treaty of arbitration, it may be useful to draw attention to the fact that, if the parties so desired, its provisions would, with the necessary adaptations, also be capable of utilization for the purposes of arbitrations between States and international organizations or between international organizations.

"In the case of arbitrations between States and foreign private corporations or other juridical entities, different legal considerations arise. However, some of the articles of the draft, if adapted, might be capable of use for this purpose also."[474]

After extensive discussions in the Sixth Committee, the General Assembly, in resolution 1262 (XIII) of 14 November 1958, took note of chapter II on arbitral procedure of the Commission's report on its tenth session; brought the draft articles on arbitral procedure to the attention of Member States for their consideration and use; and invited Governments to send to the Secretary-General any comments they may wish to make on the draft, and in particular on their experience in the drawing up of arbitral agreements and the conduct

---

[471] See *Yearbook of the International Law Commission, 1958*, vol. II, document A/CN.4/113.
[472] See *Yearbook of the International Law Commission, 1958*, vol. II, document A/3859, paras. 15 and 22-43.
[473] See *Yearbook of the International Law Commission, 1958*, vol. II, document A/3859, para. 17.
[474] See *Yearbook of the International Law Commission, 1958*, vol. II, document A/3859, footnote 16.

of arbitral procedure, with a view to facilitating a review of the matter by the United Nations at an appropriate time.

11. Diplomatic intercourse and immunities

In the course of its first session, in 1949, the Commission selected diplomatic intercourse and immunities as one of the topics for codification without, however, including it in the list of topics to which it gave priority. At its fifth session, in 1953, the Commission was apprised of General Assembly resolution 685 (VII) of 5 December 1952, by which the Assembly requested the Commission to undertake, as soon as it considered possible, the codification of diplomatic intercourse and immunities and to treat it as a priority topic.

At its sixth session, in 1954, the Commission decided to initiate work on the subject and appointed A. E. F. Sandström as Special Rapporteur. The Commission considered this topic at its ninth and tenth sessions, in 1957 and 1958, respectively. In connection with its work on this topic, the Commission had before it the reports of the Special Rapporteur,[475] information provided by Governments[476] as well as a document prepared by the Secretariat.[477]

At its ninth session, in 1957, on the basis of the report by the Special Rapporteur,[478] the Commission, adopted on first reading a set of draft articles with commentaries. The draft was circulated to Governments for comment and was also included in the report submitted by the Commission to the Assembly's twelfth session, in 1957. At its tenth session, in 1958, the Commission adopted the final draft on diplomatic intercourse and immunities consisting of forty-five draft articles, with commentaries.[479] In submitting this final draft to the General Assembly, the Commission recommended that the

---

[475] See *Yearbook of the International Law Commission, 1955*, vol. II, document A/CN.4/91; and ibid., *1958*, vol. II, document A/CN.4/116/Add.1 and 2.

[476] Document A/CN.4/114 and Add.1-6 incorporated in *Yearbook of the International Law Commission, 1958*, vol. II, document A/3859, annex; and document A/CN.4/116.

[477] See *Yearbook of the International Law Commission, 1956*, vol. II, document A/CN.4/98. In addition, the Secretariat published for the use of the Commission in its work on diplomatic and consular intercourse and immunities a volume in the *United Nations Legislative Series* entitled *"Laws and Regulations Regarding Diplomatic and Consular Privileges and Immunities"* (ST/LEG/SER.B/7, United Nations publication, Sales No. 58.V.3), which was supplemented by an additional volume in 1963 (ST/LEG/SER.B/13, United Nations publication, Sales No. 63.V.5).

[478] See *Yearbook of the International Law Commission, 1955*, vol. II, document A/CN.4/91.

[479] See *Yearbook of the International Law Commission, 1958*, vol. II, document A/3859, para. 53.

General Assembly recommend the draft to Member States with a view to the conclusion of a convention.[480]

The Commission pointed out that the draft dealt only with permanent diplomatic missions. The Commission had, however, asked the Special Rapporteur to study and, at one of its future sessions, make a report on other forms of diplomatic relations, that is, so-called "ad hoc diplomacy", covering itinerant envoys, diplomatic conferences and special missions sent to a State for limited purposes. The Commission's report also referred to relations between States and international organizations and the privileges and immunities of such organizations. In this respect, the Commission simply remarked that these matters were, as regards most of these organizations, governed by special conventions.[481]

During the Sixth Committee's debate, in 1958, on the report of the International Law Commission, some representatives expressed doubts as to whether it was desirable to codify by convention the rules regarding diplomatic privileges and immunities. It was argued that the matter was adequately governed by custom and usage and that regulation by convention would introduce an element of rigidity. An attempt to lay down strict treaty rules on the subject, it was also contended, might even result in the reduction of the privileges and immunities at present enjoyed in practice by members of diplomatic missions. A restatement of current usage would for these reasons be preferable to regulation by convention.[482]

The majority of members, however, favoured codifying the subject by convention, but were divided into two groups regarding the procedure to be followed. One group proposed that the preparation of a convention should be entrusted to the Sixth Committee; the other group preferred the convening of a conference of plenipotentiaries for that purpose. The General Assembly, by resolution 1288 (XIII) of 5 December 1958, deferred action until its fourteenth session, in 1959, at which it finally endorsed the recommendation of the Commission and decided, in resolution 1450 (XIV) of 7 December 1959, to convene a conference of plenipotentiaries not later than the spring of 1961. The Commission's final report on diplomatic intercourse and immunities, containing the draft articles, was referred to the conference by the Assembly. A year later, by resolution 1504 (XV) of 12 December 1960, the Assembly also referred to the conference

---

[480] See *Yearbook of the International Law Commission, 1958,* vol. II, document A/3859, para. 50.
[481] See *Yearbook of the International Law Commission, 1958,* vol. II, document A/3859, paras. 51 and 52.
[482] See *Official Records of the General Assembly, Thirteenth Session, Annexes,* agenda item 56, document A/4007.

three draft articles on special missions (*see page 140*) approved by the Commission at its twelfth session, in 1960, so that they could be considered together with the draft articles on permanent diplomatic relations.

The United Nations Conference on Diplomatic Intercourse and Immunities met in Vienna from 2 March to 14 April 1961.[483] It was attended by delegates from eighty-one countries, seventy-five of which were Members of the United Nations and six of related agencies or parties to the Statute of the International Court of Justice. The Conference set up a Committee of the Whole, to which it referred the substantive items on its agenda, namely, consideration of the question of diplomatic intercourse and immunities, consideration of draft articles on special missions, and the adoption of instruments regarding the matters considered and of the Final Act of the Conference. The draft articles on special missions were referred by the Committee of the Whole to a Subcommittee on Special Missions.

The Conference adopted a convention entitled the "Vienna Convention on Diplomatic Relations",[484] consisting of fifty-three articles and covering most major aspects of permanent diplomatic relations between States. It also adopted an Optional Protocol concerning Acquisition of Nationality[485] and an Optional Protocol concerning the Compulsory Settlement of Disputes.[486] The texts of the Convention and Optional Protocols are reproduced in annex V, section C. By a resolution adopted by the Conference, the subject of special missions was referred back to the General Assembly with the recommendation that the Assembly entrust to the International Law Commission the task of further study of the topic (*see page 140*).

The Final Act of the Conference was signed on 18 April 1961. The Convention and Optional Protocols remained open for signature until 31 October 1961 at the Federal Ministry for Foreign Affairs of Austria and subsequently, until 31 March 1962, at United Nations Headquarters. They remain open for accession at any time by all Members of the United Nations or of any of the specialized agencies or Parties to the Statute of the International Court of Justice, and by any other State invited by the General Assembly to become a party. The Convention and the two Optional Protocols entered into force on 24 April 1964. By 7 October 2003, 180 States were parties to the Vienna Convention on Diplomatic Relations, fifty States were parties

---

[483] See *Official Records of the United Nations Conference on Diplomatic Intercourse and Immunities, Vienna, 2 March-14 April 1961*, vol. I (United Nations publication, Sales No. 61.X.2); and ibid., vol. II (United Nations publication, Sales No. 62.X.I).
[484] United Nations, *Treaty Series,* vol. 500, p. 95.
[485] United Nations, *Treaty Series,* vol. 500, p. 223.
[486] United Nations, *Treaty Series,* vol. 500, p. 241.

to the Optional Protocol concerning Acquisition of Nationality and sixty-two States were parties to the Optional Protocol concerning the Compulsory Settlement of Disputes.

12. Consular intercourse and immunities

At its first session, in 1949, the Commission selected the subject of consular intercourse and immunities as one of the topics for codification without, however, including it in the list of topics to which it gave priority. At its seventh session, in 1955, the Commission decided to begin the study of this topic and appointed Jaroslav Zourek as Special Rapporteur.

The Commission considered this topic at its eighth session in 1956, and from its tenth session, in 1958, to its thirteenth session, in 1961. In connection with its work on this topic, the Commission had before it the reports of the Special Rapporteur[487] and information provided by Governments.[488]

At its twelfth session, in 1960, the Commission adopted on first reading sixty-five draft articles, together with commentaries, and transmitted the draft to Governments for their comments. At its thirteenth session, in 1961, the Commission adopted a final draft on consular relations, consisting of seventy-one articles accompanied by commentaries.[489] In submitting the final draft to the General Assembly, the Commission recommended to the Assembly that it convene an international conference of plenipotentiaries to study the Commission's draft and conclude one or more conventions on the subject.[490]

The General Assembly, in resolution 1685 (XVI) of 18 December 1961, noted "with satisfaction that the draft articles on consular relations prepared by the International Law Commission constitute a good basis for the preparation of a convention on that subject",

---

[487] For the reports of the Special Rapporteur, see *Yearbook of the International Law Commission, 1957,* vol. II, document A/CN.4/108; ibid., *1960,* vol. II, document A/CN.4/131; and ibid., *1961,* vol. II, document A/CN.4/137.

[488] Document A/CN.4/136 and Add.1-11 incorporated in *Yearbook of the International Law Commission, 1961,* vol. II, document A/4843, annex I. In addition, the Secretariat published for the use of the Commission in its work on diplomatic and consular intercourse and immunities a volume in the *United Nations Legislative Series* entitled *"Laws and Regulations Regarding Diplomatic and Consular Privileges and Immunities"* (ST/LEG/SER.B/7, United Nations publication, Sales No. 58.V.3), which was supplemented by an additional volume in 1963 (ST/LEG/SER.B/13, United Nations publication, Sales No. 63.V.5).

[489] See *Yearbook of the International Law Commission, 1961,* vol. II, document A/4843, para. 37.

[490] See *Yearbook of the International Law Commission, 1961,* vol. II, document A/4843, para. 27.

decided that an international conference of plenipotentiaries should be convened at Vienna at the beginning of March 1963, and referred to the Conference the report adopted by the Commission containing draft articles on consular relations. At the same time, in order "to provide an opportunity for completing the preparatory work by further expressions and exchanges of views concerning the draft articles at the seventeenth [1962] session", the Assembly also requested Member States to submit written comments on the draft articles, by 1 July 1962, for circulation to Governments prior to the beginning of the seventeenth session, and decided to place on the provisional agenda of that session the item "Consular relations".

In 1962, after a discussion on the draft articles on consular relations in the Sixth Committee, the General Assembly, by resolution 1813 (XVII) of 18 December 1962, requested the Secretary-General to transmit to the conference of plenipotentiaries the summary records and documentation relating to the consideration of this item at the Assembly's seventeenth session, and invited States intending to participate in the conference to submit to the Secretary-General as soon as possible, for circulation to Governments, any amendment to the draft articles which they might wish to propose in advance of the conference.

The United Nations Conference on Consular Relations, which was attended by delegates of ninety-five States, met at Vienna from 4 March to 22 April 1963.[491] The Conference assigned consideration of the draft articles prepared by the International Law Commission, and certain additional proposals, to two main committees, each composed of all the participating States. After the articles and proposals had been dealt with in the main committees, they were referred to a drafting committee, which prepared texts for submission to the Conference meeting in plenary session. The Conference adopted the Vienna Convention on Consular Relations,[492] consisting of seventy-nine articles, an Optional Protocol concerning Acquisition of Nationality[493] and an Optional Protocol concerning the Compulsory Settlement of Disputes,[494] the texts of which are reproduced in annex V, section D.

The Final Act of the Conference was signed on 24 April 1963. The Convention and Optional Protocols remained open for signature until 31 October 1963 at the Federal Ministry for Foreign Affairs of

---

[491] See *Official Records of the United Nations Conference on Consular Relations,* vol. I (United Nations publication, Sales No. 63.X.2); and ibid., vol. II (United Nations publication, Sales No. 64.X.I).
[492] United Nations, *Treaty Series,* vol. 596, p. 261.
[493] United Nations, *Treaty Series,* vol. 596, p. 469.
[494] United Nations, *Treaty Series,* vol. 596, p. 487.

Austria and subsequently, until 31 March 1964, at United Nations Headquarters. They remain open for accession by all Members of the United Nations or of any of the specialized agencies or Parties to the Statute of the International Court of Justice, and by any other State invited by the General Assembly to become a party. The Convention and both Optional Protocols came into force on 19 March 1967. By 7 October 2003, 165 States were parties to the Vienna Convention on Consular Relations, thirty-nine States were parties to the Optional Protocol concerning Acquisition of Nationality and forty-six States were parties to the Optional Protocol concerning the Compulsory Settlement of Disputes.

13. Extended participation in general multilateral treaties concluded under the auspices of the League of Nations

By resolution 1766 (XVII) of 20 November 1962, the General Assembly requested the International Law Commission to study the question of participation of new States in certain general multilateral treaties, concluded under the auspices of the League of Nations, which by their terms authorized the Council of the League to invite additional States to become parties but to which States that had not been so invited by the League Council before the dissolution of the League were unable to become parties for want of an invitation. This problem had originally been brought to the attention of the Assembly by the International Law Commission. In the report on its fourteenth session, in 1962, the Commission had pointed out that certain difficulties stood in the way of finding a speedy and satisfactory solution to this problem through the medium of the draft articles on the law of treaties, and it therefore suggested that consideration should be given to the possibility of solving the problem more expeditiously by other procedures, such as administrative action by the depositary and a resolution of the General Assembly, to the terms of which the assent of all the States entitled to a voice in the matter might be obtained.[495]

In accordance with General Assembly resolution 1766 (XVII), the Commission resumed consideration of the question at its fifteenth session, in 1963. After examining the arrangements which were made in 1946 on the occasion of the dissolution of the League of Nations and the assumption by the United Nations of some of its functions and powers in relation to treaties concluded under the auspices of the League, the Commission reached the conclusion that the General

---

[495] See *Yearbook of the International Law Commission, 1962*, vol. II, document A/5209, pp. 168 and 169.

Assembly appeared to be entitled, if it so desired, to designate an organ of the United Nations to assume and fulfil the powers which, under the participation clauses of the treaties in question, were formerly exercisable by the Council of the League. This procedure, which was endorsed by the Commission as a simplified and expeditious solution for achieving the object of extending participation in the treaties in question, was accordingly referred to by the Commission, in its report to the General Assembly, in listing various alternate methods which might be adopted. The Commission also observed in its report that a number of the treaties concerned might hold no interest for States and suggested that this aspect of the matter be further examined by the competent authorities. In addition, the Commission suggested that the General Assembly take steps to initiate the examination of those treaties with a view to determining what action might be necessary to adapt them to contemporary conditions.[496]

On the basis of the conclusions reached by the Commission, the General Assembly, in resolution 1903 (XVIII) of 18 November 1963, decided that the Assembly was the appropriate organ of the United Nations to exercise the power conferred on the League Council by twenty-one general multilateral treaties of a technical and non-political character concluded under the auspices of the League of Nations to invite States to accede to those treaties; it also placed on record the assent to that decision by those Members of the United Nations which are parties to the treaties concerned.

By the same resolution, the General Assembly requested the Secretary-General: (a) to bring the terms of the resolution to the notice of any party not a Member of the United Nations; (b) to transmit the resolution to Member States which are parties to those treaties; (c) to consult, where necessary, with these States and the United Nations organs and specialized agencies concerned as to whether any of the treaties in question have ceased to be in force, have been superseded, have otherwise ceased to be of interest for accession by additional States, or require action to adapt them to contemporary conditions; and (d) to report to the Assembly at its nineteenth session, in 1964. Finally, the Assembly requested the Secretary-General to invite "each State which is a Member of the United Nations or member of a specialized agency or a party to the Statute of the International Court of Justice, or has been designated for this purpose by the General Assembly, and which otherwise is not eligible to become a party to the treaties in question, to accede thereto

---

[496] See *Yearbook of the International Law Commission, 1963*, vol. II, document A/5509, para. 50.

by depositing an instrument of accession with the Secretary-General of the United Nations".

At its twentieth session, in 1965, the General Assembly considered a report of the Secretary-General[497] submitted in pursuance of resolution 1903 (XVIII), and adopted, on 5 November 1965, resolution 2021 (XX) in which it recognized that nine treaties "listed in the annex to the present resolution may be of interest for accession by additional States" and drew the "attention of the parties to the desirability of adapting some of these treaties to contemporary conditions, particularly in the event that new parties should so request".

14. Law of treaties

At its first session, in 1949, the Commission selected the law of treaties as a topic for codification to which it gave priority. The Commission appointed J. L. Brierly, Sir Hersch Lauterpacht, Sir Gerald Fitzmaurice and Sir Humphrey Waldock as the successive Special Rapporteurs for the topic at its first, fourth, seventh and thirteenth sessions, in 1949, 1952, 1955 and 1961, respectively. The Commission considered the topic at its second, third, eighth, eleventh and thirteenth to eighteenth sessions, in 1950, 1951, 1956, 1959 and from 1961 to 1966, respectively. In connection with its work on the topic, the Commission had before it the reports of the Special Rapporteurs,[498] information provided by Governments[499] as well as documents prepared by the Secretariat.[500]

---

[497] See *Official Records of the General Assembly, Twentieth Session, Annexes*, agenda item 88, document A/5759 and Add.l.

[498] For the reports of James L. Brierly, see *Yearbook of the International Law Commission, 1950*, vol. II, document A/CN.4/23; ibid., *1951*, vol. II, document A/CN.4/43; and ibid., *1952*, vol. II, document A/CN.4/54 and Corr.1. For the reports of H. Lauterpacht, see *Yearbook of the International Law Commission, 1953*, vol. II, document A/CN.4/63; and ibid., *1954*, vol. II, document A/CN.4/87 and Corr.1. For the reports of Sir Gerald Fitzmaurice, see *Yearbook of the International Law Commission, 1956*, vol. II, document A/CN.4/101; ibid., *1957*, vol. II, document A/CN.4/107; ibid., *1958*, vol. II, document A/CN.4/115 and Corr.1; ibid., *1959*, vol. II, document A/CN.4/120; and ibid., *1960*, vol. II, document A/CN.4/130. For the reports of Sir Humphrey Waldock, see *Yearbook of the International Law Commission, 1962*, vol. II, document A/CN.4/144 and Add.1; ibid., *1963*, vol. II, document A/CN.4/156 and Add.1-3; ibid., *1964*, vol. II, A/CN.4/167 and Add.1-3; ibid., *1965*, vol. II, A/CN.4/177 and Add.1 and 2; and ibid., *1966*, vol. II, document A/CN.4/183 and Add.1-4 and A/CN.4/186 and Add.1-7.

[499] See *Yearbook of the International Law Commission, 1950*, vol. II, document A/CN.4/19; and documents A/CN.4/175 and Add.1-5 and A/CN.4/182 and Add.1-3 incorporated in *Yearbook of the International Law Commission, 1966*, vol. II, document A/6309/Rev.1, annex.

[500] See *Yearbook of the International Law Commission, 1959*, vol. II, document A/CN.4/121; ibid., *1963*, vol. II, document A/CN.4/154; ibid., *1965*, vol. II,

The Commission had originally envisaged its work on the law of treaties as taking the form of "a code of a general character", rather than of one or more international conventions. In its report on its eleventh session, in 1959, to the General Assembly, the Commission stated:

"In short, the law of treaties is not itself dependent on treaty, but is part of general customary international law. Queries might arise if the law of treaties were embodied in a multilateral convention, but some States did not become parties to the convention, or became parties to it and then subsequently denounced it; for they would in fact be or remain bound by the provisions of the treaty in so far as these embodied customary international law de lege lata. No doubt this difficulty arises whenever a convention embodies rules of customary international law. In practice, this often does not matter. In the case of the law of treaties it might matter — for the law of treaties is itself the basis of the force and effect of all treaties. It follows from all this that if it were ever decided to cast the Code, or any part of it, in the form of an international convention, considerable drafting changes, and possibly the omission of some material, would almost certainly be required."[501]

At its thirteenth session, in 1961, the Commission changed the scheme of its work from a mere expository statement of the law of treaties to the preparation of draft articles capable of serving as a basis for an international convention. This decision was explained as follows by the Commission in its report on its fourteenth session, in 1962:

"First, an expository code, however well formulated, cannot in the nature of things be so effective as a convention for consolidating the law; and the consolidation of the law of treaties is of particular importance at the present time when so many new States have recently become members of the international community. Secondly, the codification of the law of treaties through a multilateral convention would give all the new States the opportunity to participate directly in the formulation of the law if they so wished; and their participation in the work of

---

document A/5687; and ibid., *1966*, vol. II, document A/CN.4/187. See also documents A/CN.4/31, A/CN.4/37 and A/CN.4/L.55. In addition, the Secretariat published a volume in the *United Nations Legislative Series* entitled *"Laws and Practices Concerning the Conclusion of Treaties with a Select Bibliography on the Law of Treaties"* (ST/LEG/SER.B/3, United Nations publication, Sales No. 1952.V.4).

[501] See *Yearbook of the International Law Commission, 1959*, vol. II, document A/4169, para. 18.

codification appears to the Commission to be extremely desirable in order that the law of treaties may be placed upon the widest and most secure foundations."[502]

The General Assembly, in resolution 1765 (XVII) of 20 November 1962, recommended that the Commission continue the work on the law of treaties, taking into account the views expressed in the Assembly and the written comments submitted by Governments.

At its fourteenth to sixteenth sessions, from 1962 to 1964, the Commission proceeded with the first reading of the draft articles and submitted the provisionally adopted draft articles to Governments for comment. The Commission completed the first reading of the draft articles at its sixteenth session, in 1964.

At its seventeenth session, in 1965, the Commission began the second reading of the draft articles in the light of the comments of Governments. It re-examined the question of the form ultimately to be given to the draft articles, and adhered to the views it had expressed in 1961 and 1962 in favour of a convention. The Commission noted that, at the General Assembly's seventeenth session, in 1962, the Sixth Committee had stated in its report that the great majority of representatives had approved the Commission's decision to give the codification of the law of treaties the form of a convention.

At its eighteenth session, in 1966, the Commission completed the second reading of the draft articles and adopted its final report on the law of treaties, setting forth seventy-five draft articles together with their commentaries.[503] In submitting the final report to the General Assembly, the Commission recommended that the Assembly should convene an international conference of plenipotentiaries to study the Commission's draft articles on the law of treaties and to conclude a convention on the subject.[504]

In drawing up the draft articles, the Commission decided to limit the scope of application of those articles to treaties concluded between States, to the exclusion of treaties between States and other subjects of international law (e.g., international organizations) and between such other subjects. It also decided not to deal with international agreements not in written form. In addition, the

---

[502] See *Yearbook of the International Law Commission, 1962*, vol. II, document A/5209, para. 17.
[503] See *Yearbook of the International Law Commission, 1966*, vol. II, document A/6309/Rev.1, paras. 22 and 38.
[504] See *Yearbook of the International Law Commission, 1966*, vol. II, document A/6309/Rev.1, para. 36.

Commission decided that the draft articles should not contain any provisions concerning the following topics: the effect of the outbreak of hostilities upon treaties; succession of States in respect of treaties; the question of the international responsibility of a State with respect to a failure to perform a treaty obligation; "most-favoured-nation clause"; and the application of treaties providing for obligations or rights to be performed or enjoyed by individuals.[505]

Following the discussion in the Sixth Committee on the report of the Commission on the work of its eighteenth session, the General Assembly by resolution 2166 (XXI) of 5 December 1966 decided to convene an international conference of plenipotentiaries to consider the law of treaties and to embody the results of its work in an international convention and such other instruments as it may deem appropriate. It requested the Secretary-General to convoke the first session of the conference early in 1968 and the second session early in 1969. By the same resolution, the Assembly invited Member States, the Secretary-General and the Directors-General of those specialized agencies which act as depositaries of treaties to submit their written comments and observations on the draft articles. The International Atomic Energy Agency also submitted written comments and observations.

The following year, on the recommendation of the Sixth Committee, the General Assembly, by resolution 2287 (XXII) of 6 December 1967, decided to convene the first session of the United Nations Conference on the Law of Treaties at Vienna in March 1968.

The first session of the United Nations Conference on the Law of Treaties was accordingly held at Vienna from 26 March to 24 May 1968 and was attended by representatives of 103 countries and observers from thirteen specialized and intergovernmental agencies. The second session was held from 9 April to 22 May 1969, also at Vienna, and was attended by representatives of 110 countries and observers from fourteen specialized and intergovernmental agencies.[506] The first session of the Conference was devoted primarily to consideration by a Committee of the Whole and by a Drafting Committee of the set of draft articles adopted by the International Law Commission. The first part of the second session was devoted to meetings of the Committee of the Whole and of the Drafting Committee, completing their consideration of articles reserved from

---

[505] See *Yearbook of the International Law Commission, 1966*, vol. II, document A/6309/Rev.1, paras. 28-35.
[506] See *Official Records of the United Nations Conference on the Law of Treaties, First Session* (United Nations publication, Sales No. 68.V.7); ibid., *Second Session* (United Nations publication, Sales No. 70.V.6); and ibid., *First and Second Sessions, Documents of the Conference* (United Nations publication, Sales No. 70.V.5).

the previous session. The remainder of the second session was devoted to thirty plenary meetings which considered the articles adopted by the Committee of the Whole and reviewed by the Drafting Committee.

The Conference adopted the Vienna Convention on the Law of Treaties[507] on 22 May 1969. The Convention is made up of a preamble, eighty-five articles and an annex.

In line with the draft articles prepared by the Commission, the Vienna Convention on the Law of Treaties applies to treaties between States, the term "treaty" being defined for the purposes of the Convention as "an international agreement concluded between States in written form and governed by international law, whether embodied in a single instrument or in two or more related instruments and whatever its particular designation". Without prejudice to any relevant rules of the organization concerned, the Convention expressly provides that it applies to any treaty which is the constituent instrument of an international organization and to any treaty adopted within an international organization. Part I of the Convention also provides that the fact that international agreements concluded between States and other subjects of international law or between such other subjects of international law, or international agreements not in written form, are not covered by the Convention shall not affect (*a*) the legal force of such agreements, (*b*) the application to them of any of the rules set forth in the Convention to which they would be subject under international law independently of the Convention, and (*c*) the application of the Convention to the relations of States as between themselves under international agreements to which other subjects of international law are also parties. Finally, it is also provided that the Convention applies only to treaties which are concluded by States after the entry into force of the Convention with regard to such States, without prejudice to the application of any of the rules set forth in the Convention to which treaties would be subject under international law independently of the Convention.

The principal matters covered in the Convention are: conclusion and entry into force of treaties (part II), including reservations and provisional application of treaties; observance, application and interpretation of treaties (part III), including treaties and third States; amendment and modification of treaties (part IV); invalidity, termination and suspension of the operation of treaties (part V), including the procedure for the application of the provisions of that part and for the settlement of disputes concerning the application or

---

[507] United Nations, *Treaty Series,* vol. 1155, p. 331.

interpretation of those provisions, and the consequences of the invalidity, termination or suspension of the operation of a treaty; miscellaneous provisions (part VI), reserving cases of State succession, State responsibility and outbreak of hostilities, as well as the case of an aggressor State, and dealing with the severance or absence of diplomatic or consular relations and the conclusion of treaties; and depositaries, notifications, corrections and registration (part VII). The conciliation procedure referred to in article 66 of part V is specified in an annex to the Convention. The text of the Convention is reproduced in annex V, section F.

The final provisions of the Convention open it for signature and for ratification or accession by all States Members of the United Nations or members of any of the specialized agencies or of the International Atomic Energy Agency or parties to the Statute of the International Court of Justice, and also by any other State invited by the General Assembly to become a party to the Convention. The Convention was opened for signature on 23 May 1969. It remained open for signature until 30 November 1969 at the Federal Ministry for Foreign Affairs of Austria and, subsequently, until 30 April 1970, at United Nations Headquarters. Signatures are subject to ratification. The Convention is open for accession by any non-signatory State entitled to become a party. It entered into force on 27 January 1980. By 20 October 2003, ninety-six States were parties to the Convention.

In addition to the Vienna Convention on the Law of Treaties, the Conference adopted two declarations (the Declaration on the Prohibition of Military, Political or Economic Coercion in the Conclusion of Treaties and the Declaration on Universal Participation in the Vienna Convention on the Law of Treaties) and five resolutions which were annexed to the Final Act of the Conference.[508]

In the Declaration on Universal Participation in the Vienna Convention on the Law of Treaties, the Conference stated its conviction that multilateral treaties which deal with the codification and progressive development of international law, or the object and purpose of which are of interest to the international community as a whole, should be open to universal participation; noted that articles 81 and 83 of the Vienna Convention on the Law of Treaties enable the General Assembly to issue special invitations to States which are not members of the United Nations or of any of the specialized agencies or of the International Atomic Energy Agency, or parties to the Statute of the International Court of Justice, to become parties to the

---

[508] See *Official Records of the United Nations Conference on the Law of Treaties, First and Second Sessions, Documents of the Conference* (United Nations publication, Sales No. 70.V.5), document A/CONF.39/26.

Convention; and invited the General Assembly to give consideration, at its twenty-fourth session, to the matter of issuing invitations in order to ensure the widest possible participation in the Vienna Convention on the Law of Treaties. At the General Assembly's twenty-fourth session, this matter was referred to the Sixth Committee, which recommended to the Assembly that the question of issuing invitations be deferred until the twenty-fifth session. The Assembly adopted this recommendation without objection. On the recommendation of the General Committee, the General Assembly further deferred the consideration of the matter in 1970, 1971, 1972 and 1973 until the following year. On 12 November 1974, the Assembly adopted resolution 3233 (XXIX) whereby it decided to invite all States to become parties to the Vienna Convention on the Law of Treaties.

15. Special missions

In submitting its final draft on diplomatic intercourse and immunities (*see pages 126 and 127*) to the General Assembly at its thirteenth session, in 1958, the Commission stated that, although the draft dealt only with permanent diplomatic missions, diplomatic relations also assumed other forms that might be placed under the heading of "ad hoc diplomacy", covering itinerant envoys, diplomatic conferences and special missions sent to a State for limited purposes. In 1958, the Commission considered that these forms of diplomacy should also be studied, in order to bring out the rules of law governing them, and accordingly requested A. E. F. Sandström, the Special Rapporteur for the topic "diplomatic intercourse and immunities", to undertake that study and to submit his report at a future session. The Commission decided at its eleventh session, in 1959, to place the question of ad hoc diplomacy as a special topic on the agenda for its twelfth session, and appointed Mr. Sandström as Special Rapporteur for the topic.

At its twelfth session, in 1960, on the basis of the Special Rapporteur's report,[509] the Commission adopted three draft articles on "special missions" together with commentaries. In the report covering the work of its twelfth session, the Commission stated that the draft should be regarded "as constituting only a preliminary survey"; the Commission, nevertheless, recommended that the General Assembly should refer the draft to the United Nations Conference on Diplomatic Intercourse and Immunities which was to meet in Vienna

---

[509] See *Yearbook of the International Law Commission, 1960*, vol. II, document A/CN.4/129.

in the spring of 1961. Article 1, paragraph 1, of the draft defines "special mission" as follows:

"The expression 'special mission' means an official mission of State representatives sent by one State to another in order to carry out a special task. It also applies to an itinerant envoy who carries out special tasks in the States to which he proceeds."[510]

At the same session, the Commission, observing that the question of "diplomatic conferences" was linked not only to that of "special missions" but also to that of "relations between States and international organizations", decided not to deal with the subject of "diplomatic conferences" for the moment.

The General Assembly, by resolution 1504 (XV) of 12 December 1960, decided that the draft articles on special missions should be referred to the Vienna Conference so that they could be considered together with the draft articles on permanent diplomatic missions.

At the Vienna Conference, the question of special missions was referred to a Subcommittee established by the Committee of the Whole. While stressing the importance of the subject of special missions, the Subcommittee noted that, because of lack of time, the draft articles on special missions had, in contrast with the usual practice, not been submitted to Governments for their comments before being drafted in final form, and that the draft articles did little more than indicate which of the rules on permanent missions applied, and which did not apply, to special missions. The Subcommittee considered that, while the basic rules might in fact be the same, it could not be assumed that such an approach necessarily covered the whole field of special missions. Following consideration of the topic by the Subcommittee and by the Committee of the Whole, the Vienna Conference adopted a resolution recommending to the General Assembly that it refer the topic back to the International Law Commission.[511]

At its sixteenth session, the General Assembly adopted resolution 1687 (XVI) of 18 December 1961, requesting the Commission to study further the subject of special missions and to report thereon to the Assembly.

During its fifteenth session, in 1963, the Commission appointed Milan Bartoš as Special Rapporteur for the topic of special missions and decided that he should prepare draft articles, based on the

---

[510] See *Yearbook of the International Law Commission, 1960*, vol. II, document A/4425, para. 38.
[511] See *Official Records of the United Nations Conference on Diplomatic Intercourse and Immunities, Vienna, 2 March-14 April 1961*, vol. II (United Nations publication, Sales No. 62.X.1), pp. 45-46 and 89-90.

provisions of the 1961 Vienna Convention on Diplomatic Relations but that he should keep in mind that special missions were, by virtue of both their functions and nature, an institution distinct from permanent missions. It was also agreed to await the Special Rapporteur's recommendations before deciding whether the draft articles should be in the form of an additional protocol to the 1961 Vienna Convention or should be embodied in a separate convention or any other appropriate form. With regard to the scope of the topic, most of the members of the Commission expressed the opinion that for the time being the question of status of government delegates to international conferences should not be covered in the study on special missions.

The Commission considered this topic from its sixteenth session, in 1964, to its nineteenth session, in 1967. In connection with its work on this topic, the Commission had before it the reports of the Special Rapporteur,[512] information provided by Governments[513] as well as a document prepared by the Secretariat.[514]

At its sixteenth session, in 1964, the Commission considered the first report of the Special Rapporteur[515] and provisionally adopted sixteen articles, which were subsequently submitted to the General Assembly and to Governments for information. At the first part of its seventeenth session, in 1965, the Commission considered the second report of the Special Rapporteur[516] and provisionally adopted twenty-eight articles, which follow on from the sixteen articles previously adopted. All draft articles adopted at the sixteenth and seventeenth sessions were submitted to the General Assembly for its consideration and were also transmitted to Governments for comment.

At its eighteenth session, in 1966, the Commission examined certain questions of a general nature affecting special missions which had arisen out of the opinions expressed in the Sixth Committee and the written comments by Governments and which it was important to settle as a preliminary to the later work on the draft articles.

---

[512] See *Yearbook of the International Law Commission, 1964,* vol. II, document A/CN.4/166; ibid., *1965,* vol. II, document A/CN.4/179; ibid., *1966,* vol. II, document A/CN.4/189 and Add.1 and 2; and ibid., *1967,* vol. II, document A/CN.4/194 and Add.1-5.

[513] Documents A/CN.4/188 and Add.1-4 as well as A/CN.4/193 and Add.1-5, all incorporated in *Yearbook of the International Law Commission, 1967,* vol. II, document A/6709/Rev.1 and Rev.1/Corr.1, annex I.

[514] See *Yearbook of the International Law Commission, 1962,* vol. II, document A/CN.4/147; and ibid., *1963,* vol. II, document A/CN.4/155.

[515] See *Yearbook of the International Law Commission, 1964,* vol. II, document A/CN.4/166.

[516] See *Yearbook of the International Law Commission, 1965,* vol. II, document A/CN.4/179.

By resolution 2167 (XXI) of 5 December 1966, the General Assembly recommended that the Commission continue its work relating to special missions with the object of presenting a final draft on the topic in its next report.

At its nineteenth session, in 1967, the Commission, after examining the Special Rapporteur's fourth report[517] and taking into account the written comments received from Governments and the views expressed in the Sixth Committee, adopted its final draft on special missions, comprising fifty draft articles, with commentaries,[518] and submitted them to the General Assembly with a recommendation "that appropriate measures be taken for the conclusion of a convention on special missions".[519]

After discussion, the Sixth Committee recommended that an item entitled "Draft convention on special missions" be placed on the provisional agenda of the General Assembly's twenty-third session with a view to the adoption of such a convention by the Assembly. By resolution 2273 (XXII) of 1 December 1967, the Assembly adopted the recommendation of the Sixth Committee and invited Member States to submit comments and observations on the draft articles.

At the General Assembly's twenty-third and twenty-fourth sessions, in 1968 and 1969, the Sixth Committee considered the item "Draft convention on special missions" on the basis of the draft adopted by the International Law Commission. At each session, Switzerland[520] was invited to participate in the relevant proceedings of the Sixth Committee as an observer without the right to vote. By resolution 2530 (XXIV) of 8 December 1969, the General Assembly, upon the recommendation of the Sixth Committee, adopted the Convention on Special Missions[521] and the Optional Protocol concerning the Compulsory Settlement of Disputes relating thereto,[522] which are reproduced in annex V, section E. On the same date, 8 December 1969, while adopting the Convention on Special Missions, the General Assembly, in resolution 2531 (XXIV), also recommended that "the sending State should waive the immunity of members of its special mission in respect of civil claims of persons in the receiving State, when it can do so without impeding the performance of the

---

[517] See *Yearbook of the International Law Commission,* 1967, vol. II, document A/CN.4/194 and Add.1-5.
[518] See *Yearbook of the International Law Commission, 1967,* vol. II, document A/6709/Rev.1 and Rev.1/Corr.l, paras. 32 and 35.
[519] See *Yearbook of the International Law Commission, 1967,* vol. II, document A/6709/Rev.1 and Rev.1/Corr.l, para. 33.
[520] Switzerland was admitted to the United Nations membership on 10 September 2002.
[521] United Nations, *Treaty Series,* vol. 1400, p. 231.
[522] United Nations, *Treaty Series,* vol. 1400, p. 339.

functions of the special mission, and that, when immunity is not waived, the sending State should use its best endeavours to bring about a just settlement of the claims". For the purposes of the Convention, a "special mission" means "a temporary mission, representing the State, which is sent by one State to another State with the consent of the latter for the purpose of dealing with it on specific questions or of performing in relation to it a specific task".

The final provisions of the Convention open it for signature and for ratification or accession by all States Members of the United Nations or members of any of the specialized agencies or of the International Atomic Energy Agency or Parties to the Statute of the International Court of Justice, and also by any other State invited by the General Assembly to become a party to the Convention. The final provisions of the Optional Protocol open it for signature and for ratification or accession by all States which may become parties to the Convention. The Convention and the Optional Protocol were opened for signature on 16 December 1969 and remained open for signature until 31 December 1970. Signatures are subject to ratification. The Convention and the Optional Protocol are open for accession by any non-signatory State entitled to become a party. The Convention and the Optional Protocol came into force on 21 June 1985. By 7 October 2003, thirty-two States had become a party to the Convention and fifteen States had become a party to the Optional Protocol.

Also by resolution 2530 (XXIV), the General Assembly decided to consider at its twenty-fifth session the question of issuing invitations in order to ensure the widest possible participation in the Convention. The Assembly deferred consideration of the matter in 1970, 1971, 1972 and 1973 until the following year. On 12 November 1974, on the recommendation of the Sixth Committee, the General Assembly adopted resolution 3233 (XXIX) whereby it noted the Declaration on Universal Participation in the Vienna Convention on the Law of Treaties, adopted by the United Nations Conference on the Law of Treaties, in which the Assembly was invited to give consideration to the matter of issuing invitations in order to ensure the widest possible participation in that Convention. The Assembly by that resolution decided to invite all States to become parties to the Convention on Special Missions and its Optional Protocol concerning the Compulsory Settlement of Disputes.

16.   Relations between States and international organizations[523]

In the course of the consideration by the Sixth Committee, during the General Assembly's thirteenth session, in 1958, of the Commission's final report on diplomatic intercourse and immunities (*see page 127*), the representative of France proposed that the General Assembly should request the Commission to include in its agenda the study of the subject of relations between States and international organizations. In support of this proposal, he pointed out that the development of international organizations had increased the number and scope of the legal problems arising out of relations between the organizations and States and that these problems had only partially been solved by special conventions governing privileges and immunities of international organizations. It was therefore necessary, he stressed, not only to codify those special conventions but also to work out general principles which would serve as a basis for the progressive development of international law in the field.

On the recommendation of the Sixth Committee, the General Assembly adopted resolution 1289 (XIII) of 5 December 1958, inviting the Commission "to give further consideration to the question of relations between States and intergovernmental international organizations at the appropriate time, after study of diplomatic intercourse and immunities, consular intercourse and immunities and ad hoc diplomacy has been completed by the United Nations and in the light of the results of that study and of the discussion in the General Assembly".

At its eleventh session, in 1959, the Commission took note of the resolution and decided to consider the question in due course. At its fourteenth session, in 1962, the Commission decided to place the question on the agenda of its next session, and appointed Abdullah El-Erian as Special Rapporteur for the topic.

At its fifteenth and sixteenth sessions, in 1963 and 1964, respectively, the Commission considered the scope of and approach to the topic of relations between States and intergovernmental organizations on the basis of the report and working papers submitted by the Special Rapporteur.[524] A majority of the Commission concluded that, while agreeing that in principle the topic of relations between States and intergovernmental organizations had a broad

---

[523] At its twentieth session, in 1968, the Commission decided to amend the title of the topic, without altering its meaning, by changing the word "intergovernmental" to "international".

[524] See *Yearbook of the International Law Commission, 1963*, vol. II, documents A/CN.4/161 and Add.1, and A/CN.4/L.103; as well as document A/CN.4/L.104.

scope, for the purpose of its immediate study "the question of diplomatic law in its application to relations between States and intergovernmental organizations should receive priority". Subsequently, the Commission concentrated its work with respect to the topic on the study of the status, privileges and immunities of representatives of States to international organizations. After completing its work on the first part of the topic, the Commission, at its twenty-eighth session, in 1976, commenced its consideration of the second part of the topic dealing with the status, privileges and immunities of international organizations, their officials, experts and other persons engaged in their activities not being representatives of States.[525]

(a) Status, privileges and immunities of representatives of States to international organizations

The Commission considered the first part of the topic from its twentieth session, in 1968, to its twenty-third session, in 1971. In connection with its consideration of the topic, the Commission had before it the reports of the Special Rapporteur,[526] information provided by Governments and international organizations[527] as well as documents prepared by the Secretariat.[528]

From its twentieth session, in 1968, to its twenty-second session, in 1970, the Commission proceeded with the first reading of the draft articles and transmitted the provisionally adopted draft articles with commentaries to Governments of Member States and Switzerland as well as the secretariats of the United Nations, the specialized agencies and the International Atomic Energy Agency for their observations.

---

[525] In order to assist the Commission in its work on the topic, the Secretariat published two volumes in the *United Nations Legislative Series* entitled *"Legislative Texts and Treaty Provisions concerning the Legal Status, Privileges and Immunities of International Organizations"* (ST/LEG/SER.B/10, United Nations publication, Sales No. 60.V.2; and ST/LEG/SER.B/11, United Nations publication, Sales No. 61.V.3).

[526] See *Yearbook of the International Law Commission, 1967,* vol. II, document A/CN.4/195 and Add.1; ibid., *1968,* vol. II, document A/CN.4/203 and Add.1-5; ibid., *1969,* vol. II, document A/CN.4/218 and Add.1; ibid., *1970,* vol. II, document A/CN.4/227 and Add.1 and 2; ibid., *1971,* vol. II (Part One), document A/CN.4/241 and Add.1-6; and documents A/CN.4/L.136, A/CN.4/L.151, A/CN.4/L.166, A/CN.4/L.171 and A/CN.4/L.173.

[527] Documents A/CN.4/221 and Add.1 and Corr.1, A/CN.4/238 and Add.1 and 2, A/CN.4/239 and Add.1-3 and A/CN.4/240 and Add.1-7, incorporated in *Yearbook of the International Law Commission, 1971,* vol. II (Part One), document A/8410/Rev.1, annex I.

[528] See *Yearbook of the International Law Commission, 1967,* vol. II, document A/CN.4/L.118 and Add.1 and 2; ibid., *1968,* vol. II, document A/CN.4/L.129; as well as documents A/CN.4/L.162/Rev.1, A/CN.4/L.163, A/CN.4/L.164, A/CN.4/L.165 and A/CN.4/L.167.

By resolutions 2501 (XXIV) of 12 November 1969 and 2634 (XXV) of 12 November 1970, the General Assembly recommended that the Commission should continue its work on relations between States and international organizations, with the object of presenting in 1971 a final draft on the topic. It was also recommended that the Commission take into account the views expressed at the General Assembly session and the written comments submitted by Governments.

At its twenty-third session, in 1971, the Commission held the second reading of the draft articles. It established a working group that studied the whole draft from the stand-point of its general economy and structure and made recommendations thereon to the Commission.[529]

At the same session, the Commission adopted the final set of eighty-two draft articles, with commentaries,[530] and submitted it to the General Assembly with a recommendation that it should convene an international conference of plenipotentiaries to study the draft articles and to conclude a convention on the subject.[531] In the light of the contents of the final draft, the title was changed to "Draft articles on the representation of States in their relations with international organizations".[532]

The scope of the draft was limited to international organizations having a universal character, to organs of such organizations in which States were parties and to conferences convened under the auspices of those organizations. Because the set of provisions on observer delegations to organs and conferences had not been included in the provisional sets of draft articles transmitted to Governments and international organizations, the Commission deemed it appropriate to present its provisions on observer delegations in the form of an annex to the final draft articles.[533]

The General Assembly, in resolution 2780 (XXVI) of 3 December 1971, expressed its desire that an international convention be elaborated and concluded expeditiously on the basis of the Commission's draft articles. By the same resolution, Member States

---

[529] For the report of the Working Group, see documents A/CN.4/L.174 and Add.1-6 and A/CN.4/L.177 and Add.1-3.
[530] See *Yearbook of the International Law Commission, 1971*, vol. II (Part One), document A/8410/Rev.1, paras. 39 and 60.
[531] See *Yearbook of the International Law Commission, 1971*, vol. II (Part One), document A/8410/Rev.1, para. 57.
[532] See *Yearbook of the International Law Commission, 1971*, vol. II (Part One), document A/8410/Rev.1, paras. 51 and 52.
[533] See *Yearbook of the International Law Commission, 1971*, vol. II (Part One), document A/8410/Rev.1, paras. 40-56.

and Switzerland were requested to submit written comments and observations on the draft articles and on the procedure to be adopted for the elaboration and conclusion of a convention on the subject. The Secretary-General and the Directors-General of the specialized agencies and the International Atomic Energy Agency were also invited to submit their written comments and observations on the draft articles.

The following year the General Assembly, by resolution 2966 (XXVII) of 14 December 1972, decided to convene the international conference as soon as practicable. In 1973 the Assembly, by resolution 3072 (XXVIII) of 30 November, decided that the conference would be held early in 1975 in Vienna.

The United Nations Conference on the Representation of States in Their Relations with International Organizations[534] was thus held at Vienna from 4 February to 14 March 1975. It was attended by representatives of eighty-one States as well as observers from two States, seven specialized and related agencies, three other intergovernmental organizations and seven national liberation movements recognized by the Organization of African Unity and/or by the League of Arab States. The Conference established a Committee of the Whole and assigned to it the consideration of the draft articles adopted by the International Law Commission. It also set up a Drafting Committee, to which it entrusted, in addition to the responsibilities for drafting and for coordinating and reviewing all the texts adopted, the preparation of the title, preamble and final clauses of the Convention, as well as the preparation of the Final Act of the Conference.

On 13 March 1975, the Conference adopted the Vienna Convention on the Representation of States in Their Relations with International Organizations of a Universal Character,[535] consisting of ninety-two articles, the text of which is reproduced in annex V, section H. The Convention was opened for signature on 14 March 1975. It remained open for signature until 30 September 1975 at the Federal Ministry of Foreign Affairs of the Republic of Austria and, subsequently, until 30 March 1976 at United Nations Headquarters. Signatures are subject to ratification. The Convention remains open

---

[534] See *Official Records of the United Nations Conference on the Representation of States in Their Relations with International Organizations, Vienna, 4 February-14 March 1975*, vol. I (United Nations publication, Sales No. 75.V.11); and ibid., vol. II (United Nations publication, Sales No. 75.V.12).
[535] See *Official Records of the United Nations Conference on the Representation of States in Their Relations with International Organizations, Vienna, 4 February-14 March 1975*, vol. II (United Nations publication, Sales No. 75.V.12), document A/CONF.67/16.

for accession by any State. It will enter into force on the thirtieth day following the date of deposit of the thirty-fifth instrument of ratification or accession. As of 20 October 2003, thirty States had become a party to the Convention.

In addition to the Vienna Convention, the Conference adopted two resolutions relating, respectively, to the status of national liberation movements recognized by the Organization of African Unity and/or by the League of Arab States and to the application of the Convention in future activities of international organizations. These resolutions are annexed to the Final Act of the Conference.[536] In light of the provisions of those resolutions, an item was placed on the agenda of the thirtieth session of the General Assembly, in 1975, entitled "Resolutions adopted by the United Nations Conference on the Representation of States in Their Relations with International Organizations: (*a*) resolution relating to the observer status of national liberation movements recognized by the Organization of African Unity and/or by the League of Arab States; (*b*) resolution relating to the application of the Convention in future activities of international organizations". From its thirtieth to thirty-fourth sessions, the General Assembly deferred consideration of the item to its next session. It considered it at its thirty-fourth, thirty-fifth, thirty-seventh, thirty-ninth,[537] forty-first, forty-third, forty-fifth, forty-seventh and forty-ninth sessions and adopted resolutions 35/167 of 15 December 1980, 37/104 of 16 December 1982, 39/76 of 13 December 1984, 41/71 of 3 December 1986, 43/160 of 9 December 1988, 45/37 of 28 November 1990 and 47/29 of 25 November 1992, and decisions 34/433 and 49/423. The General Assembly by its decision 49/423 deferred the consideration of the subject matter to its future session.

(b)   Status, privileges and immunities of international organizations

At its twenty-eighth session, in 1976, the Commission requested the Special Rapporteur for the topic, Abdullah El-Erian, to prepare a preliminary report to enable it to take the necessary decisions and to define its course of action on the second part of the topic of relations between States and international organizations, namely, the status, privileges and immunities of international organizations and their

---

[536] See *Official Records of the United Nations Conference on the Representation of States in Their Relations with International Organizations, Vienna, 4 February-14 March 1975*, vol. II (United Nations publication, Sales No. 75.V.12), document A/CONF.67/15.

[537] Since the thirty-ninth session of the General Assembly, the subject matter of the item has been confined to the observer status of national liberation movements recognized by the Organization of African Unity and/or by the League of Arab States.

officials, experts and other persons engaged in their activities who are not representatives of States.

At its twenty-ninth session, in 1977, the Commission decided to authorize the Special Rapporteur to continue his study on the lines indicated in his preliminary report[538] and to prepare a further report having regard to the views expressed and the questions raised during the debate at the twenty-ninth session. It also decided to authorize the Special Rapporteur to seek additional information and expressed the hope that he would carry out his research in the customary manner, namely by investigating the agreements and practices of international organizations, whether within or outside the United Nations system, as well as the legislation and practice of States.

In its resolution 32/151 of 19 December 1977, the General Assembly endorsed the conclusions reached by the Commission regarding the second part of the topic of relations between States and international organizations.

At the thirtieth session of the Commission, in 1978, the Commission approved the conclusions and recommendations set out in the second report of the Special Rapporteur[539] that:

(a) General agreement existed both in the Commission and in the Sixth Committee of the General Assembly on the desirability of the Commission taking up the study of the second part of the topic "Relations between States and international organizations";

(b) The Commission's work on the second part of the topic should proceed with great prudence;

(c) For the purposes of its initial work on the second part of the topic, the Commission should adopt a broad outlook, inasmuch as the study should include regional organizations. The final decision on whether to include such organizations in the eventual codification could be taken only when the study was completed;

(d) The same broad outlook should be adopted in connection with the subject matter of the study, inasmuch as the question of priority would have to be deferred until the study was completed.

At its thirty-first session, in 1979, the Commission appointed Leonardo Díaz-Gonzalez as Special Rapporteur for this part of the topic.

---

[538] See *Yearbook of the International Law Commission, 1977,* vol. II (Part One), document A/CN.4/304.
[539] See *Yearbook of the International Law Commission, 1978,* vol. II (Part One), document A/CN.4/311 and Add.1.

The Commission considered the topic on the basis of the reports of the new Special Rapporteur,[540] as well as documents prepared by the Secretariat,[541] at its thirty-fifth, thirty-seventh, thirty-ninth, forty-second and forty-third sessions, in 1983, 1985, 1987, 1990 and 1991, respectively. The Commission proceeded with the first reading of the draft articles on the basis of the fourth, fifth and sixth reports of the Special Rapporteur[542] at its forty-second and forty-third sessions, in 1990 and 1991, respectively.

At its forty-fourth session, in 1992, the Commission noted that the Planning Group had established a Working Group to review the progress so far achieved on the topic and to make a recommendation as to whether the Commission should continue with it and, if in the affirmative, in what direction. The Commission observed that the discussion of the first part of the topic, dealing with the status, privileges and immunities of representatives of States to international organizations, had resulted in draft articles which had formed the basis of the 1975 Convention on the Representation of States in Their Relations with International Organizations of a Universal Character. States had been slow to ratify the Convention or adhere to it and doubts had therefore arisen as to the advisability of continuing the work undertaken in 1976 on the second part of the topic, dealing with the status, privileges and immunities of international organizations and their personnel, a matter which seemed to a large extent covered by existing agreements. The Commission also noted that the passage of time had failed to bring any sign of increased acceptance of the Convention and the Commission had not given very active consideration to the topic. Eight reports had been presented by two successive Special Rapporteurs and all of the 22 articles contained therein had been referred to the Drafting Committee, but the Committee had not taken any action on them. Neither in the Commission nor in the Sixth Committee had the view been expressed that the topic should be more actively considered. Under the circumstances, the Commission, accepting the recommendation of the Planning Group that the topic should not be pursued further for the time being, decided not to pursue further during the current term of

---

[540] See *Yearbook of the International Law Commission, 1983*, vol. II (Part One), document A/CN.4/370; ibid., *1985*, vol. II (Part One), document A/CN.4/391 and Add.l; ibid., *1986*, vol. II (Part One), document A/CN.4/401; ibid., *1989*, vol. II (Part One), document A/CN.4/424; and ibid., *1991*, vol. II (Part One), documents A/CN.4/438 and A/CN.4/439.

[541] See *Yearbook of the International Law Commission, 1985*, vol. II (Part One), addendum, document A/CN.4/L.383 and Add.1-3.

[542] See *Yearbook of the International Law Commission, 1989*, vol. II (Part One), document A/CN.4/424; and ibid., *1991*, vol. II (Part One), documents A/CN.4/438 and A/CN.4/439.

office of its members the consideration of the topic, unless the General Assembly decided otherwise.

The General Assembly, in resolution 47/33 of 25 November 1992, endorsed the above decision of the Commission.

17. Successions of States and Governments

At its first session, in 1949, the Commission selected the subject of succession of States and Governments as one of the topics for codification without, however, including it in the list of topics to which it gave priority. At its fourteenth session, in 1962, the Commission was apprised of General Assembly resolution 1686 (XVI) of 18 December 1961, recommending that the Commission include on its priority list the topic of succession of States and Governments. In principle, all members of the Commission were in favour of including the topic on its priority list, but there were divergent views concerning the scope of the topic and the best approach to its study. The Commission decided to set up a Subcommittee on the Succession of States and Governments whose task was to submit to the Commission a preliminary report containing suggestions on the scope of the subject, the method of approach to the study and the means of providing the necessary documentation.[543]

At its fifteenth session, in 1963, the Commission considered and unanimously approved the report of the Subcommittee.[544] In the opinion of the Commission, the priority given to the study of the question of State succession was fully justified, and it was agreed that the question of the succession of Governments would, for the time being, be considered only to the extent necessary to supplement the study on State succession. Several members of the Commission stressed the importance which State succession had for new States and for the international community in view of the phenomenon of decolonization, and agreed with the Subcommittee's view that special attention should be given in the study to the problems of concern to new States.

The Commission expressed its agreement with the broad outline, the order of priority of the headings and the detailed division of the topic recommended by the Subcommittee: succession in respect of

---

[543] The Subcommittee had before it the studies prepared by the Secretariat published in *Yearbook of the International Law Commission, 1962,* vol. II, documents A/CN.4/149 and Add.1, A/CN.4/150 and A/CN.4/151.
[544] See *Yearbook of the International Law Commission, 1963,* vol. II, document A/5509, annex II. At that session, the Commission had also before it a study prepared by the Secretariat. See *Yearbook of the International Law Commission, 1963,* vol. II, document A/CN.4/157.

treaties; succession in respect of rights and duties resulting from other sources than treaties (revised in 1968 to read "succession of States in respect of matters other than treaties") and succession in respect of membership of international organizations. The Commission approved the Subcommittee's recommendations concerning the relationship between the topic of State succession and other topics on the Commission's agenda, in particular that the succession in respect of treaties would be considered in connection with the succession of States rather than in the context of the law of treaties.

The objectives proposed by the Subcommittee — a survey and evaluation of the current state of the law and practice in the matter of State succession and the preparation of draft articles on the topic in the light of new developments in international law — were approved by all members of the Commission. The Commission appointed Manfred Lachs as Special Rapporteur for the topic.

The General Assembly, in resolution 1902 (XVIII) of 18 November 1963, recommended that the Commission should "continue its work on the succession of States and Governments, taking into account the views expressed at the eighteenth session of the General Assembly, the report of the Subcommittee on the Succession of States and Governments and the comments which may be submitted by Governments, with appropriate reference to the views of States which have achieved independence since the Second World War".

Following the resignation of Mr. Lachs, the Commission decided, at its nineteenth session, in 1967, to deal with the three aspects of the topic in accordance with the broad outline of the subject laid down in the report of the Subcommittee in 1963. The Commission appointed Special Rapporteurs for the first two aspects of the topic, succession in respect of treaties and succession of States in respect of matters other than treaties, and decided to leave aside for the time being the third aspect, succession in respect of membership of international organizations, without assigning it to a Special Rapporteur. It was considered that the third aspect related both to succession in respect of treaties and to relations between States and international organizations. In accordance with the decision taken in 1963, it was agreed to give priority to the study of State succession, considering the study of succession of Governments only to the extent necessary to supplement the study of State succession.

(a) Succession of States in respect of treaties

The Commission considered the sub-topic at its twentieth, twenty-second, twenty-fourth and twenty-sixth sessions, in 1968, 1970, 1972 and 1974, respectively. The Commission appointed Sir Humphrey

Waldock and Sir Francis Vallat as the successive Special Rapporteurs for the sub-topic at its nineteenth and twenty-fifth sessions, in 1967 and 1973, respectively. In connection with its consideration of the topic, the Commission had before it the reports of the Special Rapporteurs,[545] information provided by Governments and international organizations[546] as well as documents prepared by the Secretariat.[547]

At its twenty-fourth session, in 1972, the Commission conducted the first reading of the draft articles on succession of States in respect of treaties. At that session, the Commission adopted on first reading a provisional draft with commentaries and, in accordance with articles 16 and 21 of its Statute, decided to transmit it to Governments of Member States for their observations.

The General Assembly, in resolution 2926 (XXVII) of 28 November 1972, recommended that the Commission should continue its work on the sub-topic in the light of comments received from Member States on the provisional draft. In resolution 3071 (XXVIII) of 30 November 1973, the General Assembly recommended that the Commission complete at its twenty-sixth session, in 1974, the second reading of the draft on succession of States in respect of treaties, in the light of comments received from Member States.

At its twenty-sixth session, in 1974, the Commission adopted the final text of the draft articles on the succession of States in respect of treaties, with commentaries,[548] and submitted it to the General Assembly with a recommendation that the General Assembly should invite Member States to submit their written comments and observations on the draft articles and should convene a conference of

---

[545] For the reports of Sir Humphrey Waldock, see *Yearbook of the International Law Commission, 1968*, vol. II, document A/CN.4/202; ibid., *1969*, vol. II, document A/CN.4/214 and Add.1 and 2; ibid., *1970*, vol. II, document A/CN.4/224 and Add.1; ibid., *1971*, vol. II (Part One), document A/CN.4/249; and ibid., *1972*, vol. II, documents A/CN.4/256 and Add.1-4 and A/CN.4/L.184. For the report of Sir Francis Vallat, see ibid., *1974*, vol. II (Part One), document A/CN.4/278 and Add.1-6.

[546] Documents A/CN.4/275 and Add.1 and 2, A/CN.4/L.205 and A/9610/Add.1 and 2 reproduced in *Yearbook of the International Law Commission, 1974*, vol. II (Part One), document A/9610/Rev.1, annex I; as well as document A/CN.4/L.213.

[547] See *Yearbook of the International Law Commission, 1968*, vol. II, document A/CN.4/200 and Add.1 and 2; ibid., *1969*, vol. II, document A/CN.4/210; ibid., *1970*, vol. II, documents A/CN.4/225 and A/CN.4/229; and ibid., *1971*, vol. II (Part Two), document A/CN.4/243 and Add.1. Furthermore, for the use of the Commission in its work on the topic, the Secretariat published a volume in the *United Nations Legislative Series* entitled *"Materials on Succession of States"* containing information related mainly to succession of States in respect of treaties (see ST/LEG/SER.B/14, United Nations publication, Sales No. 68.V.5). A supplement thereto was published in 1972 as a document of the twenty-fourth session of the Commission (document A/CN.4/263).

[548] See *Yearbook of the Internatiomal Law Commission, 1974*, vol. II (Part One), document A/9610/Rev.1, paras. 43 and 85.

plenipotentiaries to study the draft articles and conclude a convention on the subject.[549]

The General Assembly, in resolution 3315 (XXIX) of 14 December 1974, invited Member States to submit their written comments and observations on the draft articles prepared by the Commission and on the procedure by which and the form in which work on the draft articles should be completed. The following year, the Assembly, by resolution 3496 (XXX) of 15 December 1975, decided to convene a conference of plenipotentiaries in 1977 to consider the draft articles and to embody the results of its work in an international convention and such other instruments as it might deem appropriate. In the resolution, the Assembly urged Member States which had not yet done so to submit as soon as possible their written comments and observations on the draft articles. On 24 November 1976, the Assembly adopted resolution 31/18 by which it decided that the United Nations Conference on Succession of States in Respect of Treaties would be held from 4 April to 6 May 1977 at Vienna.

The Conference was held as scheduled but, having been unable to conclude its work in the time available, it recommended on 6 May 1977 that the General Assembly decide to reconvene the Conference in the first half of 1978 for a final session.[550]

The resumed session of the Conference, approved by General Assembly resolution 32/47 of 8 December 1977, was held at Vienna from 31 July to 23 August 1978.[551]

The delegations of one hundred States participated in the Conference (eighty-nine States in the 1977 session and ninety-four States in the resumed session). Two States were represented by observers at each of the 1977 and resumed sessions. In addition, the United Nations Council for Namibia[552] participated in the Conference and the Palestine Liberation Organization and the South West Africa People's Organization (SWAPO) were represented by observers, SWAPO at the 1977 session only. Four specialized and related

---

[549] See *Yearbook of the Internatiomal Law Commission, 1974,* vol. II (Part One), document A/9610/Rev.l, para. 84.

[550] See *Official Records of the United Nations Conference on Succession of States in Respect of Treaties, Vienna, 4 April-6 May 1977 and 31 July-23 August 1978*, vol. III, Documents of the Conference, First and Resumed Sessions (United Nations publication, Sales No. 79.V.10), Report of the Conference (1977 session), document A/CONF.80/15, para. 26.

[551] See *Official Records of the United Nations Conference on Succession of States in Respect of Treaties, Vienna, 4 April-6 May 1977 and 31 July-23 August 1978*, vol. I (United Nations publication, Sales No. 78.V.8); ibid., vol. II (United Nations publication, Sales No. 79.V.9); and ibid., vol. III (United Nations publication, Sales No. 79.V.10).

[552] Namibia was admitted to the United Nations membership on 23 April 1990.

agencies and one other intergovernmental organization sent observers to the 1977 session and two other intergovernmental organizations to both the 1977 and resumed sessions.

The Conference assigned to a Committee of the Whole the consideration of the draft articles adopted by the International Law Commission and entrusted to a Drafting Committee, in addition to its responsibilities for drafting and coordinating and reviewing all texts adopted, with the preparation of the title, preamble and final clauses of the Convention and the Final Act of the Conference. The Conference also established an Informal Consultations Group for the purpose of considering draft articles 6, 7 and 12 and, at the resumed session, an Ad hoc Group on Peaceful Settlement of Disputes. The Conference, on 22 August 1978, adopted the Vienna Convention on Succession of States in Respect of Treaties[553] consisting of a preamble, fifty articles and an annex, the text of which is reproduced in annex V, section I. The Convention retains, to a considerable degree, the structure and the text of the draft articles adopted by the International Law Commission. The annex to the Convention specifies the conciliation procedure to which article 42 of the Convention relates.

The Final Act of the Conference, of which five resolutions adopted by the Conference form an integral part, was signed on 23 August 1978. The Convention was opened for signature on 23 August 1978 until 28 February 1979 at the Federal Ministry for Foreign Affairs of the Republic of Austria and, subsequently, until 31 August 1979 at United Nations Headquarters. Signatures are subject to ratification. The Convention remains open for accession by any State. The Convention entered into force on 6 November 1996. As of 27 October 2003, seventeen States had become a party to the Convention.

Of the five resolutions adopted by the Conference, one, relating to incompatible treaty obligations and rights arising from a uniting of States, recommends that in such cases the successor States and the other States parties to the treaties in question make every effort to resolve the matter by mutual agreement. In another resolution, concerning Namibia, the Conference resolved that the relevant articles of the Convention shall be interpreted, in the case of Namibia, in conformity with United Nations resolutions on the question of Namibia and that South Africa was not the predecessor State of the future independent State of Namibia.[554]

---

[553] United Nations, *Treaty Series,* vol. 1946, p. 3.
[554] See *Official Records of the United Nations Conference on Succession of States in Respect of Treaties, Vienna, 4 April-6 May 1977 and 31 July-23 August 1978,* vol.

(b) Succession of States in respect of matters other than treaties

At its nineteenth session, in 1967, the Commission appointed Mohammed Bedjaoui as Special Rapporteur for the sub-topic of succession in respect of rights and duties resulting from sources other than treaties.[555]

The Commission considered this sub-topic at its twentieth, twenty-first, twenty-fifth and from its twenty-seventh to thirty-third sessions, in 1968, 1969, 1973 and from 1975 to 1981, respectively. In connection with its consideration of this topic, the Commission had before it the reports of the Special Rapporteur,[556] information provided by Governments[557] as well as documents prepared by the Secretariat.[558]

At its twenty-fifth session, in 1973, the Commission decided to limit its study for the time being to only one category of public property, namely property of the State. At the same session, it began the first reading of the draft articles.

The Commission completed the first reading of the draft articles on succession of States in respect of State property and State debts at its thirty-first session, in 1979, and on succession in respect of State archives, at its following session, in 1980. In accordance with articles 16 and 21 of its Statute, the draft articles adopted by the Commission on first reading were transmitted, through the Secretary-General, to Governments of Member States for their observations.

III, Documents of the Conference, First and Resumed Sessions (United Nations publication, Sales No. 79.V.10), document A/CONF.80/32, Annex.

[555] At its twentieth session, in 1968, the Commission decided to delete from the title of the topic all reference to sources in order to avoid any ambiguity regarding its delimitation, adopting as the new title "Succession in respect of matters other than treaties."

[556] See *Yearbook of the International Law Commission, 1968,* vol. II, document A/CN.4/204; ibid., *1969,* vol. II, document A/CN.4/216/Rev.1; ibid., *1970,* vol. II, document A/CN.4/226; ibid., *1971,* vol. II (Part One), document A/CN.4/247 and Add.1; ibid., *1972,* vol. II, document A/CN.4/259; ibid., *1973,* vol. II, document A/CN.4/267; ibid., *1974,* vol. II (Part One), document A/CN.4/282; ibid., *1976,* vol. II (Part One), document A/CN.4/292; ibid., *1977,* vol. II (Part One), document A/CN.4/301 and Add.1; ibid., *1978,* vol. II (Part One), document A/CN.4/313; ibid., *1979,* vol. II (Part One), document A/CN.4/322 and Add.1 and 2; ibid., *1980,* vol. II (Part One), document A/CN.4/333; and ibid., *1981,* vol. II (Part One), document A/CN.4/345 and Add. 1-3.

[557] Document A/CN.4/338 and Add.1-4 published in *Yearbook of the International Law Commission, 1981,* vol. II (Part Two), annex I.

[558] See *Yearbook of the International Law Commission, 1970,* vol. II, document A/CN.4/232. Furthermore, apart from the volume in the *United Nations Legislative Series* entitled *"Materials on Succession of States"* and supplement thereto (*see above*), the Secretariat published a separate volume in the *United Nations Legislative Series* containing exclusively materials provided by Governments on succession of States in respect of matters other than treaties (ST/LEG/SER.B/17, United Nations publication, Sales No. 77.V.9).

The General Assembly, in paragraph 4 (*a*) of resolution 35/163 of 15 December 1980, recommended that, taking into account the written comments of Governments and views expressed in debates in the General Assembly, the Commission should, at its thirty-third session, complete the second reading of the draft articles on succession of States in respect of matters other than treaties adopted at its thirty-first and thirty-second sessions.

At its thirty-third session, in 1981, the Commission re-examined the draft articles in the light of the comments of Governments and adopted the final text of its draft articles on succession of States in respect of State property, archives and debts, as a whole, with commentaries.[559] In accordance with its Statute, the Commission submitted the final draft articles to the General Assembly with a recommendation that the Assembly should convene a conference of plenipotentiaries to study the draft articles and conclude a convention on the subject.[560]

The General Assembly, in resolution 36/113 of 10 December 1981, decided to convene an international conference of plenipotentiaries to consider the draft articles on succession of States in respect of State property, archives and debts, and to embody the results of its work in an international convention and such other instruments as it might deem appropriate. In that resolution, the General Assembly also invited Member States to submit their written comments and observations on the final draft articles. In resolution 37/11 of 15 November 1982, the General Assembly decided that the United Nations Conference on Succession of States in respect of State Property, Archives and Debts would be held from 1 March to 8 April 1983 at Vienna.

The Conference was accordingly held at Vienna from 1 March to 8 April 1983. The delegations of ninety States participated in the Conference, as did also Namibia, represented by the United Nations Council for Namibia. In addition, the Palestine Liberation Organization, the African National Congress of South Africa and the Pan Africanist Congress of Azania were represented at the Conference. Two specialized and related agencies and two other intergovernmental organizations were represented by observers.

The Conference had before it written comments of Governments on the final draft articles on succession of States in respect of State property, archives and debts pursuant to General Assembly resolution

---

[559] See *Yearbook of the International Law Commission, 1981*, vol. II (Part Two), paras. 61 and 87.
[560] See *Yearbook of the International Law Commission, 1981*, vol. II (Part Two), para. 86.

36/113 of 10 December 1981, as well as comments made orally on the draft articles in the Sixth Committee of the General Assembly at the thirty-sixth and thirty-seventh sessions of the Assembly. The comments were contained in an analytical compilation prepared by the Secretariat of the United Nations.[561]

The Conference assigned to the Committee of the Whole the consideration of the draft articles on succession of States in respect of State property, archives and debts adopted by the International Law Commission. It entrusted to the Drafting Committee, in addition to the responsibility of drafting and coordinating and reviewing all the texts adopted, the preparation of the title, preamble and final clauses of the Convention, as well as the preparation of the Final Act of the Conference. The Conference, on 7 April 1983, adopted the Vienna Convention on Succession of States in respect of State Property, Archives and Debts,[562] consisting of a preamble, fifty-one articles and an annex, the text of which is reproduced in annex V, section J. The Annex to the Convention specifies the conciliation procedure to which article 43 of the Convention relates. The Convention was opened for signature on that date until 31 December 1983 at the Federal Ministry for Foreign Affairs of the Republic of Austria and, subsequently, until 30 June 1984 at United Nations Headquarters. The Convention is subject to ratification. The Convention remains open for accession by any State. The Convention shall enter into force on the thirtieth day following the date of the deposit of the fifteenth instrument of ratification or accession. As of 27 October 2003, six States had become a party to the Convention.

The Final Act of the Conference, of which six resolutions adopted by the Conference form an integral part, was signed on 8 April 1983. One of the resolutions adopted by the Conference recognizes that the provisions of the Convention may not in any circumstances impair the exercise of the lawful right to self-determination and independence, in accordance with the Purposes and Principles of the Charter of the United Nations and the Declaration on Principles of International Law concerning Friendly Relations and Cooperation among States in accordance with the Charter of the United Nations, for peoples struggling against colonialism, alien domination, alien occupation, racial discrimination and *apartheid* and recognizes that the peoples in question possess permanent

---

[561] Document A/CONF.117/5 and Add.1.
[562] See *Official Records of the United Nations Conference on Succession of States in Respect of State Property, Archives and Debts, Vienna, 1 March-8 April 1983*, vol. II, Summary records of the plenary meetings and of the meetings of the Committee of the Whole (United Nations publication, Sales No. 94.V.6), document A/CONF/117/14.

sovereignty over their resources and natural wealth and their rights to development, to information concerning their history and to the conservation of their cultural heritage. Another resolution, concerning Namibia, provides that the relevant articles of the Convention shall be interpreted, in the case of Namibia, in conformity with United Nations resolutions on the question of Namibia and that, in consequence, all the rights of the future independent State of Namibia should be reserved.[563]

At its forty-seventh session, in 1995, the Commission took up another aspect of the topic of succession of States and Governments, namely "Nationality in relation to the succession of States" (*see Part III.A, section 24*).

18. Question of the protection and inviolability of diplomatic agents and other persons entitled to special protection under international law

At the twenty-third session of the Commission, in 1971, it was suggested that the Commission should consider whether it would be possible to produce draft articles regarding such crimes as the murder, kidnapping and assaults upon diplomats and other persons entitled to special protection under international law. Though recognizing the importance and the urgency of the matter, the Commission had to defer its decision in view of the priority that had to be given to another existing topic. In considering its programme of work for 1972, however, the Commission decided that, if the General Assembly requested it to do so, it would prepare at its 1972 session a set of draft articles on that subject.

The General Assembly, in resolution 2780 (XXVI) of 3 December 1971, requested the Commission to study as soon as possible the question of the protection and inviolability of diplomatic agents and other persons entitled to special protection under international law with a view to preparing a set of draft articles dealing with offences committed against such agents and persons for submission to the Assembly at the earliest date which the Commission would consider appropriate. It also requested the Secretary-General to invite comments from Member States on the

---

[563] See *Official Records of the United Nations Conference on Succession of States in Respect of State Property, Archives and Debts, Vienna, 1 March-8 April 1983*, vol. II, Summary records of the plenary meetings and of the meetings of the Committee of the Whole (United Nations publication, Sales No. 94.V.6), document A/CONF.117/15.

question of the protection of diplomats and to transmit them to the Commission.

At its twenty-fourth session, in 1972, the Commission, after an initial general discussion, set up a Working Group to review the problem involved and prepare a set of draft articles for submission to the Commission.[564] This step, in contrast with the traditional procedure of appointing a Special Rapporteur to make a study of the subject and prepare draft articles, was based on the view of most of the members who participated in the general discussion that the subject was one of sufficient urgency and importance to justify the Commission adopting a more expeditious method of producing a set of draft articles for submission to the General Assembly at its twenty-seventh session.

At the conclusion of the initial stage of its work, the Working Group submitted to the Commission a first report[565] containing a set of twelve draft articles on the prevention and punishment of crimes against diplomatic agents and other internationally protected persons. Following the Commission's consideration of the draft articles, the Working Group revised them and referred them back to the Commission in two further reports.[566] The Commission considered those reports and provisionally adopted the draft of twelve articles, which it submitted to the General Assembly as well as to Governments for comments.

The General Assembly, in resolution 2926 (XXVII) of 28 November 1972, decided to consider at its twenty-eighth session the draft convention on the prevention and punishment of crimes against diplomatic agents and other internationally protected persons with a view to the final elaboration of such a convention by the Assembly. It also invited States and the specialized agencies and interested intergovernmental organizations to submit their written comments and observations on the draft articles prepared by the Commission.

At the twenty-eighth session of the General Assembly, in 1973, the Sixth Committee considered the provisions of the draft convention in two stages.[567] In the first stage, it considered all the

---

[564] At that session, the Commission had before it observations of Member States, transmitted to the Commission in accordance with General Assembly resolution 2780 (XXVI) of 3 December 1971 (document A/CN.4/253 and Add.1-5 incorporated in *Yearbook of the International Law Commission, 1972*, vol. II, document A/8710/Rev.1, annex), a working paper containing the text of a draft convention prepared by the delegation of Uruguay (document A/C.6/L.822) as well as a working paper by a member of the Commission, Richard D. Kearney (see *Yearbook of the International Law Commission, 1972*, vol. II, document A/CN.4/L.182).

[565] Document A/CN.4/L.186.

[566] Documents A/CN.4/L.188 and Add.1 and A/CN.4/L.189.

[567] See *Official Records of the General Assembly, Twenty-eighth Session, Annexes,*

draft articles and the new articles proposed as well as the preamble and the final clauses and, except for article 9 which it decided to delete, referred them to a Drafting Committee either in their original form or in amended form, together with amendments submitted, as appropriate. In a second stage, it considered and adopted, in their original form or in amended form, the texts recommended by the Drafting Committee. The Drafting Committee was then entrusted with the coordination and further review of the text as a whole, before its adoption by the Sixth Committee for recommendation to the General Assembly. On 14 December 1973, the General Assembly adopted the Convention on the Prevention and Punishment of Crimes against Internationally Protected Persons, including Diplomatic Agents,[568] consisting of a preamble and twenty articles, annexed to resolution 3166 (XXVIII) of 14 December 1973. The text of the Convention, together with that of resolution 3166 (XXVIII),[569] is reproduced in annex V, section G.

The Convention, which is subject to ratification, was opened for signature by all States at United Nations Headquarters until 31 December 1974. It remains open for accession by any State. The Convention came into force on 20 February 1977. As of 3 November 2003, one hundred forty-three States had become a party to the Convention.

19. The most-favoured-nation clause

The topic of the most-favoured-nation clause was first raised in 1964 when the Commission was examining the question of treaties and third States. After considering the matter, the Commission concluded that it did not think it advisable to deal with the most-favoured-nation clause in the codification of the general law of treaties, although it felt that such clauses might at some future time appropriately form the subject of a special study.

At its nineteenth session, in 1967, in view of the manageable scope of the topic, of the interest expressed in it by representatives in the Sixth Committee and of the fact that the clarification of its legal aspects might be of assistance to the work of the United Nations Commission on International Trade Law, the Commission decided to place on its programme of work the topic of the most-favoured-nation clause in the law of treaties.

---

agenda item 90, document A/9407.
[568] United Nations, *Treaty Series*, vol. 1035, p. 167.
[569] Resolution 3166 (XXVIII) of 14 December 1973 requires, in its paragraph 6, that it be always published together with the Convention annexed thereto.

By resolution 2272 (XXII) of 1 December 1967, the General Assembly recommended that the Commission should study the topic of most-favoured-nation clauses in the law of treaties.

The Commission considered this topic at its twentieth, twenty-first, twenty-fifth, twenty-seventh, twenty-eighth and thirtieth sessions, in 1968, 1969, 1973, 1975, 1976 and 1978, respectively. The Commission appointed Endre Ustor and Nikolai A. Ushakov as the successive Special Rapporteurs for the topic at its nineteenth and twenty-ninth sessions, in 1967 and 1977, respectively. In connection with its consideration of the topic, the Commission had before it the working paper and reports of the Special Rapporteurs,[570] information provided by Governments and international organizations[571] as well as a document prepared by the Secretariat.[572]

At its twentieth session, in 1968, after a general discussion on the matter, the Commission instructed the Special Rapporteur, Mr. Ustor, not to confine his studies to the domain of international trade but to explore the major fields of application of the clause. The Commission considered that it should clarify the scope and effect of the clause as a legal institution in the context of all aspects of its practical application.

The Commission proceeded with the first reading of the draft articles at its twenty-fifth, twenty-seventh and twenty-eighth sessions, in 1973, 1975 and 1976. At its twenty-eighth session, in 1976, the Commission decided to transmit the draft articles adopted on first reading, through the Secretary-General, to Governments of Member States for their observations in accordance with articles 16 and 21 of its Statute.

The General Assembly, in resolution 31/97 of 15 December 1976, welcomed the completion of the first reading of the draft articles and recommended that the Commission should conclude the second reading of them at its thirtieth session in the light of comments received from Member States, from organs of the United

---

[570] For the working paper and reports of Endre Ustor, see *Yearbook of the International Law Commission, 1968,* vol. II, document A/CN.4/L.127; ibid., *1969,* vol. II, document A/CN.4/213; ibid., *1970,* vol. II, document A/CN.4/228 and Add.1; ibid., *1972,* vol. II, document A/CN.4/257 and Add.1; ibid., *1973,* vol. II, document A/CN.4/266; ibid., *1974,* vol. II (Part One), document A/CN.4/280; ibid., *1975,* vol. II, document A/CN.4/286; and ibid., *1976,* vol. II (Part One), document A/CN.4/293 and Add.1. For the report of Nikolai A. Ushakov, see ibid., *1978,* vol. II (Part One), document A/CN.4/309 and Add.1 and 2.

[571] Documents A/CN.4/308 and Add.1, Add.1/Corr.1 and Add.2 as well as A/CN.4/L.268 incorporated in *Yearbook of the International Law Commission, 1978,* vol. II (Part Two), annex.

[572] See *Yearbook of the International Law Commission, 1973,* vol. II, document A/CN.4/269.

Nations which had competence on the subject matter and from interested intergovernmental organizations. This recommendation was reiterated by the Assembly in its resolution 32/151 of 19 December 1977.

At its thirtieth session in 1978, the Commission re-examined the draft articles on the basis of the first report submitted by the new Special Rapporteur, Mr. Ushakov,[573] comments received from Member States and international organizations and proposals submitted by certain members of the Commission for additional articles as follows: article 21 *bis*, "The most-favoured-nation clause in relation to arrangements between developing countries";[574] article A, "The most-favoured-nation clause and treatment extended in accordance with the Charter of Economic Rights and Duties of States";[575] article 21 *ter* "The most-favoured-nation clause and treatment extended under commodity agreements";[576] article 23 *bis* "The most-favoured-nation clause in relation to treatment extended by one member of a customs union to another member"[577] and article 28 entitled "Settlement of disputes" with an annex.[578]

At the same session, the Commission adopted the final text of thirty draft articles, with commentaries, on most-favoured-nation clauses.[579] The text of the final draft is reproduced in annex IV, section 6.

In considering the relationship between the most-favoured-nation clause and the different levels of economic development, the Commission found that the operation of the clause in the sphere of economic relations, with particular reference to the developing countries, was not a matter that lent itself easily to codification of international law in the sense in which that term was used in article 15 of the Statute of the Commission, because the requirements for that process described therein, namely, extensive State practice, precedents and doctrine, were not easily discernible. The Commission, therefore, attempted to enter into the field of progressive development by adopting, inter alia, article 24, which was based on the proposal for a new article 21 *bis* mentioned above. The Commission, however, did not agree on the appropriateness of

---

[573] See *Yearbook of the International Law Commission, 1978*, vol. II (Part One), document A/CN.4/309 and Add.1 and 2.
[574] Document A/CN.4/L.266.
[575] Document A/CN.4/L.264.
[576] Document A/CN.4/L.265.
[577] Document A/CN.4/L.267.
[578] Document A/CN.4/L.270.
[579] See *Yearbook of the International Law Commission, 1978*, vol. II (Part Two), paras. 45 and 74.

including in its final draft further provisions based on the two proposals for additional articles A and 21 *ter* and decided instead to bring their texts to the attention of the General Assembly so that Member States might take them into account as appropriate when undertaking the final codification of the topic. With regard to the question of most-favoured-nation clauses in relation to customs unions and similar associations of States, on which a proposal for a new article 23 *bis* had been submitted, the Commission, bearing in mind the inconclusiveness of the comments made thereon and the lack of time, agreed not to include an article on a customs union exception in the final draft. It was understood that the silence of the draft articles could not be interpreted as an implicit recognition of the existence or non-existence of such a rule but should, rather, be interpreted to mean that the ultimate decision was one to be taken by the States to which the draft was submitted, at the final stage of the codification of the topic. Likewise, the Commission decided not to include in its final draft a provision on the settlement of disputes such as that contained in the proposal for an additional article 28 but to refer the question to the General Assembly and Member States, and, ultimately, to the body which might be entrusted with the task of finalizing the draft articles.[580]

The Commission decided, in conformity with article 23 of its Statute, to recommend to the General Assembly that the draft articles should be recommended to Member States with a view to the conclusion of a convention on the subject.[581]

The General Assembly, by its resolution 33/139 of 19 December 1978, inter alia, invited all States, organs of the United Nations which have competence on the subject matter and interested intergovernmental organizations to submit their written comments on the draft articles on most-favoured-nation clauses adopted by the International Law Commission as well as on those provisions relating to such clauses on which the Commission was unable to take decisions. The Assembly also requested States to comment on the Commission's recommendation regarding the conclusion of a convention on the subject. The Assembly reiterated these invitations at its thirty-fifth, thirty-sixth, thirty-eighth and fortieth sessions, in 1980, 1981, 1983 and 1985.[582]

---

[580] See *Yearbook of the International Law Commission, 1978*, vol. II (Part Two), paras. 47-72.

[581] See *Yearbook of the International Law Commission, 1978*, vol. II (Part Two), para. 73.

[582] General Assembly resolutions 35/161 of 15 December 1980, 36/111 of 10 December 1981, 38/127 of 19 December 1983 and 40/65 of 11 December 1985.

By its decision 43/429 of 9 December 1988, the General Assembly, noting the complexity of codification or progressive development of the international law on most-favoured-nation clauses, and considering that additional time should be given to Governments for thorough study of the draft articles and for determining their respective positions on the most appropriate procedure for future work, decided to include the item in the provisional agenda of its forty-sixth session, in 1991.

The General Assembly, at its forty-sixth session, in 1991, gave further consideration to the topic. In its decision 46/416 of 9 December 1991, the Assembly, having noted with appreciation the valuable work done by the Commission on the most-favoured-nation clauses, as well as the observations and comments of Member States, of organs of the United Nations, of the specialized agencies and of interested intergovernmental organizations, decided to bring the draft articles on most-favoured-nations clauses, as contained in the report of the Commission on the work of its thirtieth session,[583] to the attention of Member States and interested intergovernmental organizations for their consideration in such cases and to the extent as they deemed appropriate.

20. Question of treaties concluded between States and international organizations or between two or more international organizations

The United Nations Conference on the Law of Treaties, held in 1969 at Vienna, adopted a resolution entitled "Resolution relating to article 1 of the Vienna Convention on the Law of Treaties", annexed to the Final Act, recommending that the General Assembly should refer to the Commission the study of the question of treaties concluded between States and international organizations or between two or more international organizations (*see page 138*). Acting on this recommendation, the General Assembly, in resolution 2501 (XXIV) of 12 November 1969, recommended that the International Law Commission should study the question, in consultation with the principal international organizations.

At its twenty-second session, in 1970, the Commission included this question in its programme of work and set up a Subcommittee to consider the preliminary problems involved in the study of the topic. The Subcommittee's report,[584] as adopted by the Commission,

---

[583] See *Yearbook of the International Law Commission, 1978*, vol. II (Part Two), para. 74.
[584] Document A/CN.4/L.155 reproduced in *Yearbook of the International Law*

requested the Secretariat to undertake certain preparatory work, in particular as regards United Nations practice, and asked the Chairman of the Subcommittee to submit to members of the Subcommittee a questionnaire concerning the method of treating the topic and its scope.

At the Commission's twenty-third session, in 1971, the Subcommittee submitted to the Commission a report,[585] containing a summary of the views expressed by members of the Subcommittee in reply to the questionnaire prepared by its Chairman, and recommendations to the Commission, in particular to appoint a Special Rapporteur for the topic and confirm the request addressed to the Secretary-General concerning certain preparatory work. The Commission considered the report and adopted it without change. At the same session, the Commission appointed Paul Reuter as Special Rapporteur for the topic.

The Commission considered the topic from its twenty-fifth to twenty-seventh and from its twenty-ninth to thirty-fourth sessions, from 1973 to 1975 and from 1977 to 1982, respectively. In connection with its consideration of the topic, the Commission had before it the reports of the Special Rapporteur,[586] information provided by Governments and international organizations[587] as well as documents prepared by the Secretariat.[588]

At its twenty-fifth session, in 1973, the Commission requested the Special Rapporteur to begin the preparation of a set of draft articles on the basis of his first two reports and the comments made during that session.

At its twenty-sixth session, in 1974, the Commission began the first reading of the draft articles, which was completed at its thirty-

---

Commission, 1970, vol. II, document A/8410/Rev.1, para. 89.

[585] See *Yearbook of the International Law Commission, 1971*, vol. II (Part Two), document A/CN.4/250, also reproduced in ibid., vol. II (Part One), document A/8410/Rev.1, annex.

[586] See *Yearbook of the International Law Commission, 1972*, vol. II, document A/CN.4/258; ibid., *1973*, vol. II, document A/CN.4/271; ibid., *1974*, vol. II (Part One), document A/CN.4/279; ibid., *1975*, vol. II, document A/CN.4/285; ibid., *1976*, vol. II (Part One), document A/CN.4/290 and Add.1; ibid., *1977*, vol. II (Part One), document A/CN.4/298; ibid., *1978*, vol. II (Part One), document A/CN.4/312; ibid., *1979*, vol. II (Part One), document A/CN.4/319; ibid., *1980*, vol. II (Part One), document A/CN.4/327; ibid., *1981*, vol. II (Part One), document A/CN.4/341 and Add.1; and ibid., *1982*, vol. II (Part One), document A/CN.4/353.

[587] Document A/CN.4/339 and Add.1-8 reproduced in *Yearbook of the International Law Commission, 1981*, vol. II (Part Two), annex II; as well as document A/CN.4/350 and Add.1-6, Add.6/Corr.1 and Add.7-11 reproduced in *Yearbook of the International Law Commission, 1982*, vol. II (Part Two), annex.

[588] Document A/CN.4/L.161 and Add.1 and 2; as well as *Yearbook of the International Law Commission, 1974*, vol. II (Part Two), documents A/CN.4/277 and A/CN.4/281.

second session, in 1980. In accordance with the decision taken by the Commission at its thirtieth session, in 1978, the Commission, upon provisional adoption of certain sets of draft articles, transmitted them to Governments and principal international organizations[589] for comments and observations, before the draft as a whole was adopted on the first reading. That procedure was seen as making it possible for the Commission to undertake the second reading without too much delay.

The General Assembly, in resolution 35/163 of 15 December 1980, invited the Commission to commence the second reading of the draft articles.

The Commission proceeded with the second reading of the draft articles at its thirty-third and thirty-fourth sessions, in 1981 and 1982, respectively, in accordance with the General Assembly recommendation contained in resolution 36/114 of 10 December 1981. At the latter session, the Commission adopted the final text of the draft articles, with commentaries, on the law of treaties between States and international organizations or between international organizations, and submitted it to the General Assembly with the recommendation that the Assembly convoke a conference to conclude a convention on the subject under article 23, subparagraph 1 (*d*) of its Statute.[590]

By resolution 37/112 of 16 December 1982, the General Assembly decided that an international convention should be concluded on the basis of the draft articles adopted by the Commission. In addition, the Assembly invited States and the principal international organizations to submit comments on the final draft as well as on other questions, such as the participation of international organizations in the conference and the solution of the problem of how international organizations would be associated with the convention.

At its thirty-eighth session, the General Assembly, by its resolution 38/139 of 19 December 1983, decided that the appropriate forum for the final consideration of the draft articles was a conference of plenipotentiaries, to be convened not earlier than 1985. It also appealed to potential participants in the Conference to undertake consultations on the draft articles and related questions prior to the thirty-ninth session of the Assembly, in order to facilitate the

---

[589] In the light of Commission practice regarding its work on the topic, the organizations in question were the United Nations and the intergovernmental organizations invited to send observers to United Nations codification conferences.
[590] See *Yearbook of the International Law Commission, 1982*, vol. II (Part Two), paras. 33 and 57.

successful conclusion of the work of the Conference. The following year the General Assembly, by resolution 39/86 of 13 December 1984, decided that the United Nations Conference on the Law of Treaties between States and International Organizations or between International Organizations would be held at Vienna from 18 February to 21 March 1986 and referred to the Conference as the basic proposal for its consideration the final set of draft articles adopted by the Commission at its thirty-fourth session, in 1982. It also appealed to participants in the Conference to organize consultations, primarily on the organization and methods of work of the Conference, including rules of procedure, and on major issues of substance, including final clauses and settlement of disputes, prior to the convening of the Conference in order to facilitate a successful conclusion of its work through the promotion of general agreement.

Informal consultations were held between 18 March and 1 May and between 8 and 12 July 1985.[591] By resolution 40/76 of 11 December 1985, the General Assembly considered that those informal consultations proved useful in enabling thorough preparation for successful conduct of the Conference. The Assembly decided to transmit to the Conference, and to recommend that it adopt, the draft rules of procedure for the Conference, worked out during the informal consultations (annex I of the resolution). Also, the Assembly decided to transmit to the Conference for its consideration and action, as appropriate, a list of draft articles of the basic proposal, for which substantive consideration was deemed necessary (annex II of the resolution). Finally, the Assembly referred to the Conference for its consideration the draft final clauses presented by the co-Chairmen of the informal consultations on which an exchange of views had been held (annex III of the resolution).

The Conference was held at Vienna from 18 February to 21 March 1986. Ninety-seven States participated in the Conference, as did also Namibia, represented by the United Nations Council for Namibia. The Palestine Liberation Organization, the African National Congress of South Africa and the Pan Africanist Congress of Azania were represented by observers. Nineteen international intergovernmental organizations, including the United Nations, were represented at the Conference.

The Conference assigned to the Committee of the Whole those draft articles of the basic proposal which required substantive consideration as well as the preparation of the preamble and the final provisions of the Convention. It referred all other draft articles of the

---

[591] The informal summing-up by the co-Chairman of the informal consultations is contained in document A/C.6/40/10.

basic proposal directly to the Drafting Committee, which was furthermore responsible for considering the draft articles referred to it by the Committee of the Whole and for coordinating and reviewing the drafting of all texts adopted, as well as for the preparation of the Final Act of the Conference.

On 20 March 1986, the Conference adopted the Vienna Convention on the Law of Treaties between States and International Organizations or between International Organizations,[592] which consists of a preamble, 86 articles and an annex. The text of the Convention is reproduced in annex V, section K.

The Convention applies to treaties between one or more States and one or more international organizations and to treaties between international organizations, the term "treaty" being defined for the purposes of the Convention as an international agreement governed by international law and concluded in written form between one or more States and one or more international organizations or between international organizations whether that agreement is embodied in a single instrument or in two or more related instruments and whatever its particular designation. The Convention does not apply to international agreements to which one or more States, one or more international organizations and one or more subjects of international law other than States or international organizations are parties, to international agreements to which one or more international organizations and one or more subjects of international law other than States or organizations are parties, to international agreements not in written form between one or more States and one or more international organizations, or between international organizations, or to international agreements between subjects of international law other than States or international organizations. That fact shall not affect (*a*) the legal force of such agreements; (*b*) the application to them of any of the rules set forth in the Convention to which they would be subject under international law independently of the Convention; or (*c*) the application of the Convention to the relations between States and international organizations or to the relations of organizations between themselves, where those relations are governed by international agreements to which other subjects of international law are also parties.

The principal matters covered in the Convention are: conclusion and entry into force of treaties (part II); observance, application and

---

[592] See *Official Records of the United Nations Conference on the Law of Treaties between States and International Organizations or between International Organizations, Vienna, 18 February-21 March 1986*, vol. II, Documents of the Conference (United Nations publication, Sales No. 94.V.5), document A/CONF.129/15.

interpretation of treaties (part III); amendment and modification of treaties (part IV); invalidity, termination and suspension of the operation of treaties (part V); miscellaneous provisions (part VI), dealing, inter alia, with the relationship of the Convention to the Vienna Convention on the Law of Treaties and reserving questions that may arise in regard to a treaty from a succession of States, from the international responsibility of a State or from the outbreak of hostilities between States, from the international responsibility of an international organization, from the termination of the existence of the organization or from the termination of participation by a State in the membership of the organization, as well as questions that may arise in regard to the establishment of obligations and rights for States members of an international organization under a treaty to which that organization is a party; and depositaries, notifications, corrections and registration (part VII). The procedures for judicial settlement, arbitration and conciliation referred to in article 66 of the Convention are specified in an annex to the Convention.

On 21 March 1986, the Convention was opened for signature, by all States, Namibia, represented by the United Nations Council for Namibia, and international organizations invited to participate in the Conference.[593] It remained open for signature until 31 December 1986 at the Federal Ministry for Foreign Affairs of the Republic of Austria and, subsequently, until 30 June 1987 at United Nations Headquarters. The Convention is subject to ratification by States and to acts of formal confirmation by international organizations. The Convention remains open for accession by any State and by any international organization which has the capacity to conclude treaties. The Convention shall enter into force on the thirtieth day following the date of deposit of the thirty-fifth instrument of ratification or accession by a State. By 4 November 2003, twenty-sixth States had deposited instruments of ratification, accession or succession.[594]

In addition to the Vienna Convention on the Law of Treaties between States and International Organizations or between International Organizations, the Conference adopted five resolutions which were annexed to the Final Act of the Conference.[595] In

---

[593] Ten international organizations, including the United Nations, had signed the Convention.
[594] Instruments of formal confirmation deposited by international organizations are not counted toward the entry into force of the Convention. By 4 November 2003, eleven international organizations had deposited instruments of formal confirmation.
[595] See *Official Records of the United Nations Conference on the Law of Treaties between States and International Organizations or between International Organizations, Vienna, 18 February-21 March 1986*, vol. II, Documents of the Conference (United Nations publication, Sales No. 94.V.5), document A/CONF.129/14.

accordance with one of the resolutions, the expenses of any arbitral tribunal and conciliation commission that may be set up under article 66 of the Convention shall be borne by the United Nations.

21. Status of the diplomatic courier and the diplomatic bag not accompanied by diplomatic courier

The General Assembly, by resolution 3501 (XXX) of 15 December 1975, while reaffirming the need for strict implementation by States of the provisions of the 1961 Vienna Convention on Diplomatic Relations, deplored instances of violations of the rules of diplomatic law and in particular of the provisions of that Convention. It further invited Member States to submit to the Secretary-General their comments and observations on ways and means to ensure the implementation of the provisions of the Convention as well as on the desirability of elaborating provisions concerning the status of the diplomatic courier.

By resolution 31/76 of 13 December 1976, the General Assembly, being concerned at continuing instances of violations of the rules of diplomatic law relating, in particular, to the status of the diplomatic courier and the diplomatic bag not accompanied by diplomatic courier, again invited Member States to comment on the desirability of elaborating provisions concerning the status of the diplomatic courier with due regard also to the question of the status of the diplomatic bag not accompanied by diplomatic courier. At the same time, the Assembly requested the International Law Commission at the appropriate time to study the proposals made or to be made by Member States on the elaboration of a protocol concerning the status of such courier and bag, which would constitute development and concretization of the Vienna Convention on Diplomatic Relations.

The Commission accordingly included in the agenda of its twenty-ninth session, in 1977, an item entitled "Proposals on the elaboration of a protocol concerning the status of the diplomatic courier and the diplomatic bag not accompanied by diplomatic courier", and established a Working Group to ascertain the most suitable ways and means of dealing with the topic. The Working Group agreed to recommend a number of conclusions to the Commission,[596] including the following: (1) the topic should be inscribed on the Commission's programme of work for study, as requested by the General Assembly; (2) the Commission should

---

[596] For the report of the Working Group, see document A/CN.4/305.

undertake the study of the topic at its next session without curtailing the time allocated for the consideration of the topics on the current programme of work to which priority had been given pursuant to the relevant recommendations of the General Assembly and the corresponding decisions of the Commission; and (3) in order to fulfill this aim, it would seem more appropriate for the Commission to adopt a procedure similar mutatis mutandis to the one it followed with respect to the protection and inviolability of diplomatic agents and other persons (*see page 160*) by having the Working Group undertake the first stage of the study of the topic and report thereon to the Commission without appointing a Special Rapporteur. The Commission approved the conclusions reached by the Working Group concerning the ways and means of dealing with the item.[597]

At its thirtieth session, in 1978, the Commission reconvened the Working Group, which studied at that session the proposals for the elaboration of a protocol as well as the relevant provisions of the 1961 Vienna Convention on Diplomatic Relations,[598] the 1963 Vienna Convention on Consular Relations,[599] the 1969 Convention on Special Missions,[600] and the 1975 Vienna Convention on the Representation of States in Their Relations with International Organizations of a Universal Character.[601] The Working Group adopted as its basic position that the relevant provisions of those conventions, if any, should form the basis for any further study of the question. The Working Group tentatively identified the relevant issues relating to the diplomatic courier and the diplomatic bag and considered the extent to which these issues were covered by the conventions. Although the issues were formulated to apply to the "diplomatic" courier and the "diplomatic" bag as requested by the General Assembly, some members of the Working Group were of the view that the issues were also relevant to other couriers and bags and should eventually be extended to them as well. The Commission included the report of the Working Group[602] in its report to the General Assembly on the session.[603]

At its thirty-third session, in 1978, the General Assembly discussed the results of the Commission's work under two separate

---

[597] See *Yearbook of the International Law Commission, 1977*, vol. II (Part Two), paras. 83 and 84.
[598] See annex V, section C (1).
[599] See annex V, section D (1).
[600] See annex V, section E (1).
[601] See annex V, section H.
[602] Document A/CN.4/L.285.
[603] See *Yearbook of the International Law Commission, 1978*, vol. II (Part Two), paras. 137-144.

agenda items in the Sixth Committee, namely "Implementation by States of the provisions of the Vienna Convention on Diplomatic Relations of 1961: report of the Secretary-General" (item 116) and "Report of the International Law Commission on the work of its thirtieth session" (item 114). In resolution 33/139 on the latter item, adopted on 19 December 1978, the General Assembly recommended that the Commission should continue the study, including those issues it had already identified, concerning the status of the diplomatic courier and the diplomatic bag not accompanied by diplomatic courier, in the light of comments made during the debate on the item in the Sixth Committee at the thirty-third session of the General Assembly and comments to be submitted by Member States, with a view to the possible elaboration of an appropriate legal instrument. With regard to the former item, the Assembly adopted, on the same day, resolution 33/140. The Assembly noted with appreciation the study by the Commission of the proposals on the elaboration of a protocol which could constitute a further development of international diplomatic law, decided that it would give further consideration to this question and expressed the view that, unless Member States indicated the desirability of an earlier consideration, it would be appropriate to do so when the International Law Commission submitted to the Assembly the results of its work on the possible elaboration of an appropriate legal instrument on the topic.

At its thirty-first session, in 1979, the Commission again re-established a Working Group, which studied issues on the status of the diplomatic courier and the diplomatic bag not accompanied by diplomatic courier. The results of the study were set out in the Commission's report to the General Assembly.[604] At the same session, the Commission decided to appoint Alexander Yankov as Special Rapporteur for the topic.

The Commission proceeded with its work on the topic from its thirty-second to thirty-eighth sessions and at its fortieth and forty-first sessions, from 1980 to 1986 and in 1988 and 1989, respectively. In connection with its consideration of the topic, the Commission had before it the reports of the Special Rapporteur,[605] information

---

[604] See *Yearbook of the International Law Commission, 1979*, vol. II (Part Two), chapter VI, sections B to D. For the report of the Working Group, see document A/CN.4/L.310.

[605] See *Yearbook of the International Law Commission, 1980*, vol. II (Part One), document A/CN.4/335; ibid., *1981*, vol. II (Part One), document A/CN.4/347 and Add.1 and 2; ibid., *1982*, vol. II (Part One), document A/CN.4/359 and Add.1; ibid., *1983*, vol. II (Part One), document A/CN.4/374 and Add.1-4; ibid., *1984*, vol. II (Part One), document A/CN.4/382; ibid., *1985*, vol. II (Part One), document A/CN.4/390; ibid., *1986*, vol. II (Part One), document A/CN.4/400; and ibid., *1988*, vol. II (Part One), document A/CN.4/417.

provided by Governments[606] as well as documents prepared by the Secretariat.[607]

The Commission began the first reading of the draft articles at its thirty-third session, in 1981, which was completed at its thirty-eighth session, in 1986. The draft adopted on first reading was transmitted, in accordance with articles 16 and 21 of the Commission's Statute, through the Secretary-General, to Governments for comments and observations.

The General Assembly, in resolutions 41/81 of 3 December 1986, and 42/156 of 7 December 1987, inter alia, urged Governments to give full attention to the request of the Commission for comments and observations on the draft articles adopted on first reading by the Commission.

At its fortieth session, in 1988, the Commission began the second reading of the draft articles. It re-examined the draft articles on the basis of the eighth report submitted by the Special Rapporteur.[608] In that report, the Special Rapporteur analysed the comments and observations of Governments in connection with each draft article and proposed the revision of certain draft articles. In his view, the elaboration of the draft articles should be based on a comprehensive approach leading to a coherent and, as much as possible, uniform regime concerning all kinds of couriers and bags. He also underscored the significance which should be attached to functional necessity as the basic factor in determining the status of all kinds of couriers and bags. These considerations of the Special Rapporteur were generally shared by the Commission.

At its forty-first session, in 1989, the Commission adopted the final text of thirty-two draft articles on the status of the diplomatic courier and the diplomatic bag not accompanied by diplomatic courier, as a whole, as well as a draft optional protocol on the status of the courier and the bag of special missions, and a draft optional protocol on the status of the courier and the bag of international organizations of a universal character, with commentaries thereto.[609]

---

[606] See *Yearbook of the International Law Commission, 1979,* vol. II (Part One), document A/CN.4/321 and Add.1-7; ibid., *1982,* vol. II (Part One), document A/CN.4/356 and Add.1-3; ibid., *1983,* vol. II (Part One), document A/CN.4/372 and Add.1 and 2; ibid., *1984,* vol. II (Part One), document A/CN.4/379 and Add.l; ibid., *1988,* vol. II (Part One), document A/CN.4/409 and Add. 1-5; and ibid., *1989,* vol. II (Part One), document A/CN.4/420.

[607] See *Yearbook of the International Law Commission, 1977,* vol. II (Part One), document A/CN.4/300, as well as working papers A/CN.4/WP.4 and 5.

[608] See *Yearbook of International Law Commission, 1988,* vol. II (Part One), document A/CN.4/417.

[609] See *Yearbook of International Law Commission, 1989,* vol. II (Part Two), paras. 30 and 72.

The texts of the final draft articles and optional protocols are reproduced in annex IV, section 7. In accordance with article 23 of its Statute, the Commission decided to recommend to the General Assembly that it convene an international conference of plenipotentiaries to study the draft articles and the optional protocols and to conclude a convention on the subject.[610]

By its resolution 44/36 of 4 December 1989, the General Assembly decided to hold at its forty-fifth session, in 1990, informal consultations, in the framework of the Sixth Committee, to study the draft articles on the status of the diplomatic courier and the diplomatic bag not accompanied by diplomatic courier, the draft optional protocols thereto, as well as the question of how to deal further with those draft instruments with a view to facilitating the reaching of a generally acceptable decision in the latter respect. Those consultations were continued at the forty-sixth and forty-seventh sessions, pursuant to General Assembly resolutions 45/43 of 28 November 1990 and 46/57 of 9 December 1991. Various proposals were made to reconcile the divergences of views which existed on some articles, in particular article 28 on the inviolability of the bag, but no agreement was reached. On the recommendation of the Sixth Committee, the General Assembly decided, by its decision 47/415 of 25 November 1992, that the informal consultations would be resumed at the fiftieth session, in 1995.

At its fiftieth session, in 1995, the General Assembly adopted decision 50/416 of 11 December 1995, by which it decided to bring the draft articles, together with the observations made during the debates on them in the Sixth Committee, to the attention of Member States, and to remind Member States of the possibility that this field of international law and any further developments within it may be subject to codification at an appropriate time in the future.

22. Jurisdictional immunities of States and their property

At its first session, in 1949, the Commission selected the subject of jurisdictional immunities of States and their property as one of the topics for codification without, however, including it in the list of topics to which it gave priority. At its twenty-ninth session, in 1977, the Commission considered possible additional topics for study. The topic "Jurisdictional immunities of States and their property" was recommended for selection in the near future for active consideration by the Commission, bearing in mind its day-to-day practical

---

[610] See *Yearbook of International Law Commission, 1989,* vol. II (Part Two), para. 66.

importance as well as its suitability for codification and progressive development.

The General Assembly, in resolution 32/151 of 19 December 1977, invited the Commission, at an appropriate time and in the light of progress made on other topics on its agenda, to commence work on the topic of jurisdictional immunities of States and their property.

At its thirtieth session, in 1978, the Commission set up a Working Group to consider the question of the future work of the Commission on the topic and to report thereon to the Commission. The Working Group submitted to the Commission a report[611] that dealt, inter alia, with general aspects of the topic and contained a number of recommendations. The Commission took note of the report of the Working Group and, on the basis of the recommendations contained therein, decided to begin its consideration of the topic "Jurisdictional immunities of States and their property". It also appointed Sompong Sucharitkul as Special Rapporteur for the topic and invited him to prepare a preliminary report at an early juncture for consideration by the Commission. The Commission, further, requested the Secretary-General to invite Governments of Member States to submit relevant materials on the topic, including national legislation, decisions of national tribunals and diplomatic and official correspondence and requested the Secretariat to prepare working papers and materials on the topic as the need arose and as requested by the Commission or the Special Rapporteur.[612]

The Commission considered the topic from its thirty-first to thirty-eighth and from its forty-first to forty-third sessions, from 1979 to 1986 and from 1989 to 1991. The Commission appointed Motoo Ogiso as the new Special Rapporteur for the topic at its thirty-ninth session, in 1987. In connection with its consideration of the topic, the Commission had before it the reports of the Special Rapporteurs[613]

---

[611] Document A/CN.4/L.279/Rev.1. Section III of the report is reproduced in *Yearbook of the International Law Commission, 1978*, vol. II (Part Two), para. 190, annex.

[612] See *Yearbook of the International Law Commission, 1978*, vol. II (Part Two), paras. 179, 180 and 188-190.

[613] For the reports of Sompong Sucharitkul, see *Yearbook of the International Law Commission, 1979*, vol. II (Part One), document A/CN.4/323; ibid., *1980*, vol. II (Part One), document A/CN.4/331 and Add.l; ibid., *1981*, vol. II (Part One), document A/CN.4/340 and Add.l; ibid., *1982*, vol. II (Part One), document A/CN.4/357; ibid., *1983*, vol. II (Part One), document A/CN.4/363 and Add.l; ibid., *1984*, vol. II (Part One), document A/CN.4/376 and Add.1 and 2; ibid., *1985*, vol. II (Part One), document A/CN.4/388; and ibid., *1986*, vol. II (Part One), document A/CN.4/396. For the reports of Motoo Ogiso, see *Yearbook of the International Law Commission, 1988*, vol. II (Part One), document A/CN.4/415; ibid., *1989*, vol. II (Part One), document A/CN.4/422 and Add.l; and ibid.. *1990*, vol. II (Part One), document A/CN.4/431.

and information provided by Governments.[614]

At its thirty-first session, in 1979, the Commission had before it a preliminary report on the topic submitted by the Special Rapporteur, Mr. Sucharitkul.[615] The report was designed to present an overall picture of the topic without proposing any solution for each or any of the substantive issues identified. During the discussion in the Commission at that session, a consensus emerged to the effect that for the immediate future the Special Rapporteur should continue his study, concentrating on general principles and thus confining the areas of initial interest to the substantive contents and constitutive elements of the general rules of jurisdictional immunities of States. It was also understood that the question of the extent of, or limitations on, the application of the rules of State immunity required an extremely careful and balanced approach, and that the exceptions identified in the preliminary report were merely noted as possible limitations, without any assessment or evaluation of their significance in State practice. It was furthermore agreed, in terms of priorities to be accorded in the treatment of the topic, that the Special Rapporteur should continue his work on the immunities of States from jurisdiction, leaving aside for the time being the question of immunity from execution of judgement. Another point which was noted was the widening functions of the State, which had enhanced the complexities of the problem of State immunities. Controversies had existed in the past concerning the divisibility of the functions of the State or the various distinctions between the activities carried on by modern States in fields of activity formerly undertaken by individuals, such as trade and finance. No generally accepted criterion for identifying the circumstances or areas in which State immunity could be invoked or accorded had been found. The greatest care was therefore called for in the treatment of this particular aspect of the topic.

The Commission began the first reading of the draft articles at its thirty-second session, in 1980, which was concluded at its thirty-eighth session, in 1986. At that session, the Commission transmitted the draft articles adopted on first reading through the Secretary-General to Governments for comments and observations in accordance with articles 16 and 21 of its Statute.

---

[614] Document A/CN.4/343 and Add.1-4, reproduced in a volume in the *United Nations Legislative Series* entitled *"Materials on Jurisdictional Immunities of States and Their Property"* (ST/LEG/SER.B/20, United Nations publication, Sales No. 81.V.10); and *Yearbook of the International Law Commission, 1988,* vol. II (Part One), document A/CN.4/410 and Add.1-5.

[615] See *Yearbook of the International Law Commission, 1979,* vol. II (Part One), document A/CN.4/323.

The General Assembly, in resolutions 41/81 of 3 December 1986 and 42/156 of 7 December 1987, inter alia, urged Governments to give full attention to the request of the Commission for comments and observations on the draft articles adopted on first reading by the Commission.

The Commission began the second reading of the draft articles based on the three reports of the new Special Rapporteur, Mr. Ogiso, at its forty-first session, in 1989, which was concluded at its forty-third session, in 1991. In his preliminary report, the Special Rapporteur analysed some of the comments and observations of Governments and proposed to revise or merge some of the draft articles based on those comments. In his second report, the Special Rapporteur gave further consideration to some of the draft articles on the basis of the written comments and observations of Governments and his analysis of relevant treaties, laws and State practice, and proposed certain revisions, additions or deletions complementary to those contained in his preliminary report. Responding to a request from some members of the Commission, the Special Rapporteur also included a brief review of the recent development of general State practice concerning State immunity. In his third report, the Special Rapporteur reviewed once again the entire set of draft articles and suggested certain reformulations, taking into account the views expressed by members of the Commission at its forty-first session, in 1989, as well as by Governments in their written comments and in the Sixth Committee of the General Assembly at its forty-fourth session.

In undertaking the second reading of the draft articles, at its forty-first session, in 1989, the Commission agreed with the Special Rapporteur that it should avoid entering yet again into a doctrinal debate on the general principles of State immunity, which had been extensively debated in the Commission and on which the views of the Commission remained divided; the Commission should instead concentrate its discussion on individual articles, so as to arrive at a consensus as to what kind of activities of the State should, or should not, enjoy immunity from jurisdiction of another State. This, in the view of the Commission, was the only pragmatic way of preparing a convention which would command wide support of the international community. The Commission also noted that the law of State jurisdictional immunity was in a state of flux as some States were in the process of amending their basic laws or had done so recently, and thus it was essential that the draft articles be given the opportunity to reflect such Government practice, and, moreover, to leave room for further development of the law of jurisdictional immunity of States.[616]

---

[616] See *Yearbook of the International Law Commission, 1989,* vol. II (Part Two),

At its forty-third session, in 1991, the Commission adopted the final text of twenty-two draft articles on the jurisdictional immunities of States and their property, with commentaries.[617] In accordance with article 23 of its Statute, the Commission submitted the draft articles to the General Assembly, together with a recommendation that the Assembly convene an international conference of plenipotentiaries to examine the draft articles and to conclude a convention on the subject.[618]

The draft articles adopted by the Commission consist of five parts as follows: *Part I*, "Introductory provisions", comprises four articles, namely, article 1 (Scope of the draft articles), article 2 (Use of terms), article 3 (Privileges and immunities not affected by the draft articles), article 4 (Non-retroactivity of the draft articles); *Part II*, "General principles", includes article 5 (State immunity), article 6 (Modalities for giving effect to State immunity), article 7 (Express consent to exercise of jurisdiction), article 8 (Effect of participation in a proceeding before a court), article 9 (Counter-claims); *Part III*, "Proceedings in which State immunity cannot be invoked", consists of article 10 (Commercial transactions), article 11 (Contracts of employment), article 12 (Personal injuries and damage to property), article 13 (Ownership, possession and use of property), article 14 (Intellectual and industrial property), article 15 (Participation in companies or other collective bodies), article 16 (Ships owned or operated by a State) and article 17 (Effect of an arbitration agreement); *Part IV*, "State immunity from measures of constraint in connection with proceedings before a court", includes article 18 (State immunity from measures of constraint) and article 19 (Specific categories of property); and *Part V*, "Miscellaneous provisions", consists of article 20 (Service of process), article 21 (Default judgement) and article 22 (Privileges and immunities during court proceedings).

As regards the question of the settlement of disputes,[619] the Commission was of the view that it could be dealt with by the proposed international conference, if the conference considered that a

---

paras. 406 and 407.
[617] See *Yearbook of the International Law Commission, 1991*, vol. II (Part Two), paras. 23 and 28.
[618] See *Yearbook of the International Law Commission, 1991*, vol. II (Part Two), para. 25.
[619] Articles 29 to 33 and the Annex dealing with the settlement of disputes, which were proposed by the former Special Rapporteur in his eighth report (see *Yearbook of the International Law Commission, 1986*, vol. II (Part One), document A/CN.4/396) but not discussed, are reproduced in the report of the Commission on the work of its forty-first session (see *Yearbook of the International Law Commission, 1989*, vol. II (Part Two), para. 611).

legal mechanism on the settlement of disputes should be provided in connection with the draft articles.[620]

The General Assembly, by its resolution 46/55 of 9 December 1991, invited States to submit their written comments and observations on the draft articles, and decided to establish at its forty-seventh session an open-ended working group of the Sixth Committee to examine, in the light of the written comments of Governments, as well as views expressed in debates at the forty-sixth session of the Assembly: (a) issues of substance arising out of the draft articles, in order to facilitate a successful conclusion of a convention through the promotion of general agreement; and (b) the question of the convening of an international conference, to be held in 1994 or subsequently, to conclude a convention on jurisdictional immunities of States and their property.

The Working Group began its work at the forty-seventh session of the General Assembly[621] and resumed it, in accordance with General Assembly decision 47/414 of 25 November 1992, at the forty-eighth session.[622] By its decision 48/413 of 9 December 1993, the General Assembly decided that consultations should be held in the framework of the Sixth Committee at its forty-ninth session, to continue consideration of the substantive issues regarding which the identification and attenuation of differences was desirable in order to facilitate the successful conclusion of a convention through general agreement; and also decided that, at its forty-ninth session, in the light of the progress thus far achieved and of the results of the said consultations, it would give full consideration to the recommendation of the International Law Commission that an international conference of plenipotentiaries be convened, to examine the draft articles on the jurisdictional immunities of States and their property and to conclude a convention on the subject.

At the forty-ninth session of the General Assembly, in 1994, the Sixth Committee, in accordance with General Assembly decision 48/413, decided to convene informal consultations. The consultations were held at six meetings, from 27 September to 3 October 1994. At the same session, the Chairman of the informal consultations introduced a document[623] containing conclusions he had drawn from the consultations.[624]

---

[620] See *Yearbook of the International Law Commission, 1991,* vol. II (Part Two), para. 26.
[621] For the report of the Working Group, see document A/C.6/47/L.10.
[622] For the report of the Working Group, see document A/C.6/48/L.4.
[623] Document A/C.6/49/L.2.
[624] See document A/49/744, paras. 3-7.

By its resolution 49/61 of 9 December 1994, the General Assembly accepted the above-cited recommendation of the International Law Commission, invited States to submit to the Secretary-General their comments on the conclusions of the Chairman of the informal consultations held pursuant to General Assembly decision 48/413 of 9 December 1993, and on the reports of the Working Group established under General Assembly resolution 46/55 of 9 December 1991 and decision 47/414 of 25 November 1992, and decided to resume consideration, at its fifty-second session, in 1997, of the issues of substance, in the light of the reports mentioned above and the comments submitted by States thereon, and to determine, at its fifty-second or fifty-third session, the arrangements for the conference, including the date and place, due consideration being given to ensuring the widest possible agreement at the conference. It further decided to include in the provisional agenda of its fifty-second session the item entitled "Convention on jurisdictional immunities of States and their property".

The item was considered at the fifty-second and fifty-third sessions of the General Assembly, in 1997 and 1998. By its resolution 52/151 of 15 December 1997, the General Assembly, inter alia, decided to consider the item again at its fifty-third session with a view to establishing a working group at its fifty-fourth session, taking into account the comments submitted by States in accordance with resolution 49/61 of 9 December 1994. By its resolution 53/98 of 8 December 1998, the General Assembly decided to establish at its fifty-fourth session, in 1999, an open-ended working group of the Sixth Committee to consider outstanding substantive issues related to the draft articles taking into account, inter alia, recent developments in State practice and legislation as well as the comments submitted by States on the topic. It also invited the International Law Commission to present any preliminary comments that it might have regarding outstanding substantive issues related to the draft articles in the light of the results of the informal consultations held in the Sixth Committee, in 1994, pursuant to General Assembly decision 48/413 of 9 December 1993.

At its fifty-first session, in 1999, the Commission established a Working Group on Jurisdictional Immunities of States and Their Property in accordance with General Assembly resolution 53/98. The Working Group concentrated its work on the five main issues identified in the conclusions of the Chairman of the informal consultations held in the Sixth Committee, in 1994 (*see above*), namely: (1) the concept of a State for purposes of immunity, (2) the criteria for determining the commercial character of a contract or transaction; (3) the concept of a State enterprise or other State entity in relation to commercial transactions; (4) contracts of employment;

and (5) measures of constraint against State property. The Working Group also considered the question of the existence or non-existence of immunity in the case of violation by a State of *jus cogens* norms of international law, which was identified as an issue that might be considered in the light of recent State practice. In its report to the Commission,[625] the Working Group made a number of suggestions regarding possible ways of solving the five issues. The Commission took note of the report of the Working Group and adopted the suggestions contained therein.

At the fifty-fourth session of the General Assembly, in 1999, an open-ended working group of the Sixth Committee established under General Assembly resolution 53/98 of 8 December 1998 considered the same five outstanding substantive issues as well as the possible form of the outcome of the work on the topic. It also considered the question identified by the Working Group of the Commission on the existence or non-existence of immunity in the case of violation by a State of *jus cogens* norms.[626] The working group continued its consideration of the future form of, and outstanding substantive issues related to, the draft articles, at the fifty-fifth session of the General Assembly, in 2000, pursuant to General Assembly resolution 54/101 of 9 December 1999.[627] As a result of the later discussions, the Chairman prepared a number of texts on the five outstanding issues as a possible basis for further discussions on the topic.[628]

By its resolution 55/150 of 12 December 2000, the General Assembly, having considered the reports of the working group of the Sixth Committee, decided to establish an Ad Hoc Committee on Jurisdictional Immunities of States and Their Property open to all States Members of the United Nations and to States members of the specialized agencies, with the mandate to further the work done, consolidate areas of agreement and resolve outstanding issues with a view to elaborating a generally acceptable instrument based on the draft articles, and also on the discussions of the working group of the Sixth Committee and their results. By its resolution 56/78 of 12 December 2001, the General Assembly decided that the Ad Hoc Committee should meet in February 2002, and that it should report to the General Assembly at its fifty-seventh session on the outcome of its work.

---

[625] See *Official Records of the General Assembly, Fifty-fourth Session, Supplement No. 10 (A/54/10)*, annex.
[626] For the report of the Working Group, see document A/C.6/54/L.12.
[627] For the report of the Working Group, see document A/C.6/55/L.12.
[628] Document A/C.6/55/L.12.

The Ad Hoc Committee on Jurisdictional Immunities of States and Their Property proceeded with its work in a Working Group of the Whole in two stages by discussing first, the five outstanding substantive issues and, second, the remainder of the draft articles with a view to identifying and resolving any further issues arising from the text.[629] This was the first time that the entire draft articles had been considered in the General Assembly since their adoption by the Commission in 1991, taking into account subsequent developments in State practice. The Working Group made substantial progress on the five substantive issues by reducing the number of outstanding issues and narrowed the divergent views with respect to the remaining issues. The Working Group decided to reflect the remaining divergent views on certain draft articles in the revised text of the draft articles contained in its report. The Ad Hoc Committee emphasized the importance of elaborating in a timely manner a generally acceptable instrument and urged States to make every effort to resolve the remaining outstanding issues in the interest of arriving at an agreement.[630]

After considering the report of the Ad Hoc Committee at its fifty-seventh session, in 2002, the General Assembly adopted resolution 57/16 of 19 November 2002 in which, noting that few issues remained outstanding and stressing the importance of uniformity and clarity in the law applicable to jurisdictional immunities of States and their property, decided that the Ad Hoc Committee should be reconvened in February 2003 and requested the Ad Hoc Committee to report to the General Assembly at its fifty-eighth session on the outcome of its work.

In 2003, the Ad Hoc Committee proceeded with the substantive discussion of the outstanding issues in a Working Group of the Whole. The Working Group established two informal consultative groups. It discussed and resolved all of the outstanding issues. The Ad Hoc Committee adopted its report[631] containing the text of the draft articles,[632] together with understandings with respect to draft articles 10 (Commercial transactions), 11 (Contracts of employment), 13 (Ownership, possession and use of property), 14 (Intellectual and

---

[629] For the report of the Ad Hoc Committee, see *Official Records of the General Assembly, Fifty-seventh Session, Supplement No. 22* (A/57/22). For the documents before the Ad Hoc Committee, see ibid., para. 7.
[630] See *Official Records of the General Assembly, Fifty-seventh Session, Supplement No. 22* (A/57/22), paras. 8-13.
[631] See *Official Records of the General Assembly, Fifty-eighth Session, Supplement No. 22* (A/58/22). For the documents before the Ad Hoc Committee, see ibid., para. 7.
[632] See *Official Records of the General Assembly, Fifty-eighth Session, Supplement No. 22* (A/58/22), annex I.

industrial property), 17 (Effect of an arbitration agreement) and 19[633] (State immunity from post-judgement measures of constraint) as well as a general understanding that the draft articles did not cover criminal proceedings.[634] The Ad Hoc Committee recommended that the General Assembly take a decision on the form of the draft articles and noted that, if the General Assembly decided to adopt the draft articles as a convention, the draft articles would need a preamble and final clauses, including a general saving provision concerning the relationship between the articles and other international agreements relating to the same subject.[635]

23. The law of the non-navigational uses of international watercourses

The General Assembly, by resolution 2669 (XXV) of 8 December 1970, recommended that the Commission should take up the study of the law of the non-navigational uses of international watercourses with a view to its progressive development and codification and, in the light of its scheduled programme of work, should consider the practicability of taking the necessary action as soon as the Commission deemed it appropriate.

At its twenty-third session, in 1971, the Commission included the subject of non-navigational uses of international watercourses in its programme of work. The Commission also agreed that, for studying the rules of international law on that subject with a view to their progressive development and codification, all relevant materials on State practice should be compiled and analysed.[636]

The General Assembly, by resolution 2780 (XXVI) of 3 December 1971, recommended that the Commission should decide upon the priority to be given to the topic.

---

[633] As renumbered (previously article 18).

[634] See *Official Records of the General Assembly, Fifty-eighth Session, Supplement No. 22* (A/58/22), annex II.

[635] See *Official Records of the General Assembly, Fifty-eighth Session, Supplement No. 22* (A/58/22), para.12.

[636] The Commission noted that a considerable amount of such material had already been published in 1963 in the Secretary-General's report entitled "Legal problems relating to the utilization and use of international rivers" (see *Yearbook of the International Law Commission, 1974*, vol. II (Part Two), document A/5409), prepared pursuant to General Assembly resolution 1401 (XIV) of 21 November 1959, as well as in a volume in the *United Nations Legislative Series* entitled *"Legislative Texts and Treaty Provisions Concerning the Utilization of International Rivers for Other Purposes Than Navigation"* (ST/LEG/SER.B/12, United Nations publication, Sales No. 63.V.4).

At its twenty-fourth session, in 1972, the Commission indicated its intention to take up the Assembly's recommendation when it came to discuss its long-term programme of work. The Commission furthermore reached the conclusion that the problem of the pollution of international waterways was of both substantial urgency and complexity. Accordingly, it requested the Secretariat to continue compiling the material relating to the topic with specific reference to the problems of the pollution of international watercourses.

At its twenty-fifth session, in 1973, the Commission gave special attention to the question of the priority to be given to the topic. It concluded, however, that a formal decision on the commencement of the substantive work should be taken after members had had an opportunity to review the supplementary report on the legal problems relating to the non-navigational uses of international watercourses being prepared by the Secretariat, which was issued in 1974.[637]

At its twenty-sixth session, in 1974, the Commission, pursuant to the recommendation contained in General Assembly resolution 3071 (XXVIII) of 30 November 1973, set up a Subcommittee to consider the question. The Subcommittee submitted a report to the Commission[638] that dealt with the nature of international watercourses and pointed out that a preliminary question to be examined was the scope of the term "international watercourses". Recognizing the variations in practice and theory, the report proposed to request States to comment on a series of questions concerning the appropriate scope of "international watercourses" to be adopted in a study of the legal aspects of their non-navigational uses. It stated that another preliminary question was the type of activities to be included within the term "non-navigational uses". Since uses could be conflicting, both on the national and on the international levels, the report proposed that the views of States should be sought as to the range of uses that the Commission should take account of in its work and as to whether certain special problems needed to be considered. Furthermore the report recommended that States be requested to reply to the questions whether the Commission should take up the problem

---

[637] The General Assembly, in resolution 2669 (XXV) of 8 December 1970, requested the Secretary-General to continue the study initiated in accordance with General Assembly resolution 1401 (XIV) in order to prepare a "supplementary report" on the legal problems relating to the question, taking into account the updated application in State practice and international adjudication of the law of international watercourses and also intergovernmental and non-governmental studies of this matter. The Secretary-General submitted a supplementary report in 1974, which was printed in *Yearbook of the International Law Commission, 1974*, vol. II (Part Two), document A/CN.4/274.
[638] Document A/CN.4/283 reproduced in *Yearbook of the International Law Commission, 1974*, vol. II (Part One), document A/9610/Rev.1, chapter V, annex.

of pollution of international watercourses at the initial stage in its study, and whether special arrangements should be made for ensuring that the Commission be provided with technical, scientific and economic advice. At the same session, the Commission adopted the report without change.

The General Assembly, by resolution 3315 (XXIX) of 14 December 1974, recommended that the Commission should continue its study of the law of the non-navigational uses of international watercourses taking into account, inter alia, comments received from Member States on the questions mentioned in the Subcommittee's report.

The Commission proceeded with its work on the topic at its twenty-eighth, thirty-first and thirty-second sessions, from its thirty-fifth to forty-third sessions and at its forty-fifth and forty-sixth sessions, in 1976, 1979 and 1980, from 1983 to 1991 and in 1993 and 1994, respectively. The Commission appointed Richard D. Kearney, Stephen M. Schwebel, Jens Evensen, Stephen McCaffrey, and Robert Rosenstock as the successive Special Rapporteurs for the topic at its twenty-sixth, twenty-ninth, thirty-fourth, thirty-seventh and forty-fourth sessions, in 1974, 1977, 1982, 1985 and 1992, respectively. In connection with its consideration of the topic, the Commission had before it the reports of the Special Rapporteurs,[639] information

---

[639] For the report of Richard D. Kearney, see *Yearbook of the International Law Commission, 1976,* vol. II (Part One), document A/CN.4/295. For the reports of Stephen M. Schwebel, see *Yearbook of the International Law Commission, 1979,* vol. II (Part One), document A/CN.4/320; ibid., *1980,* vol. II (Part One), document A/CN.4/332 and Add.1; and ibid., *1982,* vol. II (Part One), document A/CN.4/348. For the reports of Jens Evensen, see *Yearbook of the International Law Commission, 1983,* vol. II (Part One), document A/CN.4/367; and ibid., *1984,* vol. II (Part One), document A/CN.4/381. For the reports of Stephen McCaffrey, see *Yearbook of the International Law Commission, 1985,* vol. II (Part One), document A/CN.4/393; ibid., *1986,* vol. II (Part One), document A/CN.4/399 and Add.1 and 2 (in his second report, the Special Rapporteur discussed the concept of "shared natural resources" which was subsequently taken up by the Commission as a separate topic. See Part III.B, section 6); ibid., *1987,* vol. II (Part One), document A/CN.4/406 and Add.1 and 2; ibid., *1988,* vol. II (Part One), document A/CN.4/412 and Add. 1 and 2; ibid., *1989,* vol. II (Part One), document A/CN.4/421 and Add.1 and 2; ibid., *1990,* vol. II (Part One), document A/CN.4/427 and Add.1; and ibid., *1991,* vol. II (Part One), document A/CN.4/436. For the reports of Robert Rosenstock, see *Yearbook of the International Law Commission, 1993,* vol. II (Part One), document A/CN.4/451; and ibid., *1994,* vol. II (Part One), document A/CN.4/462.

provided by Governments[640] as well as documents prepared by the Secretariat.[641]

At its twenty-eighth session, in 1976, the Commission held a general debate on the topic which led to agreement in the Commission that the question of determining the scope of the term "international watercourses" did not need to be pursued at the outset of the work. Instead, attention should be devoted to beginning the formulation of general principles applicable to legal aspects of the uses of those watercourses. In so doing, every effort should be made to devise rules which would maintain a delicate balance between rules too detailed to be generally applicable and rules too general to be effective. Furthermore, the rules should be designed to promote the adoption of regimes for individual international rivers and for that reason should have a residual character. Effort should also be devoted to making the rules as widely acceptable as possible and the sensitivity of States regarding their interests in water must be taken into account.

At its thirty-second session, in 1980, the Commission began the first reading of the draft articles. It decided to use, at least in the early stages of its work on the topic, the provisional working hypothesis recommended by the Drafting Committee as to the meaning of the term "international watercourse system".[642]

At its forty-third session, in 1991, the Commission adopted on first reading the draft articles as a whole. In accordance with articles

---

[640] See *Yearbook of the International Law Commission, 1976*, vol. II (Part One), document A/CN.4/294 and Add.1; ibid., *1978*, vol. II (Part One), document A/CN.4/314; ibid., *1979*, vol. II (Part One), document A/CN.4/324; ibid., *1980*, vol. II (Part One), document A/CN.4/329 and Add.1; ibid., *1982*, vol. II (Part One), document A/CN.4/352 and Add.1; and ibid., *1993*, vol. II (Part One), document A/CN.4/447 and Add.1-3.

[641] Apart from the documents mentioned above, see also *Yearbook of the International Law Commission, 1971*, vol. II (Part Two), document A/CN.4/244/Rev.1; ibid., *1973*, vol. II, document A/CN.4/270; as well as document A/CN.4/L.241.

[642] The hypothesis was contained in a note which reads as follows:

"A watercourse system is formed of hydrographic components such as rivers, lakes, canals, glaciers and ground water constituting by virtue of their physical relationship a unitary whole; thus, any use affecting waters in one part of the system may affect waters in another part.

"An 'international watercourse system' is a watercourse system, components of which are situated in two or more States.

"To the extent that parts of the waters in one State are not affected by or do not affect uses of waters in another State, they shall not be treated as being included in the international watercourse system. Thus, to the extent that the uses of the waters of the system have an effect on one another, to that extent the system is international, but only to that extent; accordingly, there is not an absolute, but a relative, international character of the watercourse." See *Yearbook of the International Law Commission, 1980*, vol. II (Part Two), para. 90.

16 and 21 of its Statute, the Commission decided to transmit the draft articles, through the Secretary-General, to Governments of Member States for comments and observations.

The General Assembly, in resolution 46/54 of 9 December 1991, expressed its appreciation to the Commission for the completion of the first reading of the draft articles on the topic and urged the Governments to present their comments and observations on the draft in writing, as requested by the Commission.

At its forty-fifth session, in 1993, and forty-sixth session, in 1994, the Commission proceeded with its second reading of the draft articles on the basis of the reports submitted by the new Special Rapporteur for the topic, Mr. Rosenstock. In his first report, [643] the Special Rapporteur analysed the written comments and observations received from Governments and raised two issues of a general character, namely whether the eventual form of the articles should be a convention or model rules, and the question of dispute settlement procedure. He also raised the possibility of including in the draft articles provisions on "unrelated confined groundwaters". At its forty-fifth session, in 1993, the Commission requested the Special Rapporteur to undertake a study on the question of "unrelated confined groundwaters" in order to determine the feasibility of incorporating them in the topic. In his second report,[644] the Special Rapporteur suggested amending certain draft articles adopted on first reading to include provisions on "unrelated confined groundwaters",[645] in order to encourage their management in a rational manner and prevent their depletion and pollution, and proposed a new article dealing with dispute settlement.

At its forty-sixth session, in 1994, having considered the second report of the Special Rapporteur, the Commission decided to refer the entire set of the draft articles to the Drafting Committee and invited it to proceed with their consideration, without the amendments on "unrelated confined groundwaters", and to submit suggestions to the Commission on how the Commission should proceed on the question of "unrelated confined groundwaters". At the same session, the Commission adopted the final text of a set of thirty-three draft

---

[643] See *Yearbook of the International Law Commission, 1993*, vol. II (Part One), document A/CN.4/451.

[644] See *Yearbook of the International Law Commission, 1994*, vol. II (Part One), document A/CN.4/462.

[645] The term "unrelated confined groundwaters" is conceived as a shared aquifer which is an independent water resource body, not contributing water to a "common terminus" via a river system, or receiving significant amounts of water from any extant surface water body. See *Yearbook of the International Law Commission, 1994*, vol. II (Part One), document A/CN.4/462, annex, para. 38.

articles on the law of the non-navigational uses of international watercourses, with commentaries, and a resolution on confined transboundary groundwater.[646] In accordance with article 23 of its Statute, the Commission submitted the draft articles and the resolution to the General Assembly, together with a recommendation that a convention on the subject be elaborated by the Assembly or by an international conference of plenipotentiaries on the basis of the draft articles.[647]

The General Assembly, by its resolution 49/52 of 9 December 1994, expressed its appreciation to the Commission for its valuable work on the law of the non-navigational uses of international watercourses, and to the successive Special Rapporteurs for their contribution to that work, invited States to submit written comments and observations on the draft articles adopted by the Commission, and decided that, at its fifty-first session, in 1996, the Sixth Committee would convene as a Working Group of the Whole, open to States Members of the United Nations or members of specialized agencies, to elaborate a framework convention on the law of the non-navigational uses of international watercourses on the basis of the draft articles adopted by the Commission in the light of the written comments and observations of States and views expressed in the debate at the forty-ninth session of the General Assembly. It also decided that the Working Group of the Whole would, without prejudice to the rules of procedure of the General Assembly, follow the methods of work and procedures outlined in the annex to the resolution, subject to any modifications which it might deem appropriate, and further decided to include in the provisional agenda of its fifty-first session an item entitled "Convention on the law of the non-navigational uses of international watercourses".

The Working Group of the Whole of the Sixth Committee held two sessions, from 7 to 25 October 1996 and from 24 March to 4 April 1997, the second having been held pursuant to General Assembly resolution 51/206 of 17 December 1996. It had before it the draft articles on the topic adopted by the Commission, and comments, observations and proposals by States. The Working Group of the Whole established a Drafting Committee. As mandated by General Assembly resolution 51/206, upon completion of its mandate, the Working Group reported directly to the General Assembly.[648]

---

[646] See *Yearbook of the International Law Commission, 1994*, vol. II (Part Two), paras. 218 and 222.
[647] See *Yearbook of the International Law Commission, 1994*, vol. II (Part Two), para. 219.
[648] For the reports of the Working Group of the Whole, see documents A/51/624 and A/51/869.

By its resolution 51/229 of 21 May 1997, the General Assembly, upon recommendation of the Working Group of the Whole, adopted the Convention on the Law of the Non-navigational Uses of International Watercourses,[649] consisting of a preamble, thirty-seven articles and an appendix on arbitration. The text of the Convention is reproduced in annex V, section L.

The Convention was open for signature by all States and by regional economic integration organizations until 20 May 2000 at United Nations Headquarters in New York. The Convention is subject to ratification, acceptance, approval or accession by States and by regional economic integration organizations. It shall enter into force on the ninetieth day following the date of deposit of the thirty-fifth instrument of ratification, acceptance, approval or accession. As of 10 November 2003, twelve States had become a party to the Convention.[650]

24. Nationality in relation to the succession of States[651]

At its forty-fifth session, in 1993, the Commission, on the basis of the recommendation of the Working Group on the long-term programme, decided to include in the Commission's agenda, subject to the approval of the General Assembly, the topic "State succession and its impact on the nationality of natural and legal persons".

The General Assembly, by its resolution 48/31 of 9 December 1993, endorsed the above decision of the Commission on the understanding that the final form to be given to the work on the topic would be decided after a preliminary study was presented to the Assembly.

At its forty-sixth session, in 1994, the Commission appointed Václav Mikulka as Special Rapporteur for the topic.

In its resolution 49/51 of 9 December 1994, the General Assembly again endorsed the decision of the Commission on the understanding reflected above and requested the Secretary-General to invite Governments to submit relevant materials including national

---

[649] For the text of the Convention, see General Assembly resolution 51/229 of 21 May 1997, annex.

[650] In accordance with article 36, paragraph 3, of the Convention, any instrument deposited by a regional economic integration organization shall not be counted as additional to those deposited by States for the purposes, inter alia, of entrance into force of the Convention.

[651] The Commission's study on the topic has proceeded under this title following the completion by the Commission of the preliminary study of the topic "State succession and its impact on the nationality of natural and legal persons" at its forty-eighth session, in 1996.

legislation, decisions of national tribunals and diplomatic and official correspondence relevant to the topic.

At its forty-seventh and forty-eighth sessions, in 1995 and 1996, respectively, the Commission convened a Working Group entrusted with the mandate to identify issues arising out of the topic, categorize those issues which were closely related thereto, give guidance to the Commission as to which issues could be most profitably pursued given contemporary concerns and present the Commission with a calendar of actions.[652] In accordance with the Working Group's conclusions,[653] the Commission recommended to the General Assembly that it take note of the completion of the preliminary study of the topic and that it request the Commission to undertake the substantive study of the topic entitled "Nationality in relation to the succession of States," on the understanding that inter alia:

(a) consideration of the question of the nationality of natural persons would be separated from that of the nationality of legal persons and that priority would be given to the former;

(b) without prejudicing a final decision, the result of the work on the question of the nationality of natural persons should take the form of a declaration of the General Assembly consisting of articles with commentaries; and

(c) the decision on how to proceed with respect to the question of the nationality of legal persons would be taken upon completion of the work on the nationality of natural persons and in the light of the comments that the General Assembly may invite States to submit to it on the practical problems raised by a succession of States in the field of legal persons.[654]

The General Assembly, in resolution 51/160 of 16 December 1996, endorsed the Commission's recommendations.

---

[652] At these sessions, the Commission considered respectively the Special Rapporteur's first and second reports (documents A/CN.4/467 and A/CN.4/474).

[653] For the report of the Working Group at the Commission's forty-seventh session, see document A/CN.4/L.507 reproduced in *Yearbook of the International Law Commission, 1995*, vol. II (Part Two), annex. For the summary of the oral report to the plenary on the work of the Working Group at the Commission's forty-eighth session, see *Yearbook of the International Law Commission, 1996*, vol. II (Part Two), paras. 78-87.

[654] See *Yearbook of the International Law Commission, 1996*, vol. II (Part Two), para. 88.

(a) Nationality of natural persons in relation to the succession of States

The Commission proceeded with its work on this part of the topic at its forty-ninth and fifty-first sessions, in 1997 and 1999, respectively, on the basis of the report of the Special Rapporteur,[655] information provided by Governments[656] and a memorandum by the Secretariat.[657]

At its forty-ninth session, in 1997, the Commission adopted on first reading a draft preamble and a set of twenty-seven draft articles on nationality of natural persons in relation to the succession of States, with commentaries. In accordance with articles 16 and 21 of its Statute, the Commission decided to transmit them, through the Secretary-General, to Governments for comments and observations.

The General Assembly, in resolution 52/156 of 15 December 1997, drew the attention of Governments to the importance for the Commission of having their views on the draft articles, and urged them to submit their comments and observations in writing.

At its fifty-first session, in 1999, the Commission decided to establish a Working Group to review the text of the draft articles adopted on first reading, taking into account comments and observations by Governments. On the basis of the report of the Chairman of the Working Group,[658] the Commission referred the draft preamble and a set of twenty-six draft articles to the Drafting Committee. Having considered the report of the Drafting Committee, the Commission adopted the final draft articles on nationality of natural persons in relation to the succession of States, with commentaries.[659] The Commission decided to recommend to the General Assembly the adoption of the draft articles in the form of a declaration.[660]

The final draft consists of a draft preamble and twenty-six draft articles divided into two parts: Part I General provisions (articles 1-19) and Part II Provisions relating to specific categories of succession of States (articles 20-26). Part II comprises four sections: Section 1 deals with succession in the case of a transfer of part of the territory; Section 2 deals with the case of unification of States; Section 3 deals with dissolution of a State; and Section 4 deals with separation of part

---

[655] Document A/CN.4/480 and Add.1.
[656] Document A/CN.4/493 and Corr.1.
[657] Document A/CN.4/497.
[658] Document A/CN.4/L.572.
[659] See *Official Records of the General Assembly, Fifty-fourth Session, Supplement No. 10* (A/54/10), paras. 42, 43, 47 and 48.
[660] See *Official Records of the General Assembly, Fifty-fourth Session, Supplement No. 10* (A/54/10), para. 44.

or parts of the territory. The text of the draft articles is reproduced in annex IV, section 10.

By its resolution 54/112 of 9 December 1999, the General Assembly decided to include in the provisional agenda of its fifty-fifth session, in 2000, an item entitled "Nationality of natural persons in relation to the succession of States", with a view to the consideration of the draft articles and their adoption as a declaration. The General Assembly also invited Governments to submit comments and observations on the question of a convention on nationality of natural persons in relation to the succession of States, with a view to the General Assembly considering the elaboration of such a convention at a future session.

By its resolution 55/153 of 12 December 2000, the Assembly took note of the articles, which were annexed to the resolution, invited Governments to take into account, as appropriate, the provisions contained in the articles in dealing with issues of nationality of natural persons in relation to the succession of States and recommended that all efforts be made for the wide dissemination of the text of the articles. It also decided to include in the provisional agenda of its fifty-ninth session, in 2004, an item entitled "Nationality of natural persons in relation to the succession of States".

(b) Nationality of legal persons in relation to the succession of States

At its fiftieth session, in 1998, the Commission considered the second part of the topic on the basis of the report of the Special Rapporteur.[661] On the suggestion of the Special Rapporteur, the Commission established a Working Group to consider the question of the possible orientation to be given to the second part of the topic, in order to facilitate the Commission's decision on this issue. The Working Group agreed that there were, in principle, two options for enlarging the scope of the study of problems falling within the second part of the topic: either expand the study of the question of the nationality of legal persons beyond the context of the succession of States, or keep the study within the context of the succession of States, but go beyond the problem of nationality to include other questions. The Working Group noted, however, that in the absence of positive comments from States, the Commission would have to conclude that States were not interested in the study of the second

---

[661] Document A/CN.4/489.

part of the topic. The preliminary conclusions of the Working Group were endorsed by the Commission.[662]

At its fifty-first session, in 1999, taking into account that no positive comments had been received from States with respect to the Commission's study of the second part of the topic, the Commission recommended to the General Assembly that, with the adoption of the draft articles on nationality of natural persons in relation to the succession of States, the work of the Commission on the topic "Nationality in relation to the succession of States" be considered concluded.[663]

25. State responsibility[664]

At its first session, in 1949, the Commission selected State responsibility as one of the topics for codification without, however, including it in the list of topics to which it gave priority. At its sixth session, in 1954, the Commission took note of General Assembly resolution 799 (VIII) of 7 December 1953, requesting the Commission to undertake, as soon as it considered it advisable, the codification of the principles of international law governing State responsibility.[665]

At its seventh session, in 1955, the Commission decided to begin the study of State responsibility and appointed F. V. García Amador as Special Rapporteur for the topic. At the next six sessions of the Commission, from 1956 to 1961, the Special Rapporteur presented six successive reports,[666] dealing, on the whole, with the question of responsibility for injuries to the persons or property of aliens.

In pursuance of General Assembly resolution 1686 (XVI) of 18 December 1961, in which the Assembly recommended that the Commission continue its work on State responsibility, the Commission, at its fourteenth session, in 1962, held a debate on its

---

[662] See *Yearbook of the International Law Commission, 1998*, vol. II (Part Two), paras. 460-468. For the report of the Working Group, see document A/CN.4/L.557.

[663] See *Official Records of the General Assembly, Fifty-fourth Session, Supplement No. 10* (A/54/10), para. 45.

[664] At its fifty-third session, in 2001, the Commission decided to amend the title of the topic to "Responsibility of States for internationally wrongful acts".

[665] The Commission also had before it the memorandum presented by its member, F. V. García Amador (see *Yearbook of the International Law Commission, 1954*, vol. II, document A/CN.4/80).

[666] See *Yearbook of the International Law Commission, 1956*, vol. II, document A/CN.4/96; ibid., *1957*, vol. II, document A/CN.4/106; ibid., *1958*, vol. II, document A/CN.4/111; ibid., *1959*, vol. II, document A/CN.4/119; ibid., *1960*, vol. II, document A/CN.4/125; and ibid., *1961*, vol. II, document A/CN.4/134 and Addendum.

programme of future work in the field of State responsibility. The idea that the topic of State responsibility should be one of those which should receive priority met with the general approval of the Commission. There were divergent views, however, concerning the best approach to the study of the question and the issues the study should cover. As a result, the Commission decided to set up a Subcommittee whose task was to submit to the Commission at its next session a preliminary report containing suggestions concerning the scope and approach of the future study.

At its fifteenth session, in 1963, the Commission considered the report of the Subcommittee on State Responsibility.[667] All members of the Commission who took part in the discussion agreed with the general conclusions of the report, namely: (1) that priority should be given to the definitions of the general rules governing the international responsibility of the State; and (2) that, in defining these general rules, the experience and material gathered in certain special sectors, especially that of responsibility for injuries to the persons or property of aliens, should not be overlooked and that careful attention should be paid to the possible repercussions which developments in international law may have had on State responsibility. The Subcommittee's suggestion that the study of the responsibility of other subjects of international law, such as international organizations, should be left aside also met with the general approval of the members of the Commission. At the same session, the Commission appointed Roberto Ago as Special Rapporteur for the topic.

The General Assembly, in resolution 1902 (XVIII) of 18 November 1963, recommended that the Commission should "continue its work on State responsibility, taking into account the views expressed at the eighteenth session of the General Assembly and the report of the Subcommittee on State Responsibility and giving due consideration to the purposes and principles enshrined in the Charter of the United Nations". In its resolution 2272 (XXII) of 1 December 1967, the General Assembly recommended that the Commission expedite the study of the topic of State responsibility and, by resolution 2400 (XXIII) of 11 December 1968, recommended that the Commission "make every effort to begin substantive work" on the topic as from its next session.

The Commission proceeded with its work on the topic at its nineteenth, twenty-first and twenty-second sessions, from its twenty-fifth to thirty-eighth sessions, at its forty-first and forty-second

---

[667] Document A/CN.4/152 reproduced in *Yearbook of the International Law Commission, 1963,* vol. II, document A/5509, annex I.

sessions and from its forty-fourth to fifty-third sessions, in 1967, 1969 and 1970, from 1973 to 1986, in 1989 and 1990 and from 1992 to 2001, respectively. Following the resignation of Roberto Ago from the Commission in 1978, the Commission appointed Willem Riphagen, Gaetano Arangio-Ruiz and James Crawford as the successive Special Rapporteurs for the topic at its thirty-first, thirty-ninth and forty-ninth sessions, in 1979, 1987 and 1997, respectively. In connection with its consideration of the topic, the Commission had before it a note and the reports of the Special Rapporteurs,[668] comments and observations received from Governments[669] as well as documents prepared by the Secretariat.[670]

At its twenty-first session, in 1969, the Commission, after examining the first report of the Special Rapporteur,[671] requested the Special Rapporteur, Mr. Ago, to prepare a report containing a first set of draft articles on the topic, the aim being "to establish, in an initial

---

[668] For a note and the reports of Roberto Ago, see *Yearbook of the International Law Commission, 1967,* vol. II, document A/CN.4/196; ibid., *1969,* vol. II, document A/CN.4/217 and Add.l; ibid., *1970,* vol. II, document A/CN.4/233; ibid., *1971,* vol. II (Part One), documents A/CN.4/217/Add.2 and A/CN.4/246 and Add.1-3; ibid., *1972,* vol. II, document A/CN.4/264 and Add.l; ibid., *1976,* vol. II (Part One), document A/CN.4/291 and Add.1 and 2; ibid., *1977,* vol. II (Part One), document A/CN.4/302 and Add.1-3; ibid., *1978,* vol. II (Part One), document A/CN.4/307 and Add.1 and 2; ibid., *1979,* vol. II (Part One), document A/CN.4/318 and Add.1-4; and ibid., *1980,* vol. II (Part One), document A/CN.4/318/Add.5-7. For the reports of Willem Riphagen, see ibid., *1980,* vol. II (Part One), document A/CN.4/330; ibid., *1981,* vol. II (Part One), document A/CN.4/344; ibid., *1982,* vol. II (Part One), document A/CN.4/354 and Add.1 and 2; ibid., *1983,* vol. II (Part One), document A/CN.4/366 and Add.l; ibid., *1984,* vol. II (Part One), document A/CN.4/380; ibid., *1985,* vol. II (Part One), document A/CN.4/389; and ibid., *1986,* vol. II (Part One), document A/CN.4/397 and Add.1. For the reports of Gaetano Arangio-Ruiz, see ibid., *1988,* vol. II (Part One), document A/CN.4/416 and Add.l; ibid., *1989,* vol. II (Part One), document A/CN.4/425 and Add.l; ibid., *1991,* vol. II (Part One), document A/CN.4/440 and Add.l; ibid., *1992,* vol. II (Part One), document A/CN.4/444 and Add.1-3; ibid., *1993,* vol. II (Part One), document A/CN.4/453 and Add.1-3; ibid., *1994,* vol. II (Part One), document A/CN.4/461 and Add.1-3; as well as document A/CN.4/469 and Add.1 and 2; and document A/CN.4/476 and Add.1. For the reports of James Crawford, see documents A/CN.4/490 and Add.1-7; A/CN.4/498 and Add.1-4; A/CN.4/507 and Add.1-4; and A/CN.4/517 and Add.1.
[669] See *Yearbook of the International Law Commission, 1980,* vol. II (Part One), document A/CN.4/328 and Add.1-4; ibid., *1981,* vol. II (Part One), document A/CN.4/342 and Add.1-4; ibid., *1982,* vol. II (Part One), document A/CN.4/351 and Add.1-3; ibid., *1983,* vol. II (Part One), document A/CN.4/362; ibid., *1988,* vol. II (Part One), document A/CN.4/414; as well as documents A/CN.4/488 and Add.1-3, and A/CN.4/492.
[670] See *Yearbook of the International Law Commission, 1964,* vol. II. documents A/CN.4/165 and A/CN.4/169; ibid., *1969,* vol. II, documents A/CN.4/208 and A/CN.4/209; ibid., *1978,* vol. II (Part One), document A/CN.4/315 (a survey of State practice, international jurisprudence and doctrine relating to "force majeure" and "fortuitous event" as circumstances precluding wrongfulness); and ibid., *1980,* vol. II (Part One), document A/CN.4/318/Add.8 (a list of the principal works cited in the reports of Mr. Ago).
[671] See *Yearbook of the International Law Commission, 1969,* vol. II, document A/CN.4/217 and Add.l.

part of the proposed draft articles, the conditions under which an act which is internationally illicit and which, as such, generates an international responsibility, can be imputed to a State".[672] The criteria laid down by the Commission as a guide for its future work on the topic were summarized as follows:

(a) The Commission intended to confine its study of international responsibility, for the time being, to the responsibility of States;

(b) The Commission would first examine the question of the responsibility of States for internationally wrongful acts. The question of responsibility arising from certain lawful acts, such as space and nuclear activities, would be examined as soon as the Commission's programme of work permitted;

(c) The Commission agreed to concentrate its study on the determination of the principles which govern the responsibility of States for internationally wrongful acts, maintaining a strict distinction between this task and that of defining the rules that place obligations on States, the violation of which may generate responsibility;

(d) The study of the international responsibility of States would comprise two broad separate phases, the first covering the origin of international responsibility and the second the content of that responsibility. The first task was to determine what facts and circumstances must be established in order to be able to impute to a State the existence of an internationally wrongful act which, as such, is a source of international responsibility. The second task was to determine the consequences attached by international law to an internationally wrongful act in different cases, in order to arrive, on this basis, at a definition of the content, forms and degrees of responsibility. Once these tasks had been accomplished, the Commission would be able to decide whether a third phase should be added in the same context, covering the examination of certain problems relating to what has been termed the "implementation" of the international responsibility of States and questions concerning the settlement of disputes with regard to the application of the rules on responsibility.

At the Commission's twenty-second session, in 1970, the Special Rapporteur presented a second report,[673] entitled "The origin of international responsibility", which examined the following general rules governing the topic as a whole: the principle of the

---

[672] See *Yearbook of the International Law Commission, 1969*, vol. II, document A/7610/Rev.1, para. 80.
[673] See *Yearbook of the International Law Commission, 1970*, vol. II, document A/CN.4/233.

internationally wrongful act as a source of responsibility; the essential conditions for the existence of an internationally wrongful act; and the capacity to commit such acts. Draft articles were submitted in respect of these fundamental rules. The Commission's discussion of the report led it to a series of conclusions as to the method, substance, and terminology essential for the continuation of its work on State responsibility.

The draft articles, which were cast in a form that would have permitted them to be used as the basis for the conclusion of a convention if so decided, related solely to the *responsibility of States for internationally wrongful acts*. The Commission fully recognized the importance not only of questions of responsibility for internationally wrongful acts, but also of questions concerning the obligation to make good any injurious consequences arising out of certain activities not prohibited by international law (especially those which, because of their nature, present certain risks). The Commission took the view, however, that the latter category of questions could not be treated jointly with the former. Being obliged to bear any injurious consequences of an activity which is itself lawful, and being obliged to face the consequences (not necessarily limited to compensation) of the breach of a legal obligation, are not comparable situations. The limitation of the draft articles to responsibility of States for internationally wrongful acts merely meant that the Commission would make its study of the topic of international liability for injurious consequences arising out of certain acts not prohibited by international law separately from that of responsibility for internationally wrongful acts, so that two matters, which, in spite of certain appearances, are quite distinct, would not be dealt with in one and the same draft. Thus, the Commission emphasized that the expression "State responsibility", which appeared in the title of the draft, was to be understood as meaning only "responsibility of States for internationally wrongful acts".

The Commission also pointed out that the purpose of the draft articles was not to define the rules imposing on States, in one sector or another of inter-State relations, obligations whose breach could be a source of responsibility and which, in a certain sense, may be described as "'primary". On the contrary, in preparing its draft the Commission undertook to define other rules which, in contradistinction to the primary rules, may be described as "secondary", inasmuch as they were aimed at determining the legal consequences of failure to fulfil obligations established by the "primary" rules. Only these "secondary" rules fall within the actual sphere of responsibility for internationally wrongful acts. This does not mean that the content, nature and scope of the obligations imposed on the State by the "primary" rules of international law are of no significance in determining the rules governing responsibility for internationally wrongful acts. The essential fact nevertheless remains that it is one thing to state a rule and the content of the obligation it imposes, and another to determine whether that obligation has been breached and what the consequences of the breach must be. Only this second aspect comes within the actual sphere of the international responsibility that is the subject matter of the draft.

The draft articles are concerned only with the determination of the rules governing the international responsibility of the State for internationally wrongful acts, that is to say, the rules that govern all the new legal relationships to which an internationally wrongful act on the part of a State may give rise in different cases. They codify the rules governing the responsibility of States for internationally wrongful acts "in general", not simply in certain particular sectors. The international responsibility of the State is made up of a set of legal situations which result from the breach of any international obligation, whether imposed by the rules governing one particular matter or by those governing another.[674]

It was on the basis of these conclusions that the Commission undertook the preparation of draft articles on the topic, beginning the first reading thereof at its twenty-fifth session, in 1973.

The General Assembly, by resolution 3071 (XXVIII) of 30 November 1973, recommended that the Commission should continue on a priority basis at its twenty-sixth session its work on State responsibility with a view to the preparation of a first set of draft articles on responsibility of States for internationally wrongful acts, and that the Commission should undertake at an appropriate time a separate study of the topic of international liability for injurious consequences arising out of the performance of other activities.

At its twenty-fifth to thirtieth sessions, from 1973 to 1978, the Commission provisionally adopted on first reading chapters I, II and III of Part One of the draft articles on State responsibility for internationally wrongful acts. In 1978, in conformity with the pertinent provisions of its Statute, the Commission requested the Governments of Member States to transmit their observations and comments on those chapters.

The General Assembly, in resolution 33/139 of 19 December 1978, endorsed this decision of the Commission.

---

[674] See *Yearbook of the International Law Commission, 1973*, vol. II, document A/9010/Rev.1, paras. 36-57.

At its thirty-second session, in 1980, the Commission provisionally adopted on first reading the whole of Part One of the draft articles, concerning "the origin of international responsibility". The Commission decided, in conformity with articles 16 and 21 of its Statute, to transmit the provisions of chapters IV and V to the Governments of Member States, through the Secretary-General, and to request them to transmit their observations and comments on those provisions. The Commission also decided to renew its request to Governments to transmit their observations and comments on chapters I, II and III.

At its forty-eighth session, in 1996, the Commission completed the first reading of Parts Two and Three of the draft articles and decided, in accordance with articles 16 and 21 of its Statute, to transmit the draft articles provisionally adopted by the Commission on first reading to Governments for comments and observations.

The General Assembly, in resolution 51/160 of 16 December 1996, expressed its appreciation to the Commission for the completion of the provisional draft articles and urged Governments to submit their comments and observations on the draft in writing, as requested by the Commission.

At its forty-ninth session, in 1997, the Commission began the second reading of the draft articles on the basis of the four reports submitted by the new Special Rapporteur, Mr. Crawford, as well as comments by Governments. At the same session, it established a working group on State Responsibility to address matters dealing with the second reading of the topic.[675]

At its fiftieth session, in 1998, the Commission held an extensive debate[676] on the issue of the treatment of State "crimes" and "delicts" in the draft articles based on the first report of the Special Rapporteur.[677] Following the debate, the Commission noted that no consensus existed on this issue and that more work needed to be done on possible ways of dealing with the substantial questions raised. It was accordingly agreed that: (a) without prejudice to the views of any member of the Commission, draft article 19 concerning international crimes and delicts would be put aside for the time being while the Commission proceeded to consider other aspects of Part One; (b) consideration should be given to whether the systematic development

---

[675] For the guidelines on the consideration of this topic on second reading adopted by the Commission on the recommendation of the Working Group, see *Yearbook of the International Law Commission, 1997*, vol. II (Part Two), para. 161. For the report of the Working Group, see document A/CN.4/L.538.

[676] See *Yearbook of the International Law Commission, 1998*, vol. II (Part Two), paras. 241-330.

[677] Document A/CN.4/490 and Add.1-7.

in the draft articles of key notions such as obligations *erga omnes*, peremptory norms (*jus cogens*) and a possible category of the most serious breaches of international obligation could be sufficient to resolve the issues raised by article 19; (c) this consideration would occur, in the first instance, in the Working Group established on this topic and also in the Special Rapporteur's second report; and (d) in the event that no consensus was achieved through this process of further consideration and debate, the Commission would return to the questions raised in the first report as to draft article 19, with a view to taking a decision thereon.[678] At the same session, the Commission established a Working Group to assist the Special Rapporteur in the consideration of various issues during the second reading of the draft articles.

The Commission completed the second reading of the draft articles at its fifty-third session, in 2001. At that session, the Commission established two Working Groups on the topic: one open-ended Working Group to deal with the main outstanding issues on the topic, and the other Working Group to consider the commentaries to the draft articles.

On the recommendation of the first Working Group, the Commission agreed as an exception to its long-standing practice in adopting draft articles on second reading to include a brief summary of the debate concerning the main outstanding issues in the light of the importance of the topic and the complexity of the issues as well as the Working Group's recommendations on those issues.[679] On the basis of the Working Group's recommendations,[680] the Commission reached the following understandings:

(a) Serious breaches of obligations to the international community as a whole: Part Two, chapter III, would be retained; article 42, paragraph 1, concerning damages reflecting the gravity of the breach would be deleted; and previous references to serious breach of an obligation owed to the international community as a whole and essential for the protection of its fundamental interests, which mostly dealt with the question of invocation as expressed by the International Court of Justice in the *Barcelona Traction* case, would be replaced with the category of peremptory norms. Use of the category of peremptory norms was preferred since it concerned the scope of secondary

---

[678] See *Yearbook of the International Law Commission, 1998*, vol. II (Part Two), para. 331.
[679] See *Official Records of the General Assembly, Fifty-sixth session, Supplement No. 10* (A/56/10), para. 44.
[680] Reproduced in *Official Records of the General Assembly, Fifty-sixth session, Supplement No. 10* (A/56/10), paras. 49, 55, 60 and 67.

obligations, and not their invocation, and the notion of peremptory norms was well established in the Vienna Convention on the Law of Treaties (*see annex V, section F*). The new formulation would not deal with trivial or minor breaches of peremptory norms, but only with serious breaches of peremptory norms. The Drafting Committee would give further consideration to aspects of consequences of serious breaches in order to simplify these, to avoid excessively vague formulas and to narrow the scope of its application to cases falling properly within the scope of the chapter.

(b) Countermeasures: It was undesirable to include all or a substantial part of the articles on countermeasures in article 23, which was devoted only to one aspect of the question. Such an attempt would overburden article 23 and could even make it incomprehensible. Article 23 would remain in chapter V of Part One and the chapter on countermeasures would remain in Part Three, but article 54, which dealt with countermeasures by States other than the injured State, would be deleted. Instead, there would be a saving clause leaving all positions on this issue unaffected. In addition, article 53 dealing with conditions relating to countermeasures, would be reconsidered and the distinction between countermeasures and provisional countermeasures would be deleted. That article would be simplified and brought substantially into line with the decisions of the arbitral tribunal in the *Air Services* case and of the International Court of Justice in the *Gabčíkovo-Nagymaros* case. Articles 51 and 52 on the obligations not subject to countermeasures and proportionality would be reconsidered, as necessary.

(c) Dispute settlement provisions: The Commission would not include provisions for a dispute settlement machinery, but would draw attention to the machinery elaborated by the Commission in the first reading draft as a possible means for settlement of disputes concerning State responsibility; and would leave it to the General Assembly to consider whether and what form of provisions for dispute settlement would be included in the event that the Assembly should decide to elaborate a convention.

(d) Form of the draft articles: The Commission, in the first instance, would recommend to the General Assembly that it take note of the draft articles and annex the text of the articles to a resolution, similar to the procedure followed by the Assembly with regard to the articles on "Nationality of natural persons in relation to the succession of States" in resolution 55/153 of 12 December 2000. The recommendation would also propose that, given the importance of the topic, in the second and later stage the Assembly should consider the adoption of a Convention on this topic, which would raise the question of dispute settlement mentioned above.

At the same session, the Commission also decided to amend the title of the topic to "Responsibility of States for internationally wrongful acts" to distinguish the topic from the responsibility of the State under internal law and from the concept of international "liability" for acts not prohibited by international law.[681]

At the same session, the Commission adopted the entire set of final draft articles on responsibility of States for internationally wrongful acts consisting of 59 articles as well as commentaries thereto.[682] The draft articles are divided into four parts, as follows: Part One. The internationally wrongful act of a State, including Chapter I. General principles, Chapter II. Attribution of conduct to a State, Chapter III. Breach of an international obligation, Chapter IV. Responsibility of a State in connection with the act of another State and Chapter V. Circumstances precluding wrongfulness; Part Two. Content of the international responsibility of a State, including Chapter I. General principles, Chapter II. Reparation for injury and Chapter III. Serious breaches of obligations under peremptory norms of general international law; Part Three. The implementation of the international responsibility of a State, including Chapter I. Invocation of the responsibility of a State and Chapter II. Countermeasures; and Part Four. General provisions. The text of the draft articles is reproduced in annex IV, section 11.

The Commission decided, in accordance with article 23 of its Statute, to recommend to the General Assembly that it take note of the draft articles on responsibility of States for internationally wrongful acts in a resolution, and that it annex the draft articles to the resolution. The Commission decided further to recommend that the General Assembly consider, at a later stage, and in the light of the importance of the topic, the possibility of convening an international conference of plenipotentiaries to examine the draft articles on responsibility of States for internationally wrongful acts with a view to concluding a convention on the topic. The Commission was of the view that the question of the settlement of disputes could be dealt with by the above-mentioned international conference, if it considered that a legal mechanism on the settlement of disputes should be provided in connection with the draft articles.[683]

---

[681] See *Official Records of the General Assembly, Fifty-sixth session, Supplement No. 10 (A/56/10)*, para. 68.
[682] See *Official Records of the General Assembly, Fifty-sixth session, Supplement No. 10 (A/56/10)*, paras. 69, 70, 76 and 77.
[683] See *Official Records of the General Assembly, Fifty-sixth session, Supplement No. 10 (A/56/10)*, paras. 72 and 73.

The General Assembly, in resolution 56/83 of 12 December 2001, as recommended by the Commission, took note of the articles on responsibility of States for internationally wrongful acts, the text of which was annexed to the resolution, commended them to the attention of Governments without prejudice to the question of their future adoption or other appropriate action, and decided to include in the provisional agenda of its fifty-ninth session, in 2004, an item entitled "Responsibility of States for internationally wrongful acts".

26. International liability for injurious consequences arising out of acts not prohibited by international law

From the outset of its work on the topic of State responsibility the Commission agreed that that topic should deal only with the consequences of internationally wrongful acts, and that, in defining the general rule concerning the principle of responsibility for internationally wrongful acts, it was necessary to adopt a formula which did not prejudge the existence of responsibility for lawful acts. That conclusion met with broad acceptance in the discussion of the Sixth Committee of the General Assembly at its twenty-fifth session, in 1970.

At its twenty-fifth session, in 1973, when the Commission started to work on the first set of draft articles on State responsibility, it referred to the matter in more definite terms: ". . . if it is thought desirable — and views to this effect have already been expressed in the past both in the International Law Commission and in the Sixth Committee of the General Assembly — the International Law Commission can undertake the study of the so-called responsibility for risk after its study on responsibility for wrongful acts has been completed, or it can do so simultaneously but separately."[684]

The General Assembly, in resolution 3071 (XXVIII) of 30 November 1973, again supported the position of the Commission and recommended that the Commission should undertake a study of the new topic "at an appropriate time". The Assembly, in resolutions 3315 (XXIX) of 14 December 1974 and 3495 (XXX) of 15 December 1975, repeated its recommendation that the Commission take up the topic "as soon as appropriate", and finally in 1976, in resolution 31/97 of 15 December, it replaced that phrase by the words "at the earliest possible time".

---

[684] See *Yearbook of the International Law Commission, 1973*, vol. II, document A/9010/Rev.1, para. 39.

Pursuant to those recommendations of the General Assembly, the Commission agreed, at its twenty-ninth session, in 1977, to undertake the study on the topic at the earliest possible time, having regard, in particular, to the progress made on the draft articles on State responsibility for internationally wrongful acts.

The General Assembly, in resolution 32/151 of 19 December 1977, endorsed the conclusion of the Commission and invited it, at an appropriate time and in the light of progress made on the draft articles on State responsibility for internationally wrongful acts and on other topics in its current programme of work, to commence work on the topic of international liability for injurious consequences arising out of acts not prohibited by international law.

At its thirtieth session, in 1978, the Commission established a working group to consider, in a preliminary manner, the scope and nature of the topic. On the basis of the recommendations made by the Working Group,[685] the Commission appointed Robert Q. Quentin-Baxter as Special Rapporteur for the topic and invited him to prepare a preliminary report at an early juncture. It also requested the Secretariat to collect and survey materials on the topic on a continuous basis.

The Commission proceeded with its work on the topic as a whole from its thirty-second to thirty-sixth sessions and from its thirty-eighth to forty-ninth sessions, from 1980 to 1984 and from 1986 to 1997, respectively. At its forty-ninth session, in 1997, the Commission decided to split the topic into two parts, prevention of transboundary damage from hazardous activities and international liability in case of loss from transboundary harm arising out of hazardous activities. Since then, the Commission has considered the two parts of the topic separately, as discussed below.

At the Commission's thirty-seventh session, in 1985, Julio Barbosa succeeded Robert Q. Quentin-Baxter as Special Rapporteur for the topic. In connection with its work on the topic, the Commission had before it the reports of the Special Rapporteurs,[686]

---

[685] For the report of the Working Group, see document A/CN.4/L.284 and Corr.1. Section II of the report is reproduced in *Yearbook of the International Law Commission, 1978,* vol. II (Part Two), para. 178, annex.

[686] For the reports of Robert Q. Quentin-Baxter, see *Yearbook of the International Law Commission, 1980,* vol. II (Part One), document A/CN.4/334 and Add.1 and 2; ibid., *1981,* vol. II (Part One), document A/CN.4/346 and Add.1 and 2; ibid., *1982,* vol. II (Part One), document A/CN.4/360; ibid., *1983,* vol. II (Part One), document A/CN.4/373; and ibid., *1984,* vol. II (Part One), document A/CN.4/383 and Add.1. For the reports of Julio Barbosa, see *Yearbook of the International Law Commission, 1985,* vol. II (Part One), document A/CN.4/394; ibid., *1986,* vol. II (Part One), document A/CN.4/402; ibid., *1987,* vol. II (Part One), document A/CN.4/405; ibid., *1988,* vol. II (Part One), document A/CN.4/413; ibid., *1989,* vol. II (Part One),

information provided by Governments and international organizations[687] as well as documents prepared by the Secretariat.[688]

At its thirty-fifth session, in 1983, the Commission agreed that the Special Rapporteur should, with the help of the Secretariat, prepare a questionnaire to be addressed to selected international organizations with a view to ascertaining whether obligations which States owed to each other, and discharged, as members of international organizations might, to that extent, fulfil or replace some of the procedures indicated in the Special Rapporteur's schematic outline contained in his third report. In compliance with this decision, a questionnaire was prepared and addressed to sixteen international organizations, selected on the basis of activities which might bear on the subject matter of the inquiry.

At its fortieth session, in 1988, the Commission began the first reading of the draft articles on the topic.

At its forty-fourth session, in 1992, the Commission established a Working Group to consider some of the general issues relating to the scope, the approach to be taken and the possible direction of the future work on the topic. On the basis of the recommendation of the Working Group,[689] the Commission decided, with regard to the scope of the topic, that, pending a final decision, the topic should be understood as comprising both issues of prevention and of remedial measures. Prevention should, however, be considered first; only after having completed its work on that first part of the topic would the Commission proceed to the question of remedial measures. Remedial measures in that context might include those designed for mitigation of harm, restoration of what had been harmed and compensation for harm caused. Thus, the draft articles should deal first with preventive measures in respect of activities creating a risk of causing transboundary harm and secondly with articles on the remedial measures when such activities had caused transboundary harm. The

---

document A/CN.4/423; ibid., *1990*, vol. II (Part One), document A/CN.4/428 and Add.1; ibid., *1991*, vol. II (Part One), document A/CN.4/437; ibid., *1992*, vol. II (Part One), document A/CN.4/443; ibid., *1993*, vol. II (Part One), document A/CN.4/450; ibid., *1994*, vol. II (Part One), document A/CN.4/459; as well as documents A/CN.4/468 and A/CN.4/475 and Add.1.

[687] See *Yearbook of the International Law Commission, 1984*, vol. II (Part One), document A/CN.4/378; as well as document A/CN.4/481 and Add.1.

[688] "Survey of State practice relevant to international liability for injurious consequences arising out of acts not prohibited by international law" (document ST/LEG/15, subsequently reissued in a slightly amended form under the symbol A/CN.4/384, reproduced in *Yearbook of the International Law Commission, 1985*, vol. II (Part One, addendum)); and "Survey of liability regimes relevant to the topic of international liability for injurious consequences arising out of acts not prohibited by international law" (document A/CN.4/471).

[689] Document A/CN.4/L.470.

Commission deferred, however, its decision on the question of the approach to be taken with regard to the nature of the articles or of the instrument to be drafted, until after the completion of the work on the topic. The articles would be considered and adopted on the basis of their merits based on their clarity and utility for the contemporary and future needs of the international community and their possible contribution to the promotion of the progressive development and codification of international law in that area. The Commission also deferred its decision on the title of the topic until after the completion of the draft articles.[690]

At its forty-sixth and forty-seventh sessions, in 1994 and 1995, the Commission provisionally adopted draft articles 1 (Scope of the present articles), 2 (Use of terms), 11 (Prior authorisation), 12 (Risk assessment), 13 (Pre-existing activities), 14 (Measures to prevent or minimize the risk), 14 bis (Non-transference of risk), 15 (Notification and information), 16 (Exchange of information), 16 bis (Information to the public), 17 (National security and industrial secrets), 18 (Consultations on preventive measures), 19 (Rights of the State likely to be affected), 20 (Factors involved in an equitable balance of interests), A (Freedom of action and the limits thereto), B (Prevention), C (Liability and compensation) and D (Cooperation), with commentaries thereto.

At its forty-seventh session, in 1995, the Commission established a Working Group to identify activities within the scope of the topic. In the light of the Working Group's report,[691] the Commission agreed that it must, in its future work on the topic, have a clear view of the kind of activities to which the draft articles on the topic apply. It took the view that it could work on the basis that the types of activities listed in various conventions dealing with issues of transboundary harm came within the scope of the topic, but that eventually, more specificity might be required in the draft articles.

At its forty-eighth session, in 1996, the Commission established a Working Group to review the topic in all its aspects in the light of the reports of the Special Rapporteur and the discussions on the topic held over the years. In its report to the Commission, the Working Group submitted a single consolidated text of draft articles and commentaries thereto which were limited in terms of the scope of the topic and residual in character.[692] The Commission was unable to

---

[690] See *Yearbook of the International Law Commission, 1992*, vol. II (Part Two), paras. 344-348.
[691] Document A/CN.4/L.510.
[692] Document A/CN.4/L.533 and Add.1 reproduced in *Yearbook of the International Law Commission, 1996*, vol. II (Part Two), annex I.

examine the draft articles at that session. It, however, decided to transmit them to the General Assembly and to Governments for comments.[693]

At its forty-ninth session, in 1997, the Commission, pursuant to General Assembly resolution 51/160 of 16 December 1996, established a Working Group to consider the question of how to proceed with the topic. The Working Group reviewed the work of the Commission on the topic since 1978. It noted that the scope and content of the topic remained unclear due to such factors as conceptual and theoretical difficulties, appropriateness of the title and the relation of the subject to the topic "State responsibility." It further noted that the Commission had dealt with two distinct, though related, issues under the topic: "prevention" and "international liability." The Working Group agreed that those issues henceforth should be dealt with separately. Noting that the work on prevention was already at an advanced stage, the Working Group believed that the Commission should proceed with its work on this aspect of the topic with a possible completion of the first reading in the near future. With respect to the second aspect, liability, the Working Group was of the view that, while retaining it, the Commission should await further comments from Governments before making any decision on the issue.[694]

At the same session, the Commission considered and adopted the Working Group's report.[695] On the basis of the recommendation of the Working Group, the Commission decided, inter alia, to proceed with its work on the topic, undertaking first prevention under the subtitle "Prevention of transboundary damage from hazardous activities".

The General Assembly, in resolution 52/156 of 15 December 1997, took note of the Commission's decision.

(a)   Prevention of transboundary damage from hazardous activities

At its forty-ninth session, in 1997, the Commission appointed Pemmaraju Sreenivasa Rao as Special Rapporteur for this part of the topic.

---

[693] See *Yearbook of the International Law Commission, 1996*, vol. II (Part Two), para. 99.
[694] See *Yearbook of the International Law Commission, 1997*, vol. II (Part Two), paras. 165-167.
[695] Document A/CN.4/L.536 reflected in *Yearbook of the International Law Commission, 1997*, vol. II (Part Two), paras. 165-167.

The Commission proceeded with its work on this part of the topic, on the basis of the reports of the Special Rapporteur[696] and information provided by Governments,[697] from its fiftieth to fifty-third sessions, from 1998 to 2001, respectively,

At its fiftieth session, in 1998, the Commission established a Working Group to ascertain whether the principles of procedure and content of the duty of prevention were appropriately reflected in the draft articles recommended by the Working Group to the Commission at its forty-eighth session, in 1996. On the basis of the Working Group's discussions, the Special Rapporteur proposed at the same session a revised text of the draft articles,[698] which the Commission referred to the Drafting Committee. The Commission considered the report of the Drafting Committee and adopted on first reading a set of seventeen draft articles on prevention of transboundary damage from hazardous activities. In accordance with articles 16 and 21 of the Statute, they were transmitted to Governments for comments and observations.

The General Assembly, in resolution 53/102 of 8 December 1998, expressed its appreciation to the Commission for the completion of the first reading of the draft articles on the prevention part of the topic and invited Governments to submit comments and observations in writing on the draft articles.

At its fifty-second session, in 2000, the Commission established a Working Group to examine the comments and observations made by States on the draft articles. On the basis of the discussion in the Working Group, the Special Rapporteur presented his third report[699] containing a draft preamble and a revised set of draft articles on prevention, along with the recommendation that they be adopted as a framework convention. Furthermore, the third report addressed questions such as the scope of the topic, its relationship with liability, the relationship between an equitable balance of interests among States concerned and the duty of prevention, as well as duality of the regimes of liability and State responsibility. The Commission considered the report and decided to refer the draft preamble and draft articles contained therein to the Drafting Committee.

At its fifty-third session, in 2001, the Commission adopted and submitted to the General Assembly the final text of draft articles on prevention of transboundary harm from hazardous activities,

---

[696] Documents A/CN.4/487 and Add.1; A/CN.4/501; and A/CN.4/510.
[697] Documents A/CN.4/509 and A/CN.4/516.
[698] Document A/CN.4/L.556 reproduced in *Yearbook of the International Law Commission, 1998*, vol. II (Part Two), footnote 12.
[699] Document A/CN.4/510.

consisting of a preamble and nineteen articles, with commentaries thereto.[700] The text of the draft articles is reproduced in annex IV, section 12. In transmitting the final draft to the General Assembly, the Commission recommended that the General Assembly elaborate a convention on the basis of the draft articles.[701]

The General Assembly, by resolution 56/82 of 12 December 2001, expressed its appreciation for the valuable work done by the Commission on the issue of prevention on the topic of international liability for injurious consequences arising out of acts not prohibited by international law (prevention of transboundary harm from hazardous activities).

(b) International liability in case of loss from transboundary harm arising out of hazardous activities

The General Assembly, in resolution 53/102 of 8 December 1998, requested the Commission, while continuing its work on prevention, to examine other issues arising out of the topic, taking into account comments made by Governments, either in writing or in the Sixth Committee, and to submit its recommendations on the future work to be done on these issues to the Sixth Committee.

In his second report,[702] the Special Rapporteur on the prevention part of the topic, dealt, apart from the issues related to the first part of the topic (prevention), with the treatment of the concept of international liability in the Commission since the topic was placed on its agenda; negotiations on liability issues in other international fora; and options with respect to the future course of action on the question of liability. The Commission considered the report at its fifty-first session, in 1999, and decided to defer the consideration of the question of international liability, pending completion of the second reading of the draft articles on the prevention of transboundary damage from hazardous activities.

The General Assembly, in resolutions 54/111 of 9 December 1999 and 55/152 of 12 December 2000, requested the Commission to resume the consideration of the liability aspects of the topic as soon as the second reading of the draft articles on prevention was finalized. The General Assembly, by resolution 56/82 of 12 December 2001, requested the Commission to resume, during its fifty-fourth session, its consideration of the liability aspects of the topic, bearing in mind

---

[700] See *Official Records of the General Assembly, Fifty-sixth Session, Supplement No. 10* (A/56/10), paras. 91, 92, 97 and 98.
[701] See *Official Records of the General Assembly, Fifty-sixth Session, Supplement No. 10* (A/56/10), para. 94
[702] Document A/CN.4/501.

the interrelationship between prevention and liability, and taking into account the developments in international law and comments by Governments.

The Commission resumed its consideration of the liability aspect of the topic at its fifty-fourth session, in 2002 (*see Part III.B, section 4*).

B. TOPICS AND SUB-TOPICS CURRENTLY UNDER CONSIDERATION BY THE COMMISSION

A brief account of the work of the International Law Commission on the topics and sub-topics currently under consideration is set out below.

1. Reservations to treaties[703]

At its forty-fifth session, in 1993, the International Law Commission, on the basis of the recommendation of a Working Group on the long-term programme of work, decided to include in the Commission's agenda, subject to the approval of the General Assembly, the topic "The law and practice relating to reservations to treaties". The Commission noted that the 1969 Vienna Convention on the Law of Treaties (*see annex V, section F*), the 1978 Vienna Convention on Succession of States in Respect of Treaties (*see annex V, section I*) and the 1986 Vienna Convention on the Law of Treaties between States and International Organizations or between International Organizations (*see annex V, section K*) set out some principles concerning reservations to treaties, but they did so in terms that were too general to act as a guide for State practice and left a number of important matters in the dark. These conventions provide ambiguous answers to the questions of differentiating between reservations and declarations of interpretation, the scope of declarations of interpretation, the validity of reservations (the conditions for the lawfulness of reservations and their applicability to another State) and the regime of objections to reservations (in particular, the admissibility and scope of objections to a reservation which is neither prohibited by the treaty nor contrary to its object and purpose). These conventions are also silent on the effect of reservations on the entry into force of treaties, problems pertaining to the particular object of some treaties (in particular the constituent instruments of international organizations and human rights treaties), reservations to codification treaties and problems resulting from particular treaty techniques (elaboration of additional protocols, bilateralization techniques). The Commission recognized the need not to challenge the regime established in articles 19 to 23 of the 1969 Vienna Convention on the Law of Treaties, but nonetheless considered that

---

[703] At its forty-seventh session, in 1995, the Commission concluded that the title of the topic should be amended to read as above rather than "The law and practice relating to reservations to treaties".

these provisions could be clarified and developed in draft protocols to existing conventions or a guide to practice.[704]

The General Assembly, in resolution 48/31 of 9 December 1993, endorsed the above decision of the International Law Commission on the understanding that the final form to be given to the work on the topic would be decided after a preliminary study was presented to the Assembly.

At its forty-sixth session, in 1994, the Commission appointed Mr. Alain Pellet as Special Rapporteur for the topic.[705]

The General Assembly, in resolution 49/51 of 9 December 1994, again endorsed the decision of the Commission on the understanding reflected above.

At its forty-seventh session, in 1995, the Commission had before it the first report[706] of the Special Rapporteur. This preliminary report provided a detailed study of the Commission's previous work on reservations and its outcome. It also provided an inventory of the problematic aspects of the topic including those relating to the ambiguities and gaps in the provisions concerning reservations contained in the Vienna Conventions on the Law of Treaties, as well as those connected with the specific object of certain treaties or provisions or arising from certain specific treaty approaches. Finally, it outlined the scope and form of the Commission's future work, guided by the preservation of what had been achieved, and proposed the form that the results of the Commission's work might take. Following the Commission's consideration of the report, the Special Rapporteur summarized the conclusions he had drawn with respect to: (1) the title of the topic, which should now read "Reservations to treaties"; (2) the form of the results of the study, which should be a guide to practice in respect of reservations; (3) the flexible way in which the Commission's work on the topic should be carried out; and (4) the consensus in the Commission that there should be no change in the relevant provisions of the Vienna Conventions. The Guide to Practice in the form of draft articles with commentaries would provide guidelines for the practice of States and international organizations in respect of reservations. These guidelines would, if necessary, be accompanied by model clauses.[707] In the view of the Commission, those conclusions constituted the results of the

---

[704] See *Yearbook of the International Law Commission, 1993*, vol. II (Part Two), paras. 427-430 and 440.
[705] See *Yearbook of the International Law Commission, 1994*, vol. II (Part Two), para. 381.
[706] Document A/CN.4/470.
[707] See *Yearbook of the International Law Commission, 1995*, vol. II (Part Two), para. 487.

preliminary study requested by the General Assembly in resolutions 48/31 of 9 December 1993 and 49/51 of 9 December 1994.[708] The Commission authorized the Special Rapporteur to prepare a detailed questionnaire on reservations to treaties to ascertain the practice of, and the problems encountered by, States and international organizations, particularly those which are depositaries of multilateral conventions.[709]

The General Assembly, in resolution 50/45 of 11 December 1995, took note of the Commission's conclusions, invited the Commission to continue its work along the lines indicated in its report and invited States and international organizations, particularly those which are depositaries, to answer the questionnaire.

At its forty-eighth session, in 1996, the Commission had before it the Special Rapporteur's second report[710] as well as a bibliography.[711] The report dealt with the issue of the unity or diversity of the legal regime of reservations to treaties, especially reservations to human rights treaties. The Special Rapporteur concluded that despite the diversity of treaties, the Vienna regime on reservations is generally applicable. Moreover, the coexistence of monitoring mechanisms does not preclude monitoring bodies from making determinations of the permissibility of reservations, even if States still can draw any consequences they wish from such determinations and react accordingly. The Special Rapporteur also proposed a draft resolution of the International Law Commission on reservations to normative multilateral treaties, including human rights treaties, which was addressed to the General Assembly for the purpose of drawing attention to and clarifying the legal aspects of the matter. The Commission did not have time to consider the report and the draft resolution. The Commission therefore deferred the debate on the topic to its next session.[712]

At its forty-ninth session, in 1997, the Commission again had before it the second report of the Special Rapporteur on the topic concerning the question of the unity or diversity of the juridical regime for reservations. Wishing to contribute to discussions taking place in other forums on the subject of reservations to normative multilateral treaties, particularly human rights treaties, the

---

[708] See *Yearbook of the International Law Commission, 1995,* vol. II (Part Two), para. 488.
[709] See *Yearbook of the International Law Commission, 1995,* vol. II (Part Two), para. 489.
[710] Document A/CN.4/477 and Add.1.
[711] Document A/CN.4/478.
[712] See *Yearbook of the International Law Commission, 1996,* vol. II (Part Two), para. 137.

Commission adopted a number of preliminary conclusions on the subject.[713] The Commission welcomed comments by Governments on these preliminary conclusions and invited monitoring bodies set up by the relevant human rights treaties to submit their comments as well.[714]

The General Assembly, in resolution 52/156 of 15 December 1997, took note of the Commission's preliminary conclusions and its invitation to all treaty bodies set up by normative multilateral treaties that might wish to do so to provide, in writing, their comments and observations on the conclusions, while drawing the attention of Governments to the importance for the International Law Commission of having their views on the preliminary conclusions.

At its fiftieth session, in 1998, the Commission had before it the Special Rapporteur's third report,[715] which dealt with the definition of reservations and interpretative declarations to treaties. The report focused on the distinction between reservations and interpretative declarations, the uncertainties of the terminology and the criteria for the distinction between the two categories. The report also dealt with the issue of "reservations" (and interpretative declarations) in respect of bilateral treaties in the light of theory and State practice. The Special Rapporteur proposed the following draft guidelines: 1.1 (Definition of reservations), 1.1.1 (Joint formulation of a reservation), 1.1.2 (Moment when a reservation is formulated), 1.1.3 (Reservations formulated when notifying territorial application), 1.1.4 (Object of reservations), 1.1.5 (Statements designed to increase the obligations of their author), 1.1.6 (Statements designed to limit the obligations of their author), 1.1.7 (Reservations relating to non-recognition), 1.1.8 (Reservations having territorial scope), 1.1.9 ("Reservations" to bilateral treaties), 1.2 (Definition of interpretative declarations), 1.2.1 (Joint formulation of interpretative declarations), 1.2.2 (Phrasing and name), 1.2.3 (Formulation of an interpretative declaration when a reservation is prohibited), 1.2.4 (Conditional interpretative declarations), 1.2.5 (General declarations of policy), 1.2.6 (Informative declarations), 1.2.7 (Interpretative declarations in respect of bilateral treaties), 1.2.8 (Legal effect of acceptance of an interpretative declaration made in respect of a bilateral treaty by the other party), 1.3.1 (Method of distinguishing between reservations and interpretative declarations) and 1.4 (Scope of definitions). The Special Rapporteur also tentatively proposed the following draft guidelines concerning the distinction between reservations and

---

[713] See *Yearbook of the International Law Commission, 1997*, vol. II (Part Two), para. 157.
[714] See *Yearbook of the International Law Commission, 1997*, vol. II (Part Two), para. 28.
[715] Document A/CN.4/491 and Add.1-6.

interpretative declarations: 1.3.0 (Criterion of reservations), 1.3.0 bis (Criterion of interpretative declarations) and 1.3.0 *ter* (Criterion of conditional interpretative declarations). After considering part of the report, the Commission referred draft guidelines 1.1, 1.1.1-1.1.8, 1.2 and 1.4 to the Drafting Committee.[716]

At the same session, the Commission provisionally adopted the following seven draft guidelines as well as the commentaries thereto: 1.1 (Definition of reservations), 1.1.1 [1.1.4][717] (Object of reservations), 1.1.2 (Instances in which reservations may be formulated), 1.1.3 [1.1.8] (Reservations having territorial scope), 1.1.4 [1.1.3] (Reservations formulated when notifying territorial application), 1.1.7 [1.1.1] (Joint formulation of a reservation) and a draft guideline with no title or number concerning the relation between the definition and the permissibility of reservations.[718]

At its fifty-first session, in 1999, the Commission again had before it part of the Special Rapporteur's third report, which it had not had time to consider at its fiftieth session, the fourth report on the topic[719] as well as a revised bibliography.[720] In the fourth report, the Special Rapporteur continued the consideration of the definition of reservations and interpretative declarations and proposed a revised version of draft guideline 1.1.7 (1.1.7 bis) (Statements of non-recognition) which was already before the Drafting Committee. After considering the reports, the Commission referred draft guidelines 1.1.9 ("Reservations" to bilateral treaties), 1.2.1 (Joint formulation of interpretative declarations), 1.2.2 (Phrasing and name), 1.2.3 (Formulation of an interpretative declaration when a reservation is prohibited), 1.2.4 (Conditional interpretative declarations), 1.2.5 (General statements of policy), 1.2.6 (Informative declarations), 1.2.7 (Interpretative declarations in respect of bilateral treaties), 1.2.8 (Legal effect of acceptance of an interpretative declaration made in respect of a bilateral treaty by the other party) and 1.3.1 (Method of distinguishing between reservations and interpretative declarations) to the Drafting Committee. The Commission noted that draft guidelines 1.3.0, 1.3.0 bis and 1.3.0 ter concerning the distinction between reservations and interpretative declarations were tentatively proposed by the Special Rapporteur for the purpose of determining a series of

---

[716] See *Yearbook of the International Law Commission, 1998*, vol. II (Part Two), para. 479.
[717] The numbers in square brackets correspond to the numbers of the draft guidelines proposed by the Special Rapporteur.
[718] See *Yearbook of the International Law Commission, 1998*, vol. II (Part Two), para. 480.
[719] Document A/CN.4/499.
[720] Document A/CN.4/478/Rev.1.

criteria stemming from the general definitions of reservations and interpretative declarations. The Commission concluded that the criteria were inherent in the definitions and that these three draft guidelines did not add a new element. The Commission decided not to refer those guidelines to the Drafting Committee but to reflect their content in the relevant commentaries to draft guidelines on this issue.[721]

At the same session, the Commission provisionally adopted the following eighteen draft guidelines as well as the commentaries thereto: 1.1.5 [1.1.6] (Statements purporting to limit the obligations of their author), 1.1.6 (Statements purporting to discharge an obligation by equivalent means), 1.2 (Definition of interpretative declarations), 1.2.1 [1.2.4] (Conditional interpretative declarations), 1.2.2 [1.2.1] (Interpretative declarations formulated jointly), 1.3 (Distinction between reservations and interpretative declarations), 1.3.1 (Method of implementation of the distinction between reservations and interpretative declarations), 1.3.2 [1.2.2] (Phrasing and name), 1.3.3 [1.2.3] (Formulation of a unilateral statement when a reservation is prohibited), 1.4 (Unilateral statements other than reservations and interpretative declarations), 1.4.1 [1.1.5] (Statements purporting to undertake unilateral commitments), 1.4.2 [1.1.6] (Unilateral statements purporting to add further elements to a treaty), 1.4.3 [1.1.7] (Statements of non-recognition), 1.4.4 [1.2.5] (General statements of policy), 1.4.5 [1.2.6] (Statements concerning modalities of implementation of a treaty at the internal level), 1.5.1 [1.1.9] (Reservations to bilateral treaties), 1.5.2 [1.2.7] (Interpretative declarations in respect of bilateral treaties) and 1.5.3 [1.2.8] (Legal effect of acceptance of an interpretative declaration made in respect of a bilateral treaty by the other party). In the light of the consideration of interpretative declarations, the Commission also adopted a new version of draft guideline 1.1.1 [1.1.4] (Object of reservations) and of the draft guideline without a title or number (which has become draft guideline 1.6 (Scope of definitions)).[722]

At its fifty-second session, in 2000, the Commission had before it the Special Rapporteur's fifth report,[723] which dealt, on the one hand, with the alternatives to reservations and interpretative declarations and, on the other hand, with the procedure regarding reservations and interpretative declarations, particularly their formulation and the question of late reservations and interpretative declarations. The

[721] See *Official Records of the General Assembly, Fifty-fourth Session, Supplement No. 10* (A/54/10), paras. 467 and 468.
[722] See *Official Records of the General Assembly, Fifty-fourth Session, Supplement No. 10* (A/54/10), para. 469.
[723] Document A/CN.4/508 and Add.1-4.

Commission was able to consider only the first part of the fifth report[724] in which the Special Rapporteur proposed the following draft guidelines: 1.1.8 (Reservations formulated under exclusionary clauses), 1.4.6 (Unilateral statements adopted under an optional clause), 1.4.7 (Restrictions contained in unilateral statements adopted under an optional clause), 1.4.8 (Unilateral statements providing for a choice between the provisions of a treaty), 1.7.1 (Alternatives to reservations), 1.7.2 (Different procedures permitting modification of the effects of the provisions of a treaty), 1.7.3 (Restrictive clauses), 1.7.4 (["Bilateralized reservations"] [Agreements between States having the same object as reservations]) and 1.7.5 (Alternative to interpretative declarations). After considering the first part of the report, the Commission referred the proposed draft guidelines to the Drafting Committee.[725]

At the same session, the Commission provisionally adopted the following five draft guidelines as well as the commentaries thereto: 1.1.8 (Reservations made under exclusionary clauses), 1.4.6 [1.4.6, 1.4.7] (Unilateral statements made under an optional clause), 1.4.7 [1.4.8] (Unilateral statements providing for a choice between the provisions of a treaty), 1.7.1 [1.7.1, 1.7.2, 1.7.3, 1.7.4] (Alternatives to reservations) and 1.7.2 [1.7.5] (Alternatives to interpretative declarations).[726] The Commission deferred consideration of the second part of the fifth report to the following session.[727]

At its fifty-third session, in 2001, the Commission again had before it the second part of the fifth report[728] relating to questions of procedure regarding reservations and interpretative declarations. The Special Rapporteur proposed the following draft guidelines: 2.2.1 (Reservations formulated when signing and formal confirmation), 2.2.2 (Reservations formulated when negotiating, adopting or authenticating the text of the treaty and formal confirmation), 2.2.3 (Non-confirmation of reservations formulated when signing [an agreement in simplified form] [a treaty that enters into force solely by being signed]), 2.2.4 (Reservations formulated when signing for which the treaty makes express provision), 2.3.1 (Reservations formulated late), 2.3.2 (Acceptance of reservations formulated late), 2.3.3 (Objection to reservations formulated late), 2.3.4 (Late

---

[724] Document A/CN.4/508 and Add.1-2.
[725] See *Official Records of the General Assembly, Fifty-fifth Session, Supplement No. 10* (A/55/10), para. 636.
[726] See *Official Records of the General Assembly, Fifty-fifth Session, Supplement No. 10* (A/55/10), para. 637.
[727] See *Official Records of the General Assembly, Fifty-fifth Session, Supplement No. 10* (A/55/10), para. 638.
[728] Document A/CN.4/508/Add.3 and Add.4.

exclusion or modification of the legal effects of a treaty by procedures other than reservations), 2.4.3 (Times at which an interpretative declaration may be formulated), 2.4.4 (Conditional interpretative declarations formulated when negotiating, adopting or authenticating or signing the text of the treaty and formal confirmation), 2.4.5 (Non-confirmation of interpretative declarations formulated when signing [an agreement in simplified form] [a treaty that enters into force solely by being signed]), 2.4.6 (Interpretative declarations formulated when signing for which the treaty makes express provision), 2.4.7 (Interpretative declarations formulated late) and 2.4.8 (Conditional interpretative declarations formulated late). After considering the report, the Commission referred the proposed draft guidelines to the Drafting Committee.[729]

At the same session, the Commission provisionally adopted the following twelve draft guidelines as well as the commentaries thereto: 2.2.1 (Formal confirmation of reservations formulated when signing a treaty), 2.2.2 [2.2.3] (Instances of non-requirement of confirmation of reservations formulated when signing a treaty), 2.2.3 [2.2.4] (Reservations formulated upon signature when a treaty expressly so provides), 2.3.1 (Late formulation of a reservation), 2.3.2 (Acceptance of the late formulation of a reservation), 2.3.3 (Objection to the late formulation of a reservation), 2.3.4 (Subsequent exclusion or modification of the legal effects of a treaty by means other than reservations), 2.4.3 (Time at which an interpretative declaration may be formulated), 2.4.4 [2.4.5] (Non-requirement of confirmation of interpretative declarations made when signing a treaty), 2.4.5 [2.4.4] (Formal confirmation of conditional interpretative declarations formulated when signing a treaty), 2.4.6 [2.4.7] (Late formulation of an interpretative declaration) and 2.4.7 [2.4.8] (Late formulation of a conditional interpretative declaration).[730]

At the fifty-third session, the Commission also had before it the Special Rapporteur's sixth report[731] relating to the modalities of formulating reservations and interpretative declarations (including their form and notification) as well as the publicity of reservations and interpretative declarations (their communication, addressees and obligations of depositaries). The Special Rapporteur proposed the following draft guidelines: 2.1.1 (Written form), 2.1.2 (Form of formal confirmation), 2.1.3 (Competence to formulate a reservation at

---

[729] See *Official Records of the General Assembly, Fifty-sixth Session, Supplement No. 10* (A/56/10), para. 113.
[730] See *Official Records of the General Assembly, Fifty-sixth Session, Supplement No. 10* (A/56/10), para. 114.
[731] Document A/CN.4/518 and Add.1-3.

the international level), 2.1.3 bis (Competence to formulate a reservation at the internal level), 2.1.4 (Absence of consequences at the international level of the violation of internal rules regarding the formulation of reservations), 2.1.5 (Communication of reservations), 2.1.6 (Procedure for communication of reservations), 2.1.7 (Functions of depositaries), 2.1.8 (Effective date of communications relating to reservations), 2.4.1 (Formulation of interpretative declarations), 2.4.1 bis (Competence to formulate an interpretative declaration at the internal level), 2.4.2 (Formulation of conditional interpretative declarations) and 2.4.9 (Communication of conditional interpretative declarations). After considering the report, the Commission referred the proposed guidelines to the Drafting Committee.[732]

At its fifty-fourth session, in 2002, the Commission had before it the Special Rapporteur's seventh report[733] relating to the formulation, modification and withdrawal of reservations and interpretative declarations. The Special Rapporteur proposed the following draft guidelines: draft guidelines: 2.1.7 bis (Case of manifestly impermissible reservations), 2.5.1 (Withdrawal of reservations), 2.5.2 (Form of withdrawal), 2.5.3 (Periodic review of the usefulness of reservations), 2.5.4 (Withdrawal of reservations held to be impermissible by a body monitoring the implementation of a treaty), three alternative versions of guideline 2.5.5 (Competence to withdraw a reservation at the international level; the third version entitled "Competence to withdraw a reservation"), 2.5.5 bis (Competence to withdraw a reservation at the internal level), 2.5.5 ter (Absence of consequences at the international level of the violation of internal rules regarding the withdrawal of reservations), two alternative versions of guideline 2.5.6 (Communication of withdrawal of a reservation), 2.5.6 bis (Procedure for communication of withdrawal of reservations), 2.5.6 ter (Functions of depositaries), 2.5.7 (Effect of withdrawal of a reservation), 2.5.8 (Effect of withdrawal of a reservation in cases of objection to the reservation and opposition to entry into force of the treaty with the reserving State or international organization), 2.5.9 (Effective date of withdrawal of a reservation, including model clauses A, B and C), 2.5.10 (Cases in which a reserving State may unilaterally set the effective date of withdrawal of a reservation), 2.5.11 (Partial withdrawal of a reservation), 2.5.11 bis (Partial withdrawal of reservations held to be impermissible by a body monitoring the implementation of a treaty), 2.5.X (Withdrawal

---

[732] See *Official Records of the General Assembly, Fifty-sixth Session, Supplement No. 10* (A/56/10), para. 155.
[733] Document A/CN.4/526 and Add.1-3. The consolidated text of all draft guidelines adopted by the Commission or proposed by the Special Rapporteur is contained in document A/CN.4/526/Add.1.

of reservations held to be impermissible by a body monitoring the implementation of a treaty) and 2.5.12 (Effect of a partial withdrawal of a reservation). After considering the report, the Commission referred the proposed draft guidelines, including the related model clauses, to the Drafting Committee with the exception of draft guidelines relating to the withdrawal of a reservation held to be impermissible by a treaty-monitoring body (i.e., 2.5.4, 2.5.11 bis and 2.5.X).

At the same session, the Commission provisionally adopted the following eleven draft guidelines as well as the commentaries thereto: 2.1.1 (Written form), 2.1.2 (Form of formal confirmation), 2.1.3 (Formulation of a reservation at the international level), 2.1.4 [2.1.3 bis, 2.1.4][734] (Absence of consequences at the international level of the violation of internal rules regarding the formulation of reservations), 2.1.5 (Communication of reservations) 2.1.6 [2.1.6, 2.1.8] (Procedure for communication of reservations), 2.1.7 (Functions of depositaries), 2.1.8 [2.1.7 bis] (Procedure in case of manifestly [impermissible] reservations),[735] 2.4.1 (Formulation of interpretative declarations), [2.4.2 [2.4.1 bis] (Formulation of an interpretative declaration at the internal level)], [2.4.7 [2.4.2, 2.4.9] (Formulation and communication of conditional interpretative declarations)].[736]

At its fifty-fifth session, in 2003, the Commission had before it the Special Rapporteur's eighth report[737] relating to withdrawal and modification of reservations and interpretative declarations as well as to the formulation of objections to reservations and interpretative declarations. The Special Rapporteur proposed the following draft guidelines: 2.3.5 (Enlargement of the scope of a reservation), 2.4.9 (Modification of interpretative declarations), 2.4.10 (Modification of a conditional interpretative declaration), 2.5.12 (Withdrawal of an interpretative declaration), 2.5.13 (Withdrawal of a conditional interpretative declaration), 2.6.1. (Definition of objections to reservations), 2.6.1 bis (Objection to late formulation of a

---

[734] The numbers in square brackets correspond to the numbers of the draft guidelines proposed by the Special Rapporteur or, as the case may be, the number of the draft guideline proposed by the Special Rapporteur which has been merged with the final draft guideline. See *Official Records of the General Assembly, Fifty-seventh Session, Supplement No. 10* (A/57/10), para. 50.
[735] The term will be reviewed by the Commission. See *Official Records of the General Assembly, Fifty-seventh Session, Supplement No. 10* (A/57/10), para. 50.
[736] See *Official Records of the General Assembly, Fifty-seventh Session, Supplement No. 10* (A/57/10), paras. 50 and 51. The two draft guidelines are in square brackets pending a decision by the Commission on the fate of all of the draft guidelines on conditional interpretative declarations.
[737] Document A/CN.4/535 and Add.1.

reservation) and 2.6.1 ter (Object of objections). In addition, he proposed three revised draft guidelines: 2.4.3 (Time at which an interpretative declaration may be formulated *or modified*), 2.4.6 (Late formulation *or modification* of an interpretative declaration), and 2.4.8 (Late formulation *or modification* of a conditional interpretative declaration),[738] so as to accommodate modification alongside the formulation of interpretative declarations.

After considering the report, the Commission decided to refer to the Drafting Committee the following proposed draft guidelines: 2.3.5 (Enlargement of the scope of a reservation), 2.4.9 (Modification of interpretative declarations), 2.4.10 (Modification of a conditional interpretative declaration), 2.5.12 (Withdrawal of an interpretative declaration) and 2.5.13 (Withdrawal of a conditional interpretative declaration).[739]

At the same session, the Commission provisionally adopted the following eleven draft guidelines (with three model clauses) as well as the commentaries thereto: 2.5.1 (Withdrawal of reservations), 2.5.2 (Form of withdrawal), 2.5.3 (Periodic review of the usefulness of reservations), 2.5.4 [2.5.5] (Formulation of the withdrawal of a reservation at the international level), 2.5.5 [2.5.5 bis, 2.5.5 ter] (Absence of consequences at the international level of the violations of internal rules regarding the withdrawal of reservations), 2.5.6 (Communication of withdrawal of a reservation), 2.5.7 [2.5.7, 2.5.8] (Effect of withdrawal of a reservation), 2.5.8 [2.5.9] (Effective date of withdrawal of a reservation, including model clauses A, B and C), 2.5.9 [2.5.10] (Cases in which a reserving State or international organization may unilaterally set the effective date of withdrawal of a reservation), 2.5.10 [2.5.11] (Partial withdrawal of a reservation) and 2.5.11 [2.5.12] (Effect of a partial withdrawal of a reservation).[740]

The work of the Commission on the topic as described above has been proceeding in accordance with the successive resolutions adopted by the General Assembly under the item relating to the report of the International Law Commission.[741]

---

[738] Revisions were proposed to guidelines 2.4.3, 2.4.6 [2.4.7] and 2.4.7 [2.4.8] provisionally adopted by the Commission at its fifty-third session, in 2001.

[739] Draft guideline 2.3.5 was referred to the Drafting Committee following a vote. See *Official Records of the General Assembly, Fifty-eighth Session, Supplement No. 10* (A/58/10), para. 328.

[740] See *Official Records of the General Assembly, Fifty-eighth Session, Supplement No. 10* (A/58/10), paras. 329 and 330.

[741] General Assembly resolutions 51/160 of 16 December 1996, 53/102 of 8 December 1998, 54/111 of 9 December 1999, 55/152 of 12 December 2000, 56/82 of 12 December 2001 and 57/21 of 19 November 2002.

2. Diplomatic protection

At its forty-seventh session, in 1995, the International Law Commission, on the basis of the recommendation of a Working Group on the long-term programme of work, decided to include in the Commission's agenda, subject to the approval of the General Assembly, the topic "Diplomatic Protection". The Commission noted that work on this topic would complement the Commission's work on State responsibility and should be of interest to all Member States. The Commission could consider, inter alia, the content and scope of the rule of exhaustion of local remedies; the rule of nationality of claims as applied to both natural and legal persons, including its relation to so-called "functional" protection; and problems of stateless persons and dual nationals. The Commission could also address the effect of dispute settlement clauses on domestic remedies and on the exercise of diplomatic protection.[742]

The General Assembly, in resolution 50/45 of 11 December 1995, took note of the Commission's suggestion to include the topic in its agenda and invited Governments to submit comments on this suggestion for consideration by the Sixth Committee of the General Assembly at its fifty-first session.

At its forty-eighth session, in 1996, the Commission adopted a general outline of the main legal issues raised under the topic, including explanatory notes, prepared by a Working Group on the long-term programme of work to assist Governments in deciding whether to approve further work. This provisional outline included the following sections:

1. Basis of, and rationale for, diplomatic protection;

2. Persons claiming diplomatic protection;

3. Protection of certain forms of State property, and individuals only incidentally;

4. Preconditions for protection;

5. Mechanisms for diplomatic protection in the absence of diplomatic relations;

6. Formal requirements of a claim to protection; and

7. Conclusiveness of claims settlements.

The Commission noted that the topic would form a companion study to the Commission's work on State responsibility. The Commission had previously considered issues relating to diplomatic

---

[742] See *Yearbook of the International Law Commission, 1995,* vol. II (Part Two), para. 501.

protection in connection with the question of responsibility for injuries to the persons or property of aliens, which was the initial focus of its work on the topic of State responsibility (*see page 194*). The Commission also noted that the present study could follow the traditional pattern of articles and commentaries, but leave for future decision the question of its final form, which could be a guide for Governments in handling international claims rather than a convention.[743]

The General Assembly, in resolution 51/160 of 16 December 1996, invited the Commission to examine further the topic and to indicate its scope and content in the light of the comments and observations made during the debate in the Sixth Committee on the report of the Commission and any written comments submitted by Governments.

At its forty-ninth session, in 1997, the Commission established a Working Group to examine further the topic and to indicate its scope and content in accordance with General Assembly resolution 51/160. The Working Group had before it the general outline adopted by the Commission at its previous session, the topical summary of the discussion held by the Sixth Committee at the fifty-first session of the General Assembly[744] and the written comments submitted by Governments.[745] The Working Group attempted to (a) clarify the scope of the topic to the extent possible; and (b) identify the issues that should be studied in the context of the topic. The Commission adopted the report submitted by the Working Group.[746]

As regards the scope of the topic, the Working Group reviewed the general outline and decided to retain only material dealing with diplomatic protection stricto sensu. Thus, the topic would address only indirect harm (harm caused to natural or legal persons whose case is taken up by a State) and not direct harm (harm caused directly to a State or its property). Section 3 of the general outline would not be included. In addition, the Working Group drew attention to the distinction between diplomatic protection properly so called, that is to say a formal claim made by a State in respect of an injury to one of its nationals which has not been redressed through local remedies, and certain diplomatic and consular activities for the assistance and protection of nationals as envisaged by articles 3 and 5, respectively, of the Vienna Convention on Diplomatic Relations (*see annex V,*

---

[743] See *Yearbook of the International Law Commission, 1996*, vol. II (Part Two), paras. 244, 245 and 248, and annex II, addendum 1.

[744] Document A/CN.4/479, sect. E.6.

[745] Document A/51/358 and Add.1.

[746] See *Yearbook of the International Law Commission, 1997*, vol. II (Part Two), pp. 60-63.

section C.1) and the Vienna Convention on Consular Relations (*see annex V, section D.1*). Finally, the Working Group recommended limiting the topic to the codification of secondary rules by addressing the requirement of an internationally wrongful act of the State as a prerequisite but not the specific content of the international legal obligation which has been violated.

As to the relevant issues, the Working Group prepared a revised outline of the content of the topic in which it identified a number of issues under four major areas for study by the Commission. The four major areas of study are covered by the following chapters of the outline:

I. Basis for diplomatic protection (the required linkage between the beneficiary and the States exercising diplomatic protection);

II. Parties to diplomatic protection (claimants and respondents in diplomatic protection);

III. Conditions under which diplomatic protection is exercised; and

IV. Consequences of diplomatic protection.

At the forty-ninth session, the Commission also appointed Mr. Mohamed Bennouna as Special Rapporteur for the topic and recommended that the Special Rapporteur submit, at the Commission's next session, a preliminary report on the basis of the revised outline.[747]

The General Assembly, in resolution 52/156 of 15 December 1997, endorsed the Commission's decision to include in its agenda the topic "Diplomatic protection".

At its fiftieth session, in 1998, the Commission had before it the preliminary report of the Special Rapporteur, which dealt with the legal nature of diplomatic protection and the nature of the rules governing the topic.[748] After considering the report, the Commission established a Working Group, chaired by the Special Rapporteur, to consider the possible conclusions which might be drawn on the basis of the discussion as to the approach to the topic and also to provide directions in respect of the issues to be covered in the second report of the Special Rapporteur. The Commission endorsed the report submitted by the Working Group.[749]

---

[747] See *Yearbook of the International Law Commission, 1997*, vol. II (Part Two), para. 190.

[748] Document A/CN.4/484.

[749] See *Yearbook of the International Law Commission, 1998*, vol. II (Part Two), paras. 107 and 110.

As regards the approach to the topic, the Working Group agreed, inter alia, to the following:

"(a) The customary law approach to diplomatic protection should form the basis for the work of the Commission on this topic;

(b) The topic will deal with secondary rules of international law relating to diplomatic protection; primary rules shall only be considered when their clarification is essential to providing guidance for a clear formulation of a specific secondary rule;

(c) The exercise of diplomatic protection is the right of the State. In the exercise of this right, the State should take into account the rights and interests of its nationals for whom it is exercising diplomatic protection;

(d) The work on diplomatic protection should take into account the development of international law in increasing recognition and protection of the rights of individuals and in providing them with more direct and indirect access to international forums to enforce their rights. The Working Group was of the view that the actual and specific effect of such developments, in the context of this topic, should be examined in the light of State practice and insofar as they relate to specific issues involved such as the nationality link requirement;

(e) The discretionary right of the State to exercise diplomatic protection does not prevent it from committing itself to its nationals to exercise such a right. In this context, the Working Group noted that some domestic laws have recognized the right of their nationals to diplomatic protection by their Governments;

(f) The Working Group believed that it would be useful to request Governments to provide the Commission with the most significant national legislation, decisions by domestic courts and State practice relevant to diplomatic protection ..."[750]

As to the second report of the Special Rapporteur, the Working Group suggested that it should concentrate on the issues raised in chapter I, "Basis for diplomatic protection", of the revised outline adopted by the Commission at its forty-ninth session.[751]

The General Assembly, in resolution 53/102 of 8 December 1998, invited Governments to submit the most relevant national legislation, decisions of domestic courts and State practice relevant to

---

[750] See *Yearbook of the International Law Commission, 1998*, vol. II (Part Two), para. 108.

[751] See *Yearbook of the International Law Commission, 1998*, vol. II (Part Two), paras. 107-110.

diplomatic protection in order to assist the Commission in its future work on the topic.

At its fifty-first session, in 1999, the Commission, following Mr. Bennouna's resignation from the Commission, appointed Christopher John R. Dugard as Special Rapporteur for the topic.[752]

At its fifty-second session, in 2000, the Commission had before it the first report of the newly appointed Special Rapporteur,[753] which consisted of three parts: (1) an introduction to diplomatic protection examining the history and scope of the topic and suggesting how the right of diplomatic protection could advance the protection of human rights; (2) proposed draft articles and commentaries; and (3) an outline of future work. The Special Rapporteur proposed the following draft articles: 1 (the scope of the draft articles), 2 (the threat or use of force), 3 (the right to exercise diplomatic protection on behalf of a national), 4 (the duty to exercise diplomatic protection in cases of injury arising from a grave breach of a *jus cogens* norm), 5 (the State of nationality), 6 (the exercise of diplomatic protection on behalf of a dual or multiple national by one State of nationality against another State of nationality), 7 (the exercise of diplomatic protection on behalf of a dual or multiple national against third States), 8 (the exercise of diplomatic protection on behalf of stateless persons and refugees) and 9 (continuous nationality and transferability of claims). After considering the report, the Commission established an open-ended informal consultation, chaired by the Special Rapporteur, on draft articles 1, 3 and 6. After considering the report of the informal consultation,[754] the Commission referred draft articles 1, 3 and 5 to 8 to the Drafting Committee, together with the report. Due to lack of time, the Commission deferred consideration of the remainder of the first report (draft article 9) to its next session.

At its fifty-third session, in 2001, the Commission had before it the remainder of the Special Rapporteur's first report as well as the second report[755] concerning the exhaustion of local remedies and future work on the topic. In the second report, the Special Rapporteur proposed the following draft articles: 10 (the exhaustion of local remedies rule), 11 (the preponderance rule concerning the distinction between "direct" and "indirect" claims for purposes of the exhaustion of local remedies rule), 12 (the exhaustion of local remedies rule as a

[752] See *Official Records of the General Assembly, Fifty-fourth Session, Supplement No. 10* (A/54/10), para. 19.
[753] Document A/CN.4/506 and Corr.1 and Add.1.
[754] See *Official Records of the General Assembly, Fifty-fifth Session, Supplement No. 10* (A/55/10), para. 495.
[755] Document A/CN.4/514 and Corr.1 and 2 (Spanish only).

procedural precondition with respect to an internationally wrongful act which is a violation of domestic law and international law) and 13 (the exhaustion of local remedies rule with respect to a denial of justice regarding a violation of domestic law). After considering the reports, the Commission referred draft articles 9, 10 and 11 to the Drafting Committee. The Commission also established an open-ended informal consultation, chaired by the Special Rapporteur,[756] to consider draft article 9 with a view to providing the Drafting Committee with guidance on its scope and formulation. Due to lack of time, the Commission deferred consideration of draft articles 12 and 13 to its next session.

At its fifty-fourth session, in 2002, the Commission had before it the remainder of the Special Rapporteur's second report relating to the exhaustion of local remedies rule as well as the third report[757] dealing with the exceptions to that rule, the question of the burden of proof and the so-called Calvo clause. In his third report, the Special Rapporteur proposed the following draft articles: 14 (exceptions to the exhaustion of local remedies rule), 15 (burden of proof), and 16 (the Calvo clause). After considering the report, the Commission decided to refer draft article 14, paragraphs (a), (b), (c) and (d) (both to be considered in connection with paragraph (a)) and (e) concerning futility, waiver and estoppel, voluntary link, territorial connection and undue delay, respectively, to the Drafting Committee. The Commission also held a general discussion, inter alia, on the scope of the study. In addition, the Commission established an open-ended informal consultation, chaired by the Special Rapporteur, on the question of the diplomatic protection of crews as well as that of corporations and shareholders.[758]

At the same session, the Commission provisionally adopted the following seven draft articles as well as the commentaries thereto: 1 (definition and scope),[759] 2 [3][760] (right to exercise diplomatic protection), 3 [5] (State of nationality),[761] 4 [9] (continuous nationality), 5 [7] (multiple nationality and claim against a third

---

[756] See *Official Records of the General Assembly, Fifty-sixth Session, Supplement No. 10* (A/56/10), para. 166.

[757] Document A/CN.4/523 and Add.1.

[758] See *Official Records of the General Assembly, Fifty-seventh Session, Supplement No. 10* (A/57/10), paras. 112-114.

[759] Paragraph 2 of this article will be reconsidered if other exceptions are included in the draft articles.

[760] The numbers in square brackets correspond to the numbers of the articles proposed by the Special Rapporteur.

[761] Article 3 will be reviewed in connection with the Commission's consideration of the diplomatic protection of legal persons.

State), 6 (multiple nationality and claim against a State of nationality) and 7 [8] (stateless persons and refugees).[762]

At its fifty-fifth session, in 2003, the Commission had before it the Special Rapporteur's fourth report[763] relating to the diplomatic protection of corporations, shareholders and other legal persons. The Special Rapporteur proposed the following draft articles on the diplomatic protection of corporations and shareholders: 17 (diplomatic protection of corporations), 18 (diplomatic protection of shareholders of corporations), 19 (classification of claims in the context of the protection of shareholders of corporations), 20 (continuous nationality of corporations), 21 (*lex specialis*) and 22 (legal persons). The Commission established a Working Group, chaired by the Special Rapporteur, on article 17, paragraph 2, and considered its report as well. After considering these reports, the Commission decided to refer draft article 17, as proposed by the Working Group, as well as draft articles 18 to 22 to the Drafting Committee.[764]

At the same session, the Commission provisionally adopted the following three draft articles as well as commentaries thereto: 8 [10] (exhaustion of local remedies), 9 [11] (category of claims) and 10 [14] (exceptions to the local remedies rule).[765]

The work of the Commission on the topic as described above has been proceeding in accordance with the successive resolutions adopted by the General Assembly under the item relating to the report of the International Law Commission. In these resolutions, the Assembly has reiterated its invitation to Governments to submit relevant materials to assist the Commission in its work on the topic.[766]

---

[762] See *Official Records of the General Assembly, Fifty-seventh Session, Supplement No. 10* (A/57/10), paras. 115 and 116.
[763] Document A/CN.4/530, Corr.1 (Spanish only) and Add.1.
[764] See *Official Records of the General Assembly, Fifty-eighth Session, Supplement No. 10* (A/58/10), paras. 67 and 68.
[765] See *Official Records of the General Assembly, Fifty-eighth Session, Supplement No. 10* (A/58/10), para. 69. These articles will be included in a future Part Four entitled "Local Remedies" and will be renumbered accordingly. The cross-reference to article 7 [8] contained in articles 8 [10] and 9 [11] will be considered further if other exceptions to the nationality rule are included in the draft articles. Article 10 [14], paragraph (d), may be reconsidered in the future with a view to its placement in a separate provision entitled "Waiver".
[766] General Assembly resolutions 54/111 of 9 December 1999, 55/152 of 12 December 2000, 56/82 of 12 December 2001 and 57/21 of 19 November 2002.

3.   Unilateral acts of States

At its forty-eighth session, in 1996, the International Law Commission, on the basis of the recommendation of a Working Group on the long-term programme of work, identified the topic of "Unilateral acts of States" as appropriate for codification and progressive development. The Working Group noted the relationship between this topic and the more general topic of "Sources of International Law" envisaged as a global topic of codification in the memorandum submitted by the Secretary-General at the first session of the Commission, in 1949.[767] The Working Group concluded that the present topic was appropriate for immediate consideration for the following reasons: (1) it is a well delimited topic which has not been studied by any international official body; (2) it has been touched upon in several judgments of the International Court of Justice (ICJ), especially the *Nuclear Tests* cases,[768] but the dicta left room for uncertainties and questions; (3) States have abundant recourse to unilateral acts and their practice can be studied with a view to drawing general legal principles; and (4) the law of treaties provides a point of departure and a scheme of reference for approaching the rules relating to unilateral acts notwithstanding the differences between the two topics. The Working Group prepared a tentative general outline of the topic, including explanatory notes, which contained the following sections: (1) Definition and typology; (2) Legal effects and application; (3) Conditions of validity; and (4) Duration, amendment and termination. The Commission adopted the report of the Working Group.[769]

The General Assembly, in resolution 51/160 of 16 December 1996, invited the Commission to examine further the topic "Unilateral acts of States" and to indicate its scope and content in the light of the comments and observations made during the debate in the Sixth Committee on the report of the Commission and any written comments that Governments may wish to submit.

At its forty-ninth session, in 1997, the Commission established a Working Group on the topic. The Working Group bore in mind the general outline for the study of unilateral acts of States prepared at the previous session as well as the topical summary of the debate held in the Sixth Committee at the fifty-first session of the General

---

[767] Document A/CN.4/1 (United Nations publication, Sales No. 48.V.1) reissued under the symbol A/CN.4/1/Rev.1 (United Nations publication, Sales No. 48.V.1(1)).
[768] *Nuclear Tests (Australia v. France, New Zealand v. France), Judgment, I.C.J. Reports 1974*, pp. 253 and 457.
[769] See *Yearbook of the International Law Commission, 1996*, vol. II (Part Two), para. 245 and annex II, addendum 3.

Assembly.[770] The Working Group concluded that the Commission's consideration of the topic, with a view to the codification and progressive development of the applicable legal rules, was advisable and feasible for the following reasons:

"(a) In their conduct in the international sphere, States frequently carry out unilateral acts with the intent to produce legal effects. The significance of such unilateral acts is constantly growing as a result of the rapid political, economic and technological changes taking place in the international community at the present time and, in particular, the great advances in the means for expressing and transmitting the attitudes and conduct of States;

(b) State practice in relation to unilateral legal acts is manifested in many forms and circumstances, has been a subject of study in many legal writings and has been touched upon in some judgments of ICJ and other international courts; there is thus sufficient material for the Commission to analyse and systematize;

(c) In the interest of legal security and to help bring certainty, predictability and stability to international relations and thus strengthen the rule of law, an attempt should be made to clarify the functioning of this kind of act and what the legal consequences are, with a clear statement of the applicable law."[771]

The Working Group also considered the scope and content of the topic. As regards the scope of the topic, the Working Group concluded that it should be limited to the unilateral acts of States that are intended to produce "legal" effects, creating, recognizing, safeguarding or modifying rights, obligations or legal situations. As to the content of the topic, the Working Group proposed a revised outline which contained the following sections: (1) Definition of unilateral legal acts of States; (2) Criteria for classifying unilateral legal acts of States; (3) Analysis of the forms, the characteristics and the effects of the most frequent unilateral acts in State practice; (4) General rules applicable to unilateral legal acts; and (5) Rules applicable to specific categories of unilateral legal acts of States.[772]

The Commission endorsed the report of the Working Group; appointed Victor Rodrígues Cedeño as Special Rapporteur for the topic; requested the Special Rapporteur to submit at its next session his first report which would include a general outline of the topic

---

[770] Document A/CN.4/479, section E.6.
[771] See *Yearbook of the International Law Commission, 1997*, vol. II (Part Two), para. 196.
[772] See *Yearbook of the International Law Commission, 1997*, vol. II (Part Two), paras. 197-210.

containing a brief description of State practice, a survey of relevant judicial decisions and literature, and a detailed scheme for the substantive development of the topic; and invited Governments to express their views on the topic, in the Sixth Committee and separately in writing, and to provide information relevant for the study of the topic.[773]

The General Assembly, in resolution 52/156 of 15 December 1997, endorsed the Commission's decision to include in its agenda the topic "Unilateral acts of States".

At its fiftieth session, in 1998, the Commission had before it the first report[774] of the Special Rapporteur the aim of which was to identify, by considering the various acts and forms of conduct of States, the constituent elements of a definition of a unilateral act of a State. The report dealt with the existence of unilateral acts of States, the criteria for identifying strictly unilateral acts of States and the legal basis for the binding character of these acts. After considering this report, the Commission decided to establish the Working Group on Unilateral acts of States.

The Working Group considered the scope of the topic, the form of work on the topic and the future work of the Special Rapporteur. As regards the scope of the topic, the Working Group endorsed the approach taken by the Special Rapporteur in his report, which was consistent with the outline adopted by the Commission at its forty-ninth session, and which limited the topic to unilateral acts of States issued for the purpose of producing international legal effects. This excluded from the topic's scope acts of States which do not produce legal effects, unilateral acts of the State which are linked to a specific legal regime and acts of other subjects of international law, such as acts of international organizations. As to the form of the work, the Working Group believed that the elaboration of draft articles with commentaries was the most appropriate way to proceed, without prejudging the final legal status of the draft articles which could be in the form of a convention, guidelines, a restatement or any other outcome. As regards future work, the Working Group recommended that the Special Rapporteur be requested to prepare a second report including: (1) draft articles on the definition of unilateral acts and the scope of the draft articles, based on the report of the Working Group concerning these issues; and (2) a further examination of the

---

[773] See *Yearbook of the International Law Commission, 1997*, vol. II (Part Two), paras. 194, 212 and 213.
[774] Document A/CN.4/486.

elaboration of unilateral acts and the conditions for their validity. The Commission endorsed the report of the Working Group.[775]

At its fifty-first session, in 1999, the Commission had before it the second report[776] of the Special Rapporteur which addressed certain questions raised by Governments in the Sixth Committee in 1998 in commenting on the report of the Commission on this topic, namely: the relationship between the unilateral acts that are the subject of this study and the international responsibility of States; unilateral acts and estoppel; and unilateral acts relating to international organizations, particularly State acts addressed to such organizations. In addition, the Special Rapporteur proposed the following draft articles: 1 (the scope of the draft articles), 2 (the definition of unilateral acts of States), 3 (the capacity of States to formulate unilateral acts), 4 (the representatives of a State for the purpose of formulating unilateral acts), 5 (subsequent confirmation of a unilateral act formulated without authorization), 6 (the validity of unilateral acts in terms of the expression of consent) and 7 (the invalidity of unilateral acts). After considering this report, the Commission decided to reconvene the Working Group on Unilateral Acts of States.

The Working Group considered the following issues concerning the way in which the Commission's work on the topic should proceed: (a) the basic elements of a workable definition of unilateral acts as a starting point for further work on the topic as well as for gathering the relevant State practice; (b) the general guidelines for gathering the relevant State practice, including a questionnaire to be sent to Governments; and (c) the direction that the work of the Special Rapporteur should take in the future. As regards the definition, the Working Group agreed that the following concept could be taken as the basic focus for the Commission's study of the topic: "A unilateral statement by a State by which such State intends to produce legal effects in its relations to one or more States or international organizations and which is notified or otherwise made known to the State or organization concerned."[777] As to relevant State practice, the Working Group established guidelines for a questionnaire to be sent to States requesting materials and inquiring about their practice with respect to unilateral acts as well as their position on certain aspects of the Commission's study of the topic.[778]

---

[775] See *Yearbook of the International Law Commission, 1998*, vol. II (Part Two), paras. 194-201.
[776] Document A/CN.4/500 and Add.1.
[777] See *Official Records of the General Assembly, Fifty-fourth session, Supplement No. 10* (A/54/10), para. 589.
[778] For replies from Governments to the questionnaire, see document A/CN.4/511. The document contains the text of the replies received as at 6 July 2000.

With respect to future work, the Working Group recommended that the Special Rapporteur: continue, taking into account the relevant State practice, formulating new draft articles; consider, in the light of the comments made in the Commission, reformulating the draft articles contained in his second report; and examine the interpretation, effects and revocability of unilateral acts. The Commission adopted the report of the Working Group as amended by the Commission.[779]

At its fifty-second session, in 2000, the Commission had before it the third report[780] of the Special Rapporteur, as well as the replies received from Governments to the questionnaire circulated in 1999.[781] In his third report, the Special Rapporteur examined some preliminary issues such as the relevance of the topic, the relationship between the draft articles on unilateral acts and the 1969 Vienna Convention on the Law of Treaties (see annex V, section F), as well as the question of estoppel and unilateral acts. The Special Rapporteur also proposed a reformulation of the draft articles contained in his second report, including: the deletion of the previous draft article 1 (Scope of the present draft articles); a new draft article 1 [2][782] (Definition of unilateral acts); a new draft article 2 [3] (Capacity of States to formulate unilateral acts); a new draft article 3 [4] (Persons authorized to formulate unilateral acts on behalf of the State); a new draft article 4 [5] (Subsequent confirmation of an act formulated by a person not authorized for that purpose); the deletion of previous draft article 6 (Expression of consent); and a new draft article 5 [7] (Invalidity of unilateral acts). The Special Rapporteur concluded that it was not necessary to include a draft article based on article 3 of the Vienna Convention on the Law of Treaties, which addresses the legal force of international agreements not within the scope of the Convention and the provisions of international law which apply to them, since the reference to unilateral acts in the present draft articles is broad enough to cover all unilateral expressions of will formulated by a State. In connection with the proposed deletion of article 6, the Special Rapporteur also examined the question of silence and the formulation of unilateral acts. After considering this report, the Commission referred draft articles 1 to 4 to the Drafting Committee and draft article 5 to the Working Group for further consideration and study.

---

[779] See *Official Records of the General Assembly, Fifty-fourth session, Supplement No. 10* (A/54/10), paras. 577-597.
[780] Document A/CN.4/505.
[781] Document A/CN.4/511.
[782] The numbers in square brackets correspond to the numbers of the draft articles proposed by the Special Rapporteur in his second report.

The Working Group did not have sufficient time to consider draft article 5 or to draw any final conclusions concerning the topic. Nonetheless, the Working Group noted that there was a strong measure of support for the following points concerning (a) the scope of the topic; (b) the structure of the draft articles; and (c) future work on the topic:

"(a) The kind of unilateral acts with which the topic should be concerned are non-dependent acts in the sense that the legal effects they produce are not pre-determined by conventional or customary law but are established as to their nature and extent, by the will of the author State.

(b) The draft articles could be structured around a distinction between general rules which may be applicable to all unilateral acts and specific rules applicable to individual categories of unilateral acts.

(c) The Special Rapporteur could initiate the study of specific categories of unilateral acts by concentrating first on those acts which create obligations for the author State (promises), without prejudice to recognizing the existence of other categories of unilateral acts such as protest, waiver and recognition, which could be addressed at a later stage."[783]

The Working Group also recommended that further work on the topic should pay particular attention to State practice and that efforts to gather relevant State practice should continue. Although it did not have time to consider the report of the Working Group, the Commission agreed that it would be useful to seek the views of Governments on points (a), (b) and (c) above.

At its fifty-third session, in 2001, the Commission had before it the fourth report[784] of the Special Rapporteur which dealt with the classification of unilateral acts as a prerequisite to the formulation of common rules for various categories of unilateral acts and the extent to which the rules of interpretation contained in the Vienna Convention on the Law of Treaties were applicable mutatis mutandis to unilateral acts. The Special Rapporteur proposed a classification of unilateral acts based on the legal effects criterion. The Special Rapporteur also proposed draft articles (a) (General rule of interpretation) and (b) (Supplementary means of interpretation) based on the provisions concerning the interpretation of treaties contained in articles 31 and 32 of the Vienna Convention. These provisions were adapted to reflect the particular nature of unilateral acts by

---

[783] See *Official Records of the General Assembly, Fifty-fifth session, Supplement No. 10* (A/55/10), para. 621.
[784] Document A/CN.4/519.

providing for a subjective rather than an objective interpretation of a unilateral act as well as a restrictive interpretation of the self-imposed restriction of sovereignty implied by the act. After considering the report, the Commission established a Working Group, chaired by the Special Rapporteur. At the recommendation of the Working Group, the Commission requested the Secretariat to circulate a questionnaire to Governments inviting them to provide further information regarding their practice of formulating and interpreting unilateral acts.[785]

At its fifty-fourth session, in 2002, the Commission had before it the fifth report[786] of the Special Rapporteur as well as the replies received from Governments[787] to the questionnaire circulated in 2001. In his fifth report, the Special Rapporteur dealt with the following: (a) the progress made on the topic; (b) the definition of unilateral acts, conditions of validity and causes of invalidity, rules of interpretation and classification of unilateral acts; (c) the possible elaboration of common rules applicable to all unilateral acts; (d) entry into force and determination of the moment at which the unilateral act begins to produce its legal effects; and (e) the structure of the draft articles as well as the future plan of work. The Special Rapporteur proposed the following draft articles: revised 5 (a) to (h) (invalidity of a unilateral act as a result of error, fraud, corruption of the State representative, coercion of the person formulating the act, coercion by the threat or use of force, a contrary peremptory norm of international law (*jus cogens*), a contrary Security Council decision, or a contrary fundamental norm of domestic law); (a) and (b) (general rule and supplementary means of interpretation); 7 (*acta sunt servanda*); 8 (non-retroactivity); and 9 (territorial application). After considering the report, the Commission established an open-ended informal consultation, chaired by the Special Rapporteur, on unilateral acts of States.[788]

At its fifty-fifth session, in 2003, the Commission had before it the sixth report[789] of the Special Rapporteur which focused on the unilateral act of recognition. After considering the report, the Commission established a Working Group, chaired by Alain Pellet, which dealt with the scope of the topic and the method of work. The

---

[785] For the replies from Governments, see document A/CN.4/524. The document contains the text of the replies received as at 14 March 2002.

[786] Document A/CN.4/525 and Add.1, Corr.1, Corr.2 (Arabic and English only) and Add.2.

[787] Document A/CN.4/524.

[788] See *Official Records of the General Assembly, Fifty-seventh Session, Supplement No. 10* (A/57/10), para. 295.

[789] Document A/CN.4/534.

Working Group made the following recommendations: (1) for the purposes of the present study, a unilateral act of a State is a statement expressing the will or consent by which that State purports to create obligations or other legal effects under international law; (2) the study will also deal with the conduct of States which may create obligations or other legal effects under international law similar to those of unilateral acts; (3) the study will propose draft articles accompanied by commentaries with respect to unilateral acts and, if appropriate, guidelines or recommendations with respect to other conduct; (4) the Special Rapporteur's report to be submitted at the Commission's next session will present State practice concerning unilateral acts and will include information originating with the author of the act or conduct as well as the reactions of other States or actors concerned; (5) the empirical information should enable the identification of rules applicable to unilateral acts *stricto sensu*, with a view to preparing draft articles accompanied by commentaries, as well as rules which might be applicable to State conduct producing similar effects; (6) the orderly classification of State practice should address the reasons for the unilateral act or conduct of the State, the criteria for the validity of the express or implied commitment of the State and the circumstances in which the unilateral commitment can be modified or withdrawn; and (7) the legal rules which may be deduced from the material submitted will be dealt with in later reports for preparing specific draft articles or recommendations. The Commission adopted the recommendations of the Working Group.[790]

The work of the Commission on the topic as described above has been proceeding in accordance with the successive resolutions adopted by the General Assembly under the item relating to the report of the International Law Commission.[791] The General Assembly has drawn the attention of Governments to the importance for the International Law Commission of having their views on various aspects of the topic and invited Governments to provide relevant information as requested by the Commission.

---

[790] See *Official Records of the General Assembly, Fifty-eighth Session, Supplement No. 10* (A/58/10), paras. 17, 244, 245, 303, 306 and 308.
[791] General Assembly resolutions 53/102 of 8 December 1998, 54/111 of 9 December 1999, 55/152 of 12 December 2000, 56/82 of 12 December 2001 and 57/21 of 19 November 2002.

4. International liability for injurious consequences arising out of acts not prohibited by international law (International liability in case of loss from transboundary harm arising out of hazardous activities)

At its fifty-third session, in 2001, the International Law Commission adopted the final draft articles on Prevention of transboundary harm from hazardous activities and thus concluded its work on the first part of the topic (*see pages 209 and 210*).

The General Assembly, in resolution 56/82 of 12 December 2001, requested the Commission to resume its consideration of the liability aspects of the topic, bearing in mind the interrelationship between prevention and liability, and taking into account the developments in international law and comments by Governments.

At its fifty-fourth session, in 2002, the Commission decided to include the topic "International liability for injurious consequences arising out of acts not prohibited by international law" on its programme of work and to begin consideration of the second part of the topic "International liability in case of loss from transboundary harm arising out of hazardous activities". The Commission established a Working Group, chaired by Pemmaraju Sreenivasa Rao, to consider the conceptual outline of the topic. The Working Group recommended continuing to limit the scope of the remainder of the topic concerning liability to the same activities that were covered under the first part of the topic concerning prevention, which would effectively link the work on the two parts of the topic. The Working Group also set out the following initial understandings on the topic: (a) a threshold would have to be determined to trigger the application of the regime on allocation of loss caused; and (b) the loss to be covered should include loss to (i) persons, (ii) property, including elements of State patrimony and national heritage, and (iii) environment within national jurisdiction. The Working Group also considered the approach to be taken regarding the role of the operator and the State in the allocation of loss. The Commission adopted the report of the Working Group, as amended by the Commission. The Commission also appointed Mr. Rao as Special Rapporteur for the topic.[792]

The General Assembly, in resolution 57/21 of 19 November 2002, took note of the Commission's decision to proceed with its work on the topic, as requested by the Assembly in resolution 56/82.

---

[792] See *Official Records of the General Assembly, Fifty-seventh Session, Supplement No. 10* (A/57/10), paras. 441-457, 517 and 519.

At its fifty-fifth session, in 2003, the Commission had before it the Special Rapporteur's first report[793] on the legal regime for allocation of loss in case of transboundary harm arising out of hazardous activities. The report reviewed the work of the Commission in previous years, analysed the liability regimes of various instruments and offered conclusions for the consideration of the Commission. After considering the report, the Commission decided to establish a Working Group, under the chairmanship of the Special Rapporteur, to assist the Special Rapporteur in considering the future orientation of the topic in the light of his report and the debate in the Commission.[794]

5. Responsibility of international organizations

At its fifty-second session, in 2000, the Commission, on the basis of the recommendation of a Working Group on the long-term programme of work, concluded that the topic "Responsibility of international organizations" was appropriate for inclusion in its long-term programme of work.[795]

The General Assembly, in resolution 55/152 of 12 December 2000, took note of the Commission's report concerning its long-term programme of work. In resolution 56/82 of 12 December 2001, the Assembly requested the Commission to begin its work on the topic.

At its fifty-fourth session, in 2002, the Commission decided to include the topic in its programme of work, to appoint Giorgio Gaja as Special Rapporteur for the topic, and to establish a Working Group on the topic.[796] The Working Group considered the following issues: (a) the scope of the topic, including the concepts of responsibility and international organizations; (b) relations between the topic of responsibility of international organizations and the articles on State responsibility; (c) questions of attribution; (d) questions of responsibility of member States for conduct that is attributed to an international organization; (e) other questions concerning the arising of responsibility for an international organization; (f) questions of content and implementation of international responsibility; (g) settlement of disputes; and (h) the practice to be taken into

---

[793] Document A/CN.4/531.
[794] See *Official Records of the General Assembly, Fifty-eighth Session, Supplement No. 10* (A/58/10), paras. 10 (c), 16, 165 and 166.
[795] See *Official Records of the General Assembly, Fifty-fifth Session, Supplement No. 10* (A/55/10), paras. 726-728 and 729 (1). For the syllabus on the topic, see ibid., annex (1).
[796] See *Official Records of the General Assembly, Fifty-seventh Session, Supplement No. 10* (A/57/10), paras. 10 (b), 18, 461-463, 517 and 519.

consideration. The Working Group recommended that the Secretariat approach international organizations with a view to collecting relevant materials, especially on questions of attribution and the responsibility of member States for conduct that is attributed to an international organization.[797] The Commission adopted the report of the Working Group.[798]

The General Assembly, in resolution 57/21 of 19 November 2002, took note of the Commission's decision to include the topic in its programme of work.

At its fifty-fifth session, in 2003, the Commission had before it the first report[799] of the Special Rapporteur dealing with the scope of the work and general principles concerning the responsibility of international organizations. The Special Rapporteur proposed the following draft articles: 1 (scope of the draft articles), 2 (use of terms) and 3 (general principles). The Commission referred draft articles 1 and 3 to the Drafting Committee and established a Working Group to consider draft article 2. The Commission considered the report of the Working Group on draft article 2 and referred the text of that article, as formulated by the Working Group, to the Drafting Committee.[800]

At the same session, the Commission provisionally adopted the following three draft articles as well as the commentaries thereto: 1 (Scope of the present draft articles), 2 (Use of terms) and 3 (General principles). The Commission also decided to establish a Working Group to assist the Special Rapporteur with regard to his next report. The Commission further decided to request the Secretariat to circulate, on an annual basis, the chapter of the Commission's report on this topic to the United Nations, its specialized agencies as well as other international organizations for comment.[801]

6. Shared natural resources

At its fifty-second session, in 2000, the Commission, on the basis of the recommendation of a Working Group on the long-term programme of work, concluded that the topic "Shared natural

---

[797] See *Official Records of the General Assembly, Fifty-seventh Session, Supplement No. 10* (A/57/10), paras. 465-488.
[798] See *Official Records of the General Assembly, Fifty-seventh Session, Supplement No. 10* (A/57/10), para. 464.
[799] Document A/CN.4/532.
[800] See *Official Records of the General Assembly, Fifty-eighth Session, Supplement No. 10* (A/58/10), paras. 43-48.
[801] See *Official Records of the General Assembly, Fifty-eighth Session, Supplement No. 10* (A/58/10), paras. 49-54.

resources of States" was appropriate for inclusion in its long-term programme of work.[802]

The General Assembly, in resolution 55/152 of 12 December 2000, took note of the Commission's report concerning its long-term programme of work. In resolution 56/82 of 12 December 2001, the Assembly requested the Commission to further consider the topic having due regard to comments made by Governments.

At its fifty-fourth session, in 2002, the International Law Commission decided to include the topic "Shared natural resources" in its programme of work, to appoint Chusei Yamada as Special Rapporteur for the topic, and to establish a Working Group to assist the Special Rapporteur.[803]

The General Assembly, in resolution 57/21 of 19 November 2002, took note of the Commission's decision to include the topic in its programme of work.

At its fifty-fifth session, in 2003, the Commission had before it the first preliminary report[804] of the Special Rapporteur which provided the background on the topic and proposed to limit its scope to the study of confined transboundary groundwaters, oil and gas, with work proceeding initially on the study of confined transboundary groundwaters. The Special Rapporteur also submitted an addendum to the report which was technical in nature and sought to provide a better understanding of what constituted confined transboundary groundwaters. The Special Rapporteur noted that the problem of shared natural resources had first been dealt with by the Commission during its codification of the law of the non-navigational uses of international watercourses (*see pages 186 (footnote 639), 188 and 189*). At the time, the Commission had decided to exclude confined groundwaters unrelated to surface waters from the topic, but nonetheless considered that a separate study was warranted due to the importance of confined groundwaters in many parts of the world. The Special Rapporteur deemed it indispensable to know exactly what such groundwaters were in order to ascertain the extent to which the principles embodied in the 1997 Convention on the Law of the Non-navigational Uses of International Watercourses (*see annex V, section L*) could be applicable. The Special Rapporteur noted that the international efforts to manage groundwaters were taking place in different forums, that the law relating to groundwaters was more akin

---

[802] See *Official Records of the General Assembly, Fifty-fifth Session, Supplement No. 10* (A/55/10), paras. 726-728 and 729 (3). For the syllabus on the topic, see ibid., annex (3).
[803] See *Official Records of the General Assembly, Fifty-seventh Session, Supplement No. 10* (A/57/10), paras. 20, 518 and 519.
[804] Document A/CN.4/533 and Add.1.

to that governing the exploitation of oil and gas, and that the Commission's work on the topic of international liability, particularly regarding the prevention aspect, would be relevant.[805]

The Commission considered the report without taking any decision with respect to the scope of the topic or the future course of work. The Commission also had an informal briefing by experts on groundwaters from the Food and Agriculture Organization and the International Association of Hydrogeologists.[806]

7. Fragmentation of international law: difficulties arising from the diversification and expansion of international law[807]

At its fifty-second session, in 2000, the Commission, on the basis of the recommendation of a Working Group on the long-term programme of work, concluded that the topic "Risks ensuing from fragmentation of international law" was appropriate for inclusion in its long-term programme of work.[808] The Commission noted that this topic was different from the other topics which it had considered. Nevertheless, the Commission expressed the view that it could contribute to a better understanding of the increasingly important issues involved in the topic. The Commission also noted that the method and outcome of work on the topic did not fall strictly within the normal form of codification, but was well within its competence and in accordance with its Statute.[809]

The General Assembly, in resolution 55/152 of 12 December 2000, took note of the Commission's report concerning its long-term programme of work. In resolution 56/82 of 12 December 2001, the Assembly requested the Commission to further consider the topic, having due regard to comments made by Governments.

At its fifty-fourth session, in 2002, the Commission decided to include the topic "Fragmentation of international law: difficulties arising from the diversification and expansion of international law" in

---

[805] See *Official Records of the General Assembly, Fifty-eighth Session, Supplement No. 10* (A/58/10), paras. 19 and 376-381.

[806] See *Official Records of the General Assembly, Fifty-eighth Session, Supplement No. 10* (A/58/10), para. 373.

[807] At its fifty-fourth session, in 2002, the Commission decided that the title of the topic should be amended to read as above rather than "Risks ensuing from the fragmentation of international law". See *Official Records of the General Assembly, Fifty-seventh Session, Supplement No. 10* (A/57/10), para. 494.

[808] See *Official Records of the General Assembly, Fifty-fifth Session, Supplement No. 10* (A/55/10), paras. 726-728 and 729 (5). For the syllabus on the topic, see ibid., annex (5).

[809] See *Official Records of the General Assembly, Fifty-fifth Session, Supplement No. 10* (A/55/10), para. 731.

its programme of work and to establish a Study Group on the topic, chaired by Bruno Simma.[810] In its report,[811] the Study Group made the following recommendations: to amend the title of the topic to its present wording; to prepare a series of studies on specific aspects of the topic to assist international judges and practitioners in coping with the consequences of the diversification of international law;[812] and to provide a "toolbox" designed to assist in solving practical problems arising from incongruities and conflicts between existing legal norms and regimes. The Study Group recommended that the following topics could be the subject of study: (*a*) the function and scope of the *lex specialis* rule and the question of "self-contained regimes"; (*b*) the interpretation of treaties in the light of "any relevant rules of international law applicable in the relations between the parties" (article 31 (3) (c) of the Vienna Convention on the Law of Treaties (*see annex V, section F*)), in the context of general developments in international law and concerns of the international community; (*c*) the application of successive treaties relating to the same subject matter (article 30 of the Vienna Convention on the Law of Treaties); (*d*) the modification of multilateral treaties between certain of the parties only (article 41 of the Vienna Convention on the Law of Treaties); and (*e*) hierarchy in international law: *jus cogens*, obligations *erga omnes*, Article 103 of the Charter of the United Nations, as conflict rules. As a first step, the Study Group recommended requesting its Chairman to undertake a study on subject (a) above. The Study Group noted that the choice of subjects for study was guided by the Commission's previous work relating to the law of treaties and the responsibility of States for internationally wrongful acts and that the Commission's work on the present topic would build upon and further develop its earlier texts.[813] The Commission adopted the report of the Study Group.[814]

The General Assembly, in resolution 57/21 of 19 November 2002, took note of the Commission's decision to include the topic in its programme of work.

At its fifty-fifth session, in 2003, the Commission appointed Martti Koskenniemi as Chairman of the Study Group, to succeed

---

[810] See *Official Records of the General Assembly, Fifty-seventh Session, Supplement No. 10* (A/57/10), paras. 10 (c), 492-493 and 518.

[811] See *Official Records of the General Assembly, Fifty-seventh Session, Supplement No. 10* (A/57/10), paras. 495-513.

[812] See *Official Records of the General Assembly, Fifty-seventh Session, Supplement No. 10* (A/57/10), para. 512.

[813] See *Official Records of the General Assembly, Fifty-seventh Session, Supplement No. 10* (A/57/10), paras. 511-513.

[814] See *Official Records of the General Assembly, Fifty-seventh Session, Supplement No. 10* (A/57/10), paras. 19 and 494.

Bruno Simma who had resigned from the Commission.[815] The Study Group established a tentative schedule of work for the remainder of the quinquennium (2004-2006), agreed upon the distribution among its members of the preparation of the studies on the remaining subjects approved by the Commission in 2002, decided upon the methodology to be adopted for the preparation of the studies, and held a preliminary discussion of an outline prepared by the new Chairman of the Study Group on the first subject identified for study, namely, "The function and scope of the *lex specialis* rule and the question of self-contained regimes". The Study Group also indicated its intention to prepare a final study covering all topics which may include the elaboration of guidelines.[816] The Commission took note of the report of the Study Group.[817]

---

[815] See *Official Records of the General Assembly, Fifty-eighth Session, Supplement No. 10* (A/58/10), paras. 10 (e) and 412.

[816] See *Official Records of the General Assembly, Fifty-eighth Session, Supplement No. 10* (A/58/10), para. 413. For the report of the Study Group submitted at this session, see ibid., paras. 415-435.

[817] See *Official Records of the General Assembly, Fifty-eighth Session, Supplement No. 10* (A/58/10), para. 414.

ANNEX I

STATUTE OF THE
INTERNATIONAL LAW COMMISSION*

Article 1

1. The International Law Commission shall have for its object the promotion of the progressive development of international law and its codification.

2. The Commission shall concern itself primarily with public international law, but is not precluded from entering the field of private international law.

CHAPTER I
ORGANIZATION OF THE INTERNATIONAL LAW COMMISSION

Article 2ᵃ

1. The Commission shall consist of thirty-four members who shall be persons of recognized competence in international law.

2. No two members of the Commission shall be nationals of the same State.

3. In case of dual nationality a candidate shall be deemed to be a national of the State in which he ordinarily exercises civil and political rights.

Article 3

The members of the Commission shall be elected by the General Assembly from a list of candidates nominated by the Governments of States Members of the United Nations.

---

* General Assembly resolution 174 (II) of 21 November 1947. The text of the Statute that was reproduced in previous editions of this publication contained the following textual differences: the term "curricula vitae" was replaced by the term "statements of qualifications" in article 6; the term "vacancy" was replaced by the term "casual vacancy" in article 11; the phrase "necessary and desirable" was replaced by the phrase "necessary or desirable" in article 18, paragraph 2; and the phrase "Conclusions defining" was replaced by the phrase "Conclusions relevant to" in article 20, subparagraph (b). The present edition of this publication reproduces the text of the Statute as adopted by the General Assembly in resolution 174 (II) which did not contain these changes.
ᵃ Text amended by General Assembly resolution 36/39 of 18 November 1981.

Article 4

Each Member may nominate for election not more than four candidates, of whom two may be nationals of the nominating State and two nationals of other States.

Article 5

The names of the candidates shall be submitted in writing by the Governments to the Secretary-General by 1 June of the year in which an election is held, provided that a Government may in exceptional circumstances substitute for a candidate whom it has nominated before 1 June another candidate whom it shall name not later than thirty days before the opening of the General Assembly.

Article 6

The Secretary-General shall as soon as possible communicate to the Governments of States Members the names submitted, as well as any curricula vitae of candidates that may have been submitted by the nominating Governments.

Article 7

The Secretary-General shall prepare the list referred to in article 3 above, comprising in alphabetical order the names of all the candidates duly nominated, and shall submit this list to the General Assembly for the purposes of the election.

Article 8

At the election the electors shall bear in mind that the persons to be elected to the Commission should individually possess the qualifications required and that in the Commission as a whole representation of the main forms of civilization and of the principal legal systems of the world should be assured.

Article 9[b]

1. Those candidates, up to the maximum number prescribed for each regional group, who obtain the greatest number of votes and not less than a majority of the votes of the Members present and voting shall be elected.

2. In the event of more than one national of the same State obtaining a sufficient number of votes for election, the one who obtains the greatest number of votes shall be elected, and, if the votes are equally divided, the elder or eldest candidate shall be elected.

---

[b] Text amended by General Assembly resolution 36/39 of 18 November 1981.

246

Article 10^c

The members of the Commission shall be elected for five years. They shall be eligible for re-election.

Article 11

In the case of a vacancy, the Commission itself shall fill the vacancy having due regard to the provisions contained in articles 2 and 8 above.

Article 12^d

The Commission shall sit at the European Office of the United Nations at Geneva. The Commission shall, however, have the right to hold meetings at other places after consultation with the Secretary-General.

Article 13^e

Members of the Commission shall be paid travel expenses, and shall also receive a special allowance, the amount of which shall be determined by the General Assembly.

Article 14

The Secretary-General shall, so far as he is able, make available staff and facilities required by the Commission to fulfil its task.

CHAPTER II
FUNCTIONS OF THE INTERNATIONAL LAW COMMISSION

Article 15

In the following articles the expression "progressive development of international law" is used for convenience as meaning the preparation of draft conventions on subjects which have not yet been regulated by international law or in regard to which the law has not yet been sufficiently developed in the practice of States. Similarly, the expression "codification of international law" is used for convenience as meaning the more precise formulation and systematization of rules of international law in fields where there already has been extensive State practice, precedent and doctrine.

---

^c Text amended by General Assembly resolution 985 (X) of 3 December 1955.
^d Text amended by General Assembly resolution 984 (X) of 3 December 1955.
^e Text amended by General Assembly resolution 485 (V) of 12 December 1950.

A. PROGRESSIVE DEVELOPMENT OF INTERNATIONAL LAW

Article 16

When the General Assembly refers to the Commission a proposal for the progressive development of international law, the Commission shall follow in general a procedure on the following lines:

(*a*) It shall appoint one of its members to be Rapporteur;

(*b*) It shall formulate a plan of work;

(*c*) It shall circulate a questionnaire to the Governments, and shall invite them to supply, within a fixed period of time, data and information relevant to items included in the plan of work;

(*d*) It may appoint some of its members to work with the Rapporteur on the preparation of drafts pending receipt of replies to this questionnaire;

(*e*) It may consult with scientific institutions and individual experts; these experts need not necessarily be nationals of Members of the United Nations. The Secretary-General will provide, when necessary and within the limits of the budget, for the expenses of these consultations of experts;

(*f*) It shall consider the drafts proposed by the Rapporteur;

(*g*) When the Commission considers a draft to be satisfactory, it shall request the Secretary-General to issue it as a Commission document. The Secretariat shall give all necessary publicity to this document which shall be accompanied by such explanations and supporting material as the Commission considers appropriate. The publication shall include any information supplied to the Commission in reply to the questionnaire referred to in subparagraph (*c*) above;

(*h*) The Commission shall invite the Governments to submit their comments on this document within a reasonable time;

(*i*) The Rapporteur and the members appointed for that purpose shall reconsider the draft, taking into consideration these comments, and shall prepare a final draft and explanatory report which they shall submit for consideration and adoption by the Commission;

(*j*) The Commission shall submit the draft so adopted with its recommendations through the Secretary-General to the General Assembly.

Article 17

1. The Commission shall also consider proposals and draft multilateral conventions submitted by Members of the United Nations, the principal organs of the United Nations other than the General Assembly, specialized agencies, or official bodies established by intergovernmental agreement to encourage the progressive

development of international law and its codification, and transmitted to it for that purpose by the Secretary-General.

2. If in such cases the Commission deems it appropriate to proceed with the study of such proposals or drafts, it shall follow in general a procedure on the following lines:

(*a*)   The Commission shall formulate a plan of work, and study such proposals or drafts, and compare them with any other proposals and drafts on the same subjects;

(*b*)   The Commission shall circulate a questionnaire to all Members of the United Nations and to the organs, specialized agencies and official bodies mentioned above which are concerned with the question, and shall invite them to transmit their comments within a reasonable time;

(*c*)   The Commission shall submit a report and its recommendations to the General Assembly. Before doing so, it may also, if it deems it desirable, make an interim report to the organ or agency which has submitted the proposal or draft;

(*d*)   If the General Assembly should invite the Commission to proceed with its work in accordance with a suggested plan, the procedure outlined in article 16 above shall apply. The questionnaire referred to in paragraph (*c*) of that article may not, however, be necessary.

B. CODIFICATION OF INTERNATIONAL LAW

Article 18

1. The Commission shall survey the whole field of international law with a view to selecting topics for codification, having in mind existing drafts, whether governmental or not.

2. When the Commission considers that the codification of a particular topic is necessary and desirable, it shall submit its recommendations to the General Assembly.

3. The Commission shall give priority to requests of the General Assembly to deal with any question.

Article 19

1. The Commission shall adopt a plan of work appropriate to each case.

2. The Commission shall, through the Secretary-General, address to Governments a detailed request to furnish the texts of laws, decrees, judicial decisions, treaties, diplomatic correspondence and other documents relevant to the topic being studied and which the Commission deems necessary.

Article 20

The Commission shall prepare its drafts in the form of articles and shall submit them to the General Assembly together with a commentary containing:

    (*a*)   Adequate presentation of precedents and other relevant data, including treaties, judicial decisions and doctrine;

    (*b*)   Conclusions defining:

        (i)   The extent of agreement on each point in the practice of States and in doctrine;

        (ii)   Divergencies and disagreements which exist, as well as arguments invoked in favour of one or another solution.

Article 21

1. When the Commission considers a draft to be satisfactory, it shall request the Secretary-General to issue it as a Commission document. The Secretariat shall give all necessary publicity to the document, including such explanations and supporting material as the Commission may consider appropriate. The publication shall include any information supplied to the Commission by Governments in accordance with article 19. The Commission shall decide whether the opinions of any scientific institution or individual experts consulted by the Commission shall be included in the publication.

2. The Commission shall request Governments to submit comments on this document within a reasonable time.

Article 22

Taking such comments into consideration, the Commission shall prepare a final draft and explanatory report, which it shall submit with its recommendations through the Secretary-General to the General Assembly.

Article 23

1. The Commission may recommend to the General Assembly:

    (*a*) To take no action, the report having already been published;

    (*b*) To take note of or adopt the report by resolution;

    (*c*) To recommend the draft to Members with a view to the conclusion of a convention;

    (*d*) To convoke a conference to conclude a convention.

2. Whenever it deems it desirable, the General Assembly may refer drafts back to the Commission for reconsideration or redrafting.

Article 24

The Commission shall consider ways and means for making the evidence of customary international law more readily available, such as the collection and publication of documents concerning State practice and of the decisions of national and international courts on questions of international law, and shall make a report to the General Assembly on this matter.

CHAPTER III
COOPERATION WITH OTHER BODIES

Article 25

1. The Commission may consult, if it considers it necessary, with any of the organs of the United Nations on any subject which is within the competence of that organ.

2. All documents of the Commission which are circulated to Governments by the Secretary-General shall also be circulated to such organs of the United Nations as are concerned. Such organs may furnish any information or make any suggestions to the Commission.

Article 26

1. The Commission may consult with any international or national organizations, official or non-official, on any subject entrusted to it if it believes that such a procedure might aid it in the performance of its functions.

2. For the purpose of distribution of documents of the Commission, the Secretary-General, after consultation with the Commission, shall draw up a list of national and international organizations concerned with questions of international law. The Secretary-General shall endeavour to include on this list at least one national organization of each Member of the United Nations.

3. In the application of the provisions of this article, the Commission and the Secretary-General shall comply with the resolutions of the General Assembly and the other principal organs of the United Nations concerning relations with Franco Spain and shall exclude both from consultations and from the list, organizations which have collaborated with the nazis and fascists.

4. The advisability of consultation by the Commission with intergovernmental organizations whose task is the codification of international law, such as those of the Pan American Union, is recognized.

ANNEX II

PRESENT AND FORMER MEMBERS OF THE
INTERNATIONAL LAW COMMISSION

Names marked with an asterisk are those of members elected in 2001
by the General Assembly for the term 1 January 2002 to 31 December
2006.[a] Names marked with two asterisks are those of members
elected by the Commission to fill vacancies during this term.

Name	Nationality[b]	Period of service[c]
*Emmanuel Akwei Addo	Ghana	1997-
Roberto Ago	Italy	1957-1978
Bola Adesumbo Ajibola	Nigeria	1987-1991
Richard Osuolale A. Akinjide	Nigeria	1982-1986
*Husain M. Al-Baharna	Bahrain	1987-
Fernando Albonico	Chile	1967-1971
Gonzalo Alcivar	Ecuador	1970-1972
George H. Aldrich	United States of America	1981
Ricardo J. Alfaro	Panama	1949-1953 1958-1959
Awn S. Al-Khasawneh	Jordan	1987-1999
*Ali Mohsen Fetais Al-Marri	Qatar	2002-
Riyadh Mahmoud Sami Al-Qaysi	Iraq	1982-1991
Gilberto Amado	Brazil	1949-1969
Gaetano Arangio-Ruiz	Italy	1985-1996

---

[a] General Assembly decision 56/311 of 7 November 2001.
[b] As designated during the term of office of a respective member.
[c] Years included in the period of service correspond to the years when a member is listed as such in the Yearbooks of the International Law Commission.

Name	Nationality[b]	Period of service[c]
*Joao Clemente Baena Soares	Brazil	1997-
Mikuin Leliel Balanda	Zaire[d]	1982-1986
Julio Barboza	Argentina	1979-1996
Yuri G. Barsegov	Union of Soviet Socialist Republics[e]	1987-1991
Milan Bartoš	Yugoslavia	1957-1973
Mohammed Bedjaoui	Algeria	1965-1981
John Alan Beesley	Canada	1987-1991
Mohamed Bennouna	Morocco	1987-1998
Ali Suat Bilge	Turkey	1972-1976
Boutros Boutros-Ghali	Egypt	1979-1991
Derek William Bowett	United Kingdom of Great Britain and Northern Ireland	1992-1996
James Leslie Brierly	United Kingdom of Great Britain and Northern Ireland	1949-1951
Herbert W. Briggs	United States of America	1962-1966
*Ian Brownlie	United Kingdom of Great Britain and Northern Ireland	1997-
Marcel Cadieux	Canada	1962-1966
Carlos Calero-Rodrigues	Brazil	1982-1996
Juan José Calle y Calle	Peru	1973-1981
*Enrique J. A. Candioti	Argentina	1997-
Jorge Castañeda	Mexico	1967-1986
Erik Castrén	Finland	1962-1971
*Choung Il Chee	Republic of Korea	2002-

---

[d] As from 17 May 1997, the designation "Zaire" was changed to the "Democratic Republic of the Congo".
[e] As at 24 December 1991, the name "Russian Federation" is used in the United Nations in place of the name the "Union of Soviet Socialist Republics".

Name	Nationality[b]	Period of service[c]
*Pedro Comissario Afonso	Mozambique	2002-
Roberto Córdova	Mexico	1949-1954
James Richard Crawford	Australia	1992-2001
Emmanuel Kodjoe Dadzie	Ghana	1977-1981
*Riad Daoudi	Syrian Arab Republic	2002-
John de Saram	Sri Lanka	1992-1996
Leonardo Díaz-González	Venezuela	1977-1991
*Christopher John Robert Dugard	South Africa	1997-
**Constantin P. Economides	Greece	1997-2001 2003-
Douglas L. Edmonds	United States of America	1954-1961
Gudmundur Eiriksson	Iceland	1987-1996
Abdullah El-Erian	Egypt, United Arab Republic and Arab Republic of Egypt[f]	1957-1958 1962-1978
Nabil Elaraby	Egypt	1994-2001
Taslim Olawale Elias	Nigeria	1962-1975
Faris El-Khouri	Syria, United Arab Republic[g]	1949-1961
Khalafalla El Rasheed Mohamed Ahmed	Sudan	1982-1986
Nihat Erim	Turkey	1959-1961
*Paula Escarameia	Portugal	2002-
Constantin Th. Eustathiades	Greece	1967-1971

---

[f] By a communication, dated 24 February 1958, the Secretary-General was informed of the establishment by Egypt and Syria of a single State, the United Arab Republic. By a communication, dated 2 September 1971, the designation "United Arab Republic" was changed to "Arab Republic of Egypt" (Egypt).
[g] By a communication, dated 24 February 1958, the Secretary-General was informed of the establishment by Egypt and Syria of a single State, the United Arab Republic. By a communication, dated 13 September 1971, the Secretary-General was informed of the official name of Syria as the "Syrian Arab Republic".

Name	Nationality[b]	Period of service[c]
Jens Evensen	Norway	1979-1984
Luigi Ferrari Bravo	Italy	1997-1998
Sir Gerald Fitzmaurice	United Kingdom of Great Britain and Northern Ireland	1955-1960
Constantin Flitan	Romania	1982-1986
*Salifou Fomba	Mali	1992-1996 2002-
Laurel B. Francis	Jamaica	1977-1991
J. P. A. François	Netherlands	1949-1961
*Giorgio Gaja	Italy	1999-
*Zdzislaw Galicki	Poland	1997-
Francisco V. García Amador	Cuba	1954-1961
Raul I. Goco	Philippines	1997-2001
Bernhard Graefrath	German Democratic Republic, Germany[h]	1987-1991
André Gros	France	1961-1963
Mehmet Güney	Turkey	1992-1996
Gerhard Hafner	Austria	1997-2001
Edvard Hambro	Norway	1972-1976
Francis Mahon Hayes	Ireland	1987-1991
Qizhi, He	China	1994-2001
Mauricio Herdocia Sacasa	Nicaragua	1997-2001
Shuhsi Hsu	China	1949-1961
Jiahua Huang	China	1985-1986
Manley O. Hudson	United States of America	1949-1953

[h] Through the accession of the German Democratic Republic to the Federal Republic of Germany with effect from 3 October 1990, the two German States have united to form one sovereign State. As from 3 October 1990, the Federal Republic of Germany acts in the United Nations under the designation "Germany".

Name	Nationality[b]	Period of service[c]
Kamil E. Idris	Sudan	1992-1996 2000-2001
*Adegoke Ajibola Ige[hh]	Nigeria	
Luis Ignacio-Pinto	Dahomey[i]	1967-1969
Jorge E. Illueca	Panama	1982-1991 1997-2001
Andreas J. Jacovides	Cyprus	1982-1996
S. P. Jagota	India	1977-1986
Eduardo Jimenez de Arechaga	Uruguay	1960-1969
**Peter C. R. Kabatsi	Uganda	1992-2001 2002-
*Maurice Kamto	Cameroon	1999-
Victor Kanga	Cameroon	1962-1964
*James Lutabanzibwa Kateka	United Republic of Tanzania	1997-
Richard D. Kearney	United States of America	1967-1976
*Fathi Kemicha	Tunisia	2002-
Thanat Khoman	Thailand	1957-1959
**Roman Anatolyevitch Kolodkin	Russian Federation	2003-
Vladimir M. Koretsky	Union of Soviet Socialist Republics[e]	1949-1951
Abdul G. Koroma	Sierra Leone	1982-1993
*Martti Koskenniemi	Finland	2002-
Feodor I. Kozhevnikov	Union of Soviet Socialist Republics[e]	1952-1953
Sergei B. Krylov	Union of Soviet Socialist Republics[e]	1954-1956
Mochtar Kusuma-Atmadja	Indonesia	1992-2001

[hh] Mr. Ige died shortly after his election.
[i] The designation "Dahomey" was changed to "Benin" on 1 December 1975.

Name	Nationality[b]	Period of service[c]
*Valery I. Kuznetsov	Russian Federation	2002
Manfred Lachs	Poland	1962-1966
José M. Lacleta Muñoz	Spain	1982-1986
Sir Hersch Lauterpacht	United Kingdom of Great Britain and Northern Ireland	1952-1954
Chieh Liu	China	1962-1966
Igor Ivanovich Lukashuk	Russian Federation	1995-2001
Antonio de Luna Garcia	Spain	1962-1966
Ahmed Mahiou	Algeria	1982-1996
Chafic Malek	Lebanon	1982-1986
*William Mansfield	New Zealand	2002-
Alfredo Martínez Moreno	El Salvador	1973-1976
**Michael J. Matheson	United States of America	2003-
Ahmed Matine-Daftary	Iran[j]	1957-1961
Stephen C. McCaffrey	United States of America	1982-1991
**Teodor Viorel Melescanu	Romania	1997-2001 2003
Václav Mikulka	Czechoslovakia, Czech Republic[k]	1992-1998
*Djamchid Momtaz	Iran (Islamic Republic of)	2000-
Zhengyu Ni	China	1982-1984
*Bernd H. Niehaus	Costa Rica	2002-
Frank X. J. C. Njenga	Kenya	1976-1991
Motoo Ogiso	Japan	1982-1991
*Didier Opertti Badan	Uruguay	1997-

---

[j] By a communication received on 14 November 1982, the Secretary-General was notified that the designation "Iran (Islamic Republic of)" should be henceforth used.
[k] As of 1 January 1993, the designation "Czechoslovakia" was changed to the "Czech Republic".

Name	Nationality[b]	Period of service[c]
Luis Padilla Nervo	Mexico	1955-1963
Radhabinod Pal	India	1952-1966
*Guillaume Pambou-Tchivounda	Gabon	1992-
Angel Modesto Paredes	Ecuador	1962-1966
John J. Parker	United States of America	1954
Stanislaw M. Pawlak	Poland	1987-1991
*Alain Pellet	France	1990-
Obed Pessou	Dahomey[i]	1962-1966
Christopher Walter Pinto	Sri Lanka	1973-1981
Syed Sharifuddin Pirzada	Pakistan	1982-1986
Robert Q. Quentin-Baxter	New Zealand	1972-1984
Alfred Ramangasoavina	Madagascar	1967-1976
*Pemmaraju Sreenivasa Rao	India	1987-
Sir Benegal N. Rau	India	1949-1951
Edilbert Razafindralambo	Madagascar	1982-1996
Paul Reuter	France	1964-1989
Willem Riphagen	Netherlands	1977-1986
Patrick Lipton Robinson	Jamaica	1992-1996
*Victor Rodrigues Cedeno	Venezuela	1997-
Shabtai Rosenne	Israel	1962-1971
*Robert Rosenstock	United States of America	1992-2003
Zenon Rossides	Cyprus	1972-1976
Emmanuel J. Roukounas	Greece	1985-1991
José María Ruda	Argentina	1964-1972
Milan Šahović	Yugoslavia	1974-1981
Carlos Salamanca Figueroa	Bolivia	1954-1956
A. E. F. Sandström	Sweden	1949-1961
Georges Scelle	France	1949-1960

Name	Nationality[b]	Period of service[c]
Stephen M. Schwebel	United States of America	1977-1980
*Bernardo Sepulveda	Mexico	1997-
César Sepúlveda Gutiérrez	Mexico	1987-1991
José Sette Câmara	Brazil	1970-1978
Jiuyong Shi	China	1987-1993
*Bruno Simma	Germany	1997-2002
Sir Ian Sinclair	United Kingdom of Great Britain and Northern Ireland	1982-1986
Nagendra Singh	India	1967-1972
Luis Solari Tudela	Peru	1987-1991
Jean Spiropoulos	Greece	1949-1957
Constantin A. Stavropoulos	Greece	1982-1984
Sompong Sucharitkul	Thailand	1977-1986
Alberto Szekely	Mexico	1992-1996
Abdul Hakim Tabibi	Afghanistan	1962-1981
Arnold J. P. Tammes	Netherlands	1967-1976
Doudou Thiam	Senegal	1970-1999
*Peter Tomka	Slovakia	1999-2002
Christian Tomuschat	Federal Republic of Germany, Germany[h]	1985-1996
Senjin Tsuruoka	Japan	1961-1981
Grigory I. Tunkin	Union of Soviet Socialist Republics[e]	1957-1966
Nikolai A. Ushakov	Union of Soviet Socialist Republics[e]	1967-1986
Endre Ustor	Hungary	1967-1976
Sir Francis Vallat	United Kingdom of Great Britain and Northern Ireland	1973-1981
Edmundo Vargas Carreno	Chile	1992-1996
Alfred Verdross	Austria	1957-1966

Name	*Nationality*[b]	*Period of service*[c]
Vladlen Vereshetin	Russian Federation	1992-1994
Stephen Verosta	Austria	1977-1981
Francisco Villagran Kramer	Guatemala	1992-1996
Sir Humphrey Waldock	United Kingdom of Great Britain and Northern Ireland	1961-1972
*Hanqin Xue	China	2002-
*Chusei Yamada	Japan	1992-
Alexander Yankov	Bulgaria	1977-1996
Mustafa Kamil Yasseen	Iraq	1960-1976
Jesús María Yepes	Colombia	1949-1953
Kisaburo Yokota	Japan	1957-1960
Jaroslav Zourek	Czechoslovakia[k]	1949-1961

ANNEX III

JURIDICAL STATUS OF THE MEMBERS OF THE INTERNATIONAL LAW COMMISSION AT THE PLACE OF ITS PERMANENT SEAT*

The Government of Switzerland, in a communiqué addressed to the Secretary-General of the United Nations, transmitted the text of the decision taken by the Swiss Federal Council regarding the juridical status of the members of the International Law Commission at Geneva, the place of its permanent seat. The text of the decision reads as follows:

"On the proposal of the Federal Political Department, the Federal Council decided on 9 May 1979 to accord, by analogy, to the members of the International Law Commission, for the duration of the Commission's sessions at Geneva, the privileges and immunities to which the Judges of the International Court of Justice are entitled while present in Switzerland. These are the privileges and immunities enjoyed by the heads of mission accredited to the international organizations at Geneva. The members of the International Law Commission will be entitled to a special red identity card."

---

* See *Yearbook of the International Law Commission*, 1979, vol. II (Part Two), document A/34/10, paras. 11-13.

ANNEX IV

DRAFTS PREPARED BY THE
INTERNATIONAL LAW COMMISSION

1. Draft Declaration on Rights and Duties of States[*]

Whereas the States of the world form a community governed by international law,

Whereas the progressive development of international law requires effective organization of the community of States,

Whereas a great majority of the States of the world have accordingly established a new international order under the Charter of the United Nations, and most of the other States of the world have declared their desire to live within this order,

Whereas a primary purpose of the United Nations is to maintain international peace and security, and the reign of law and justice is essential to the realization of this purpose, and

Whereas it is therefore desirable to formulate certain basic rights and duties of States in the light of new developments of international law and in harmony with the Charter of the United Nations,

The General Assembly of the United Nations adopts and proclaims this Declaration on Rights and Duties of States:

Article 1

Every State has the right to independence and hence to exercise freely, without dictation by any other State, all its legal powers, including the choice of its own form of government.

Article 2

Every State has the right to exercise jurisdiction over its territory and over all persons and things therein, subject to the immunities recognized by international law.

Article 3

Every State has the duty to refrain from intervention in the internal or external affairs of any other State.

---

[*] Text adopted by the Commission at its first session, in 1949, and submitted to the General Assembly as a part of the Commission's report covering the work of that session. The report, which also contains commentaries and observations on the draft declaration, appears in *Yearbook of the International Law Commission, 1949*. Text reproduced as it appears in the annex to General Assembly resolution 375 (IV) of 6 December 1949.

Article 4

Every State has the duty to refrain from fomenting civil strife in the territory of another State, and to prevent the organization within its territory of activities calculated to foment such civil strife.

Article 5

Every State has the right to equality in law with every other State.

Article 6

Every State has the duty to treat all persons under its jurisdiction with respect for human rights and fundamental freedoms, without distinction as to race, sex, language, or religion.

Article 7

Every State has the duty to ensure that conditions prevailing in its territory do not menace international peace and order.

Article 8

Every State has the duty to settle its disputes with other States by peaceful means in such a manner that international peace and security, and justice, are not endangered.

Article 9

Every State has the duty to refrain from resorting to war as an instrument of national policy, and to refrain from the threat or use of force against the territorial integrity or political independence of another State, or in any other manner inconsistent with international law and order.

Article 10

Every State has the duty to refrain from giving assistance to any State which is acting in violation of article 9, or against which the United Nations is taking preventive or enforcement action.

Article 11

Every State has the duty to refrain from recognizing any territorial acquisition by another State acting in violation of article 9.

Article 12

Every State has the right of individual or collective self-defence against armed attack.

Article 13

Every State has the duty to carry out in good faith its obligations arising from treaties and other sources of international law, and it may not invoke provisions in its constitution or its laws as an excuse for failure to perform this duty.

Article 14

Every State has the duty to conduct its relations with other States in accordance with international law and with the principle that the sovereignty of each State is subject to the supremacy of international law.

2. Principles of International Law Recognized in the Charter of the Nürnberg Tribunal and in the Judgment of the Tribunal*

Principle I

Any person who commits an act which constitutes a crime under international law is responsible therefor and liable to punishment.

Principle II

The fact that internal law does not impose a penalty for an act which constitutes a crime under international law does not relieve the person who committed the act from responsibility under international law.

Principle III

The fact that a person who committed an act which constitutes a crime under international law acted as Head of State or responsible Government official does not relieve him from responsibility under international law.

Principle IV

The fact that a person acted pursuant to order of his Government or of a superior does not relieve him from responsibility under international law, provided a moral choice was in fact possible to him.

Principle V

Any person charged with a crime under international law has the right to a fair trial on the facts and law.

Principle VI

The crimes hereinafter set out are punishable as crimes under international law:

(*a*) Crimes against peace:

(i) Planning, preparation, initiation or waging of a war of aggression or a war in violation of international treaties, agreements or assurances;

---

* Text adopted by the Commission at its second session, in 1950 and submitted to the General Assembly as a part of the Commission's report covering the work of that session. The report, which also contains commentaries on the principles, appears in *Yearbook of the International Law Commission, 1950*, vol. II.

(ii) Participation in a common plan or conspiracy for the accomplishment of any of the acts mentioned under (i).

(*b*) War crimes:

Violations of the laws or customs of war which include, but are not limited to, murder, ill-treatment or deportation to slave-labour or for any other purpose of civilian population of or in occupied territory, murder or ill-treatment of prisoners of war, of persons on the seas, killing of hostages, plunder of public or private property, wanton destruction of cities, towns, or villages, or devastation not justified by military necessity.

(*c*) Crimes against humanity:

Murder, extermination, enslavement, deportation and other inhuman acts done against any civilian population, or persecutions on political, racial or religious grounds, when such acts are done or such persecutions are carried on in execution of or in connection with any crime against peace or any war crime.

Principle VII

Complicity in the commission of a crime against peace, a war crime, or a crime against humanity as set forth in Principle VI is a crime under international law.

3. Draft Code of Offences (1954 and 1996)

(a) Draft Code of Offences against the Peace and Security of Mankind (1954)*

Article 1

Offences against the peace and security of mankind, as defined in this Code, are crimes under international law, for which the responsible individuals shall be punished.

Article 2

The following acts are offences against the peace and security of mankind:

(1) Any act of aggression, including the employment by the authorities of a State of armed force against another State for any purpose other than national or collective self-defence or in pursuance of a decision or recommendation of a competent organ of the United Nations.

---

* Text adopted by the Commission at its sixth session, in 1954, and submitted to the General Assembly as a part of the Commission's report covering the work of that session. The report, which also contains commentaries on the draft articles, appears in *Yearbook of the International Law Commission, 1954*, vol. II.

(2) Any threat by the authorities of a State to resort to an act of aggression against another State.

(3) The preparation by the authorities of a State of the employment of armed force against another State for any purpose other than national or collective self-defence or in pursuance of a decision or recommendation of a competent organ of the United Nations.

(4) The organization, or the encouragement of the organization, by the authorities of a State, of armed bands within its territory or any other territory for incursions into the territory of another State, or the toleration of the organization of such bands in its own territory, or the toleration of the use by such armed bands of its territory as a base of operations or as a point of departure for incursions into the territory of another State, as well as direct participation in or support of such incursions.

(5) The undertaking or encouragement by the authorities of a State of activities calculated to foment civil strife in another State, or the toleration by the authorities of a State of organized activities calculated to foment civil strife in another State.

(6) The undertaking or encouragement by the authorities of a State of terrorist activities in another State, or the toleration by the authorities of a State of organized activities calculated to carry out terrorist acts in another State.

(7) Acts by the authorities of a State in violation of its obligations under a treaty which is designed to ensure international peace and security by means of restrictions or limitations on armaments, or on military training, or on fortifications, or of other restrictions of the same character.

(8) The annexation by the authorities of a State of territory belonging to another State, by means of acts contrary to international law.

(9) The intervention by the authorities of a State in the internal or external affairs of another State, by means of coercive measures of an economic or political character in order to force its will and thereby obtain advantages of any kind.

(10) Acts by the authorities of a State or by private individuals committed with intent to destroy, in whole or in part, a national, ethnic, racial or religious group as such, including:

    (i)   Killing members of the group;

    (ii)   Causing serious bodily or mental harm to members of the group;

    (iii)   Deliberately inflicting on the group conditions of life calculated to bring about its physical destruction in whole or in part;

(iv)   Imposing measures intended to prevent births within the group;

(v)   Forcibly transferring children of the group to another group.

(11)   Inhuman acts such as murder, extermination, enslavement, deportation or persecutions, committed against any civilian population on social, political, racial, religious or cultural grounds by the authorities of a State or by private individuals acting at the instigation or with the toleration of such authorities.

(12)   Acts in violation of the laws or customs of war.

(13)   Acts which constitute:

(i) Conspiracy to commit any of the offences defined in the preceding paragraphs of this article; or

(ii)   Direct incitement to commit any of the offences defined in the preceding paragraphs of this article; or

(iii)   Complicity in the commission of any of the offences defined in the preceding paragraphs of this article; or

(iv)   Attempts to commit any of the offences defined in the preceding paragraphs of this article.

Article 3

The fact that a person acted as Head of State or as responsible government official does not relieve him of responsibility for committing any of the offences defined in this Code.

Article 4

The fact that a person charged with an offence defined in this Code acted pursuant to an order of his Government or of a superior does not relieve him of responsibility in international law if, in the circumstances at the time, it was possible for him not to comply with that order.

(b) Draft Code of Crimes against the Peace and Security of Mankind (1996)[*]

PART ONE
GENERAL PROVISIONS

Article 1

Scope and application of the present Code

1. The present Code applies to the crimes against the peace and security of mankind set out in part two.

2. Crimes against the peace and security of mankind are crimes under international law and punishable as such, whether or not they are punishable under national law.

Article 2

Individual responsibility

1. A crime against the peace and security of mankind entails individual responsibility.

2. An individual shall be responsible for the crime of aggression in accordance with article 16.

3. An individual shall be responsible for a crime set out in article 17, 18, 19 or 20 if that individual:

(*a*) Intentionally commits such a crime;

(*b*) Orders the commission of such a crime which in fact occurs or is attempted;

(*c*) Fails to prevent or repress the commission of such a crime in the circumstances set out in article 6;

(*d*) Knowingly aids, abets or otherwise assists, directly and substantially, in the commission of such a crime, including providing the means for its commission;

(*e*) Directly participates in planning or conspiring to commit such a crime which in fact occurs;

(*f*) Directly and publicly incites another individual to commit such a crime which in fact occurs;

(*g*) Attempts to commit such a crime by taking action commencing the execution of a crime which does not in fact occur because of circumstances independent of his intentions.

---

[*] Text adopted by the Commission at its forty-eighth session, in 1996, and submitted to the General Assembly as a part of the Commission's report covering the work of that session. The report, which also contains commentaries on the draft articles, appears in *Yearbook of the International Law Commission, 1996*, vol. II (Part Two).

Article 3

Punishment

An individual who is responsible for a crime against the peace and security of mankind shall be liable to punishment. The punishment shall be commensurate with the character and gravity of the crime.

Article 4

Responsibility of States

The fact that the present Code provides for the responsibility of individuals for crimes against the peace and security of mankind is without prejudice to any question of the responsibility of States under international law.

Article 5

Order of a Government or a superior

The fact that an individual charged with a crime against the peace and security of mankind acted pursuant to an order of a Government or a superior does not relieve him of criminal responsibility, but may be considered in mitigation of punishment if justice so requires.

Article 6

Responsibility of the superior

The fact that a crime against the peace and security of mankind was committed by a subordinate does not relieve his superiors of criminal responsibility, if they knew or had reason to know, in the circumstances at the time, that the subordinate was committing or was going to commit such a crime and if they did not take all necessary measures within their power to prevent or repress the crime.

Article 7

Official position and responsibility

The official position of an individual who commits a crime against the peace and security of mankind, even if he acted as head of State or Government, does not relieve him of criminal responsibility or mitigate punishment.

Article 8

Establishment of jurisdiction

Without prejudice to the jurisdiction of an international criminal court, each State Party shall take such measures as may be necessary to establish its jurisdiction over the crimes set out in articles 17, 18, 19 and 20, irrespective of where or by whom those crimes were committed. Jurisdiction over the crime set out in article 16 shall rest with an international criminal court. However, a State referred to in article 16 is not precluded from trying its nationals for the crime set out in that article.

Article 9

Obligation to extradite or prosecute

Without prejudice to the jurisdiction of an international criminal court, the State Party in the territory of which an individual alleged to have committed a crime set out in article 17, 18, 19 or 20 is found shall extradite or prosecute that individual.

Article 10

Extradition of alleged offenders

1. To the extent that the crimes set out in articles 17, 18, 19 and 20 are not extraditable offences in any extradition treaty existing between States Parties, they shall be deemed to be included as such therein. States Parties undertake to include those crimes as extraditable offences in every extradition treaty to be concluded between them.

2. If a State Party which makes extradition conditional on the existence of a treaty receives a request for extradition from another State Party with which it has no extradition treaty, it may at its option consider the present Code as the legal basis for extradition in respect of those crimes. Extradition shall be subject to the conditions provided in the law of the requested State.

3. States Parties which do not make extradition conditional on the existence of a treaty shall recognize those crimes as extraditable offences between themselves subject to the conditions provided in the law of the requested State.

4. Each of those crimes shall be treated, for the purpose of extradition between States Parties, as if it had been committed not only in the place in which it occurred but also in the territory of any other State Party.

Article 11

Judicial guarantees

1. An individual charged with a crime against the peace and security of mankind shall be presumed innocent until proved guilty and shall be entitled without discrimination to the minimum guarantees due to all human beings with regard to the law and the facts and shall have the rights:

    (*a*)   In the determination of any charge against him, to have a fair and public hearing by a competent, independent and impartial tribunal duly established by law;

    (*b*)   To be informed promptly and in detail in a language which he understands of the nature and cause of the charge against him;

(*c*)   To have adequate time and facilities for the preparation of his defence and to communicate with counsel of his own choosing;

(*d*)   To be tried without undue delay;

(*e*)   To be tried in his presence, and to defend himself in person or through legal assistance of his own choosing; to be informed, if he does not have legal assistance, of this right; and to have legal assistance assigned to him and without payment by him if he does not have sufficient means to pay for it;

(*f*)   To examine, or have examined, the witnesses against him and to obtain the attendance and examination of witnesses on his behalf under the same conditions as witnesses against him;

(*g*)   To have the free assistance of an interpreter if he cannot understand or speak the language used in court;

(*h*)   Not to be compelled to testify against himself or to confess guilt.

2. An individual convicted of a crime shall have the right to his conviction and sentence being reviewed according to law.

Article 12

Non bis in idem

1. No one shall be tried for a crime against the peace and security of mankind of which he has already been finally convicted or acquitted by an international criminal court.

2. An individual may not be tried again for a crime of which he has been finally convicted or acquitted by a national court except in the following cases:

(*a*)   By an international criminal court, if:

    (i)   The act which was the subject of the judgement in the national court was characterized by that court as an ordinary crime and not as a crime against the peace and security of mankind; or

    (ii)   The national court proceedings were not impartial or independent or were designed to shield the accused from international criminal responsibility or the case was not diligently prosecuted;

(*b*)   By a national court of another State, if:

    (i)   The act which was the subject of the previous judgement took place in the territory of that State; or

    (ii)   That State was the main victim of the crime.

3. In the case of a subsequent conviction under the present Code, the court, in passing sentence, shall take into account the extent to which

any penalty imposed by a national court on the same person for the same act has already been served.

Article 13

Non-retroactivity

1. No one shall be convicted under the present Code for acts committed before its entry into force.

2. Nothing in this article precludes the trial of anyone for any act which, at the time when it was committed, was criminal in accordance with international law or national law.

Article 14

Defences

The competent court shall determine the admissibility of defences in accordance with the general principles of law, in the light of the character of each crime.

Article 15

Extenuating circumstances

In passing sentence, the court shall, where appropriate, take into account extenuating circumstances in accordance with the general principles of law.

PART TWO

CRIMES AGAINST THE PEACE AND SECURITY OF MANKIND

Article 16

Crime of aggression

An individual who, as leader or organizer, actively participates in or orders the planning, preparation, initiation or waging of aggression committed by a State shall be responsible for a crime of aggression.

Article 17

Crime of genocide

A crime of genocide means any of the following acts committed with intent to destroy, in whole or in part, a national, ethnic, racial or religious group, as such:

(a) Killing members of the group;

(b) Causing serious bodily or mental harm to members of the group;

(c) Deliberately inflicting on the group conditions of life calculated to bring about its physical destruction in whole or in part;

(d) Imposing measures intended to prevent births within the group;

(e) Forcibly transferring children of the group to another group.

Article 18

Crimes against humanity

A crime against humanity means any of the following acts, when committed in a systematic manner or on a large scale and instigated or directed by a Government or by any organization or group:

(a) Murder;

(b) Extermination;

(c) Torture;

(d) Enslavement;

(e) Persecution on political, racial, religious or ethnic grounds;

(f) Institutionalized discrimination on racial, ethnic or religious grounds involving the violation of fundamental human rights and freedoms and resulting in seriously disadvantaging a part of the population;

(g) Arbitrary deportation or forcible transfer of population;

(h) Arbitrary imprisonment;

(i) Forced disappearance of persons;

(j) Rape, enforced prostitution and other forms of sexual abuse;

(k) Other inhumane acts which severely damage physical or mental integrity, health or human dignity, such as mutilation and severe bodily harm.

Article 19

Crimes against United Nations and associated personnel

1. The following crimes constitute crimes against the peace and security of mankind when committed intentionally and in a systematic manner or on a large scale against United Nations and associated personnel involved in a United Nations operation with a view to preventing or impeding that operation from fulfilling its mandate:

(a) Murder, kidnapping or other attack upon the person or liberty of any such personnel;

(b) Violent attack upon the official premises, the private accommodation or the means of transportation of any such personnel likely to endanger his or her person or liberty.

2. This article shall not apply to a United Nations operation authorized by the Security Council as an enforcement action under Chapter VII of the Charter of the United Nations in which any of the

personnel are engaged as combatants against organized armed forces and to which the law of international armed conflict applies.

Article 20

War crimes

Any of the following war crimes constitutes a crime against the peace and security of mankind when committed in a systematic manner or on a large scale:

(*a*) Any of the following acts committed in violation of international humanitarian law:

(i) Wilful killing;

(ii) Torture or inhuman treatment, including biological experiments;

(iii) Wilfully causing great suffering or serious injury to body or health;

(iv) Extensive destruction and appropriation of property, not justified by military necessity and carried out unlawfully and wantonly;

(v) Compelling a prisoner of war or other protected person to serve in the forces of a hostile Power;

(vi) Wilfully depriving a prisoner of war or other protected person of the rights of fair and regular trial;

(vii) Unlawful deportation or transfer of unlawful confinement of protected persons;

(viii) Taking of hostages;

(*b*) Any of the following acts committed wilfully in violation of international humanitarian law and causing death or serious injury to body or health:

(i) Making the civilian population or individual civilians the object of attack;

(ii) Launching an indiscriminate attack affecting the civilian population or civilian objects in the knowledge that such attack will cause excessive loss of life, injury to civilians or damage to civilian objects;

(iii) Launching an attack against works or installations containing dangerous forces in the knowledge that such attack will cause excessive loss of life, injury to civilians or damage to civilian objects;

(iv) Making a person the object of attack in the knowledge that he is hors de combat;

(v) The perfidious use of the distinctive emblem of the red cross, red crescent or red lion and sun or of other recognized protective signs;

(*c*)   Any of the following acts committed wilfully in violation of international humanitarian law:

(i) The transfer by the Occupying Power of parts of its own civilian population into the territory it occupies;

(ii) Unjustifiable delay in the repatriation of prisoners of war or civilians;

(*d*)   Outrages upon personal dignity in violation of international humanitarian law, in particular humiliating and degrading treatment, rape, enforced prostitution and any form of indecent assault;

(*e*)   Any of the following acts committed in violation of the laws or customs of war:

(i) Employment of poisonous weapons or other weapons calculated to cause unnecessary suffering;

(ii) Wanton destruction of cities, towns or villages, or devastation not justified by military necessity;

(iii) Attack, or bombardment, by whatever means, of undefended towns, villages, dwellings or buildings or of demilitarized zones;

(iv) Seizure of, destruction of or wilful damage done to institutions dedicated to religion, charity and education, the arts and sciences, historic monuments and works of art and science;

(v) Plunder of public or private property;

(*f*)   Any of the following acts committed in violation of international humanitarian law applicable in armed conflict not of an international character:

(i) Violence to the life, health and physical or mental well-being of persons, in particular murder as well as cruel treatment such as torture, mutilation or any form of corporal punishment;

(ii) Collective punishments;

(iii) Taking of hostages;

(iv) Acts of terrorism;

(v) Outrages upon personal dignity, in particular humiliating and degrading treatment, rape, enforced prostitution and any form of indecent assault;

(vi) Pillage;

(vii) The passing of sentences and the carrying out of executions without previous judgement pronounced by a regularly constituted court, affording all the judicial guarantees which are generally recognized as indispensable;

(g) In the case of armed conflict, using methods or means of warfare not justified by military necessity with the intent to cause widespread, long-term and severe damage to the natural environment and thereby gravely prejudice the health or survival of the population and such damage occurs.

4. Draft Convention on the Elimination of Future Statelessness[*]

PREAMBLE

Whereas the Universal Declaration of Human Rights proclaims that "everyone has the right to a nationality",

Whereas the Economic and Social Council has recognized that the problem of stateless persons demands "the taking of joint and separate action by Member nations in cooperation with the United Nations to ensure that everyone shall have an effective right to a nationality",

Whereas statelessness often results in suffering and hardship shocking to conscience and offensive to the dignity of man,

Whereas statelessness is frequently productive of friction between States,

Whereas statelessness is inconsistent with the existing principle which postulates nationality as a condition of the enjoyment by the individual of certain rights recognized by international law,

Whereas the practice of many States has increasingly tended to the progressive elimination of statelessness,

Whereas it is imperative, by international agreement, to eliminate the evils of statelessness,

The Contracting Parties

Hereby agree as follows:

Article 1

A person who would otherwise be stateless shall acquire at birth the nationality of the Party in whose territory he is born.

Article 2

For the purpose of article 1, a foundling, so long as his place of birth is unknown, shall be presumed to have been born in the territory of the Party in which he is found.

---

[*] Text adopted by the Commission at its sixth session, in 1954, and submitted to the General Assembly as a part of the Commission's report covering the work of that session. The report, which also contains commentaries on the draft articles, appears in *Yearbook of the International Law Commission, 1954*, vol. II.

Article 3

For the purpose of article 1, birth on a vessel shall be deemed to have taken place within the territory of the State whose flag the vessel flies. Birth on an aircraft shall be considered to have taken place within the territory of the State where the aircraft is registered.

Article 4

If a child is not born in the territory of a State which is a Party to this Convention he shall, if otherwise stateless, acquire the nationality of the Party of which one of his parents is a national. The nationality of the father shall prevail over that of the mother.

Article 5

If the law of a Party entails loss of nationality as a consequence of any change in the personal status of a person such as marriage, termination of marriage, legitimation, recognition or adoption, such loss shall be conditional upon acquisition of another nationality.

Article 6

The change or loss of the nationality of a spouse or of a parent shall not entail the loss of nationality by the other spouse or by the children unless they have or acquire another nationality.

Article 7

1. Renunciation shall not result in loss of nationality unless the person renouncing it has or acquires another nationality.

2. A person who seeks naturalization in a foreign country or who obtains an expatriation permit for that purpose shall not lose his nationality unless he acquires the nationality of that foreign country.

3. A person shall not lose his nationality, so as to become stateless, on the ground of departure, stay abroad, failure to register or on any other similar ground.

Article 8

A Party may not deprive its nationals of their nationality by way of penalty or on any other ground if such deprivation renders them stateless.

Article 9

A Party may not deprive any person or group of persons of their nationality on racial, ethnic, religious or political grounds.

Article 10

1. Every treaty providing for the transfer of a territory shall include provisions for ensuring that, subject to the exercise of the right of option, the inhabitants of that territory shall not become stateless.

2. In the absence of such provisions, a State to which territory is transferred, or which otherwise acquires territory, or a new State

formed on territory previously belonging to another State or States, shall confer its nationality upon the inhabitants of such territory unless they retain their former nationality by option or otherwise or have or acquire another nationality.

Article 11

1. The Parties undertake to establish, within the framework of the United Nations, an agency to act, when it deems appropriate, on behalf of stateless persons before Governments or before the tribunal referred to in paragraph 2.

2. The Parties undertake to establish, within the framework of the United Nations, a tribunal which shall be competent to decide any dispute between them concerning the interpretation or application of this Convention and to decide complaints presented by the agency referred to in paragraph 1 on behalf of a person claiming to have been denied nationality in violation of the provisions of the Convention.

3. If, within two years after the entry into force of the Convention, the agency or the tribunal referred to in paragraphs I and 2 has not been established by the Parties, any of the Parties shall have the right to request the General Assembly to establish such agency or tribunal.

4. The Parties agree that any dispute between them concerning the interpretation or application of the Convention shall, if not referred to the tribunal provided for in paragraph 2, be submitted to the International Court of Justice.

Article 12

1. The present Convention, having been approved by the General Assembly, shall until ... (a year after the approval of the General Assembly) be open for signature on behalf of any Member of the United Nations and of any non-member State to which an invitation to sign is addressed by the General Assembly.

2. The present Convention shall be ratified, and the instruments of ratification shall be deposited with the Secretary-General of the United Nations.

3. After ... (the above date) the present Convention may be acceded to on behalf of any Member of the United Nations and of any non-member State which has received an invitation as aforesaid. Instruments of accession shall be deposited with the Secretary-General of the United Nations.

Article 13

1. At the time of signature, ratification or accession any State may make a reservation permitting it to postpone, for a period not exceeding two years, the application of the Convention pending the enactment of necessary legislation.

2. No other reservations to the present Convention shall be admissible.

Article 14

1. The present Convention shall enter into force on the ninetieth day following the date of the deposit of the ... (e.g., third or sixth) instrument of ratification or accession.

2. For each State ratifying or acceding to the present Convention subsequently to the latter date, the Convention shall enter into force on the ninetieth day following the deposit of the instrument of ratification or accession by that State.

Article 15

Any Party to the present Convention may denounce it at any time by a written notification addressed to the Secretary-General of the United Nations. Such denunciation shall take effect for the said Party one year after the date of its receipt by the Secretary-General.

Article 16

The Secretary-General of the United Nations shall notify all Members of the United Nations and the non-member States referred to in article 12 of the following particulars:

(*a*) Signatures, ratifications and accessions under article 12;

(*b*) Reservations under article 13;

(*c*) The date upon which the present Convention enters into force in pursuance of article 14;

(*d*) Denunciations under article 15.

Article 17

1. The present Convention shall be deposited with the Secretariat of the United Nations.

2. A certified copy of the Convention shall be transmitted to all Members of the United Nations and to the non-member States referred to in article 12.

Article 18

The present Convention shall be registered by the Secretary-General of the United Nations on the date of its entry into force.

5. Model Rules on Arbitral Procedure[*]

PREAMBLE

The undertaking to arbitrate is based on the following fundamental rules:

1. Any undertaking to have recourse to arbitration in order to settle a dispute between States constitutes a legal obligation which must be carried out in good faith.

2. Such an undertaking results from agreement between the parties and may relate to existing disputes or to disputes arising subsequently.

3. The undertaking must be embodied in a written instrument, whatever the form of the instrument may be.

4. The procedures suggested to States Parties to a dispute by these model rules shall not be compulsory unless the States concerned have agreed, either in the *compromis* or in some other undertaking, to have recourse thereto.

5. The parties shall be equal in all proceedings before the arbitral tribunal.

THE EXISTENCE OF A DISPUTE AND THE SCOPE OF THE UNDERTAKING TO ARBITRATE

Article 1

1. If, before the constitution of the arbitral tribunal, the parties to an undertaking to arbitrate disagree as to the existence of a dispute, or as to whether the existing dispute is wholly or partly within the scope of the obligation to go to arbitration, such preliminary question shall, at the request of any of the parties and failing agreement between them upon the adoption of another procedure, be brought before the International Court of Justice for decision by means of its summary procedure.

2. The Court shall have the power to indicate, if it considers that circumstances so require, any provisional measures which ought to be taken to preserve the respective rights of either party.

3. If the arbitral tribunal has already been constituted, any dispute concerning arbitrability shall be referred to it.

---

[*] Text adopted by the Commission at its tenth session, in 1958, and submitted to the General Assembly as a part of the Commission's report covering the work of that session. The report, which also contains commentaries on the model rules, appears in *Yearbook of the International Law Commission, 1958*, vol. II.

Article 2

1. Unless there are earlier agreements which suffice for the purpose, for example in the undertaking to arbitrate itself, the parties having recourse to arbitration shall conclude a *compromis* which shall specify, as a minimum:

(*a*) The undertaking to arbitrate according to which the dispute is to be submitted to the arbitrators;

(*b*) The subject matter of the dispute and, if possible, the points on which the parties are or are not agreed;

(*c*) The method of constituting the tribunal and the number of arbitrators.

2. In addition, the *compromis* shall include any other provisions deemed desirable by the parties, in particular:

(i) The rules of law and the principles to be applied by the tribunal, and the right, if any, conferred on it to decide *ex aequo et bono* as though it had legislative functions in the matter;

(ii) The power, if any, of the tribunal to make recommendations to the parties;

(iii) Such power as may be conferred on the tribunal to make its own rules of procedure;

(iv) The procedure to be followed by the tribunal; provided that, once constituted, the tribunal shall be free to override any provisions of the *compromis* which may prevent it from rendering its award;

(v) The number of members required for the constitution of a quorum for the conduct of the hearings;

(vi) The majority required for the award;

(vii) The time limit within which the award shall be rendered;

(viii) The right of the members of the tribunal to attach dissenting or individual opinions to the award, or any prohibition of such opinions;

(ix) The languages to be employed in the course of the proceedings;

(x) The manner in which the costs and disbursements shall be apportioned;

(xi) The services which the International Court of Justice may be asked to render.

This enumeration is not intended to be exhaustive.

Article 3

1. Immediately after the request made by one of the States Parties to the dispute for the submission of the dispute to arbitration, or after the decision on the arbitrability of the dispute, the parties to an undertaking to arbitrate shall take the necessary steps, either by means of the compromis or by special agreement, in order to arrive at the constitution of the arbitral tribunal.

2. If the tribunal is not constituted within three months from the date of the request made for the submission of the dispute to arbitration, or from the date of the decision on arbitrability, the President of the International Court of Justice shall, at the request of either party, appoint the arbitrators not yet designated. If the President is prevented from acting or is a national of one of the parties, the appointments shall be made by the Vice-President. If the Vice-President is prevented from acting or is a national of one of the parties, the appointments shall be made by the oldest member of the Court who is not a national of either party.

3. The appointments referred to in paragraph 2 shall, after consultation with the parties, be made in accordance with the provisions of the *compromis* or of any other instrument consequent upon the undertaking to arbitrate. In the absence of such provisions, the composition of the tribunal shall, after consultation with the parties, be determined by the President of the International Court of Justice or by the judge acting in his place. It shall be understood that in this event the number of the arbitrators must be uneven and should preferably be five.

4. Where provision is made for the choice of a president of the tribunal by the other arbitrators, the tribunal shall be deemed to be constituted when the president is selected. If the president has not been chosen within two months of the appointment of the arbitrators, he shall be designated in accordance with the procedure prescribed in paragraph 2.

5. Subject to the special circumstances of the case, the arbitrators shall be chosen from among persons of recognized competence in international law.

Article 4

1. Once the tribunal has been constituted, its composition shall remain unchanged until the award has been rendered.

2. A party may, however, replace an arbitrator appointed by it, provided that the tribunal has not yet begun its proceedings. Once the proceedings have begun, an arbitrator appointed by a party may not be replaced except by mutual agreement between the parties.

3. Arbitrators appointed by mutual agreement between the parties, or by agreement between arbitrators already appointed, may not be changed after the proceedings have begun, save in exceptional circumstances. Arbitrators appointed in the manner provided for in article 3, paragraph 2, may not be changed even by agreement between the parties.

4. The proceedings are deemed to have begun when the president of the tribunal or the sole arbitrator has made the first procedural order.

Article 5

If, whether before or after the proceedings have begun, a vacancy should occur on account of the death, incapacity or resignation of an arbitrator, it shall be filled in accordance with the procedure prescribed for the original appointment.

Article 6

1. A party may propose the disqualification of one of the arbitrators on account of a fact arising subsequently to the constitution of the tribunal. It may only propose the disqualification of one of the arbitrators on account of a fact arising prior to the constitution of the tribunal if it can show that the appointment was made without knowledge of that fact or as a result of fraud. In either case, the decision shall be taken by the other members of the tribunal.

2. In the case of a sole arbitrator or of the president of the tribunal, the question of disqualification shall, in the absence of agreement between the parties, be decided by the International Court of Justice on the application of one of them.

3. Any resulting vacancy or vacancies shall be filled in accordance with the procedure prescribed for the original appointments.

Article 7

Where a vacancy has been filled after the proceedings have begun, the proceedings shall continue from the point they had reached at the time the vacancy occurred. The newly appointed arbitrator may, however, require that the oral proceedings shall be recommenced from the beginning, if these have already been started.

POWERS OF THE TRIBUNAL AND THE PROCESS OF ARBITRATION

Article 8

1. When the undertaking to arbitrate or any supplementary agreement contains provisions which seem sufficient for the purpose of a *compromis*, and the tribunal has been constituted, either party may submit the dispute to the tribunal by application. If the other party refuses to answer the application on the ground that the provisions above referred to are insufficient, the tribunal shall decide whether there is already sufficient agreement between the parties on

the essential elements of a *compromis* as set forth in article 2. In the case of an affirmative decision, the tribunal shall prescribe the necessary measures for the institution or continuation of the proceedings. In the contrary case, the tribunal shall order the parties to complete or conclude the *compromis* within such time limits as it deems reasonable.

2. If the parties fail to agree or to complete the *compromis* within the time limit fixed in accordance with the preceding paragraph, the tribunal, within three months after the parties report failure to agree — or after the decision, if any, on the arbitrability of the dispute — shall proceed to hear and decide the case on the application of either party.

Article 9

The arbitral tribunal, which is the judge of its own competence, has the power to interpret the *compromis* and the other instruments on which that competence is based.

Article 10

1. In the absence of any agreement between the parties concerning the law to be applied, the tribunal shall apply:

(*a*) International conventions, whether general or particular, establishing rules expressly recognized by the contesting States;

(*b*) International custom, as evidence of a general practice accepted as law;

(*c*) The general principles of law recognized by civilized nations;

(*d*) Judicial decisions and the teachings of the most highly qualified publicists of the various nations, as subsidiary means for the determination of rules of law.

2. If the agreement between the parties so provides, the tribunal may also decide *ex aequo et bono*.

Article 11

The tribunal may not bring in a finding of *non liquet* on the ground of the silence or obscurity of the law to be applied.

Article 12

1. In the absence of any agreement between the parties concerning the procedure of the tribunal, or if the rules laid down by them are insufficient, the tribunal shall be competent to formulate or complete the rules of procedure.

2. All decisions shall be taken by a majority vote of the members of the tribunal.

Article 13

If the languages to be employed are not specified in the *compromis*, this question shall be decided by the tribunal.

Article 14

1. The parties shall appoint agents before the tribunal to act as intermediaries between them and the tribunal.

2. They may retain counsel and advocates for the prosecution of their rights and interests before the tribunal.

3. The parties shall be entitled through their agents, counsel or advocates to submit in writing and orally to the tribunal any arguments they may deem expedient for the prosecution of their case. They shall have the right to raise objections and incidental points. The decisions of the tribunal on such matters shall be final.

4. The members of the tribunal shall have the right to put questions to agents, counsel or advocates, and to ask them for explanations. Neither the questions put nor the remarks made during the hearing are to be regarded as an expression of opinion by the tribunal or by its members.

Article 15

1. The arbitral procedure shall in general comprise two distinct phases: pleadings and hearing.

2. The pleadings shall consist in the communication by the respective agents to the members of the tribunal and to the opposite party of memorials, counter-memorials and, if necessary, of replies and rejoinders. Each party must attach all papers and documents cited by it in the case.

3. The time limits fixed by the *compromis* may be extended by mutual agreement between the parties, or by the tribunal when it deems such extension necessary to enable it to reach a just decision.

4. The hearing shall consist in the oral development of the parties' arguments before the tribunal.

5. A certified true copy of every document produced by either party shall be communicated to the other party.

Article 16

1. The hearing shall be conducted by the president. It shall be public only if the tribunal so decides with the consent of the parties.

2. Records of the hearing shall be kept and signed by the president, registrar or secretary; only those so signed shall be authentic.

Article 17

1. After the tribunal has closed the written pleadings, it shall have the right to reject any papers and documents not yet produced which either party may wish to submit to it without the consent of the other

party. The tribunal shall, however, remain free to take into consideration any such papers and documents which the agents, advocates or counsel of one or other of the parties may bring to its notice, provided that they have been made known to the other party. The latter shall have the right to require a further extension of the written pleadings so as to be able to give a reply in writing.

2. The tribunal may also require the parties to produce all necessary documents and to provide all necessary explanations. It shall take note of any refusal to do so.

Article 18

1. The tribunal shall decide as to the admissibility of the evidence that may be adduced, and shall be the judge of its probative value. It shall have the power, at any stage of the proceedings, to call upon experts and to require the appearance of witnesses. It may also, if necessary, decide to visit the scene connected with the case before it.

2. The parties shall cooperate with the tribunal in dealing with the evidence and in the other measures contemplated by paragraph 1. The tribunal shall take note of the failure of any party to comply with the obligations of this paragraph.

Article 19

In the absence of any agreement to the contrary implied by the undertaking to arbitrate or contained in the *compromis*, the tribunal shall decide on any ancillary claims which it considers to be inseparable from the subject matter of the dispute and necessary for its final settlement.

Article 20

The tribunal, or in case of urgency its president subject to confirmation by the tribunal, shall have the power to indicate, if it considers that circumstances so require, any provisional measures which ought to be taken to preserve the respective rights of either party.

Article 21

1. When, subject to the control of the tribunal, the agents, advocates and counsel have completed their presentation of the case, the proceedings shall be formally declared closed.

2. The tribunal shall, however, have the power, so long as the award has not been rendered, to reopen the proceedings after their closure, on the ground that new evidence is forthcoming of such a nature as to constitute a decisive factor, or if it considers, after careful consideration, that there is a need for clarification on certain points.

Article 22

1. Except where the claimant admits the soundness of the defendant's case, discontinuance of the proceedings by the claimant party shall not be accepted by the tribunal without the consent of the defendant.

2. If the case is discontinued by agreement between the parties, the tribunal shall take note of the fact.

Article 23

If the parties reach a settlement, it shall be taken note of by the tribunal. At the request of either party, the tribunal may, if it thinks fit, embody the settlement in an award.

Article 24

The award shall normally be rendered within the period fixed by the *compromis*, but the tribunal may decide to extend this period if it would otherwise be unable to render the award.

Article 25

1. Whenever one of the parties has not appeared before the tribunal, or has failed to present its case, the other party may call upon the tribunal to decide in favour of its case.

2. The arbitral tribunal may grant the defaulting party a period of grace before rendering the award.

3. On the expiry of this period of grace, the tribunal shall render an award after it has satisfied itself that it has jurisdiction. It may only decide in favour of the submissions of the party appearing, if satisfied that they are well founded in fact and in law.

DELIBERATIONS OF THE TRIBUNAL

Article 26

The deliberations of the tribunal shall remain secret.

Article 27

1. All the arbitrators shall participate in the decisions.

2. Except in cases where the *compromis* provides for a quorum, or in cases where the absence of an arbitrator occurs without the permission of the president of the tribunal, the arbitrator who is absent shall be replaced by an arbitrator nominated by the President of the International Court of Justice. In the case of such replacement the provisions of article 7 shall apply.

Article 28

1. The award shall be rendered by a majority vote of the members of the tribunal. It shall be drawn up in writing and shall bear the date on which it was rendered. It shall contain the names of the arbitrators and shall be signed by the president and by the members of the tribunal who have voted for it. The arbitrators may not abstain from voting.

2. Unless otherwise provided in the *compromis*, any member of the tribunal may attach his separate or dissenting opinion to the award.

3. The award shall be deemed to have been rendered when it has been read in open court, the agents of the parties being present or having been duly summoned to appear.

4. The award shall immediately be communicated to the parties.

Article 29

The award shall, in respect of every point on which it rules, state the reasons on which it is based.

Article 30

Once rendered, the award shall be binding upon the parties. It shall he carried out in good faith immediately, unless the tribunal has allowed a time limit for the carrying out of the award or of any part of it.

Article 31

During a period of one month after the award has been rendered and communicated to the parties, the tribunal may, either of its own accord or at the request of either party, rectify any clerical, typographical or arithmetical error in the award, or any obvious error of a similar nature.

Article 32

The arbitral award shall constitute a definitive settlement of the dispute.

INTERPRETATION OF THE AWARD

Article 33

1. Any dispute between the parties as to the meaning and scope of the award shall, at the request of either party and within three months of the rendering of the award, be referred to the tribunal which rendered the award.

2. If, for any reason, it is found impossible to submit the dispute to the tribunal which rendered the award, and if within the above-mentioned time limit the parties have not agreed upon another

solution, the dispute may be referred to the International Court of Justice at the request of either party.

3. In the event of a request for interpretation, it shall be for the tribunal or for the International Court of Justice, as the case may be, to, decide whether and to what extent execution of the award shall be stayed pending a decision on the request.

Article 34

Failing a request for interpretation, or after a decision on such a request has been made, all pleadings and documents in the case shall be deposited by the president of the tribunal with the International Bureau of the Permanent Court of Arbitration or with another depositary selected by agreement between the parties.

VALIDITY AND ANNULMENT OF THE AWARD

Article 35

The validity of an award may be challenged by either party on one or more of the following grounds:

(*a*)   That the tribunal has exceeded its powers;

(*b*)   That there was corruption on the part of a member of the tribunal;

(*c*)   That there has been a failure to state the reasons for the award or a serious departure from a fundamental rule of procedure;

(*d*)   That the undertaking to arbitrate or the *compromis* is a nullity.

Article 36

1. If, within three months of the date on which the validity of the award is contested, the parties have not agreed on another tribunal, the International Court of Justice shall be competent to declare the total or partial nullity of the award on the application of either party.

2. In the cases covered by article 35, subparagraphs (*a*) and (*c*), validity must be contested within six months of the rendering of the award, and in the cases covered by subparagraphs (*b*) and (*d*) within six months of the discovery of the corruption or of the facts giving rise to the claim of nullity, and in any case within ten years of the rendering of the award.

3. The Court may, at the request of the interested party, and if circumstances so require, grant a stay of execution pending the final decision on the application for annulment.

Article 37

If the award is declared invalid by the International Court of Justice, the dispute shall be submitted to a new tribunal constituted by agreement between the parties, or, failing such agreement, in the manner provided by article 3.

Article 38

1. An application for the revision of the award may be made by either party on the ground of the discovery of some fact of such a nature as to constitute a decisive factor, provided that when the award was rendered that fact was unknown to the tribunal and to the party requesting revision, and that such ignorance was not due to the negligence of the party requesting revision.

2. The application for revision must be made within six months of the discovery of the new fact, and in any case within ten years of the rendering of the award.

3. In the proceedings for revision, the tribunal shall, in the first instance, make a finding as to the existence of the alleged new fact and rule on the admissibility of the application.

4. If the tribunal finds the application admissible, it shall then decide on the merits of the dispute.

5. The application for revision shall, whenever possible, be made to the tribunal which rendered the award.

6. If, for any reason, it is not possible to make the application to the tribunal which rendered the award, it may, unless the parties otherwise agree, be made by either of them to the International Court of Justice.

7. The tribunal or the Court may, at the request of the interested party, and if circumstances so require, grant a stay of execution pending the final decision on the application for revision.

6. Draft Articles on Most-Favoured-Nation Clauses*

Article 1

Scope of the present articles

The present articles apply to most-favoured-nation clauses contained in treaties between States.

Article 2

Use of terms

1. For the purposes of the present articles:

---

* Text adopted by the Commission at its thirtieth session, in 1978, and submitted to the General Assembly as a part of the Commission's report covering the work of that session. The report, which also contains commentaries on the draft articles, appears in *Yearbook of the International Law Commission, 1978*, vol. II, Part Two.

(*a*) "treaty" means an international agreement concluded between States in written form and governed by international law, whether embodied in a single instrument or in two or more related instruments and whatever its particular designation;

(*b*) "granting State" means a State which has undertaken to accord most-favoured-nation treatment;

(*c*) "beneficiary State" means a State to which a granting State has undertaken to accord most-favoured-nation treatment;

(*d*) "third State" means any State other than the granting State or the beneficiary State;

(*e*) "condition of compensation" means a condition providing for compensation of any kind agreed between the granting State and the beneficiary State, in a treaty containing a most-favoured-nation clause or otherwise;

(*f*) "condition of reciprocal treatment" means a condition of compensation providing for the same or, as the case may be, equivalent treatment by the beneficiary State of the granting State or of persons or things in a determined relationship with it as that extended by the granting State to a third State or to persons or things in the same relationship with that third State.

2. The provisions of paragraph 1 regarding the use of terms in the present articles are without prejudice to the use of those terms or to the meanings which may be given to them in the internal law of any State.

Article 3

Clauses not within the scope of the present articles

The fact that the present articles do not apply to a clause on most-favoured treatment other than a most-favoured-nation clause referred to in article 4 shall not affect:

(*a*) the legal effect of such a clause;

(*b*) the application to it of any of the rules set forth in the present articles to which it would be subject under international law independently of the present articles.

Article 4

Most-favoured-nation clause

A most-favoured-nation clause is a treaty provision whereby a State undertakes an obligation towards another State to accord most-favoured-nation treatment in an agreed sphere of relations.

Article 5

Most-favoured-nation treatment

Most-favoured-nation treatment is treatment accorded by the granting State to the beneficiary State, or to persons or things in a determined relationship with that State, not less favourable than treatment extended by the granting State to a third State or to persons or things in the same relationship with that third State.

Article 6

Clauses in international agreements between States to which other subjects of international law are also parties

Notwithstanding the provisions of articles 1, 2, 4 and 5, the present articles shall apply to the relations of States as between themselves under an international agreement containing a clause on most-favoured-nation treatment to which other subjects of international law are also parties.

Article 7

Legal basis of most-favoured-nation treatment

Nothing in the present articles shall imply that a State is entitled to be accorded most-favoured-nation treatment by another State otherwise than on the basis of an international obligation undertaken by the latter State.

Article 8

The source and scope of most-favoured-nation treatment

1. The right of the beneficiary State to most-favoured-nation treatment arises only from the most-favoured-nation clause referred to in article 4, or from the clause on most-favoured-nation treatment referred to in article 6, in force between the granting State and the beneficiary State.

2. The most-favoured-nation treatment to which the beneficiary State, for itself or for the benefit of persons or things in a determined relationship with it, is entitled under a clause referred to in paragraph 1 is determined by the treatment extended by the granting State to a third State or to persons or things in the same relationship with that third State.

Article 9

Scope of rights under a most-favoured-nation clause

1. Under a most-favoured-nation clause the beneficiary State acquires, for itself or for the benefit of persons or things in a determined relationship with it, only those rights which fall within the limits of the subject matter of the clause.

2. The beneficiary State acquires the rights under paragraph 1 only in respect of persons or things which are specified in the clause or implied from its subject matter.

Article 10

Acquisition of rights under a most-favoured-nation clause

1. Under a most-favoured-nation clause the beneficiary State acquires the right to most-favoured-nation treatment only if the granting State extends to a third State treatment within the limits of the subject matter of the clause.

2. The beneficiary State acquires rights under paragraph 1 in respect of persons or things in a determined relationship with it only if they:

(*a*)   belong to the same category of persons or things as those in a determined relationship with a third State which benefit from the treatment extended to them by the granting State and

(*b*)   have the same relationship with the beneficiary State as the persons and things referred to in subparagraph (a) have with that third State.

Article 11

Effect of a most-favoured-nation clause not made subject to compensation

If a most-favoured-nation clause is not made subject to a condition of compensation, the beneficiary State acquires the right to most-favoured-nation treatment without the obligation to accord any compensation to the granting State.

Article 12

Effect of a most-favoured-nation clause made subject to compensation

If a most-favoured-nation clause is made subject to a condition of compensation, the beneficiary State acquires the right to most-favoured-nation treatment only upon according the agreed compensation to the granting State.

Article 13

Effect of a most-favoured-nation clause made subject to reciprocal treatment

If a most-favoured-nation clause is made subject to a condition of reciprocal treatment, the beneficiary State acquires the right to most-favoured-nation treatment only upon according the agreed reciprocal treatment to the granting State.

Article 14

Compliance with agreed terms and conditions

The exercise of rights arising under a most-favoured-nation clause for the beneficiary State or for persons or things in a determined relationship with that State is subject to compliance with the relevant terms and conditions laid down in the treaty containing the clause or otherwise agreed between the granting State and the beneficiary State.

Article 15

Irrelevance of the fact that treatment is extended to a third State against compensation

The acquisition without compensation of rights by the beneficiary State, for itself or for the benefit of persons or things in a determined relationship with it, under a most-favoured-nation clause not made subject to a condition of compensation is not affected by the mere fact that the treatment by the granting State of a third State or of persons or things in the same relationship with that third State has been extended against compensation.

Article 16

Irrelevance of limitations agreed between the granting State and a third State

The acquisition of rights by the beneficiary State, for itself or for the benefit of persons or things in a determined relationship with it, under a most-favoured-nation clause is not affected by the mere fact that the treatment by the granting State of a third State or of persons or things in the same relationship with that third State has been extended under an international agreement between the granting State and the third State limiting the application of that treatment to relations between them.

Article 17

Irrelevance of the fact that treatment is extended to a third State under a bilateral or a multilateral agreement

The acquisition of rights by the beneficiary State, for itself or for the benefit of persons or things in a determined relationship with it, under a most-favoured-nation clause is not affected by the mere fact that the treatment by the granting State of a third State or of persons or things in the same relationship with that third State has been extended under an international agreement, whether bilateral or multilateral.

Article 18

Irrelevance of the fact that treatment is extended to a third State as national treatment

The acquisition of rights by the beneficiary State, for itself or for the benefit of persons or things in a determined relationship with it, under a most-favoured-nation clause is not affected by the mere fact that the treatment by the granting State of a third State or of persons or things in the same relationship with that third State has been extended as national treatment.

Article 19

Most-favoured-nation treatment and national or other treatment with respect to the same subject matter

1. The right of the beneficiary State, for itself or for the benefit of persons or things in a determined relationship with it, to most-favoured-nation treatment under a most-favoured-nation clause is not affected by the mere fact that the granting State has agreed to accord as well to that beneficiary State national treatment or other treatment with respect to the same subject matter as that of the most-favoured-nation clause.

2. The right of the beneficiary State, for itself or for the benefit of persons or things in a determined relationship with it, to most-favoured-nation treatment under a most-favoured-nation clause is without prejudice to national treatment or other treatment which the granting State has accorded to that beneficiary State with respect to the same subject matter as that of the most-favoured-nation clause.

Article 20

Arising of rights under a most-favoured-nation clause

1. The right of the beneficiary State, for itself or for the benefit of persons or things in a determined relationship with it, to most-favoured-nation treatment under a most-favoured-nation clause not made subject to a condition of compensation arises at the moment when the relevant treatment is extended by the granting State to a third State or to persons or things in the same relationship with that third State.

2. The right of the beneficiary State, for itself or for the benefit of persons or things in a determined relationship with it, to most-favoured-nation treatment under a most-favoured-nation clause made subject to a condition of compensation arises at the moment when the relevant treatment is extended by the granting State to a third State or to persons or things in the same relationship with that third State and the agreed compensation is accorded by the beneficiary State to the granting State.

3. The right of the beneficiary State, for itself or for the benefit of persons or things in a determined relationship with it, to most-favoured-nation treatment under a most-favoured-nation clause made subject to a condition of reciprocal treatment arises at the moment when the relevant treatment is extended by the granting State to a third State or to persons or things in the same relationship with that third State and the agreed reciprocal treatment is accorded by the beneficiary State to the granting State.

Article 21

Termination or suspension of rights under a most-favoured-nation clause

1. The right of the beneficiary State, for itself or for the benefit of persons or things in a determined relationship with it, to most-favoured-nation treatment under a most-favoured-nation clause is terminated or suspended at the moment when the extension of the relevant treatment by the granting State to a third State or to persons or things in the same relationship with that third State is terminated or suspended.

2. The right of the beneficiary State, for itself or for the benefit of persons or things in a determined relationship with it, to most-favoured-nation treatment under a most-favoured-nation clause made subject to a condition of compensation is equally terminated or suspended at the moment of termination or suspension by the beneficiary State of the agreed compensation.

3. The right of the beneficiary State for itself or for the benefit of persons or things in a determined relationship with it, to most-favoured-nation treatment under a most-favoured-nation clause made subject to a condition of reciprocal treatment is equally terminated or suspended at the moment of termination or suspension by the beneficiary State of the agreed reciprocal treatment.

Article 22

Compliance with the laws and regulations of the granting State

The exercise of rights arising under a most-favoured-nation clause for the beneficiary State or for persons or things in a determined relationship with that State is subject to compliance with the relevant laws and regulations of the granting State. Those laws and regulations, however, shall not be applied in such a manner that the treatment of the beneficiary State or of persons or things in a determined relationship with that State is less favourable than that of the third State or of persons or things in the same relationship with that third State.

Article 23

The most-favoured-nation clause in relation to treatment under a generalized system of preferences

A beneficiary State is not entitled, under a most-favoured-nation clause, to treatment extended by a developed granting State to a developing third State on a non-reciprocal basis within a scheme of generalized preferences, established by that granting State, which conforms with a generalized system of preferences recognized by the international community of States as a whole or, for the States members of a competent international organization, adopted in accordance with its relevant rules and procedures.

Article 24

The most-favoured-nation clause in relation to arrangements between developing States

A developed beneficiary State is not entitled under a most-favoured-nation clause to any preferential treatment in the field of trade extended by a developing granting State to a developing third State in conformity with the relevant rules and procedures of a competent international organization of which the States concerned are members.

Article 25

The most-favoured-nation clause in relation to treatment extended to facilitate frontier traffic

1. A beneficiary State other than a contiguous State is not entitled under a most-favoured-nation clause to the treatment extended by the granting State to a contiguous third State in order to facilitate frontier traffic.

2. A contiguous beneficiary State is entitled under a most-favoured-nation clause to treatment not less favourable than the treatment extended by the granting State to a contiguous third State in order to facilitate frontier traffic only if the subject-matter of the clause is the facilitation of frontier traffic.

Article 26

The most-favoured-nation clause in relation to rights and facilities extended to a landlocked third State

1. A beneficiary State other than a landlocked State is not entitled under a most-favoured-nation clause to rights and facilities extended by the granting State to a landlocked third State in order to facilitate its access to and from the sea.

2. A landlocked beneficiary State is entitled under a most-favoured-nation clause to the rights and facilities extended by the granting State to a landlocked third State in order to facilitate its access to and

from the sea only if the subject matter of the clause is the facilitation of access to and from the sea.

Article 27

Cases of State succession, State responsibility and outbreak of hostilities

The provisions of the present articles shall not prejudge any question that may arise in regard to a most-favoured-nation clause from a succession of States or from the international responsibility of a State or from the outbreak of hostilities between States.

Article 28

Non-retroactivity of the present articles

1. Without prejudice to the application of any rule set forth in the present articles to which most-favoured-nation clauses would be subject under international law independently of these articles, they apply only to a most-favoured-nation clause in a treaty which is concluded by States after the entry into force of the present articles with regard to such States.

2. Without prejudice to the application of any rule set forth in the present articles to which clauses on most-favoured-nation treatment would be subject under international law independently of these articles, they apply to the relations of States as between themselves only under a clause on most-favoured-nation treatment contained in an international agreement which is concluded by States and other subjects of international law after the entry into force of the present articles with regard to such States.

Article 29

Provisions otherwise agreed

The present articles are without prejudice to any provision on which the granting State and the beneficiary State may otherwise agree.

Article 30

New rules of international law in favour of developing countries

The present articles are without prejudice to the establishment of new rules of international law in favour of developing countries.

7. Draft Articles on the Status of the Diplomatic Courier and the Diplomatic Bag Not Accompanied by Diplomatic Courier and Draft Optional Protocols*

(a) Draft Articles on the Status of the Diplomatic Courier and the Diplomatic Bag Not Accompanied by Diplomatic Courier

PART I

GENERAL PROVISIONS

Article 1

Scope of the present articles

The present articles apply to the diplomatic courier and the diplomatic bag employed for the official communications of a State with its missions, consular posts or delegations, wherever situated, and for the official communications of those missions, consular posts or delegations with the sending State or with each other.

Article 2

Couriers and bags not within the scope of the present articles

The fact that the present articles do not apply to couriers and bags employed for the official communications of special missions or international organizations shall not affect:

(*a*) the legal status of such couriers and bags;

(*b*) the application to such couriers and bags of any rules set forth in the present articles which would be applicable under international law independently of the present articles.

Article 3

Use of terms

1. For the purposes of the present articles:

(1) "diplomatic courier" means a person duly authorized by the sending State, either on a regular basis or for a special occasion as a courier ad hoc, as:

(*a*) a diplomatic courier within the meaning of the Vienna Convention on Diplomatic Relations of 18 April 1961;

---

* Text adopted by the Commission at its forty-first session, in 1989, and submitted to the General Assembly as a part of the Commission's report covering the work of that session. The report, which also contains commentaries on the draft articles and draft optional protocols thereto, appears in *Yearbook of the International Law Commission, 1989*, vol. II (Part Two).

(*b*) a consular courier within the meaning of the Vienna Convention on Consular Relations of 24 April 1963; or

(*c*) a courier of a permanent mission, a permanent observer mission, a delegation or an observer delegation within the meaning of the Vienna Convention on the Representation of States in Their Relations with International Organizations of a Universal Character of 14 March 1975;

who is entrusted with the custody, transportation and delivery of the diplomatic bag and is employed for the official communications referred to in article 1;

(2) "diplomatic bag" means the packages containing official correspondence, and documents or articles intended exclusively for official use, whether accompanied by diplomatic courier or not, which are used for the official communications referred to in article 1 and which bear visible external marks of their character as:

(*a*) a diplomatic bag within the meaning of the Vienna Convention on Diplomatic Relations of 18 April 1961;

(*b*) a consular bag within the meaning of the Vienna Convention on Consular Relations of 24 April 1963; or

(*c*) a bag of a permanent mission, a permanent observer mission, a delegation or an observer delegation within the meaning of the Vienna Convention on the Representation of States in Their Relations with International Organizations of a Universal Character of 14 March 1975;

(3) "sending State" means a State dispatching a diplomatic bag to or from its missions, consular posts or delegations;

(4) "receiving State" means a State having on its territory missions, consular posts or delegations of the sending State which receive or dispatch a diplomatic bag;

(5) "transit State" means a State through whose territory a diplomatic courier or a diplomatic bag passes in transit;

(6) "mission" means:

(*a*) a permanent diplomatic mission within the meaning of the Vienna Convention on Diplomatic Relations of 18 April 1961; and

(*b*) a permanent mission or a permanent observer mission within the meaning of the Vienna Convention on the Representation of States in Their Relations with International Organizations of a Universal Character of 14 March 1975;

(7) "consular post" means a consulate-general, consulate, vice-consulate or consular agency within the meaning of the Vienna Convention on Consular Relations of 24 April 1963;

(8) "delegation" means a delegation or an observer delegation within the meaning of the Vienna Convention on the Representation of States in Their Relations with International Organizations of a Universal Character of 14 March 1975;

(9) "international organization" means an intergovernmental organization.

2. The provisions of paragraph 1 regarding the use of terms in the present articles are without prejudice to the use of those terms or to the meanings which may be given to them in other international instruments or the internal law of any State.

Article 4

Freedom of official communications

1. The receiving State shall permit and protect the official communications of the sending State, effected through the diplomatic courier or the diplomatic bag, as referred to in article 1.

2. The transit State shall accord to the official communications of the sending State, effected through the diplomatic courier or the diplomatic bag, the same freedom and protection as is accorded by the receiving State.

Article 5

Duty to respect the laws and regulations of the receiving State and the transit State

1. The sending State shall ensure that the privileges and immunities accorded to its diplomatic courier and diplomatic bag are not used in a manner incompatible with the object and purpose of the present articles.

2. Without prejudice to the privileges and immunities accorded to him, it is the duty of the diplomatic courier to respect the laws and regulations of the receiving State and the transit State.

Article 6

Non-discrimination and reciprocity

1. In the application of the provisions of the present articles, the receiving State or the transit State shall not discriminate as between States.

2. However, discrimination shall not be regarded as taking place:

(a) where the receiving State or the transit State applies any of the provisions of the present articles restrictively because of a restrictive application of that provision to its diplomatic courier or diplomatic bag by the sending State;

(b) where States by custom or agreement extend to each other more favourable treatment with respect to their diplomatic couriers and diplomatic bags than is required by the present articles.

PART II
STATUS OF THE DIPLOMATIC COURIER AND THE CAPTAIN OF A SHIP OR AIRCRAFT ENTRUSTED WITH THE DIPLOMATIC BAG

Article 7

Appointment of the diplomatic courier

Subject to the provisions of articles 9 and 12, the sending State or its missions, consular posts or delegations may freely appoint the diplomatic courier.

Article 8

Documentation of the diplomatic courier

The diplomatic courier shall be provided with an official document indicating his status and essential personal data, including his name and, where appropriate, his official position or rank, as well as the number of packages constituting the diplomatic bag which is accompanied by him and their identification and destination.

Article 9

Nationality of the diplomatic courier

1. The diplomatic courier should in principle be of the nationality of the sending State.

2. The diplomatic courier may not be appointed from among persons having the nationality of the receiving State except with the consent of that State, which may be withdrawn at any time. However, when the diplomatic courier is performing his functions in the territory of the receiving State, withdrawal of consent shall not take effect until he has delivered the diplomatic bag to its consignee.

3. The receiving State may reserve the right provided for in paragraph 2 also with regard to:

(*a*) nationals of the sending State who are permanent residents of the receiving State;

(*b*) nationals of a third State who are not also nationals of the sending State.

Article 10

Functions of the diplomatic courier

The functions of the diplomatic courier consist in taking custody of the diplomatic bag entrusted to him and transporting and delivering it to its consignee.

Article 11

End of the functions of the diplomatic courier

The functions of the diplomatic courier come to an end, inter alia, upon:

(*a*) fulfilment of his functions or his return to the country of origin;

(*b*) notification by the sending State to the receiving State and, where necessary, the transit State that his functions have been terminated;

(*c*) notification by the receiving State to the sending State that, in accordance with paragraph 2 of article 12, it ceases to recognize him as a diplomatic courier.

Article 12

The diplomatic courier declared persona non grata or not acceptable

1. The receiving State may, at any time and without having to explain its decision, notify the sending State that the diplomatic courier is persona non grata or not acceptable. In any such case, the sending State shall, as appropriate, either recall the diplomatic courier or terminate his functions to be performed in the receiving State. A person may be declared non grata or not acceptable before arriving in the territory of the receiving State.

2. If the sending State refuses or fails within a reasonable period to carry out its obligations under paragraph 1, the receiving State may cease to recognize the person concerned as a diplomatic courier.

Article 13

Facilities accorded to the diplomatic courier

1. The receiving State or the transit State shall accord to the diplomatic courier the facilities necessary for the performance of his functions.

2. The receiving State or the transit State shall, upon request and to the extent practicable, assist the diplomatic courier in obtaining temporary accommodation and in establishing contact through the telecommunications network with the sending State and its missions, consular posts or delegations, wherever situated.

Article 14

Entry into the territory of the receiving State or the transit State

1. The receiving State or the transit State shall permit the diplomatic courier to enter its territory in the performance of his functions.

2. Visas, where required, shall be granted by the receiving State or the transit State to the diplomatic courier as promptly as possible.

Article 15

Freedom of movement

Subject to its laws and regulations concerning zones entry into which is prohibited or regulated for reasons of national security, the receiving State or the transit State shall ensure to the diplomatic courier such freedom of movement and travel in its territory as is necessary for the performance of his functions.

Article 16

Personal protection and inviolability

The diplomatic courier shall be protected by the receiving State or the transit State in the performance of his functions. He shall enjoy personal inviolability and shall not be liable to any form of arrest or detention.

Article 17

Inviolability of temporary accommodation

1. The temporary accommodation of the diplomatic courier carrying a diplomatic bag shall, in principle, be inviolable. However:

(a) prompt protective action may be taken if required in case of fire or other disaster;

(b) inspection or search may be undertaken where serious grounds exist for believing that there are in the temporary accommodation articles the possession, import or export of which is prohibited by the law or controlled by the quarantine regulations of the receiving State or the transit State.

2. In the case referred to in paragraph 1 (a), measures necessary for the protection of the diplomatic bag and its inviolability shall be taken.

3. In the case referred to in paragraph 1 (b), inspection or search shall be conducted in the presence of the diplomatic courier and on condition that it be effected without infringing the inviolability either of the person of the diplomatic courier or of the diplomatic bag and would not unduly delay or impede the delivery of the diplomatic bag. The diplomatic courier shall be given the opportunity to communicate with his mission in order to invite a member of that mission to be present when the inspection or search takes place.

4. The diplomatic courier shall, to the extent practicable, inform the authorities of the receiving State or the transit State of the location of his temporary accommodation.

Article 18

Immunity from jurisdiction

1. The diplomatic courier shall enjoy immunity from the criminal jurisdiction of the receiving State or the transit State in respect of acts performed in the exercise of his functions.

2. He shall also enjoy immunity from the civil and administrative jurisdiction of the receiving State or the transit State in respect of acts performed in the exercise of his functions. This immunity shall not extend to an action for damages arising from an accident involving a vehicle the use of which may have entailed the liability of the courier to the extent that those damages are not recoverable from insurance. Pursuant to the laws and regulations of the receiving State or the transit State, the courier shall, when driving a motor vehicle, be required to have insurance coverage against third-party risks.

3. No measures of execution may be taken in respect of the diplomatic courier, except in cases where he does not enjoy immunity under paragraph 2 and provided that the measures concerned can be taken without infringing the inviolability of his person, his temporary accommodation or the diplomatic bag entrusted to him.

4. The diplomatic courier is not obliged to give evidence as a witness on matters connected with the exercise of his functions. He may, however, be required to give evidence on other matters, provided that this would not unduly delay or impede the delivery of the diplomatic bag.

5. The immunity of the diplomatic courier from the jurisdiction of the receiving State or the transit State does not exempt him from the jurisdiction of the sending State.

Article 19

Exemption from customs duties, dues and taxes

1. The receiving State or the transit State shall, in accordance with such laws and regulations as it may adopt, permit entry of articles for the personal use of the diplomatic courier carried in his personal baggage and grant exemption from all customs duties, taxes and related charges on such articles other than charges levied for specific services rendered.

2. The diplomatic courier shall, in the performance of his functions, be exempt in the receiving State or the transit State from all dues and taxes, national, regional or municipal, except for indirect taxes of a kind which are normally incorporated in the price of goods or services and charges levied for specific services rendered.

Article 20

Exemption from examination and inspection

1. The diplomatic courier shall be exempt from personal examination.

2. The personal baggage of the diplomatic courier shall be exempt from inspection, unless there are serious grounds for believing that it contains articles not for the personal use of the diplomatic courier or articles the import or export of which is prohibited by the law or controlled by the quarantine regulations of the receiving State or the transit State. An inspection in such a case shall be conducted in the presence of the diplomatic courier.

Article 21

Beginning and end of privileges and immunities

1. The diplomatic courier shall enjoy privileges and immunities from the moment he enters the territory of the receiving State or the transit State in order to perform his functions, or, if he is already in the territory of the receiving State, from the moment he begins to exercise his functions.

2. The privileges and immunities of the diplomatic courier shall cease at the moment when he leaves the territory of the receiving State or the transit State, or on the expiry of a reasonable period in which to do so. However, the privileges and immunities of the diplomatic courier ad hoc who is a resident of the receiving State shall cease at the moment when he has delivered to the consignee the diplomatic bag in his charge.

3. Notwithstanding paragraph 2, immunity shall continue to subsist with respect to acts performed by the diplomatic courier in the exercise of his functions.

Article 22

Waiver of immunities

1. The sending State may waive the immunities of the diplomatic courier.

2. The waiver shall, in all cases, be express and shall be communicated in writing to the receiving State or the transit State.

3. However, the initiation of proceedings by the diplomatic courier shall preclude him from invoking immunity from jurisdiction in respect of any counterclaim directly connected with the principal claim.

4. The waiver of immunity from jurisdiction in respect of judicial proceedings shall not be held to imply waiver of immunity in respect of the execution of the judgement or decision, for which a separate waiver shall be necessary.

5. If the sending State does not waive the immunity of the diplomatic courier in respect of a civil action, it shall use its best endeavours to bring about an equitable settlement of the case.

Article 23

Status of the captain of a ship or aircraft entrusted with the diplomatic bag

1. The captain of a ship or aircraft in commercial service which is scheduled to arrive at an authorized port of entry may be entrusted with the diplomatic bag.

2. The captain shall be provided with an official document indicating the number of packages constituting the bag entrusted to him, but he shall not be considered to be a diplomatic courier.

3. The receiving State shall permit a member of a mission, consular post or delegation of the sending State to have unimpeded access to the ship or aircraft in order to take possession of the bag directly and freely from the captain or to deliver the bag directly and freely to him.

PART III
STATUS OF THE DIPLOMATIC BAG

Article 24

Identification of the diplomatic bag

1. The packages constituting the diplomatic bag shall bear visible external marks of their character.

2. The packages constituting the diplomatic bag, if not accompanied by a diplomatic courier, shall also bear visible indications of their destination and consignee.

Article 25

Contents of the diplomatic bag

1. The diplomatic bag may contain only official correspondence, and documents or articles intended exclusively for official use.

2. The sending State shall take appropriate measures to prevent the dispatch through its diplomatic bag of items other than those referred to in paragraph 1.

Article 26

Transmission of the diplomatic bag by postal service or any mode of transport

The conditions governing the use of the postal service or of any mode of transport, established by the relevant international or national rules, shall apply to the transmission of the packages constituting the diplomatic bag in such a manner as to ensure the best possible facilities for the dispatch of the bag.

Article 27

Safe and rapid dispatch of the diplomatic bag

The receiving State or the transit State shall facilitate the safe and rapid dispatch of the diplomatic bag and shall, in particular, ensure that such dispatch is not unduly delayed or impeded by formal or technical requirements.

Article 28

Protection of the diplomatic bag

1. The diplomatic bag shall be inviolable wherever it may be; it shall not be opened or detained and shall be exempt from examination directly or through electronic or other technical devices.

2. Nevertheless, if the competent authorities of the receiving State or the transit State have serious reason to believe that the consular bag contains something other than the correspondence, documents or articles referred to in paragraph 1 of article 25, they may request that the bag be opened in their presence by an authorized representative of the sending State. If this request is refused by the authorities of the sending State, the bag shall be returned to its place of origin.

Article 29

Exemption from customs duties and taxes

The receiving State or the transit State shall, in accordance with such laws and regulations as it may adopt, permit the entry, transit and departure of the diplomatic bag and grant exemption from customs duties, taxes and related charges other than charges for storage, cartage and similar services rendered.

PART IV
MISCELLANEOUS PROVISIONS

Article 30

Protective measures in case of force majeure or other exceptional circumstances

1. Where, because of reasons of force majeure or other exceptional circumstances, the diplomatic courier, or the captain of a ship or aircraft in commercial service to whom the diplomatic bag has been entrusted, or any other member of the crew, is no longer able to maintain custody of the bag, the receiving State or the transit State shall inform the sending State of the situation and take appropriate measures with a view to ensuring the integrity and safety of the bag until the authorities of the sending State recover possession of it.

2. Where, because of reasons of force majeure or other exceptional circumstances, the diplomatic courier or the unaccompanied diplomatic bag is present in the territory of a State not initially foreseen as a transit State, that State, where aware of the situation, shall accord to the courier and the bag the protection provided for under the present articles and, in particular, extend facilities for their prompt and safe departure from its territory.

Article 31

Non-recognition of States or Governments or absence of diplomatic or consular relations

The State on whose territory an international organization has its seat or an office or a meeting of an international organ or a conference is held shall grant the facilities, privileges and immunities accorded under the present articles to the diplomatic courier and the diplomatic bag of a sending State directed to or from its mission or delegation, notwithstanding the non-recognition of one of those States or its Government by the other State or the non-existence of diplomatic or consular relations between them.

Article 32

Relationship between the present articles and other conventions and agreements

1. The present articles shall, as between Parties to them and to the conventions listed in subparagraph (1) of paragraph 1 of article 3, supplement the rules on the status of the diplomatic courier and the diplomatic bag contained in those conventions.

2. The provisions of the present articles are without prejudice to other international agreements in force as between Parties to them.

3. Nothing in the present articles shall preclude the Parties thereto from concluding international agreements relating to the status of the diplomatic courier and the diplomatic bag not accompanied by diplomatic courier, provided that such new agreements are not incompatible with the object and purpose of the present articles and do not affect the enjoyment by the other Parties to the present articles of their rights or the performance of their obligations under the present articles.

(b) Draft Optional Protocol One on the Status of the Courier and the Bag of Special Missions

The States Parties to the present Protocol and to the articles on the status of the diplomatic courier and the diplomatic bag not accompanied by diplomatic courier, hereinafter referred to as "the articles",

Have agreed as follows:

Article I

The articles also apply to a courier and a bag employed for the official communications of a State with its special missions within the meaning of the Convention on Special Missions of 8 December 1969, wherever situated, and for the official communications of those missions with the sending State or with its other missions, consular posts or delegations.

Article II

For the purposes of the articles:

(*a*) "mission" also means a special mission within the meaning of the Convention on Special Missions of 8 December 1969;

(*b*) "diplomatic courier" also means a person duly authorized by the sending State as a courier of a special mission within the meaning of the Convention on Special Missions of 8 December 1969 who is entrusted with the custody, transportation and delivery of a diplomatic bag and is employed for the official communications referred to in article I of the present Protocol;

(*c*) "diplomatic bag" also means the packages containing official correspondence, and documents or articles intended exclusively for official use, whether accompanied by a courier or not, which are used for the official communications referred to in article I of the present Protocol and which bear visible external marks of their character as a bag of a special mission within the meaning of the Convention on Special Missions of 8 December 1969.

Article III

1. The present Protocol shall, as between Parties to it and to the Convention on Special Missions of 8 December 1969, supplement the rules on the status of the diplomatic courier and the diplomatic bag contained in that Convention.

2. The provisions of the present Protocol are without prejudice to other international agreements in force as between parties to them.

3. Nothing in the present Protocol shall preclude the Parties thereto from concluding international agreements relating to the status of the diplomatic courier and the diplomatic bag not accompanied by diplomatic courier, provided that such new agreements are not incompatible with the object and purpose of the articles and do not affect the enjoyment by the other Parties to the articles of their rights or the performance of their obligations under the articles.

(c) Draft Optional Protocol Two on the Status of the Courier and the Bag of International Organizations of a Universal Character

The States Parties to the present Protocol and to the articles on the status of the diplomatic courier and the diplomatic bag not accompanied by diplomatic courier, hereinafter referred to as "the articles",

Have agreed as follows:

Article I

The articles also apply to a courier and a bag employed for the official communications of an international organization of a universal character:

(*a*) with its missions and offices, wherever situated, and for the official communications of those missions and offices with each other;

(*b*) with other international organizations of a universal character.

Article II

For the purposes of the articles:

(*a*) "diplomatic courier" also means a person duly authorized by the international organization as a courier who is entrusted with the custody, transportation and delivery of the bag and is employed for the official communications referred to in article I of the present Protocol;

(*b*) "diplomatic bag" also means the packages containing official correspondence, and documents or articles intended exclusively for official use, whether accompanied by a courier or not, which are used for the official communications referred to in article I of the present Protocol and which bear visible external marks of their character as a bag of an international organization.

Article III

1. The present Protocol shall, as between Parties to it and to the Convention on the Privileges and Immunities of the United Nations of 13 February 1946 or the Convention on the Privileges and Immunities of the Specialized Agencies of 21 November 1947, supplement the rules on the status of the diplomatic courier and the diplomatic bag contained in those Conventions.

2. The provisions of the present Protocol are without prejudice to other international agreements in force as between parties to them.

3. Nothing in the present Protocol shall preclude the Parties thereto from concluding international agreements relating to the status of the diplomatic courier and the diplomatic bag not accompanied by diplomatic courier, provided that such new agreements are not incompatible with the object and purpose of the articles and do not affect the enjoyment by the other Parties to the articles of their rights or the performance of their obligations under the articles.

8. Draft Articles on Jurisdictional Immunities of States and Their Property*

PART I

INTRODUCTION

Article 1

Scope of the present articles

The present articles apply to the immunity of a State and its property from the jurisdiction of the courts of another State.

Article 2

Use of terms

1. For the purposes of the present articles:

(*a*) "court" means any organ of a State, however named, entitled to exercise judicial functions;

(*b*) "State" means:

(i) the State and its various organs of government;

(ii) constituent units of a federal State;

(iii) political subdivisions of the State which are entitled to perform acts in the exercise of the sovereign authority of the State;

(iv) agencies or instrumentalities of the State and other entities, to the extent that they are entitled to perform acts in the exercise of the sovereign authority of the State;

(v) representatives of the State acting in that capacity;

(*c*) "commercial transaction" means:

(i) any commercial contract or transaction for the sale of goods or supply of services;

(ii) any contract for a loan or other transaction of a financial nature, including any obligation of guarantee or of indemnity in respect of any such loan or transaction;

(iii) any other contract or transaction of a commercial, industrial, trading or professional nature, but not including a contract of employment of persons.

2. In determining whether a contract or transaction is a "commercial transaction" under paragraph 1 (*c*), reference should be made primarily to the nature of the contract or transaction, but its purpose

---

* Text adopted by the Commission at its forty-third session, in 1991, and submitted to the General Assembly as a part of the Commission's report covering the work of that session. The report, which also contains commentaries on the draft articles, appears in *Yearbook of the International Law Commission, 1991*, vol. II (Part Two).

should also be taken into account if, in the practice of the State which is a party to it, that purpose is relevant to determining the non-commercial character of the contract or transaction.

3. The provisions of paragraphs 1 and 2 regarding the use of terms in the present articles are without prejudice to the use of those terms or to the meanings which may be given to them in other international instruments or in the internal law of any State.

Article 3

Privileges and immunities not affected by the present articles

1. The present articles are without prejudice to the privileges and immunities enjoyed by a State under international law in relation to the exercise of the functions of:

(*a*) its diplomatic missions, consular posts, special missions, missions to international organizations, or delegations to organs of international organizations or to international conferences; and

(*b*) persons connected with them.

2. The present articles are likewise without prejudice to privileges and immunities accorded under international law to Heads of State *ratione personae*.

Article 4

Non-retroactivity of the present articles

Without prejudice to the application of any rules set forth in the present articles to which jurisdictional immunities of States and their property are subject under international law independently of the present articles, the articles shall not apply to any question of jurisdictional immunities of States or their property arising in a proceeding instituted against a State before a court of another State prior to the entry into force of the present articles for the States concerned.

PART II
GENERAL PRINCIPLES

Article 5

State immunity

A State enjoys immunity, in respect of itself and its property, from the jurisdiction of the courts of another State subject to the provisions of the present articles.

Article 6

Modalities for giving effect to State immunity

1. A State shall give effect to State immunity under article 5 by refraining from exercising jurisdiction in a proceeding before its courts against another State and to that end shall ensure that its courts determine on their own initiative that the immunity of that other State under article 5 is respected.

2. A proceeding before a court of a State shall be considered to have been instituted against another State if that other State:

(*a*) is named as a party to that proceeding; or

(*b*) is not named as a party to the proceeding but the proceeding in effect seeks to affect the property, rights, interests or activities of that other State.

Article 7

Express consent to exercise of jurisdiction

1. A State cannot invoke immunity from jurisdiction in a proceeding before a court of another State with regard to a matter or case if it has expressly consented to the exercise of jurisdiction by the court with regard to the matter or case:

(*a*) by international agreement;

(*b*) in a written contract; or

(*c*) by a declaration before the court or by a written communication in a specific proceeding.

2. Agreement by a State for the application of the law of another State shall not be interpreted as consent to the exercise of jurisdiction by the courts of that other State.

Article 8

Effect of participation in a proceeding before a court

1. A State cannot invoke immunity from jurisdiction in a proceeding before a court of another State if it has:

(*a*) itself instituted the proceeding; or

(*b*) intervened in the proceeding or taken any other step relating to the merits. However, if the State satisfies the court that it could not have acquired knowledge of facts on which a claim to immunity can be based until after it took such a step, it can claim immunity based on those facts, provided it does so at the earliest possible moment.

2. A State shall not be considered to have consented to the exercise of jurisdiction by a court of another State if it intervenes in a proceeding or takes any other step for the sole purpose of:

(*a*) invoking immunity; or

(*b*) asserting a right or interest in property at issue in the proceeding.

3. The appearance of a representative of a State before a court of another State as a witness shall not be interpreted as consent by the former State to the exercise of jurisdiction by the court.

4. Failure on the part of a State to enter an appearance in a proceeding before a court of another State shall not be interpreted as consent by the former State to the exercise of jurisdiction by the court.

Article 9

Counterclaims

1. A State instituting a proceeding before a court of another State cannot invoke immunity from the jurisdiction of the court in respect of any counterclaim arising out of the same legal relationship or facts as the principal claim.

2. A State intervening to present a claim in a proceeding before a court of another State cannot invoke immunity from the jurisdiction of the court in respect of any counterclaim arising out of the same legal relationship or facts as the claim presented by the State.

3. A State making a counterclaim in a proceeding instituted against it before a court of another State cannot invoke immunity from the jurisdiction of the court in respect of the principal claim.

PART III
PROCEEDINGS IN WHICH STATE IMMUNITY CANNOT BE INVOKED

Article 10

Commercial transactions

1. If a State engages in a commercial transaction with a foreign natural or juridical person and, by virtue of the applicable rules of private international law, differences relating to the commercial transaction fall within the jurisdiction of a court of another State, the State cannot invoke immunity from that jurisdiction in a proceeding arising out of that commercial transaction.

2. Paragraph 1 does not apply:

(*a*) in the case of a commercial transaction between States; or

(*b*) if the parties to the commercial transaction have expressly agreed otherwise.

3. The immunity from jurisdiction enjoyed by a State shall not be affected with regard to a proceeding which relates to a commercial transaction engaged in by a State enterprise or other entity established by the State which has an independent legal personality and is capable of:

(*a*) suing or being sued; and

(*b*) acquiring, owning or possessing and disposing of property, including property which the State has authorized it to operate or manage.

Article 11

Contracts of employment

1. Unless otherwise agreed between the States concerned, a State cannot invoke immunity from jurisdiction before a court of another State which is otherwise competent in a proceeding which relates to a contract of employment between the State and an individual for work performed or to be performed, in whole or in part, in the territory of that other State.

2. Paragraph 1 does not apply if:

(*a*) the employee has been recruited to perform functions closely related to the exercise of governmental authority;

(*b*) the subject of the proceeding is the recruitment, renewal of employment or reinstatement of an individual;

(*c*) the employee was neither a national nor a habitual resident of the State of the forum at the time when the contract of employment was concluded;

(*d*) the employee is a national of the employer State at the time when the proceeding is instituted; or

(*e*) the employer State and the employee have otherwise agreed in writing, subject to any considerations of public policy conferring on the courts of the State of the forum exclusive jurisdiction by reason of the subject-matter of the proceeding.

Article 12

Personal injuries and damage to property

Unless otherwise agreed between the States concerned, a State cannot invoke immunity from jurisdiction before a court of another State which is otherwise competent in a proceeding which relates to pecuniary compensation for death or injury to the person, or damage to or loss of tangible property, caused by an act or omission which is alleged to be attributable to the State, if the act or omission occurred in whole or in part in the territory of that other State and if the author of the act or omission was present in that territory at the time of the act or omission.

Article 13

Ownership, possession and use of property

Unless otherwise agreed between the States concerned, a State cannot invoke immunity from jurisdiction before a court of another State which is otherwise competent in a proceeding which relates to the determination of:

(*a*) any right or interest of the State in, or its possession or use of, or any obligation of the State arising out of its interest in, or its possession or use of, immovable property situated in the State of the forum;

(*b*) any right or interest of the State in movable or immovable property arising by way of succession, gift or *bona vacantia*; or

(*c*) any right or interest of the State in the administration of property, such as trust property, the estate of a bankrupt or the property of a company in the event of its winding-up.

Article 14

Intellectual and industrial property

Unless otherwise agreed between the States concerned, a State cannot invoke immunity from jurisdiction before a court of another State which is otherwise competent in a proceeding which relates to:

(*a*) the determination of any right of the State in a patent, industrial design, trade name or business name, trade mark, copyright or any other form of intellectual or industrial property, which enjoys a measure of legal protection, even if provisional, in the State of the forum; or

(*b*) an alleged infringement by the State, in the territory of the State of the forum, of a right of the nature mentioned in subparagraph (*a*) which belongs to a third person and is protected in the State of the forum.

Article 15

Participation in companies or other collective bodies

1. A State cannot invoke immunity from jurisdiction before a court of another State which is otherwise competent in a proceeding which relates to its participation in a company or other collective body, whether incorporated or unincorporated, being a proceeding concerning the relationship between the State and the body or the other participants therein, provided that the body:

(*a*) has participants other than States or international organizations; and

(*b*) is incorporated or constituted under the law of the State of the forum or has its seat or principal place of business in that State.

2. A State can, however, invoke immunity from jurisdiction in such a proceeding if the States concerned have so agreed or if the parties to the dispute have so provided by an agreement in writing or if the instrument establishing or regulating the body in question contains provisions to that effect.

Article 16

Ships owned or operated by a State

1. Unless otherwise agreed between the States concerned, a State which owns or operates a ship cannot invoke immunity from jurisdiction before a court of another State which is otherwise competent in a proceeding which relates to the operation of that ship, if at the time the cause of action arose, the ship was used for other than government non-commercial purposes.

2. Paragraph 1 does not apply to warships and naval auxiliaries nor does it apply to other ships owned or operated by a State and used exclusively on government non-commercial service.

3. For the purposes of this article, "proceeding which relates to the operation of that Ship" means, inter alia, any proceeding involving the determination of a claim in respect of:

    (*a*) collision or other accidents of navigation;

    (*b*) assistance, salvage and general average;

    (*c*) repairs, supplies or other contracts relating to the ship;

    (*d*) consequences of pollution of the marine environment.

4. Unless otherwise agreed between the States concerned, a State cannot invoke immunity from jurisdiction before a court of another State which is otherwise competent in a proceeding which relates to the carriage of cargo on board a ship owned or operated by that State if, at the time the cause of action arose, the ship was used for other than government non-commercial purposes.

5. Paragraph 4 does not apply to any cargo carried on board the ships referred to in paragraph 2 nor does it apply to any cargo owned by a State and used or intended for use exclusively for government non-commercial purposes.

6. States may plead all measures of defence, prescription and limitation of liability which are available to private ships and cargoes and their owners.

7. If in a proceeding there arises a question relating to the government and non-commercial character of a ship owned or operated by a State or cargo owned by a State, a certificate signed by a diplomatic representative or other competent authority of that State and communicated to the court shall serve as evidence of the character of that ship or cargo.

Article 17

Effect of an arbitration agreement

If a State enters into an agreement in writing with a foreign natural or juridical person to submit to arbitration differences relating to a commercial transaction, that State cannot invoke immunity from jurisdiction before a court of another State which is otherwise competent in a proceeding which relates to:

(*a*) the validity or interpretation of the arbitration agreement;

(*b*) the arbitration procedure; or

(*c*) the setting aside of the award;

unless the arbitration agreement otherwise provides.

PART IV
STATE IMMUNITY FROM MEASURES OF CONSTRAINT IN CONNECTION WITH PROCEEDINGS BEFORE A COURT

Article 18

State immunity from measures of constraint

1. No measures of constraint, such as attachment, arrest and execution, against property of a State may be taken in connection with a proceeding before a court of another State unless and except to the extent that:

(*a*) the State has expressly consented to the taking of such measures as indicated:

    (i)   by international agreement;

    (ii)   by an arbitration agreement or in a written contract; or

    (iii)   by a declaration before the court or by a written communication after a dispute between the parties has arisen;

(*b*) the State has allocated or earmarked property for the satisfaction of the claim which is the object of that proceeding; or

(*c*) the property is specifically in use or intended for use by the State for other than government non-commercial purposes and is in the territory of the State of the forum and has a connection with the claim which is the object of the proceeding or with the agency or instrumentality against which the proceeding was directed.

2. Consent to the exercise of jurisdiction under article 7 shall not imply consent to the taking of measures of constraint under paragraph 1, for which separate consent shall be necessary.

Article 19

Specific categories of property

1. The following categories, in particular, of property of a State shall not be considered as property specifically in use or intended for use by the State for other than government non-commercial purposes under paragraph 1 (c) of article 18:

(*a*) property, including any bank account, which is used or intended for use for the purposes of the diplomatic mission of the State or its consular posts, special missions, missions to international organizations, or delegations to organs of international organizations or to international conferences;

(*b*) property of a military character or used or intended for use for military purposes;

(*c*) property of the central bank or other monetary authority of the State;

(*d*) property forming part of the cultural heritage of the State or part of its archives and not placed or intended to be placed on sale;

(*e*) property forming part of an exhibition of objects of scientific, cultural or historical interest and not placed or intended to be placed on sale.

2. Paragraph 1 is without prejudice to paragraph 1 (*a*) and (*b*) of article 18.

PART V
MISCELLANEOUS PROVISIONS

Article 20
Service of process

1. Service of process by writ or other document instituting a proceeding against a State shall be effected:

(*a*) in accordance with any applicable international convention binding on the State of the forum and the State concerned; or

(*b*) in the absence of such a convention:

(i) by transmission through diplomatic channels to the Ministry of Foreign Affairs of the State concerned; or

(ii) by any other means accepted by the State concerned, if not precluded by the law of the State of the forum.

2. Service of process referred to in paragraph 1 (*b*) (i) is deemed to have been effected by receipt of the documents by the Ministry of Foreign Affairs.

3. These documents shall be accompanied, if necessary, by a translation into the official language, or one of the official languages, of the State concerned.

4. Any State that enters an appearance on the merits in a proceeding instituted against it may not thereafter assert that service of process did not comply with the provisions of paragraphs 1 and 3.

Article 21
Default judgement

1. A default judgement shall not be rendered against a State unless the court has found that:

(*a*) the requirements laid down in paragraphs 1 and 3 of article 20 have been complied with;

(*b*) a period of not less than four months has expired from the date on which the service of the writ or other document instituting a proceeding has been effected or deemed to have been effected in accordance with paragraphs 1 and 2 of article 20; and

(*c*) the present articles do not preclude it from exercising jurisdiction.

2. A copy of any default judgement rendered against a State, accompanied if necessary by a translation into the official language or one of the official languages of the State concerned, shall be transmitted to it through one of the means specified in paragraph 1 of article 20 and in accordance with the provisions of that paragraph.

3. The time-limit for applying to have a default judgement set aside shall not be less than four months and shall begin to run from the date on which the copy of the judgement is received or is deemed to have been received by the State concerned.

Article 22

Privileges and immunities during court proceedings

1. Any failure or refusal by a State to comply with an order of a court of another State enjoining it to perform or refrain from performing a specific act or to produce any document or disclose any other information for the purposes of a proceeding shall entail no consequences other than those which may result from such conduct in relation to the merits of the case. In particular, no fine or penalty shall be imposed on the State by reason of such failure or refusal.

2. A State shall not be required to provide any security, bond or deposit, however described, to guarantee the payment of judicial costs or expenses in any proceeding to which it is a party before a court of another State.

9. Draft Statute for an International Criminal Court, Annex and Appendices I to III[*]

(*a*) Draft Statute for an International Criminal Court

The States Parties to this Statute,

---

[*] Text adopted by the Commission at its forty-sixth session, in 1994, and submitted to the General Assembly as a part of the Commission's report covering the work of that session. The report, which also contains commentaries on the draft articles, appears in *Yearbook of the International Law Commission, 1994*, vol. II (Part Two).

Desiring to further international cooperation to enhance the effective prosecution and suppression of crimes of international concern, and for that purpose to establish an international criminal court;

Emphasizing that such a court is intended to exercise jurisdiction only over the most serious crimes of concern to the international community as a whole;

Emphasizing further that such a court is intended to be complementary to national criminal justice systems in cases where such trial procedures may not be available or may be ineffective;

Have agreed as follows:

PART ONE
ESTABLISHMENT OF THE COURT

Article 1

The Court

There is established an International Criminal Court ("the Court"), whose jurisdiction and functioning shall be governed by the provisions of this Statute.

Article 2

Relationship of the Court to the United Nations

The President, with the approval of the States Parties to this Statute ("States Parties"), may conclude an agreement establishing an appropriate relationship between the Court and the United Nations.

Article 3

Seat of the Court

1. The seat of the Court shall be established at ... in ... ("the host State").

2. The President, with the approval of the States Parties, may conclude an agreement with the host State establishing the relationship between that State and the Court.

3. The Court may exercise its powers and functions on the territory of any State Party and, by special agreement, on the territory of any other State.

Article 4

Status and legal capacity

1. The Court is a permanent institution open to States Parties in accordance with this Statute. It shall act when required to consider a case submitted to it.

2. The Court shall enjoy in the territory of each State Party such legal capacity as may be necessary for the exercise of its functions and the fulfilment of its purposes.

Article 5

Organs of the Court

The Court consists of the following organs:

(*a*) A Presidency, as provided in article 8;

(*b*) An Appeals Chamber, Trial Chambers and other chambers, as provided in article 9;

(*c*) A Procuracy, as provided in article 12;

(*d*) A Registry, as provided in article 13.

Article 6

Qualification and election of judges

1. The judges of the Court shall be persons of high moral character, impartiality and integrity who possess the qualifications required in their respective countries for appointment to the highest judicial offices, and have, in addition:

(*a*) Criminal trial experience;

(*b*) Recognized competence in international law.

2. Each State Party may nominate for election not more than two persons, of different nationality, who possess the qualification referred to in paragraph 1 (*a*) or that referred to in paragraph 1 (*b*), and who are willing to serve as may be required on the Court.

3. Eighteen judges shall be elected by an absolute majority vote of the States Parties by secret ballot. Ten judges shall first be elected, from among the persons nominated as having the qualification referred to in paragraph 1 (*a*). Eight judges shall then be elected, from among the persons nominated as having the qualification referred to in paragraph 1 (*b*).

4. No two judges may be nationals of the same State.

5. States Parties should bear in mind in the election of the judges that the representation of the principal legal systems of the world should be assured.

6. Judges hold office for a term of nine years and, subject to paragraph 7 and article 7, paragraph 2, are not eligible for re-election. A judge shall, however, continue in office in order to complete any case the hearing of which has commenced.

7. At the first election, six judges chosen by lot shall serve for a term of three years and are eligible for re-election; six judges chosen by lot shall serve for a term of six years; and the remainder shall serve for a term of nine years.

8. Judges nominated as having the qualification referred to in paragraphs 1 (*a*) or 1 (*b*), as the case may be, shall be replaced by persons nominated as having the same qualification.

Article 7

Judicial vacancies

1. In the event of a vacancy, a replacement judge shall be elected in accordance with article 6.

2. A judge elected to fill a vacancy shall serve for the remainder of the predecessor's term, and if that period is less than five years is eligible for re-election for a further term.

Article 8

The Presidency

1. The President, the first and second Vice-Presidents and two alternate Vice-Presidents shall be elected by an absolute majority of the judges. They shall serve for a term of three years or until the end of their term of office as judges, whichever is earlier.

2. The first or second Vice-President, as the case may be, may act in place of the President in the event that the President is unavailable or disqualified. An alternate Vice-President may act in place of either Vice-President as required.

3. The President and the Vice-Presidents shall constitute the Presidency which shall be responsible for:

(*a*) The due administration of the Court;

(*b*) The other functions conferred on it by this Statute.

4. Unless otherwise indicated, pre-trial and other procedural functions conferred under this Statute on the Court may be exercised by the Presidency in any case where a chamber of the Court is not seized of the matter.

5. The Presidency may, in accordance with the Rules, delegate to one or more judges the exercise of a power vested in it under article 26, paragraphs 3, 27, paragraphs 5, 28, 29 or 30, paragraph 3, in relation to a case, during the period before a trial chamber is established for that case.

Article 9

Chambers

1. As soon as possible after each election of judges to the Court, the Presidency shall in accordance with the Rules constitute an Appeals Chamber consisting of the President and six other judges, of whom at least three shall be judges elected from among the persons nominated as having the qualification referred to in article 6, paragraph 1 (*b*). The President shall preside over the Appeals Chamber.

2. The Appeals Chamber shall be constituted for a term of three years. Members of the Appeals Chamber shall, however, continue to sit on the Chamber in order to complete any case the hearing of which has commenced.

3. Judges may be renewed as members of the Appeals Chamber for a second or subsequent term.

4. Judges not members of the Appeals Chamber shall be available to serve on Trial Chambers and other chambers required by this Statute, and to act as substitute members of the Appeals Chamber in the event that a member of that Chamber is unavailable or disqualified.

5. The Presidency shall nominate in accordance with the Rules five such judges to be members of the Trial Chamber for a given case. A Trial Chamber shall include at least three judges elected from among the persons nominated as having the qualification referred to in article 6, paragraph 1 (*a*).

6. The Rules may provide for alternate judges to be nominated to attend a trial and to act as members of the Trial Chamber in the event that a judge dies or becomes unavailable during the course of the trial.

7. No judge who is a national of a complainant State or of a State of which the accused is a national shall be a member of a chamber dealing with the case.

Article 10

Independence of the judges

1. In performing their functions, the judges shall be independent.

2. Judges shall not engage in any activity which is likely to interfere with their judicial functions or to affect confidence in their independence. In particular, they shall not while holding the office of judge be a member of the legislative or executive branches of the Government of a State, or of a body responsible for the investigation or prosecution of crimes.

3. Any question as to the application of paragraph 2 shall be decided by the Presidency.

4. On the recommendation of the Presidency, the States Parties may by a two-thirds majority decide that the workload of the Court requires that the judges should serve on a full-time basis. In that case:

(*a*) Existing judges who elect to serve on a full-time basis shall not hold any other office or employment;

(*b*) Judges subsequently elected shall not hold any other office or employment.

Article 11

Excusing and disqualification of judges

1. The Presidency at the request of a judge may excuse that judge from the exercise of a function under this Statute.

2. Judges shall not participate in any case in which they have previously been involved in any capacity or in which their impartiality might reasonably be doubted on any ground, including an actual, apparent or potential conflict of interest.

3. The Prosecutor or the accused may request the disqualification of a judge under paragraph 2.

4. Any question as to the disqualification of a judge shall be decided by an absolute majority of the members of the Chamber concerned. The challenged judge shall not take part in the decision.

Article 12

The Procuracy

1. The Procuracy is an independent organ of the Court responsible for the investigation of complaints brought in accordance with this Statute and for the conduct of prosecutions. A member of the Procuracy shall not seek or act on instructions from any external source.

2. The Procuracy shall be headed by the Prosecutor, assisted by one or more Deputy Prosecutors, who may act in place of the Prosecutor in the event that the Prosecutor is unavailable. The Prosecutor and the Deputy Prosecutors shall be of different nationalities. The Prosecutor may appoint such other qualified staff as may be required.

3. The Prosecutor and Deputy Prosecutors shall be persons of high moral character and have high competence and experience in the prosecution of criminal cases. They shall be elected by secret ballot by an absolute majority of the States Parties, from among candidates nominated by States Parties. Unless a shorter term is otherwise decided on at the time of their election, they shall hold office for a term of five years and are eligible for re-election.

4. The States Parties may elect the Prosecutor and Deputy Prosecutors on the basis that they are willing to serve as required.

5. The Prosecutor and Deputy Prosecutors shall not act in relation to a complaint involving a person of their own nationality.

6. The Presidency may excuse the Prosecutor or a Deputy Prosecutor at their request from acting in a particular case, and shall decide any question raised in a particular case as to the disqualification of the Prosecutor or a Deputy Prosecutor.

7. The staff of the Procuracy shall be subject to Staff Regulations drawn up by the Prosecutor.

Article 13

The Registry

1. On the proposal of the Presidency, the judges by an absolute majority by secret ballot shall elect a Registrar, who shall be the principal administrative officer of the Court. They may in the same manner elect a Deputy Registrar.

2. The Registrar shall hold office for a term of five years, is eligible for re-election and shall be available on a full-time basis. The Deputy Registrar shall hold office for a term of five years or such shorter term as may be decided on, and may be elected on the basis that the Deputy Registrar is willing to serve as required.

3. The Presidency may appoint or authorize the Registrar to appoint such other staff of the Registry as may be necessary.

4. The staff of the Registry shall be subject to Staff Regulations drawn up by the Registrar.

Article 14

Solemn undertaking

Before first exercising their functions under this Statute, judges and other officers of the Court shall make a public and solemn undertaking to do so impartially and conscientiously.

Article 15

Loss of office

1. A judge, the Prosecutor or other officer of the Court who is found to have committed misconduct or a serious breach of this Statute, or to be unable to exercise the functions required by this Statute because of long-term illness or disability, shall cease to hold office.

2. A decision as to the loss of office under paragraph 1 shall be made by secret ballot:

   (*a*) In the case of the Prosecutor or a Deputy Prosecutor, by an absolute majority of the States Parties;

   (*b*) In any other case, by a two-thirds majority of the judges.

3. The judge, the Prosecutor or any other officer whose conduct or fitness for office is impugned shall have full opportunity to present evidence and to make submissions but shall not otherwise participate in the discussion of the question.

Article 16

Privileges and immunities

1. The judges, the Prosecutor, the Deputy Prosecutors and the staff of the Procuracy, the Registrar and the Deputy Registrar shall enjoy the privileges, immunities and facilities of a diplomatic agent within

the meaning of the Vienna Convention on Diplomatic Relations of 16 April 1961.

2. The staff of the Registry shall enjoy the privileges, immunities and facilities necessary to the performance of their functions.

3. Counsel, experts and witnesses before the Court shall enjoy the privileges and immunities necessary to the independent exercise of their duties.

4. The judges may by an absolute majority decide to revoke a privilege or waive an immunity conferred by this article, other than an immunity of a judge, the Prosecutor or Registrar as such. In the case of other officers and staff of the Procuracy or Registry, they may do so only on the recommendation of the Prosecutor or Registrar, as the case may be.

Article 17

Allowances and expenses

1. The President shall receive an annual allowance.

2. The Vice-Presidents shall receive a special allowance for each day they exercise the functions of the President.

3. Subject to paragraph 4, the judges shall receive a daily allowance during the period in which they exercise their functions. They may continue to receive a salary payable in respect of another position occupied by them consistently with article 10.

4. If it is decided under article 10, paragraph 4, that judges shall thereafter serve on a full-time basis, existing judges who elect to serve on a full-time basis, and all judges subsequently elected, shall be paid a salary.

Article 18

Working languages

The working languages of the Court shall be English and French.

Article 19

Rules of the Court

1. Subject to paragraphs 2 and 3, the judges may by an absolute majority make rules for the functioning of the Court in accordance with this Statute, including rules regulating:

(a) The conduct of investigations;

(b) The procedure to be followed and the rules of evidence to be applied;

(c) Any other matter which is necessary for the implementation of this Statute.

2. The initial Rules of the Court shall be drafted by the judges within six months of the first elections for the Court, and submitted to a

conference of States Parties for approval. The judges may decide that a rule subsequently made under paragraph 1 should also be submitted to a conference of States Parties for approval.

3. In any case to which paragraph 2 does not apply, rules made under paragraph 1 shall be transmitted to States Parties and may be confirmed by the Presidency unless, within six months after transmission, a majority of States Parties have communicated in writing their objections.

4. A rule may provide for its provisional application in the period prior to its approval or confirmation. A rule not approved or confirmed shall lapse.

PART THREE

JURISDICTION OF THE COURT

Article 20

Crimes within the jurisdiction of the Court

The Court has jurisdiction in accordance with this Statute with respect to the following crimes:

(*a*) The crime of genocide;

(*b*) The crime of aggression;

(*c*) Serious violations of the laws and customs applicable in armed conflict;

(*d*) Crimes against humanity;

(*e*) Crimes, established under or pursuant to the treaty provisions listed in the Annex, which, having regard to the conduct alleged, constitute exceptionally serious crimes of international concern.

Article 21

Preconditions to the exercise of jurisdiction

1. The Court may exercise its jurisdiction over a person with respect to a crime referred to in article 20 if:

(*a*) In a case of genocide, a complaint is brought under article 25, paragraph 1;

(*b*) In any other case, a complaint is brought under article 25, paragraph 2, and the jurisdiction of the Court with respect to the crime is accepted under article 22:

(i) By the State which has custody of the suspect with respect to the crime ("the custodial State");

(ii) By the State on the territory of which the act or omission in question occurred.

2. If, with respect to a crime to which paragraph 1 (*b*) applies, the custodial State has received, under an international agreement, a request from another State to surrender a suspect for the purposes of

prosecution, then, unless the request is rejected, the acceptance by the requesting State of the Court's jurisdiction with respect to the crime is also required.

Article 22

Acceptance of the jurisdiction of the Court
for the purposes of article 21

1. A State Party to this Statute may:

(*a*) At the time it expresses its consent to be bound by the Statute, by declaration lodged with the depositary; or

(*b*) At a later time, by declaration lodged with the Registrar;

accept the jurisdiction of the Court with respect to such of the crimes referred to in article 20 as it specifies in the declaration.

2. A declaration may be of general application, or may be limited to particular conduct or to conduct committed during a particular period of time.

3. A declaration may be made for a specified period, in which case it may not be withdrawn before the end of that period, or for an unspecified period, in which case it may be withdrawn only upon giving six months' notice of withdrawal to the Registrar. Withdrawal does not affect proceedings already commenced under this Statute.

4. If under article 21 the acceptance of a State which is not a party to this Statute is required, that State may, by declaration lodged with the Registrar, consent to the Court exercising jurisdiction with respect to the crime.

Article 23

Action by the Security Council

1. Notwithstanding article 21, the Court has jurisdiction in accordance with this Statute with respect to crimes referred to in article 20 as a consequence of the referral of a matter to the Court by the Security Council acting under Chapter VII of the Charter of the United Nations.

2. A complaint of or directly related to an act of aggression may not be brought under this Statute unless the Security Council has first determined that a State has committed the act of aggression which is the subject of the complaint.

3. No prosecution may be commenced under this Statute arising from a situation which is being dealt with by the Security Council as a threat to or breach of the peace or an act of aggression under Chapter VII of the Charter, unless the Security Council otherwise decides.

Article 24

Duty of the Court as to jurisdiction

The Court shall satisfy itself that it has jurisdiction in any case brought before it.

PART FOUR
INVESTIGATION AND PROSECUTION

Article 25

Complaint

1. A State Party which is also a Contracting Party to the Convention on the Prevention and Punishment of the Crime of Genocide of 9 December 1948 may lodge a complaint with the Prosecutor alleging that a crime of genocide appears to have been committed.

2. A State Party which accepts the jurisdiction of the Court under article 22 with respect to a crime may lodge a complaint with the Prosecutor alleging that such a crime appears to have been committed.

3. As far as possible a complaint shall specify the circumstances of the alleged crime and the identity and whereabouts of any suspect, and be accompanied by such supporting documentation as is available to the complainant State.

4. In a case to which article 23, paragraph 1, applies, a complaint is not required for the initiation of an investigation.

Article 26

Investigation of alleged crimes

1. On receiving a complaint or upon notification of a decision of the Security Council referred to in article 23, paragraph 1, the Prosecutor shall initiate an investigation unless the Prosecutor concludes that there is no possible basis for a prosecution under this Statute and decides not to initiate an investigation, in which case the Prosecutor shall so inform the Presidency.

2. The Prosecutor may:

   (*a*) Request the presence of and question suspects, victims and witnesses;

   (*b*) Collect documentary and other evidence;

   (*c*) Conduct on-site investigations;

   (*d*) Take necessary measures to ensure the confidentiality of information or the protection of any person;

   (*e*) As appropriate, seek the cooperation of any State or of the United Nations.

3. The Presidency may, at the request of the Prosecutor, issue such subpoenas and warrants as may be required for the purposes of an investigation, including a warrant under article 28, paragraph 1, for the provisional arrest of a suspect.

4. If, upon investigation and having regard, inter alia, to the matters referred to in article 35, the Prosecutor concludes that there is no sufficient basis for a prosecution under this Statute and decides not to file an indictment, the Prosecutor shall so inform the Presidency giving details of the nature and basis of the complaint and of the reasons for not filing an indictment.

5. At the request of a complainant State or, in a case to which article 23, paragraph 1, applies, at the request of the Security Council, the Presidency shall review a decision of the Prosecutor not to initiate an investigation or not to file an indictment, and may request the Prosecutor to reconsider the decision.

6. A person suspected of a crime under this Statute shall:

(*a*) Prior to being questioned, be informed that the person is a suspect and of the rights:

(i) To remain silent, without such silence being a consideration in the determination of guilt or innocence;

(ii) To have the assistance of counsel of the suspect's choice or, if the suspect lacks the means to retain counsel, to have legal assistance assigned by the Court;

(*b*) Not be compelled to testify or to confess guilt;

(*c*) If questioned in a language other than a language the suspect understands and speaks, be provided with competent interpretation services and with a translation of any document on which the suspect is to be questioned.

Article 27

Commencement of prosecution

1. If upon investigation the Prosecutor concludes that there is a prima facie case, the Prosecutor shall file with the Registrar an indictment containing a concise statement of the allegations of fact and of the crime or crimes with which the suspect is charged.

2. The Presidency shall examine the indictment and any supporting material and determine:

(*a*) Whether a prima facie case exists with respect to a crime within the jurisdiction of the Court; and

(*b*) Whether, having regard, inter alia, to the matters referred to in article 35, the case should on the information available be heard by the Court.

If so, it shall confirm the indictment and establish a trial chamber in accordance with article 9.

3. If, after any adjournment that may be necessary to allow additional material to be produced, the Presidency decides not to confirm the indictment, it shall so inform the complainant State or, in a case to which article 23, paragraph 1, applies, the Security Council.

4. The Presidency may at the request of the Prosecutor amend the indictment, in which case it shall make any necessary orders to ensure that the accused is notified of the amendment and has adequate time to prepare a defence.

5. The Presidency may make any further orders required for the conduct of the trial, including an order:

(*a*) Determining the language or languages to be used during the trial;

(*b*) Requiring the disclosure to the defence, within a sufficient time before the trial to enable the preparation of the defence, of documentary or other evidence available to the Prosecutor, whether or not the Prosecutor intends to rely on that evidence;

(*c*) Providing for the exchange of information between the Prosecutor and the defence, so that both parties are sufficiently aware of the issues to be decided at the trial;

(*d*) Providing for the protection of the accused, victims and witnesses and of confidential information.

Article 28

Arrest

1. At any time after an investigation has been initiated, the Presidency may at the request of the Prosecutor issue a warrant for the provisional arrest of a suspect if:

(*a*) There is probable cause to believe that the suspect may have committed a crime within the jurisdiction of the Court; and

(*b*) The suspect may not be available to stand trial unless provisionally arrested.

2. A suspect who has been provisionally arrested is entitled to release from arrest if the indictment has not been confirmed within 90 days of the arrest, or such longer time as the Presidency may allow.

3. As soon as practicable after the confirmation of the indictment, the Prosecutor shall seek from the Presidency a warrant for the arrest and transfer of the accused. The Presidency shall issue such a warrant unless it is satisfied that:

(*a*) The accused will voluntarily appear for trial; or

(*b*) There are special circumstances making it unnecessary for the time being to issue the warrant.

4. A person arrested shall be informed at the time of arrest of the reasons for the arrest and shall be promptly informed of any charges.

Article 29

Pre-trial detention or release

1. A person arrested shall be brought promptly before a judicial officer of the State where the arrest occurred. The judicial officer shall determine, in accordance with the procedures applicable in that State, that the warrant has been duly served and that the rights of the accused have been respected.

2. A person arrested may apply to the Presidency for release pending trial. The Presidency may release the person unconditionally or on bail if it is satisfied that the accused will appear at the trial.

3. A person arrested may apply to the Presidency for a determination of the lawfulness under this Statute of the arrest or detention. If the Presidency decides that the arrest or detention was unlawful, it shall order the release of the accused, and may award compensation.

4. A person arrested shall be held, pending trial or release on bail, in an appropriate place of detention in the arresting State, in the State in which the trial is to be held or if necessary, in the host State.

Article 30

Notification of the indictment

1. The Prosecutor shall ensure that a person who has been arrested is personally served, as soon as possible after being taken into custody, with certified copies of the following documents, in a language understood by that person:

   (*a*) In the case of a suspect provisionally arrested, a statement of the grounds for the arrest;

   (*b*) In any other case, the confirmed indictment;

   (*c*) A statement of the accused's rights under this Statute.

2. In any case to which paragraph 1 (*a*) applies, the indictment shall be served on the accused as soon as possible after it has been confirmed.

3. If, 60 days after the indictment has been confirmed, the accused is not in custody pursuant to a warrant issued under article 28, paragraph 3, or for some reason the requirements of paragraph 1 cannot be complied with, the Presidency may on the application of the Prosecutor prescribe some other manner of bringing the indictment to the attention of the accused.

Article 31

Persons made available to assist in a prosecution

1. The Prosecutor may request a State Party to make persons available to assist in a prosecution in accordance with paragraph 2.

2. Such persons should be available for the duration of the prosecution, unless otherwise agreed. They shall serve at the direction

of the Prosecutor, and shall not seek or receive instructions from any Government or source other than the Prosecutor in relation to their exercise of functions under this article.

3. The terms and conditions on which persons may be made available under this article shall be approved by the Presidency on the recommendation of the Prosecutor.

PART FIVE

THE TRIAL

Article 32

Place of trial

Unless otherwise decided by the Presidency, the place of the trial will be the seat of the Court.

Article 33

Applicable law

The Court shall apply:

(*a*) This Statute;

(*b*) Applicable treaties and the principles and rules of general international law;

(*c*) To the extent applicable, any rule of national law.

Article 34

Challenges to jurisdiction

Challenges to the jurisdiction of the Court may be made, in accordance with the Rules:

(*a*) Prior to or at the commencement of the hearing, by an accused or any interested State; and

(*b*) At any later stage of the trial, by an accused.

Article 35

Issues of admissibility

The Court may, on application by the accused or at the request of an interested State at any time prior to the commencement of the trial, or of its own motion, decide, having regard to the purposes of this Statute set out in the preamble, that a case before it is inadmissible on the ground that the crime in question:

(*a*) Has been duly investigated by a State with jurisdiction over it, and the decision of that State not to proceed to a prosecution is apparently well-founded;

(*b*) Is under investigation by a State which has or may have jurisdiction over it, and there is no reason for the Court to take any further action for the time being with respect to the crime; or (*c*) Is not of such gravity to justify further action by the Court.

Article 36

Procedure under articles 34 and 35

1. In proceedings under articles 34 and 35, the accused and the complainant State have the right to be heard.

2. Proceedings under articles 34 and 35 shall be decided by the Trial Chamber, unless it considers, having regard to the importance of the issues involved, that the matter should be referred to the Appeals Chamber.

Article 37

Trial in the presence of the accused

1. As a general rule, the accused should be present during the trial.

2. The Trial Chamber may order that the trial proceed in the absence of the accused if:

(*a*) The accused is in custody, or has been released pending trial, and for reasons of security or the ill-health of the accused it is undesirable for the accused to be present;

(*b*) The accused is continuing to disrupt the trial; or

(*c*) The accused has escaped from lawful custody under this Statute or has broken bail.

3. The Chamber shall, if it makes an order under paragraph 2, ensure that the rights of the accused under this Statute are respected, and in particular:

(*a*) That all reasonable steps have been taken to inform the accused of the charge; and

(*b*) That the accused is legally represented, if necessary by a lawyer appointed by the Court.

4. In cases where a trial cannot be held because of the deliberate absence of an accused, the Court may establish, in accordance with the Rules, an Indictment Chamber for the purpose of:

(*a*) Recording the evidence;

(*b*) Considering whether the evidence establishes a prima facie case of a crime within the jurisdiction of the Court; and

(*c*) Issuing and publishing a warrant of arrest in respect of an accused against whom a prima facie case is established.

5. If the accused is subsequently tried under this Statute:

(*a*) The record of evidence before the Indictment Chamber shall be admissible;

(*b*) Any judge who was a member of the Indictment Chamber may not be a member of the Trial Chamber.

Article 38

Functions and powers of the Trial Chamber

1. At the commencement of the trial, the Trial Chamber shall:

   (*a*) Have the indictment read;

   (*b*) Ensure that articles 27, paragraph 5 (*b*), and 30 have been complied with sufficiently in advance of the trial to enable adequate preparation of the defence;

   (*c*) Satisfy itself that the other rights of the accused under this Statute have been respected; and

   (*d*) Allow the accused to enter a plea of guilty or not guilty.

2. The Chamber shall ensure that a trial is fair and expeditious and is conducted in accordance with this Statute and the Rules, with full respect for the rights of the accused and due regard for the protection of victims and witnesses.

3. The Chamber may, subject to the Rules, hear charges against more than one accused arising out of the same factual situation.

4. The trial shall be held in public, unless the Chamber determines that certain proceedings be in closed session in accordance with article 43, or for the purpose of protecting confidential or sensitive information which is to be given in evidence.

5. The Chamber shall, subject to this Statute and the Rules have, *inter alia*, the power on the application of a party or of its own motion, to:

   (*a*) Issue a warrant for the arrest and transfer of an accused who is not already in the custody of the Court;

   (*b*) Require the attendance and testimony of witnesses;

   (*c*) Require the production of documentary and other evidentiary materials;

   (*d*) Rule on the admissibility or relevance of evidence;

   (*e*) Protect confidential information;

   (*f*) Maintain order in the course of a hearing.

6. The Chamber shall ensure that a complete record of the trial, which accurately reflects the proceedings, is maintained and preserved by the Registrar.

Article 39

Principle of legality *(*nullum crimen sine lege*)*

An accused shall not be held guilty:

   (*a*) In the case of a prosecution with respect to a crime referred to in article 20, subparagraphs (*a*) to (*d*), unless the act or omission in question constituted a crime under international law;

(b) In the case of a prosecution with respect to a crime referred to in article 20, subparagraph (e), unless the treaty in question was applicable to the conduct of the accused;

at the time the act or omission occurred.

Article 40

Presumption of innocence

An accused shall be presumed innocent until proved guilty in accordance with the law. The onus is on the Prosecutor to establish the guilt of the accused beyond reasonable doubt.

Article 41

Rights of the accused

1. In the determination of any charge under this Statute, the accused is entitled to a fair and public hearing, subject to article 43, and to the following minimum guarantees:

(a) To be informed promptly and in detail, in a language which the accused understands, of the nature and cause of the charge;

(b) To have adequate time and facilities for the preparation of the defence, and to communicate with counsel of the accused's choosing;

(c) To be tried without undue delay;

(d) Subject to article 37, paragraph 2, to be present at the trial, to conduct the defence in person or through legal assistance of the accused's choosing, to be informed, if the accused does not have legal assistance, of this right and to have legal assistance assigned by the Court, without payment if the accused lacks sufficient means to pay for such assistance;

(e) To examine, or have examined, the prosecution witnesses and to obtain the attendance and examination of witnesses for the defence under the same conditions as witnesses for the prosecution;

(f) If any of the proceedings of or documents presented to the Court are not in a language the accused understands and speaks, to have, free of any cost, the assistance of a competent interpreter and such translations as are necessary to meet the requirements of fairness;

(g) Not to be compelled to testify or to confess guilt.

2. Exculpatory evidence that becomes available to the Procuracy prior to the conclusion of the trial shall be made available to the defence. In case of doubt as to the application of this paragraph or as to the admissibility of the evidence, the Trial Chamber shall decide.

Article 42

Non bis in idem

1. No person shall be tried before any other court for acts constituting a crime of the kind referred to in article 20 for which that person has already been tried by the Court.

2. A person who has been tried by another court for acts constituting a crime of the kind referred to in article 20 may be tried under this Statute only if:

(*a*) The acts in question were characterized by that court as an ordinary crime and not as a crime which is within the jurisdiction of the Court; or

(*b*) The proceedings in the other court were not impartial or independent or were designed to shield the accused from international criminal responsibility or the case was not diligently prosecuted.

3. In considering the penalty to be imposed on a person convicted under this Statute, the Court shall take into account the extent to which a penalty imposed by another court on the same person for the same act has already been served.

Article 43

Protection of the accused, victims and witnesses

The Court shall take necessary measures available to it to protect the accused, victims and witnesses and may to that end conduct closed proceedings or allow the presentation of evidence by electronic or other special means.

Article 44

Evidence

1. Before testifying, each witness shall, in accordance with the Rules, give an undertaking as to the truthfulness of the evidence to be given by that witness.

2. States Parties shall extend their laws of perjury to cover evidence given under this Statute by their nationals, and shall cooperate with the Court in investigating and where appropriate prosecuting any case of suspected perjury.

3. The Court may require to be informed of the nature of any evidence before it is offered so that it may rule on its relevance or admissibility.

4. The Court shall not require proof of facts of common knowledge but may take judicial notice of them.

5. Evidence obtained by means of a serious violation of this Statute or of other rules of international law shall not be admissible.

Article 45

Quorum and judgement

1. At least four members of the Trial Chamber must be present at each stage of the trial.

2. The decisions of the Trial Chamber shall be taken by a majority of the judges. At least three judges must concur in a decision as to conviction or acquittal and as to the sentence to be imposed.

3. If after sufficient time for deliberation a Chamber which has been reduced to four judges is unable to agree on a decision, it may order a new trial.

4. The deliberations of the Court shall be and remain secret.

5. The judgement shall be in writing and shall contain a full and reasoned statement of the findings and conclusions. It shall be the sole judgement issued, and shall be delivered in open court.

Article 46

Sentencing

1. In the event of a conviction, the Trial Chamber shall hold a further hearing to hear any evidence relevant to sentence, to allow the Prosecutor and the defence to make submissions and to consider the appropriate sentence to be imposed.

2. In imposing sentence, the Trial Chamber should take into account such factors as the gravity of the crime and the individual circumstances of the convicted person.

Article 47

Applicable penalties

1. The Court may impose on a person convicted of a crime under this Statute one or more of the following penalties:

   (a) A term of life imprisonment, or of imprisonment for a specified number of years;

   (b) A fine.

2. In determining the length of a term of imprisonment or the amount of a fine to be imposed, the Court may have regard to the penalties provided for by the law of:

   (a) The State of which the convicted person is a national;

   (b) The State where the crime was committed;

   (c) The State which had custody of and jurisdiction over the accused.

3. Fines paid may be transferred, by order of the Court, to one or more of the following:

   (a) The Registrar, to defray the costs of the trial;

   (b) A State of which the nationals were the victims of the crime;

(*c*) A trust fund established by the Secretary-General of the United Nations for the benefit of victims of crime.

PART SIX

APPEAL AND REVIEW

Article 48

Appeal against judgement or sentence

1. The Prosecutor and the convicted person may, in accordance with the Rules, appeal against a decision under articles 45 or 47 on grounds of procedural error, error of fact or of law, or disproportion between the crime and the sentence.

2. Unless the Trial Chamber otherwise orders, a convicted person shall remain in custody pending an appeal.

Article 49

Proceedings on appeal

1. The Appeals Chamber has all the powers of the Trial Chamber.

2. If the Appeals Chamber finds that the proceedings appealed from were unfair or that the decision is vitiated by error of fact or law, it may:

(*a*) If the appeal is brought by the convicted person, reverse or amend the decision, or, if necessary, order a new trial;

(*b*) If the appeal is brought by the Prosecutor against an acquittal, order a new trial.

3. If in an appeal against sentence the Chamber finds that the sentence is manifestly disproportionate to the crime, it may vary the sentence in accordance with article 47.

4. The decision of the Chamber shall be taken by a majority of the judges, and shall be delivered in open court. Six judges constitute a quorum.

5. Subject to article 50, the decision of the Chamber shall be final.

Article 50

Revision

1. The convicted person or the Prosecutor may, in accordance with the Rules, apply to the Presidency for revision of a conviction on the ground that evidence has been discovered which was not available to the applicant at the time the conviction was pronounced or affirmed and which could have been a decisive factor in the conviction.

2. The Presidency shall request the Prosecutor or the convicted person, as the case may be, to present written observations on whether the application should be accepted.

341

3. If the Presidency is of the view that the new evidence could lead to the revision of the conviction, it may:

   (*a*) Reconvene the Trial Chamber;

   (*b*) Constitute a new Trial Chamber; or

   (*c*) Refer the matter to the Appeals Chamber;

with a view to the Chamber determining, after hearing the parties, whether the new evidence should lead to a revision of the conviction.

PART SEVEN

INTERNATIONAL COOPERATION AND JUDICIAL ASSISTANCE

Article 51

Cooperation and judicial assistance

1. States Parties shall cooperate with the Court in connection with criminal investigations and proceedings under this Statute.

2. The Registrar may transmit to any State a request for cooperation and judicial assistance with respect to a crime, including, but not limited to:

   (*a*) The identification and location of persons;

   (*b*) The taking of testimony and the production of evidence;

   (*c*) The service of documents;

   (*d*) The arrest or detention of persons;

   (*e*) Any other request which may facilitate the administration of justice, including provisional measures as required.

3. Upon receipt of a request under paragraph 2:

   (*a*) In a case covered by article 21, paragraph 1 (a), all States Parties;

   (*b*) In any other case, States Parties which have accepted the jurisdiction of the Court with respect to the crime in question;

shall respond without undue delay to the request.

Article 52

Provisional measures

1. In case of need, the Court may request a State to take necessary provisional measures, including the following:

   (*a*) To provisionally arrest a suspect;

   (*b*) To seize documents or other evidence; or

   (*c*) To prevent injury to or the intimidation of a witness or the destruction of evidence.

2. The Court shall follow up a request under paragraph 1 by providing, as soon as possible and in any case within 28 days, a formal request for assistance complying with article 57.

Article 53

Transfer of an accused to the Court

1. The Registrar shall transmit to any State on the territory of which the accused may be found a warrant for the arrest and transfer of an accused issued under article 28, and shall request the cooperation of that State in the arrest and transfer of the accused.

2. Upon receipt of a request under paragraph 1:

   (a) All States Parties:

       (i) In a case covered by article 21, paragraph 1 (a); or

       (ii) Which have accepted the jurisdiction of the Court with respect to the crime in question;

   shall, subject to paragraphs 5 and 6, take immediate steps to arrest and transfer the accused to the Court;

   (b) In the case of a crime to which article 20, subparagraph (e), applies, a State Party which is a party to the treaty in question but which has not accepted the Court's jurisdiction with respect to that crime shall, if it decides not to transfer the accused to the Court, forthwith take all necessary steps to extradite the accused to a requesting State or refer the case to its competent authorities for the purpose of prosecution;

   (c) In any other case, a State Party shall consider whether it can, in accordance with its legal procedures, take steps to arrest and transfer the accused to the Court, or whether it should take steps to extradite the accused to a requesting State or refer the case to its competent authorities for the purpose of prosecution.

3. The transfer of an accused to the Court constitutes, as between States Parties which accept the jurisdiction of the Court with respect to the crime, sufficient compliance with a provision of any treaty requiring that a suspect be extradited or the case referred to the competent authorities of the requested State for the purpose of prosecution.

4. A State Party which accepts the jurisdiction of the Court with respect to the crime shall, as far as possible, give priority to a request under paragraph 1 over requests for extradition from other States.

5. A State Party may delay complying with paragraph 2 if the accused is in its custody or control and is being proceeded against for a serious crime, or serving a sentence imposed by a court for a crime. It shall within 45 days of receiving the request inform the Registrar of the reasons for the delay. In such cases, the requested State:

   (a) May agree to the temporary transfer of the accused for the purpose of standing trial under this Statute; or (*b*) Shall comply with paragraph 2 after the prosecution has been completed or abandoned or the sentence has been served, as the case may be.

6. A State Party may, within 45 days of receiving a request under paragraph 1, file a written application with the Registrar requesting the Court to set aside the request on specified grounds. Pending a decision of the Court on the application, the State concerned may delay complying with paragraph 2 but shall take any provisional measures necessary to ensure that the accused remains in its custody or control.

Article 54

Obligation to extradite or prosecute

In a case of a crime referred to in article 20, subparagraph (*e*), a custodial State Party to this Statute which is a party to the treaty in question but which has not accepted the Court's jurisdiction with respect to the crime for the purposes of article 21, paragraph 1 (*b*) (i), shall either take all necessary steps to extradite the suspect to a requesting State for the purpose of prosecution or refer the case to its competent authorities for that purpose.

Article 55

Rule of speciality

1. A person transferred to the Court under article 53 shall not be subject to prosecution or punishment for any crime other than that for which the person was transferred.

2. Evidence provided under this Part shall not, if the State when providing it so requests, be used as evidence for any purpose other than that for which it was provided, unless this is necessary to preserve the right of an accused under article 41, paragraph 2.

3. The Court may request the State concerned to waive the requirements of paragraphs 1 or 2, for the reasons and purposes specified in the request.

Article 56

Cooperation with States not parties to this Statute

States not parties to this Statute may assist in relation to the matters referred to in this Part on the basis of comity, a unilateral declaration, an ad hoc arrangement or other agreement with the Court.

Article 57

Communications and documentation

1. Requests under this Part shall be in writing, or be forthwith reduced to writing, and shall be between the competent national

authority and the Registrar. States Parties shall inform the Registrar of the name and address of their national authority for this purpose.

2. When appropriate, communications may also be made through the International Criminal Police Organization.

3. A request under this Part shall include the following, as applicable:

(*a*) A brief statement of the purpose of the request and of the assistance sought, including the legal basis and grounds for the request;

(*b*) Information concerning the person who is the subject of the request on the evidence sought, in sufficient detail to enable identification;

(*c*) A brief description of the essential facts underlying the request; and

(*d*) Information concerning the complaint or charge to which the request relates and of the basis for the Court's jurisdiction.

4. A requested State which considers the information provided insufficient to enable the request to be complied with may seek further particulars.

PART EIGHT
ENFORCEMENT

Article 58

Recognition of judgements

States Parties undertake to recognize the judgements of the Court.

Article 59

Enforcement of sentences

1. A sentence of imprisonment shall be served in a State designated by the Court from a list of States which have indicated to the Court their willingness to accept convicted persons.

2. If no State is designated under paragraph 1, the sentence of imprisonment shall be served in a prison facility made available by the host State.

3. A sentence of imprisonment shall be subject to the supervision of the Court in accordance with the Rules.

Article 60

Pardon, parole and commutation of sentences

1. If, under a generally applicable law of the State of imprisonment, a person in the same circumstances who had been convicted for the same conduct by a court of that State would be eligible for pardon, parole or commutation of sentence, the State shall so notify the Court.

2. If a notification has been given under paragraph 1, the prisoner may apply to the Court in accordance with the Rules, seeking an order for pardon, parole or commutation of the sentence.

3. If the Presidency decides that an application under paragraph 2 is apparently well-founded, it shall convene a Chamber of five judges to consider and decide whether in the interests of justice the person convicted should be pardoned or paroled or the sentence commuted, and on what basis.

4. When imposing a sentence of imprisonment, a Chamber may stipulate that the sentence is to be served in accordance with specified laws as to pardon, parole or commutation of sentence of the State of imprisonment. The consent of the Court is not required to subsequent action by that State in conformity with those laws, but the Court shall be given at least 45 days' notice of any decision which might materially affect the terms or extent of the imprisonment.

5. Except as provided in paragraphs 3 and 4, a person serving a sentence imposed by the Court is not to be released before the expiry of the sentence.

(b) Annex
Crimes pursuant to treaties (see art. 20, subpara. (*e*))

1. Grave breaches of:

(*a*) The Geneva Convention for the Amelioration of the Condition of the Wounded and Sick in Armed Forces in the Field of 12 August 1949, as defined by article 50 of that Convention;

(*b*) The Geneva Convention for the Amelioration of the Condition of Wounded, Sick and Shipwrecked Members of Armed Forces at Sea of 12 August 1949, as defined by article 51 of that Convention;

(*c*) The Geneva Convention relative to the Treatment of Prisoners of War of 12 August 1949, as defined by article 130 of that Convention;

(*d*) The Geneva Convention relative to the Protection of Civilian Persons in Time of War of 12 August 1949, as defined by article 147 of that Convention;

(*e*) Protocol Additional to the Geneva Conventions of 12 August 1949, and relating to the protection of victims of international armed conflicts (Protocol I) of 8 June 1977, as defined by article 85 of that Protocol.

2. The unlawful seizure of aircraft as defined by article 1 of the Convention for the Suppression of Unlawful Seizure of Aircraft of 16 December 1970.

3. The crimes defined by article 1 of the Convention for the Suppression of Unlawful Acts against the Safety of Civil Aviation of 23 September 1971.

4. Apartheid and related crimes as defined by article II of the International Convention on the Suppression and Punishment of the Crime of Apartheid of 30 November 1973.

5. The crimes defined by article 2 of the Convention on the Prevention and Punishment of Crimes against Internationally Protected Persons, including Diplomatic Agents of 14 December 1973.

6. Hostage-taking and related crimes as defined by article 1 of the International Convention against the Taking of Hostages of 17 December 1979.

7. The crime of torture made punishable pursuant to article 4 of the Convention against Torture and Other Cruel, Inhuman or Degrading Treatment or Punishment of 10 December 1984.

8. The crimes defined by article 3 of the Convention for the Suppression of Unlawful Acts against the Safety of Maritime Navigation and by article 2 of the Protocol for the Suppression of Unlawful Acts against the Safety of Fixed Platforms located on the Continental Shelf, both of 10 March 1988.

9. Crimes involving illicit traffic in narcotic drugs and psychotropic substances as envisaged by article 3, paragraph 1, of the United Nations Convention against Illicit Traffic in Narcotic Drugs and Psychotropic Substances of 20 December 1988 which, having regard to article 2 of the Convention, are crimes with an international dimension.

(c) Appendix I
Possible Clauses of a Treaty to Accompany
the Draft Statute

1. The Commission envisages that the statute will be attached to a treaty between States Parties. That treaty would provide for the establishment of the court, and for the supervision of its administration by the States Parties. It would also deal with such matters as financing, entry into force, etc., as is required for any new instrument creating an entity such as the court.

2. The standard practice of the Commission is not to draft final clauses for its draft articles, and for that reason it has not sought to draft a set of clauses for a covering treaty which would contain clauses of that kind. However, in discussions in the Sixth Committee of the General Assembly, a number of the matters which it will be necessary to resolve in concluding such a treaty were discussed, and

the Commission felt that it may be useful to outline some possible options for dealing with them.

3. Issues that will need to be dealt with include the following:

(a) *Entry into force*: The statute of the court is intended to reflect and represent the interests of the international community as a whole in relation to the prosecution of certain most serious crimes of international concern. In consequence, the statute and its covering treaty should require a substantial number of States Parties before it enters into force.

(b) *Administration*: The administration of the court as an entity is entrusted to the Presidency (see art. 8). However States Parties will need to meet from time to time to deal with such matters as the finances and administration of the court, and to consider periodic reports from the court, etc. The means by which States Parties will act together will need to be established.

(c) *Financing*: Detailed consideration must be given to financial issues at an early stage of any discussion of the proposed court. There are essentially two possibilities: direct financing by the States Parties or total or partial financing by the United Nations. United Nations financing is not necessarily excluded in the case of a separate entity in relationship with the United Nations (such as the Human Rights Committee). The statute is drafted in such a way as to minimize the costs of establishment of the court itself. On the other hand, a number of members stressed that investigations and prosecutions under the statute could be expensive. Arrangements will also have to be made to cover the costs of imprisonment of persons convicted under the statute.

(d) *Amendment and review of the statute*: The covering treaty must of course provide for amendment of the statute. It should, in the Commission's view, provide for a review of the statute, at the request of a specified number of States Parties after, say, five years. One issue that will arise in considering amendment or review will be the question whether the list of crimes contained in the annex should be revised so as to incorporate new conventions establishing crimes. This may include such instruments in the course of preparation as the draft Code of Crimes against the Peace and Security of Mankind, and the proposed convention on the protection of United Nations peacekeepers.

(e) *Reservations*: Whether or not the statute would be considered to be "a constituent instrument of an international organization" within the meaning of article 20, paragraph 3, of the Vienna Convention of the Law of Treaties, it is certainly closely analogous to a constituent instrument, and the considerations which led the drafters to require the consent of the "competent organ of that organization" under article 20, paragraph 3, apply in rather similar fashion to it. The draft statute has been constructed as an overall scheme, incorporating important balances and qualifications in relation to the working of the court: it is intended to operate as a whole. These considerations tend to support the view that reservations to the statute and its accompanying treaty should either not be permitted, or should be limited in scope. This is of course a matter for States Parties to consider in the context of negotiations for the conclusion of the statute and its accompanying treaty.

(f) *Settlement of disputes*: The court will of course have to determine its own jurisdiction (see arts. 24 and 34), and will accordingly have to deal with any issues of interpretation and application of the statute which arise in the exercise of that jurisdiction. Consideration will need to be given to ways in which other disputes, with regard to the interpretation and implementation of the treaty embodying the statute, arising between States Parties, should be resolved.

(d) Appendix II
Relevant Treaty Provisions Mentioned in the Annex
(see art. 20, subpara. (*e*))

1. Geneva Convention for the amelioration of the condition of the wounded and sick in armed forces in the field of 12 August 1949

Article 50

Grave breaches to which the preceding article relates shall be those involving any of the following acts, if committed against persons or property protected by the Convention: wilful killing, torture or inhuman treatment, including biological experiments, wilfully causing great suffering or serious injury to body or health, and extensive destruction and appropriation of property, not justified by military necessity and carried out unlawfully and wantonly.

2. Geneva Convention for the amelioration of the conditions of wounded, sick and shipwrecked members of armed forces at sea of 12 August 1949

Article 51

Grave breaches to which the preceding article relates shall be those involving any of the following acts, if committed against persons or property protected by the Convention: wilful killing, torture or inhuman treatment, including biological experiments, wilfully causing great suffering or serious injury to body or health and extensive destruction and appropriation of property, not justified by military necessity and carried out unlawfully and wantonly.

3. Geneva Convention Relative to the Treatment of Prisoners of War of 12 August 1949

Article 130

Grave breaches to which the preceding article relates shall be those involving any of the following acts, if committed against persons or property protected by the Convention: wilful killing, torture or inhuman treatment, including biological experiments, wilfully causing great suffering or serious injury to body or health, compelling a prisoner of war to serve in the forces of the hostile Power, or wilfully depriving a prisoner of war of the rights of fair and regular trial prescribed in this Convention.

4. Geneva Convention Relative to the Protection of Civilian Persons in Time of War, 12 August 1949

Article 147

Grave breaches to which the preceding article relates shall be those involving any of the following acts, if committed against persons or property protected by the present Convention: wilful killing, torture or inhuman treatment, including biological experiments, wilfully causing great suffering or serious injury to body or health, unlawful deportation or transfer or unlawful confinement of a protected person, compelling a protected person to serve in the forces of a hostile Power, or wilfully depriving a protected person of the rights of fair and regular trial prescribed in the present Convention, taking of hostages and extensive destruction and appropriation of property, not justified by military necessity and carried out unlawfully and wantonly.

5. Protocol Additional to the Geneva Conventions of 12 August 1949, and relating to the protection of victims of international armed conflicts (Protocol I)

Article 85

Repression of breaches of this Protocol

1. The provisions of the Conventions relating to the repression of breaches and grave breaches, supplemented by this Section, shall apply to the repression of breaches and grave breaches of this Protocol.

2. Acts described as grave breaches in the Conventions are grave breaches of this Protocol if committed against persons in the power of an adverse party protected by articles 44, 45 and 73 of this Protocol, or against the wounded, sick and shipwrecked of the adverse party

who are protected by this Protocol, or against those medical or religious personnel, medical units or medical transports which are under the control of the adverse party and are protected by this Protocol.

3. In addition to the grave breaches defined in Article 11, the following acts shall be regarded as grave breaches of this Protocol, when committed wilfully, in violation of the relevant provisions of this Protocol, and causing death or serious injury to body or health:

(a) Making the civilian population or individual civilians the object of attack;

(b) Launching an indiscriminate attack affecting the civilian population or civilian objects in the knowledge that such attack will cause excessive loss of life, injury to civilians or damage to civilian objects, as defined in article 57, paragraph 2 (a) (iii);

(c) Launching an attack against works or installations containing dangerous forces in the knowledge that such attack will cause excessive loss of life, injury to civilians or damage to civilian objects, as defined in article 57, paragraph 2 (a) (iii);

(d) Making non-defended localities and demilitarized zones the object of attack;

(e) Making a person the object of attack in the knowledge that he is *hors de combat*;

(f) The perfidious use, in violation of article 37, of the distinctive emblem of the red cross, red crescent or red lion and sun or of other protective signs recognized by the Conventions or this Protocol.

4. In addition to the grave breaches defined in the preceding paragraphs and in the Conventions, the following shall be regarded as grave breaches of this Protocol, when committed wilfully and in violation of the Conventions or the Protocol:

(a) The transfer by the Occupying Power of parts of its own civilian population into the territory it occupies, or the deportation or transfer of all or parts of the population of the occupied territory within or outside this territory, in violation of Article 49 of the Fourth Convention;

(b) Unjustifiable delay in the repatriation of prisoners of war or civilians;

(c) Practices of apartheid and other inhuman and degrading practices involving outrages upon personal dignity, based on racial discrimination;

(d) Making the clearly-recognized historic monuments, works of art or places of worship which constitute the cultural or spiritual heritage of peoples and to which special protection has been given

351

by special arrangement, for example, within the framework of a competent international organization, the object of attack, causing as a result, extensive destruction thereof, where there is no evidence of the violation by the adverse Party of Article 53, subparagraph (*b*), and when such historic monuments, works of art and places of worship are not located in the immediate proximity of military objectives;

(*e*) Depriving a person protected by the Conventions or referred to in paragraph 2 of this article of the rights of fair and regular trial.

5. Without prejudice to the application of the Conventions and of this Protocol, grave breaches of these instruments shall be regarded as war crimes.

6. Convention for the Suppression of Unlawful Seizure of Aircraft

Article 1

Any person who on board an aircraft in flight:

(*a*) unlawfully, by force or threat thereof, or by any other form of intimidation, seizes, or exercises control of, that aircraft, or attempts to perform any such act; or

(*b*) is an accomplice of a person who performs or attempts to perform any such act; or

commits an offence (hereinafter referred to as "the offence").

7. Convention for the Suppression of Unlawful Acts against the Safety of Civil Aviation

Article 1

1. Any person commits an offence if he unlawfully and intentionally:

(*a*) performs an act of violence against a person on board an aircraft in flight if that act is likely to endanger the safety of that aircraft; or

(*b*) destroys an aircraft in service or causes damage to such an aircraft which renders it incapable of flight or which is likely to endanger its safety in flight; or

(*c*) places or causes to be placed on an aircraft in service, by any means whatsoever, a device or substance which is likely to destroy that aircraft, or to cause damage to it which renders it incapable of flight, or to cause damage to it which is likely to endanger its safety in flight; or

(*d*) destroys or damages air navigation facilities or interferes with their operation, if any such act is likely to endanger the safety of aircraft in flight; or (*e*) communicates information which he knows to be false, thereby endangering the safety of an aircraft in flight.

2. Any person also commits an offence if he:

(*a*) attempts to commit any of the offences mentioned in paragraph 1 of this article; or

(*b*) is an accomplice of a person who commits or attempts to commit any such offence.

8. International Convention on the Suppression and Punishment of the Crime of apartheid

Article II

For the purpose of the present Convention, the term "the crime of apartheid", which shall include similar policies and practices of racial segregation and discrimination as practised in southern Africa, shall apply to the following inhuman acts committed for the purpose of establishing and maintaining domination by one racial group of persons over any other racial group of persons and systematically oppressing them:

(*a*) Denial to a member or members of a racial group or groups of the right to life and liberty of person:

(i) By murder of members of a racial group or groups;

(ii) By the infliction upon the members of a racial group or groups of serious bodily or mental harm, by the infringement of their freedom or dignity, or by subjecting them to torture or to cruel, inhuman or degrading treatment or punishment;

(iii) By arbitrary arrest and illegal imprisonment of the members of a racial group or groups;

(*b*) Deliberate imposition on a racial group or groups of living conditions calculated to cause its or their physical destruction in whole or in part;

(*c*) Any legislative measures and other measures calculated to prevent a racial group or groups from participation in the political, social, economic and cultural life of the country and the deliberate creation of conditions preventing the full development of such a group or groups, in particular by denying to members of a racial group or groups basic human rights and freedoms, including the right to work, the right to form recognized trade unions, the right to education, the right to leave and to return to their country, the right to a nationality, the right to freedom of movement and residence, the right to freedom of opinion and expression, and the right to freedom of peaceful assembly and association;

(*d*) Any measures, including legislative measures, designed to divide the population along racial lines by the creation of separate reserves and ghettos for the members of a racial group or groups, the prohibition of mixed marriages among members of various racial groups, the expropriation of landed property belonging to a racial group or groups or to members thereof;

(*e*) Exploitation of the labour of the members of a racial group or groups, in particular by submitting them to forced labour;

(*f*) Persecution of organizations and persons, by depriving them of fundamental rights and freedoms, because they oppose apartheid.

9. Convention on the Prevention and Punishment of Crimes against internationally protected persons, including diplomatic agents

Article 2

1. The intentional commission of:

(*a*) A murder, kidnapping or other attack upon the person or liberty of an internationally protected person;

(*b*) A violent attack upon the official premises, the private accommodation or the means of transport of an internationally protected person likely to endanger his person or liberty; and

(*c*) A threat to commit any such attack;

(*d*) An attempt to commit any such attack;

(*e*) An act constituting participation as an accomplice in any such attack;

shall be made by each State Party a crime under its internal law.

2. Each State Party shall make these crimes punishable by appropriate penalties which take into account their grave nature.

3. Paragraphs 1 and 2 of this article in no way derogate from the obligations of States Parties under international law to take all appropriate measures to prevent other attacks on the person, freedom or dignity of an internationally protected person.

10. International Convention against the Taking of Hostages

Article 1

1. Any person who seizes or detains and threatens to kill, to injure or to continue to detain another person (hereinafter referred to as the "hostage") in order to compel a third patty, namely, a State, an international intergovernmental organization, a natural or juridical person, or a group of persons, to do or abstain from doing any act as an explicit or implicit condition for the release of the hostage commits the offence of taking of hostages ("hostage-taking") within the meaning of this Convention.

2. Any person who:

(*a*) Attempts to commit an act of hostage-taking; or

(*b*) Participates as an accomplice of anyone who commits or attempts to commit an act of hostage-taking;

likewise commits an offence for the purposes of this Convention.

11. Convention against Torture and Other Cruel, Inhuman or Degrading Treatment or Punishment

Article 1

1. For the purposes of this Convention, the term "torture" means any act by which severe pain or suffering, whether physical or mental, is intentionally inflicted on a person for such purposes as obtaining from him or a third person information or a confession, punishing him for an act he or a third person has committed or is suspected of having committed, or intimidating or coercing him or a third person, or for any reason based on discrimination of any kind, when such pain or suffering is infected by or at the instigation of or with the consent or acquiescence of a public official or other person acting in an official capacity. It does not include pain or suffering arising only from, inherent in, or incidental to lawful sanctions.

2. This article is without prejudice to any international instrument or national legislation which does or may contain provisions of wider application.

...

Article 4

1. Each State Party shall ensure that all acts of torture are offences under its criminal law. The same shall apply to an attempt to commit torture and to an act by any person which constitutes complicity or participation in torture.

2. Each State Party shall make these offences punishable by appropriate penalties which take into account their grave nature.

12. Convention for the Suppression of Unlawful Acts against the Safety of Maritime Navigation

Article 3

1. Any person commits an offence if that person unlawfully and intentionally:

(*a*) seizes or exercises control over a ship by force or threat thereof or any other form of intimidation; or

(*b*) performs an act of violence against a person on board a ship if that act is likely to endanger the safe navigation of that ship; or

(*c*) destroys a ship or causes damage to a ship or to its cargo which is likely to endanger the safe navigation of that ship; or

(*d*) places or causes to be placed on a ship, by any means whatsoever, a device or substance which is likely to destroy that ship, or cause damage to that ship or its cargo which endangers or is likely to endanger the safe navigation of that ship; or

(*e*) destroys or seriously damages maritime navigational facilities or seriously interferes with their operation, if any such act is likely to endanger the safe navigation of a ship; or

(*f*) communicates information which he knows to be false, thereby endangering the safe navigation of a ship; or

(*g*) injures or kills any person, in connection with the commission or the attempted commission of any of the offences set forth in subparagraphs (*a*) to (*f*).

2. Any person also commits an offence if that person:

(*a*) attempts to commit any of the offences set forth in paragraph 1; or

(*b*) abets the commission of any of the offences set forth in paragraph 1 perpetrated by any person or is otherwise an accomplice of a person who commits such an offence; or

(*c*) threatens with or without a condition, as is provided for under national law, aimed at compelling a physical or juridical person to do or refrain from doing any act, to commit any of the offences set forth in paragraph 1, subparagraphs (*b*), (*c*) and (*e*), if that threat is likely to endanger the safe navigation of the ship in question.

13. Protocol for the Suppression of Unlawful Acts against the Safety of Fixed Platforms Located on the Continental Shelf

Article 2

1. Any person commits an offence if that person unlawfully and intentionally:

(*a*) seizes or exercises control over a fixed platform by force or threat thereof or any other form of intimidation; or

(*b*) performs an act of violence against a person on board a fixed platform if that act is likely to endanger its safety; or

(*c*) destroys a fixed platform or causes damage to it which is likely to endanger its safety; or

(*d*) places or causes to be placed on a fixed platform, by any means whatsoever, a device or substance which is likely to destroy that fixed platform or likely to endanger its safety; or

(*e*) injures or kills any person in connection with the commission or the attempted commission of any of the offences set forth in subparagraphs (*a*) to (*d*).

2. Any person also commits an offence if that person:

(*a*) attempts to commit any of the offences set forth in paragraph 1; or (*b*) abets the commission of any such offences perpetrated by any person or is otherwise an accomplice of a person who commits such an offence; or

(*c*) threatens, with or without a condition, as is provided for under national law, aimed at compelling a physical or juridical person to do or refrain from doing any act, to commit any of the offences set forth in paragraph 1, subparagraphs (*b*) and (*c*), if that threat is likely to endanger the safety of the fixed platform.

14. United Nations Convention against Illicit Traffic in Narcotic Drugs and Psychotropic Substances

Article 2

Scope of the Convention

1. The purpose of this Convention is to promote cooperation among the Parties so that they may address more effectively the various aspects of illicit traffic in narcotic drugs and psychotropic substances having an international dimension. In carrying out their obligations under the Convention, the Parties shall take necessary measures, including legislative and administrative measures, in conformity with the fundamental provisions of their respective domestic legislative systems.

2. The Parties shall carry out their obligations under this Convention in a manner consistent with the principles of sovereign equality and territorial integrity of States and that of non-intervention in the domestic affairs of other States.

3. A Party shall not undertake in the territory of another Party the exercise of jurisdiction and performance of functions which are exclusively reserved for the authorities of that other Party by its domestic law.

Article 3

Offences and sanctions

1. Each party shall adopt such measures as may be necessary to establish as criminal offences under its domestic law, when committed intentionally:

    (*a*) (i) The production, manufacture, extraction, preparation, offering, offering for sale, distribution, sale, delivery on any terms whatsoever, brokerage, dispatch, dispatch in transit, transport, importation or exportation of any narcotic drug or any psychotropic substance contrary to the provisions of the 1961 Convention, the 1961 Convention as amended or the 1971 Convention;

    (ii) The cultivation of opium poppy, coca bush or cannabis plant for the purpose of the production of narcotic drugs contrary to the provisions of the 1961 Convention and the 1961 Convention as amended;

(iii) The possession or purchase of any narcotic drug or psychotropic substance for the purpose of any of the activities enumerated in (i) above;

(iv) The manufacture, transport or distribution of equipment, materials or of substances listed in Table I and Table II, knowing that they are to be used in or for the illicit cultivation, production or manufacture of narcotic drugs or psychotropic substances;

(v) The organization, management or financing of any of the offences enumerated in (i), (ii), (iii) or (iv) above;

(*b*) (i) The conversion or transfer of property, knowing that such property is derived from any offence or offences established in accordance with subparagraph (*a*) of this paragraph, or from an act of participation in such offence or offences, for the purpose of concealing or disguising the illicit origin of the property or of assisting any person who is involved in the commission of such an offence or offences to evade the legal consequences of his actions;

(ii) The concealment or disguise of the true nature, source, location, disposition, movement, rights with respect to, or ownership of property, knowing that such property is derived from an offence or offences established in accordance with subparagraph (*a*) of this paragraph or from an act of participation in such an offence or offences;

(*c*) Subject to its constitutional principles and the basic concepts of its legal system:

(i) The acquisition, possession or use of property, knowing, at the time of receipt, that such property was derived from an offence or offences established in accordance with subparagraph (*a*) of this paragraph or from an act of participation in such offence or offences;

(ii) The possession of equipment or materials or substances listed in Table I and Table II, knowing that they are being or are to be used in or for the illicit cultivation, production or manufacture of narcotic drugs or psychotropic substances;

(iii) Publicly inciting or inducing others, by any means, to commit any of the offences established in accordance with this article or to use narcotic drugs or psychotropic substances illicitly;

(iv) Participation in, association or conspiracy to commit, attempts to commit and aiding, abetting, facilitating and counselling the commission of any of the offences established in accordance with this article.

(e) Appendix III
Outline of Possible Ways whereby a Permanent International Criminal Court may Enter into Relationship with the United Nations

1. The way in which a permanent international criminal court may enter into relationship with the United Nations must necessarily be considered in connection with the method adopted for its creation.

2. In this respect, two hypotheses may be envisaged: (*a*) the court becomes part of the organic structure of the United Nations; (*b*) the court does not become part of the organic structure of the United Nations.

A. The court becomes part of the organic structure of the United Nations

3. Under this hypothesis the court, as a result of the very act of its creation, is already in relationship with the United Nations. This may be achieved in two ways.

1. THE COURT AS A PRINCIPAL ORGAN OF THE UNITED NATIONS

4. This solution would attach the maximum weight to the creation of the court by placing it on the same level with the other principal organs of the United Nations and, in particular, ICJ. It would also facilitate the ipso jure jurisdiction of the court over certain international crimes. Under this solution, the financing of the court would be provided for under the regular budget of the Organization.

5. On the other hand, this solution could give rise to potential obstacles in that it would require an amendment to the Charter of the United Nations under Chapter XVIII (Arts. 108-109). It should be noted, in this connection, that there is no precedent for the creation of any additional principal organ in the history of the Organization.

2. THE COURT AS A SUBSIDIARY ORGAN OF THE UNITED NATIONS

6. By contrast, there is a well-developed practice whereby United Nations principal organs create subsidiary organs under the relevant provisions of the Charter of the United Nations (in particular, Arts. 22 and 29), for the performance of functions conferred upon them or upon the Organization as a whole by the Charter. There is practice along these lines even in the jurisdictional field. An early example is the establishment of the Administrative Tribunal of the United

Nations.[a] A more recent example is the creation of the International Tribunal for the Prosecution of Persons Responsible for Serious Violations of International Humanitarian Law Committed in the Territory of the Former Yugoslavia since 1991 (hereinafter referred to as the "International Tribunal").[b]

7. Normally and as concerns most fields of competence, the establishment of a subsidiary organ is essentially auxiliary in nature. The subsidiary organ's decisions will usually be in the nature of recommendations which the relevant principal organ is free to accept or reject.

8. In the judicial field, however, the subsidiary nature of an organ reflects itself mainly in the fact that its very existence, as well as the cessation of its functions, depends upon the relevant principal organ of the Organization. As regards the exercise of its functions, however, the very nature of the latter (judicial) makes them incompatible with the existence of hierarchical powers on the part of the principal organ which established the court or tribunal. Therefore, the principal organ has no power to reject or amend the decisions of the tribunal or court established. This was clearly ruled by ICJ as regards the Administrative Tribunal of the United Nations[c] and also arises from certain articles of the statute of the International Tribunal (arts. 13, 15, 25, 26, etc.).[d]

9. As regards financing, the activities of a subsidiary organ of the Organization are financed from United Nations sources, whether budgetary allocations, assessed contributions or voluntary contributions.[e]

10. It should also be noted that, occasionally, the General Assembly has set up tribunals as subsidiary organs, on the basis of provisions contained in treaties concluded outside the United Nations. This was the case of the United Nations Tribunal for Libya and the United Nations Tribunal for Eritrea.[f] Although the matters dealt with by these tribunals were, broadly speaking, part of the generic competence of the General Assembly under Article 10 of the Charter of the United Nations, the provision which led to their creation was contained in annex XI, paragraph 3, of the Treaty of Peace with Italy.

---

[a] General Assembly resolution 351 A (IV) of 9 December 1949.
[b] See Security Council resolutions 808 (1993) of 22 February 1993 and 827 (1993) of 25 May 1993.
[c] *Effect of awards of compensation made by the United Nations Administrative Tribunal, Advisory Opinion, I.C.J. Reports 1954*, p. 62.
[d] Document S/25704, annex.
[e] See, for example, General Assembly resolution 48/251 of 14 April 1994.
[f] Set up, respectively, by General Assembly resolutions 388 A (V) of 15 December 1950 and 530 (VI) of 29 January 1952.

11. The cases referred to in the preceding paragraph should be distinguished from those referred to in paragraphs 15 to 17 below in which the General Assembly undertakes certain functions with respect to organs established by the parties to a multilateral treaty.

B. The Court does not become part of the organic structure of the United Nations and is set up by a treaty

12. Under this hypothesis the court would be created by a treaty binding on States Parties thereto. There are two possible ways whereby such a court could be brought into relationship with the United Nations: by means of an agreement between the court and the United Nations; or by means of a resolution of a United Nations organ (such as the General Assembly).

1. THE COURT COMES INTO RELATIONSHIP WITH
THE UNITED NATIONS BY MEANS OF AN AGREEMENT
BETWEEN THE COURT AND THE UNITED NATIONS

13. Cooperation agreements are the typical way whereby specialized agencies and analogous bodies enter into relationship with the United Nations under Articles 57 and 63 of the Charter of the United Nations. Agreements are concluded between the specialized agency concerned and the Economic and Social Council and are subject to the approval of the General Assembly. The agreements regulate, inter alia, matters of cooperation with the United Nations in the respective fields of action of each specialized agency and questions related to a common system as regards personnel policies. Each specialized agency constitutes an autonomous international organization with its own budget and financial resources.

14. A case in point is article XVI of the statute of IAEA,[g] dealing with "Relationship with other organizations" which provides that the Board of Governors, with the approval of the General Conference, is authorized to enter into an agreement or agreements establishing an appropriate relationship between IAEA and the United Nations and any other organizations the work of which is related to that of IAEA. The Agreement governing the relationship between the United Nations and IAEA was approved by the General Assembly.[h] The Agreement, inter alia, regulates the submission of reports by IAEA to the United Nations, the exchange of information and documents, matters of reciprocal representation, consideration of items in the respective agendas, cooperation with the Security Council and ICJ,

---

[g] United Nations, *Treaty Series*, vol. 276, p. 3.
[h] General Assembly resolution 1145 (XII) of 14 November 1957, annex.

coordination and cooperation matters, budgetary and financial arrangements and personnel arrangements.

15. The conclusion of an international agreement with the United Nations is also the way being envisaged by the Preparatory Commission for the International Seabed Authority and for the International Tribunal for the Law of the Sea to bring the projected tribunal into relationship with the United Nations. The final draft of that agreement[i] contemplates, inter alia, matters of legal relationship and mutual recognition, cooperation and coordination, relations with ICJ, relations with the Security Council, reciprocal representation, exchange of information and documents, reports to the United Nations, administrative cooperation and personnel arrangements. The draft agreement would also recognize "the desirability of establishing close budgetary and financial relationships with the United Nations in order that the administrative operations of the United Nations and the International Tribunal shall be carried out in the most efficient and economical manner possible, and that the maximum measure of coordination and uniformity with respect to these operations shall be secured".

2. THE COURT COMES INTO RELATIONSHIP WITH THE UNITED NATIONS BY MEANS OF A RESOLUTION OF A UNITED NATIONS ORGAN

16. Finally, a court created by a multilateral treaty could also be brought into relationship with the United Nations by means of a resolution of a United Nations organ. In the case of a permanent international criminal court such a resolution could be adopted by the General Assembly, perhaps with the concurrent involvement of the Security Council.

17. It is in the field of the protection of human rights that international practice offers the most relevant examples of treaty organs coming into relationship with the United Nations by means of a General Assembly resolution. Typically, the treaty creating the organ already contains some provisions resorting to the United Nations for the performance of certain functions under the treaty, for example, the role of the Secretary-General in circulating invitations to States Parties for the election of the treaty organ, requests to the Secretary-General to provide the necessary staff and facilities for the effective performance of the functions of the treaty organ, and so forth. The United Nations, in its turn, takes such functions upon itself, by a resolution of the General Assembly which "adopts and

---

[i] See document LOS/PCN/SCN.4/WP.16/Add.4.

opens for signature and ratification" the multilateral convention in question. Such a procedure has been followed, for instance, in the case of the International Covenant on Economic, Social and Cultural Rights, the International Covenant on Civil and Political Rights and the Optional Protocol to the International Covenant on Civil and Political Rights; the International Convention on the Elimination of All Forms of Racial Discrimination; and the Convention against Torture and Other Cruel, Inhuman or Degrading Treatment or Punishment.

18. The adoption of such resolutions will usually have financial implications for the United Nations, making necessary the intervention of the Fifth Committee in the decision-making process. For instance, in the case of the Human Rights Committee, article 36 of the International Covenant on Civil and Political Rights provides that

> The Secretary-General of the United Nations shall provide the necessary staff and facilities for the effective performance of the functions of the Committee under the present Covenant,

and also article 35 provides that

> The Members of the Committee shall, with the approval of the General Assembly of the United Nations, receive emoluments from United Nations resources on such terms and conditions as the General Assembly may decide, having regard to the importance of the Committee's responsibilities.

19. The International Convention on the Elimination of All Forms of Racial Discrimination establishing the Committee on the Elimination of Racial Discrimination and the Convention against Torture and Other Cruel, Inhuman or Degrading Treatment or Punishment establishing the Committee against Torture both provide that the secretariat of the Committees (staff and facilities) shall be provided by the Secretary-General of the United Nations (see art. 10, paras. 3-4 and art. 18, para. 3, respectively), even though the Convention against Torture and Other Cruel, Inhuman or Degrading Treatment or Punishment provides in article 18, paragraph 5, that

> 5. The States Parties shall be responsible for expenses incurred in connection with the holding of meetings of the States Parties and of the Committee, including reimbursement to the United Nations for any expenses, such as the cost of staff and facilities, incurred by the United Nations ....

Unlike the International Covenant on Civil and Political Rights, however, these two conventions place upon the States Parties and not upon the United Nations the expenses of the members of the committee while they are in the performance of their duties (see art. 8, para. 6 and art. 17, para. 7, respectively).

20. In practice the General Assembly may accept, with regard to such committees created by treaty, additional obligations to those already contained in the treaties concerned. Thus, by resolution 47/111, the General Assembly

> 9. *Endorses* the amendments to the International Convention on the Elimination of All Forms of Racial Discrimination and the Convention against Torture and Other Cruel, Inhuman or Degrading Treatment or Punishment and requests the Secretary-General:
>
> (*a*) To take the appropriate measures to provide for the financing of the committees established under the conventions from the regular budget of the United Nations, beginning with the budget for the biennium 1994-1995;
>
> ...

10. Nationality of Natural Persons in relation to the Succession of States[*]

PREAMBLE

Considering that problems of nationality arising from succession of States concern the international community,

Emphasizing that nationality is essentially governed by internal law within the limits set by international law,

Recognizing that in matters concerning nationality, due account should be taken both of the legitimate interests of States and those of individuals,

Recalling that the Universal Declaration of Human Rights of 1948[a] proclaimed the right of every person to a nationality,

Recalling also that the International Covenant on Civil and Political Rights of 1966[b] and the Convention on the Rights of the Child of 1989[c] recognize the right of every child to acquire a nationality,

Emphasizing that the human rights and fundamental freedoms of persons whose nationality may be affected by a succession of States must be fully respected,

---

[*] Text adopted by the Commission at its fifty-first session, in 1999, and submitted to the General Assembly as a part of the Commission's report covering the work of that session. The report, which also contains commentaries on the draft articles, appears in *Official Records of the General Assembly, Fifty-fourth Session, Supplement No. 10* (A/54/10). Text reproduced as it appears in the annex to General Assembly resolution 55/153 of 12 December 2000.

[a] General Assembly resolution 217 A (III) of 10 December 1948.

[b] See General Assembly resolution 2200 A (XXI) of 16 December 1966, annex.

[c] General Assembly resolution 44/25 of 20 November 1989, annex.

Bearing in mind the provisions of the Convention on the reduction of statelessness of 1961,[d] the Vienna Convention on Succession of States in Respect of Treaties of 1978[e] and the Vienna Convention on Succession of States in Respect of State Property, Archives and Debts of 1983,[f]

Convinced of the need for the codification and progressive development of the rules of international law concerning nationality in relation to the succession of States as a means for ensuring greater juridical security for States and for individuals,

PART I.   GENERAL PROVISIONS

Article 1

Right to a nationality

Every individual who, on the date of the succession of States, had the nationality of the predecessor State, irrespective of the mode of acquisition of that nationality, has the right to the nationality of at least one of the States concerned, in accordance with the present articles.

Article 2

Use of terms

For the purposes of the present articles:

(*a*) "Succession of States" means the replacement of one State by another in the responsibility for the international relations of territory;

(*b*) "Predecessor State" means the State which has been replaced by another State on the occurrence of a succession of States;

(*c*) "Successor State" means the State which has replaced another State on the occurrence of a succession of States;

(*d*) "State concerned" means the predecessor State or the successor State, as the case may be;

(*e*) "Third State" means any State other than the predecessor State or the successor State;

(*f*) "Person concerned" means every individual who, on the date of the succession of States, had the nationality of the predecessor State and whose nationality may be affected by such succession;

(*g*) "Date of the succession of States" means the date upon which the successor State replaced the predecessor State in the

---

[d] United Nations, *Treaty Series*, vol. 989, No. 14458.
[e] Ibid., vol. 1946, No. 33356.
[f] See A/CONF.117/14.

responsibility for the international relations of the territory to which the succession of States relates.

Article 3

Cases of succession of States covered by the present articles

The present articles apply only to the effects of a succession of States occurring in conformity with international law and, in particular, with the principles of international law embodied in the Charter of the United Nations.

Article 4

Prevention of statelessness

States concerned shall take all appropriate measures to prevent persons who, on the date of the succession of States, had the nationality of the predecessor State from becoming stateless as a result of such succession.

Article 5

Presumption of nationality

Subject to the provisions of the present articles, persons concerned having their habitual residence in the territory affected by the succession of States are presumed to acquire the nationality of the successor State on the date of such succession

Article 6

Legislation on nationality and other connected issues

Each State concerned should, without undue delay, enact legislation on nationality and other connected issues arising in relation to the succession of States consistent with the provisions of the present articles. It should take all appropriate measures to ensure that persons concerned will be apprised, within a reasonable time period, of the effect of its legislation on their nationality, of any choices they may have thereunder, as well as of the consequences that the exercise of such choices will have on their status.

Article 7

Effective date

The attribution of nationality in relation to the succession of States, as well as the acquisition of nationality following the exercise of an option, shall take effect on the date of such succession, if persons concerned would otherwise be stateless during the period between the date of the succession of States and such attribution or acquisition of nationality.

Article 8

Persons concerned having their habitual residence
in another State

1. A successor State does not have the obligation to attribute its nationality to persons concerned who have their habitual residence in another State and also have the nationality of that or any other State.

2. A successor State shall not attribute its nationality to persons concerned who have their habitual residence in another State against the will of the persons concerned unless they would otherwise become stateless.

Article 9

Renunciation of the nationality of another State as a
condition for attribution of nationality

When a person concerned who is qualified to acquire the nationality of a successor State has the nationality of another State concerned, the former State may make the attribution of its nationality dependent on the renunciation by such person of the nationality of the latter State. However, such requirement shall not be applied in a manner which would result in rendering the person concerned stateless, even if only temporarily.

Article 10

Loss of nationality upon the voluntary acquisition
of the nationality of another State

1. A predecessor State may provide that persons concerned who, in relation to the succession of States, voluntarily acquire the nationality of a successor State shall lose its nationality.

2. A successor State may provide that person concerned who, in relation to the succession of States, voluntarily acquire the nationality of another successor State or, as the case may be, retain the nationality of the predecessor State shall lose its nationality acquired in relation to such succession.

Article 11

Respect for the will of persons concerned

1. States concerned shall give consideration to the will of persons concerned whenever those persons are qualified to acquire the nationality of two or more States concerned.

2. Each State concerned shall grant a right to opt for its nationality to persons concerned who have appropriate connection with that State if those persons would otherwise become stateless as a result of the succession of States.

3. When persons entitled to the right of option have exercised such right, the State whose nationality they have opted for shall attribute its nationality to such persons.

4. When persons entitled to the right of option have exercised such right, the State whose nationality they have renounced shall withdraw its nationality from such persons, unless they would thereby become stateless.

5. States concerned should provide a reasonable time limit for the exercise of the right of option.

Article 12

Unity of a family

Where the acquisition or loss of nationality in relation to the succession of States would impair the unity of a family, States concerned shall take all appropriate measures to allow that family to remain together or to be reunited.

Article 13

Child born after the succession of States

A child of a person concerned, born after the date of the succession of States, who has not acquired any nationality, has the right to the nationality of the State concerned on whose territory that child was born.

Article 14

Status of habitual residents

1. The status of persons concerned as habitual residents shall not be affected by the succession of States.

2. A State concerned shall take all necessary measures to allow persons concerned who, because of events connected with the succession of States, were forced to leave their habitual residence on its territory to return thereto.

Article 15

Non-discrimination

States concerned shall not deny persons concerned the right to retain or acquire a nationality or the right of option upon the succession of States by discriminating on any ground.

Article 16

Prohibition of arbitrary decisions concerning nationality issues

Persons concerned shall not be arbitrarily deprived of the nationality of the predecessor State, or arbitrarily denied the right to acquire the nationality of the successor State or any right of option, to which they are entitled in relation to the succession of States.

Article 17

Procedures relating to nationality issues

Applications relating to the acquisition, retention or renunciation of nationality or to the exercise of the right of option, in relation to the succession of States, shall be processed without undue delay. Relevant decisions shall be issued in writing and shall be open to effective administrative or judicial review.

Article 18

Exchange of information, consultation and negotiation

1. States concerned shall exchange information and consult in order to identify any detrimental effects on persons concerned with respect to their nationality and other connected issues regarding their status as a result of the succession of States.

2. States concerned shall, when necessary, seek a solution to eliminate or mitigate such detrimental effects by negotiation and, as appropriate, through agreement.

Article 19

Other States

1. Nothing in the present articles requires States to treat persons concerned having no effective link with a State concerned as nationals of that State, unless this would result in treating those persons as if they were stateless.

2. Nothing in the present articles precludes States from treating persons concerned, who have become stateless as a result of the succession of States, as nationals of the State concerned whose nationality they would be entitled to acquire or retain, if such treatment is beneficial to those persons.

PART II. PROVISIONS RELATING TO SPECIFIC CATEGORIES OF SUCCESSION OF STATES

Section 1. Transfer of part of the territory

Article 20

Attribution of the nationality of the successor State and withdrawal of the nationality of the predecessor State

When part of the territory of a State is transferred by that State to another State, the successor State shall attribute its nationality to the persons concerned who have their habitual residence in the transferred territory and the predecessor State shall withdraw its nationality from such persons, unless otherwise indicated by the exercise of the right of option which such persons shall be granted.

The predecessor State shall not, however, withdraw its nationality before such persons acquire the nationality of the successor State.

Section 2. Unification of States

Article 21

Attribution of the nationality of the successor State

Subject to the provisions of article 8, when two or more States unite and so form one successor State, irrespective of whether the successor State is a new State or whether its personality is identical to that of one of the States which have united, the successor State shall attribute its nationality to all persons who, on the date of the succession of States, had the nationality of a predecessor State.

Section 3. Dissolution of a State

Article 22

Attribution of the nationality of the successor States

When a State dissolves and ceases to exist and the various parts of the territory of the predecessor State form two or more successor States, each successor State shall, unless otherwise indicated by the exercise of a right of option, attribute its nationality to:

(*a*) Persons concerned having their habitual residence in its territory; and

(*b*) Subject to the provisions of article 8:

(i) Persons concerned not covered by subparagraph (a) having an appropriate legal connection with a constituent unit of the predecessor State that has become part of that successor State;

(ii) Persons concerned not entitled to a nationality of any State concerned under subparagraphs (*a*) and (*b*) (i) having their habitual residence in a third State, who were born in or, before leaving the predecessor State, had their last habitual residence in what has become the territory of that successor State or having any other appropriate connection with that successor State.

Article 23

Granting of the right of option by the successor States

1. Successor States shall grant a right of option to persons concerned covered by the provisions of article 22 who are qualified to acquire the nationality of two or more successor States.

2. Each successor State shall grant a right to opt for its nationality to persons concerned who are not covered by the provisions of article 22.

Section 4. Separation of part or parts of the territory

Article 24

Attribution of the nationality of the successor State

When part or parts of the territory of a State separate from that State and form one or more successor States while the predecessor State continues to exist, a successor State shall, unless otherwise indicated by the exercise of a right of option, attribute its nationality to:

(*a*) Persons concerned having their habitual residence in its territory; and

(*b*) Subject to the provisions of article 8:

(i) Persons concerned not covered by subparagraph (*a*) having an appropriate legal connection with a constituent unit of the predecessor State that has become part of that successor State;

(ii) Persons concerned not entitled to a nationality of any State concerned under subparagraphs (*a*) and (*b*) (i) having their habitual residence in a third State, who were born in or, before leaving the predecessor State, had their last habitual residence in what has become the territory of that successor State or having any other appropriate connection with that successor State.

Article 25

Withdrawal of the nationality of the predecessor State

1. The predecessor State shall withdraw its nationality from persons concerned qualified to acquire the nationality of the successor State in accordance with article 24. It shall not, however, withdraw its nationality before such persons acquire the nationality of the successor State.

2. Unless otherwise indicated by the exercise of a right of option, the predecessor State shall not, however, withdraw its nationality from persons referred to in paragraph 1 who:

(*a*) Have their habitual residence in its territory;

(*b*) Are not covered by subparagraph (*a*) and have an appropriate legal connection with a constituent unit of the predecessor State that has remained part of the predecessor State;

(*c*) Have their habitual residence in a third State, and were born in or, before leaving the predecessor State, had their last habitual residence in what has remained part of the territory of the predecessor State or have any other appropriate connection with that State.

Article 26

Granting of the right of option by the predecessor and the successor States

Predecessor and successor States shall grant a right of option to all persons concerned covered by the provisions of article 24 and paragraph 2 of article 25 who are qualified to have the nationality of both the predecessor and successor States or of two or more successor States.

11. Responsibility of States for Internationally Wrongful Acts[*]

PART ONE

THE INTERNATIONALLY WRONGFUL ACT OF A STATE

CHAPTER I

GENERAL PRINCIPLES

Article 1

Responsibility of a State for its internationally wrongful acts

Every internationally wrongful act of a State entails the international responsibility of that State.

Article 2

Elements of an internationally wrongful act of a State

There is an internationally wrongful act of a State when conduct consisting of an action or omission:

(a) Is attributable to the State under international law; and

(b) Constitutes a breach of an international obligation of the State.

Article 3

Characterization of an act of a State as internationally wrongful

The characterization of an act of a State as internationally wrongful is governed by international law. Such characterization is not affected by the characterization of the same act as lawful by internal law.

---

[*] Text adopted by the Commission at its fifty-third session, in 2001, and submitted to the General Assembly as a part of the Commission's report covering the work of that session. The report, which also contains commentaries on the draft articles, appears in *Official Records of the General Assembly, Fifty-sixth Session, Supplement No. 10* (A/56/10). Text reproduced as it appears in the annex to General Assembly resolution 56/83 of 12 December 2001.

CHAPTER II
ATTRIBUTION OF CONDUCT TO A STATE

Article 4

Conduct of organs of a State

1. The conduct of any State organ shall be considered an act of that State under international law, whether the organ exercises legislative, executive, judicial or any other functions, whatever position it holds in the organization of the State, and whatever its character as an organ of the central Government or of a territorial unit of the State.

2. An organ includes any person or entity which has that status in accordance with the internal law of the State.

Article 5

Conduct of persons or entities exercising elements of governmental authority

The conduct of a person or entity which is not an organ of the State under article 4 but which is empowered by the law of that State to exercise elements of the governmental authority shall be considered an act of the State under international law, provided the person or entity is acting in that capacity in the particular instance.

Article 6

Conduct of organs placed at the disposal of a State by another State

The conduct of an organ placed at the disposal of a State by another State shall be considered an act of the former State under international law if the organ is acting in the exercise of elements of the governmental authority of the State at whose disposal it is placed.

Article 7

Excess of authority or contravention of instructions

The conduct of an organ of a State or of a person or entity empowered to exercise elements of the governmental authority shall be considered an act of the State under international law if the organ, person or entity acts in that capacity, even if it exceeds its authority or contravenes instructions.

Article 8

Conduct directed or controlled by a State

The conduct of a person or group of persons shall be considered an act of a State under international law if the person or group of persons is in fact acting on the instructions of, or under the direction or control of, that State in carrying out the conduct.

Article 9

Conduct carried out in the absence or default of the official authorities

The conduct of a person or group of persons shall be considered an act of a State under international law if the person or group of persons is in fact exercising elements of the governmental authority in the absence or default of the official authorities and in circumstances such as to call for the exercise of those elements of authority.

Article 10

Conduct of an insurrectional or other movement

1. The conduct of an insurrectional movement which becomes the new Government of a State shall be considered an act of that State under international law.

2. The conduct of a movement, insurrectional or other, which succeeds in establishing a new State in part of the territory of a pre-existing State or in a territory under its administration shall be considered an act of the new State under international law.

3. This article is without prejudice to the attribution to a State of any conduct, however related to that of the movement concerned, which is to be considered an act of that State by virtue of articles 4 to 9.

Article 11

Conduct acknowledged and adopted by a State as its own

Conduct which is not attributable to a State under the preceding articles shall nevertheless be considered an act of that State under international law if and to the extent that the State acknowledges and adopts the conduct in question as its own.

CHAPTER III
BREACH OF AN INTERNATIONAL OBLIGATION

Article 12

Existence of a breach of an international obligation

There is a breach of an international obligation by a State when an act of that State is not in conformity with what is required of it by that obligation, regardless of its origin or character.

Article 13

International obligation in force for a State

An act of a State does not constitute a breach of an international obligation unless the State is bound by the obligation in question at the time the act occurs.

Article 14

Extension in time of the breach of an international obligation

1. The breach of an international obligation by an act of a State not having a continuing character occurs at the moment when the act is performed, even if its effects continue.

2. The breach of an international obligation by an act of a State having a continuing character extends over the entire period during which the act continues and remains not in conformity with the international obligation.

3. The breach of an international obligation requiring a State to prevent a given event occurs when the event occurs and extends over the entire period during which the event continues and remains not in conformity with that obligation.

Article 15

Breach consisting of a composite act

1. The breach of an international obligation by a State through a series of actions or omissions defined in aggregate as wrongful occurs when the action or omission occurs which, taken with the other actions or omissions, is sufficient to constitute the wrongful act.

2. In such a case, the breach extends over the entire period starting with the first of the actions or omissions of the series and lasts for as long as these actions or omissions are repeated and remain not in conformity with the international obligation.

CHAPTER IV
RESPONSIBILITY OF A STATE IN CONNECTION WITH THE ACT OF ANOTHER STATE

Article 16

Aid or assistance in the commission of an internationally wrongful act

A State which aids or assists another State in the commission of an internationally wrongful act by the latter is internationally responsible for doing so if:

(*a*) That State does so with knowledge of the circumstances of the internationally wrongful act; and

(*b*) The act would be internationally wrongful if committed by that State.

Article 17

Direction and control exercised over the commission of an internationally wrongful act

A State which directs and controls another State in the commission of an internationally wrongful act by the latter is internationally responsible for that act if:

(*a*) That State does so with knowledge of the circumstances of the internationally wrongful act; and

(*b*) The act would be internationally wrongful if committed by that State.

Article 18

Coercion of another State

A State which coerces another State to commit an act is internationally responsible for that act if:

(*a*) The act would, but for the coercion, be an internationally wrongful act of the coerced State; and

(*b*) The coercing State does so with knowledge of the circumstances of the act.

Article 19

Effect of this chapter

This chapter is without prejudice to the international responsibility, under other provisions of these articles, of the State which commits the act in question, or of any other State.

CHAPTER V
CIRCUMSTANCES PRECLUDING WRONGFULNESS

Article 20

Consent

Valid consent by a State to the commission of a given act by another State precludes the wrongfulness of that act in relation to the former State to the extent that the act remains within the limits of that consent.

Article 21

Self-defence

The wrongfulness of an act of a State is precluded if the act constitutes a lawful measure of self-defence taken in conformity with the Charter of the United Nations.

Article 22

Countermeasures in respect of an internationally wrongful act

The wrongfulness of an act of a State not in conformity with an international obligation towards another State is precluded if and to the extent that the act constitutes a countermeasure taken against the latter State in accordance with chapter II of part three.

Article 23

Force majeure

1. The wrongfulness of an act of a State not in conformity with an international obligation of that State is precluded if the act is due to force majeure, that is the occurrence of an irresistible force or of an unforeseen event, beyond the control of the State, making it materially impossible in the circumstances to perform the obligation.

2. Paragraph 1 does not apply if:

(*a*) The situation of force majeure is due, either alone or in combination with other factors, to the conduct of the State invoking it; or

(*b*) The State has assumed the risk of that situation occurring.

Article 24

Distress

1. The wrongfulness of an act of a State not in conformity with an international obligation of that State is precluded if the author of the act in question has no other reasonable way, in a situation of distress, of saving the author's life or the lives of other persons entrusted to the author's care.

2. Paragraph 1 does not apply if:

(*a*) The situation of distress is due, either alone or in combination with other factors, to the conduct of the State invoking it; or

(*b*) The act in question is likely to create a comparable or greater peril.

Article 25

Necessity

1. Necessity may not be invoked by a State as a ground for precluding the wrongfulness of an act not in conformity with an international obligation of that State unless the act:

(*a*) Is the only way for the State to safeguard an essential interest against a grave and imminent peril; and

(*b*) Does not seriously impair an essential interest of the State or States towards which the obligation exists, or of the international community as a whole.

2. In any case, necessity may not be invoked by a State as a ground for precluding wrongfulness if:

(*a*) The international obligation in question excludes the possibility of invoking necessity; or

(*b*) The State has contributed to the situation of necessity.

Article 26

Compliance with peremptory norms

Nothing in this chapter precludes the wrongfulness of any act of a State which is not in conformity with an obligation arising under a peremptory norm of general international law.

Article 27

Consequences of invoking a circumstance precluding wrongfulness

The invocation of a circumstance precluding wrongfulness in accordance with this chapter is without prejudice to:

(*a*) Compliance with the obligation in question, if and to the extent that the circumstance precluding wrongfulness no longer exists;

(*b*) The question of compensation for any material loss caused by the act in question.

PART TWO

CONTENT OF THE INTERNATIONAL RESPONSIBILITY OF A STATE

CHAPTER I

GENERAL PRINCIPLES

Article 28

Legal consequences of an internationally wrongful act

The international responsibility of a State which is entailed by an internationally wrongful act in accordance with the provisions of part one involves legal consequences as set out in this part.

Article 29

Continued duty of performance

The legal consequences of an internationally wrongful act under this part do not affect the continued duty of the responsible State to perform the obligation breached.

Article 30

Cessation and non-repetition

The State responsible for the internationally wrongful act is under an obligation:

(a) To cease that act, if it is continuing;

(b) To offer appropriate assurances and guarantees of non-repetition, if circumstances so require.

Article 31

Reparation

1. The responsible State is under an obligation to make full reparation for the injury caused by the internationally wrongful act.

2. Injury includes any damage, whether material or moral, caused by the internationally wrongful act of a State.

Article 32

Irrelevance of internal law

The responsible State may not rely on the provisions of its internal law as justification for failure to comply with its obligations under this part.

Article 33

Scope of international obligations set out in this part

1. The obligations of the responsible State set out in this part may be owed to another State, to several States, or to the international community as a whole, depending in particular on the character and content of the international obligation and on the circumstances of the breach.

2. This part is without prejudice to any right, arising from the international responsibility of a State, which may accrue directly to any person or entity other than a State.

CHAPTER II
REPARATION FOR INJURY

Article 34

Forms of reparation

Full reparation for the injury caused by the internationally wrongful act shall take the form of restitution, compensation and satisfaction, either singly or in combination, in accordance with the provisions of this chapter.

Article 35

Restitution

A State responsible for an internationally wrongful act is under an obligation to make restitution, that is, to re-establish the situation which existed before the wrongful act was committed, provided and to the extent that restitution:

(a) Is not materially impossible;

(*b*) Does not involve a burden out of all proportion to the benefit deriving from restitution instead of compensation.

Article 36

Compensation

1. The State responsible for an internationally wrongful act is under an obligation to compensate for the damage caused thereby, insofar as such damage is not made good by restitution.

2. The compensation shall cover any financially assessable damage including loss of profits insofar as it is established.

Article 37

Satisfaction

1. The State responsible for an internationally wrongful act is under an obligation to give satisfaction for the injury caused by that act insofar as it cannot be made good by restitution or compensation.

2. Satisfaction may consist in an acknowledgement of the breach, an expression of regret, a formal apology or another appropriate modality.

3. Satisfaction shall not be out of proportion to the injury and may not take a form humiliating to the responsible State.

Article 38

Interest

1. Interest on any principal sum due under this chapter shall be payable when necessary in order to ensure full reparation. The interest rate and mode of calculation shall be set so as to achieve that result.

2. Interest runs from the date when the principal sum should have been paid until the date the obligation to pay is fulfilled.

Article 39

Contribution to the injury

In the determination of reparation, account shall be taken of the contribution to the injury by wilful or negligent action or omission of the injured State or any person or entity in relation to whom reparation is sought.

CHAPTER III
SERIOUS BREACHES OF OBLIGATIONS UNDER PEREMPTORY NORMS OF GENERAL INTERNATIONAL LAW

Article 40
Application of this chapter

1. This chapter applies to the international responsibility which is entailed by a serious breach by a State of an obligation arising under a peremptory norm of general international law.

2. A breach of such an obligation is serious if it involves a gross or systematic failure by the responsible State to fulfil the obligation.

Article 41
Particular consequences of a serious breach of an obligation under this chapter

1. States shall cooperate to bring to an end through lawful means any serious breach within the meaning of article 40.

2. No State shall recognize as lawful a situation created by a serious breach within the meaning of article 40, nor render aid or assistance in maintaining that situation.

3. This article is without prejudice to the other consequences referred to in this part and to such further consequences that a breach to which this chapter applies may entail under international law.

PART THREE
THE IMPLEMENTATION OF THE INTERNATIONAL RESPONSIBILITY OF A STATE

CHAPTER I
INVOCATION OF THE RESPONSIBILITY OF A STATE

Article 42
Invocation of responsibility by an injured State

A State is entitled as an injured State to invoke the responsibility of another State if the obligation breached is owed to:

(a) That State individually; or

(b) A group of States including that State, or the international community as a whole, and the breach of the obligation:

(i) Specifically affects that State; or

(ii) Is of such a character as radically to change the position of all the other States to which the obligation is owed with respect to the further performance of the obligation.

Article 43

Notice of claim by an injured State

1. An injured State which invokes the responsibility of another State shall give notice of its claim to that State.

2. The injured State may specify in particular:

    (a) The conduct that the responsible State should take in order to cease the wrongful act, if it is continuing;

    (b) What form reparation should take in accordance with the provisions of part two.

Article 44

Admissibility of claims

The responsibility of a State may not be invoked if:

   (a) The claim is not brought in accordance with any applicable rule relating to the nationality of claims;

   (b) The claim is one to which the rule of exhaustion of local remedies applies and any available and effective local remedy has not been exhausted.

Article 45

Loss of the right to invoke responsibility

The responsibility of a State may not be invoked if:

   (a) The injured State has validly waived the claim;

   (b) The injured State is to be considered as having, by reason of its conduct, validly acquiesced in the lapse of the claim.

Article 46

Plurality of injured States

Where several States are injured by the same internationally wrongful act, each injured State may separately invoke the responsibility of the State which has committed the internationally wrongful act.

Article 47

Plurality of responsible States

1. Where several States are responsible for the same internationally wrongful act, the responsibility of each State may be invoked in relation to that act.

2. Paragraph 1:

    (a) Does not permit any injured State to recover, by way of compensation, more than the damage it has suffered;

    (b) Is without prejudice to any right of recourse against the other responsible States.

Article 48

Invocation of responsibility by a State other than an injured State

1. Any State other than an injured State is entitled to invoke the responsibility of another State in accordance with paragraph 2 if:

   (a) The obligation breached is owed to a group of States including that State, and is established for the protection of a collective interest of the group; or

   (b) The obligation breached is owed to the international community as a whole.

2. Any State entitled to invoke responsibility under paragraph 1 may claim from the responsible State:

   (a) Cessation of the internationally wrongful act, and assurances and guarantees of non-repetition in accordance with article 30; and

   (b) Performance of the obligation of reparation in accordance with the preceding articles, in the interest of the injured State or of the beneficiaries of the obligation breached.

3. The requirements for the invocation of responsibility by an injured State under articles 43, 44 and 45 apply to an invocation of responsibility by a State entitled to do so under paragraph 1.

CHAPTER II
COUNTERMEASURES

Article 49

Object and limits of countermeasures

1. An injured State may only take countermeasures against a State which is responsible for an internationally wrongful act in order to induce that State to comply with its obligations under part two.

2. Countermeasures are limited to the non-performance for the time being of international obligations of the State taking the measures towards the responsible State.

3. Countermeasures shall, as far as possible, be taken in such a way as to permit the resumption of performance of the obligations in question.

Article 50

Obligations not affected by countermeasures

1. Countermeasures shall not affect:

   (a) The obligation to refrain from the threat or use of force as embodied in the Charter of the United Nations;

   (b) Obligations for the protection of fundamental human rights;

(*c*) Obligations of a humanitarian character prohibiting reprisals;

(*d*) Other obligations under peremptory norms of general international law.

2. A State tiling countermeasures is not relieved from fulfilling its obligations:

(*a*) Under any dispute settlement procedure applicable between it and the responsible State;

(*b*) To respect the inviolability of diplomatic or consular agents, premises, archives and documents.

Article 51

Proportionality

Countermeasures must be commensurate with the injury suffered, taking into account the gravity of the internationally wrongful act and the rights in question.

Article 52

Conditions relating to resort to countermeasures

1. Before taking countermeasures, an injured State shall:

(*a*) Call upon the responsible State, in accordance with article 43, to fulfil its obligations under part two;

(*b*) Notify the responsible State of any decision to take countermeasures and offer to negotiate with that State.

2. Notwithstanding paragraph 1 (*b*), the injured State may take such urgent countermeasures as are necessary to preserve its rights.

3. Countermeasures may not be taken, and if already taken must be suspended without undue delay if:

(*a*) The internationally wrongful act has ceased; and

(*b*) The dispute is pending before a court or tribunal which has the authority to make decisions binding on the parties.

4. Paragraph 3 does not apply if the responsible State fails to implement the dispute settlement procedures in good faith.

Article 53

Termination of countermeasures

Countermeasures shall be terminated as soon as the responsible State has complied with its obligations under part two in relation to the internationally wrongful act.

Article 54

Measures taken by States other than an injured State

This chapter does not prejudice the right of any State, entitled under article 48, paragraph 1, to invoke the responsibility of another State, to take lawful measures against that State to ensure cessation of the breach and reparation in the interest of the injured State or of the beneficiaries of the obligation breached.

PART FOUR

GENERAL PROVISIONS

Article 55

Lex specialis

These articles do not apply where and to the extent that the conditions for the existence of an internationally wrongful act or the content or implementation of the international responsibility of a State are governed by special rules of international law.

Article 56

Questions of State responsibility not regulated by these articles

The applicable rules of international law continue to govern questions concerning the responsibility of a State for an internationally wrongful act to the extent that they are not regulated by these articles.

Article 57

Responsibility of an international organization

These articles are without prejudice to any question of the responsibility under international law of an international organization, or of any State for the conduct of an international organization.

Article 58

Individual responsibility

These articles are without prejudice to any question of the individual responsibility under international law of any person acting on behalf of a State.

Article 59

Charter of the United Nations

These articles are without prejudice to the Charter of the United Nations.

12. Prevention of Transboundary Harm
from Hazardous Activities*

The States Parties,

Having in mind Article 13, paragraph 1 (a), of the Charter of the United Nations, which provides that the General Assembly shall initiate studies and make recommendations for the purpose of encouraging the progressive development of international law and its codification,

Bearing in mind the principle of permanent sovereignty of States over the natural resources within their territory or otherwise under their jurisdiction or control,

Bearing also in mind that the freedom of States to carry on or permit activities in their territory or otherwise under their jurisdiction or control is not unlimited,

Recalling the Rio Declaration on Environment and Development of 13 June 1992,

Recognizing the importance of promoting international cooperation,

Have agreed as follows:

Article 1

Scope

The present articles apply to activities not prohibited by international law which involve a risk of causing significant transboundary harm through their physical consequences.

Article 2

Use of terms

For the purposes of the present articles:

(*a*) "Risk of causing significant transboundary harm" includes risks taking the form of a high probability of causing significant transboundary harm and a low probability of causing disastrous transboundary harm;

(*b*) "Harm" means harm caused to persons, property or the environment;

(*c*) "Transboundary harm" means harm caused in the territory of or in other places under the jurisdiction or control of a State other

---

* Text adopted by the Commission at its fifty-third session, in 2001, and submitted to the General Assembly as a part of the Commission's report covering the work of that session. The report, which also contains commentaries on the draft articles, appears in *Official Records of the General Assembly, Fifty-sixth Session, Supplement No. 10* (A/56/10).

than the State of origin, whether or not the States concerned share a common border;

(*d*) "State of origin" means the State in the territory or otherwise under the jurisdiction or control of which the activities referred to in article 1 are planned or are carried out;

(*e*) "State likely to be affected" means the State or States in the territory of which there is the risk of significant transboundary harm or which have jurisdiction or control over any other place where there is such a risk;

(*f*) "States concerned" means the State of origin and the State likely to be affected.

Article 3

Prevention

The State of origin shall take all appropriate measures to prevent significant transboundary harm or at any event to minimize the risk thereof.

Article 4

Cooperation

States concerned shall cooperate in good faith and, as necessary, seek the assistance of one or more competent international organizations in preventing significant transboundary harm or at any event in minimizing the risk thereof.

Article 5

Implementation

States concerned shall take the necessary legislative, administrative or other action, including the establishment of suitable monitoring mechanisms to implement the provisions of the present articles.

Article 6

Authorization

1. The State of origin shall require its prior authorization for:

(*a*) Any activity within the scope of the present articles carried out in its territory or otherwise under its jurisdiction or control;

(*b*) Any major change in an activity referred to in subparagraph (*a*);

(*c*) Any plan to change an activity which may transform it into one falling within the scope of the present articles.

2. The requirement of authorization established by a State shall be made applicable in respect of all pre-existing activities within the scope of the present articles. Authorizations already issued by the State for pre-existing activities shall be reviewed in order to comply with the present articles.

3. In case of a failure to conform to the terms of the authorization, the State of origin shall take such actions as appropriate, including where necessary terminating the authorization.

Article 7

Assessment of risk

Any decision in respect of the authorization of an activity within the scope of the present articles shall, in particular, be based on an assessment of the possible transboundary harm caused by that activity, including any environmental impact assessment.

Article 8

Notification and information

1. If the assessment referred to in article 7 indicates a risk of causing significant transboundary harm, the State of origin shall provide the State likely to be affected with timely notification of the risk and the assessment and shall transmit to it the available technical and all other relevant information on which the assessment is based.

2. The State of origin shall not take any decision on authorization of the activity pending the receipt, within a period not exceeding six months, of the response from the State likely to be affected.

Article 9

Consultations on preventive measures

1. The States concerned shall enter into consultations, at the request of any of them, with a view to achieving acceptable solutions regarding measures to be adopted in order to prevent significant transboundary harm or at any event to minimize the risk thereof. The States concerned shall agree, at the commencement of such consultations, on a reasonable time frame for the consultations.

2. The States concerned shall seek solutions based on an equitable balance of interests in the light of article 10.

3. If the consultations referred to in paragraph 1 fail to produce an agreed solution, the State of origin shall nevertheless take into account the interests of the State likely to be affected in case it decides to authorize the activity to be pursued, without prejudice to the rights of any State likely to be affected.

Article 10

Factors involved in an equitable balance of interests

In order to achieve an equitable balance of interests as referred to in paragraph 2 of article 9, the States concerned shall take into account all relevant factors and circumstances, including:

(*a*) The degree of risk of significant transboundary harm and of the availability of means of preventing such harm, or minimizing the risk thereof or repairing the harm;

(*b*) The importance of the activity, taking into account its overall advantages of a social, economic and technical character for the State of origin in relation to the potential harm for the State likely to be affected;

(*c*) The risk of significant harm to the environment and the availability of means of preventing such harm, or minimizing the risk thereof or restoring the environment;

(*d*) The degree to which the State of origin and, as appropriate, the State likely to be affected are prepared to contribute to the costs of prevention;

(*e*) The economic viability of the activity in relation to the costs of prevention and to the possibility of carrying out the activity elsewhere or by other means or replacing it with an alternative activity;

(*f*) The standards of prevention which the State likely to be affected applies to the same or comparable activities and the standards applied in comparable regional or international practice.

Article 11

Procedures in the absence of notification

1. If a State has reasonable grounds to believe that an activity planned or carried out in the State of origin may involve a risk of causing significant transboundary harm to it, it may request the State of origin to apply the provision of article 8. The request shall be accompanied by a documented explanation setting forth its grounds.

2. In the event that the State of origin nevertheless finds that it is not under an obligation to provide a notification under article 8, it shall so inform the requesting State within a reasonable time, providing a documented explanation setting forth the reasons for such finding. If this finding does not satisfy that State, at its request, the two States shall promptly enter into consultations in the manner indicated in article 9.

3. During the course of the consultations, the State of origin shall, if so requested by the other State, arrange to introduce appropriate and feasible measures to minimize the risk and, where appropriate, to suspend the activity in question for a reasonable period.

Article 12

Exchange of information

While the activity is being carried out, the States concerned shall exchange in a timely manner all available information concerning that activity relevant to preventing significant transboundary harm or at any event minimizing the risk thereof. Such an exchange of information shall continue until such time as the States concerned consider it appropriate even after the activity is terminated.

Article 13

Information to the public

States concerned shall, by such means as are appropriate, provide the public likely to be affected by an activity within the scope of the present articles with relevant information relating to that activity, the risk involved and the harm which might result and ascertain their views.

Article 14

National security and industrial secrets

Data and information vital to the national security of the State of origin or to the protection of industrial secrets or concerning intellectual property may be withheld, but the State of origin shall cooperate in good faith with the State likely to be affected in providing as much information as possible under the circumstances.

Article 15

Non-discrimination

Unless the States concerned have agreed otherwise for the protection of the interests of persons, natural or juridical, who may be or are exposed to the risk of significant transboundary harm as a result of an activity within the scope of the present articles, a State shall not discriminate on the basis of nationality or residence or place where the injury might occur, in granting to such persons, in accordance with its legal system, access to judicial or other procedures to seek protection or other appropriate redress.

Article 16

Emergency preparedness

The State of origin shall develop contingency plans for responding to emergencies, in cooperation, where appropriate, with the State likely to be affected and competent international organizations.

Article 17

Notification of an emergency

The State of origin shall, without delay and by the most expeditious means, at its disposal, notify the State likely to be affected of an emergency concerning an activity within the scope of the present articles and provide it with all relevant and available information.

The present ar̶t̶i̶c̶l̶e̶s̶ ... n incurred
by States under relevant t̶r̶e̶a̶t̶ ... international
law.

Article 19

Settlement of disputes

1. Any dispute concerning the interpretation or application of the present articles shall be settled expeditiously through peaceful means of settlement chosen by mutual agreement of the parties to the dispute, including negotiations, mediation, conciliation, arbitration or judicial settlement.

2. Failing an agreement on the means for the peaceful settlement of the dispute within a period of six months, the parties to the dispute shall, at the request of any of them, have recourse to the establishment of an impartial fact-finding commission.

3. The Fact-finding Commission shall be composed of one member nominated by each party to the dispute and, in addition, a member not having the nationality of any of the parties to the dispute chosen by the nominated members who shall serve as Chairperson.

4. If more than one State is involved on one side of the dispute and those States do not agree on a common member of the Commission and each of them nominates a member, the other party to the dispute has the right to nominate an equal number of members of the Commission.

5. If the members nominated by the parties to the dispute are unable to agree on a Chairperson within three months of the request for the establishment of the Commission, any party to the dispute may request the Secretary-General of the United Nations to appoint the Chairperson who shall not have the nationality of any of the parties to the dispute. If one of the parties to the dispute fails to nominate a member within three months of the initial request pursuant to paragraph 2, any other party to the dispute may request the Secretary-General of the United Nations to appoint a person who shall not have the nationality of any of the parties to the dispute. The person so appointed shall constitute a single-member Commission.

6. The Commission shall adopt its report by a majority vote, unless it is a single-member Commission, and shall submit that report to the parties to the dispute setting forth its findings and recommendations, which the parties to the dispute shall consider in good faith.